# Leadership in Literacy
## Capacity Building and the Ifè Program

## SIL International® Publications in Language Use and Education

7

Publications in Language Use and Education began as Publications in Sociolinguistics, a venue for works covering a broad range of topics in sociolinguistics, and has been expanded to include topics in mother tongue literacy, multilingual education, educational anthropology, and a variety of other issues and topics related to language and education.

**Managing Editor**
Eric Kindberg

**Volume Editor**
George Huttar
Joyce Park

**Copy Editors**
Bonnie Brown
Chewlan Lastufka
Dirk Kievit

**Production Staff**
Lois Gourley, Composition Director
Judy Benjamin, Compositor
Barbara Alber, Cover Design

**Cover Photograph**
JeDene Reeder

# Leadership in Literacy
## Capacity Building and the Ifè Program

JeDene Reeder

SIL International®
Dallas, Texas

© 2017 by SIL International®
Library of Congress Catalog No: 2017941257
ISBN: 978-1-55671-389-7
ISSN: 1545-0074

Printed in the United States of America

All rights reserved

No part of this publication may be reproduced, stored in a retrieval system, or transmitted in any form or by any means—electronic, mechanical, photocopy, recording, or otherwise—without the express permission of SIL International®. However, short passages, generally understood to be within the limits of fair use, may be quoted without permission.

Copies of this and other publications of SIL International® may be obtained through distributors such as Amazon, Barnes & Noble, other worldwide distributors and, for select volumes, www.sil.org/resources/publications:

SIL International Publications
7500 W. Camp Wisdom Road
Dallas, TX 75236-5629 USA

General inquiry: publications_intl@sil.org
Pending order inquiry: sales_intl@sil.org
www.sil.org/resources/publications

# Contents

Acronyms and Abbreviations .................................................................. ix
Transcription Conventions..................................................................... xi
Preface.................................................................................................. xiii
1 Introduction ........................................................................................ 1
   1.1 Perspectives and concepts ............................................................. 2
      1.1.1 Leadership............................................................................ 3
      1.1.2 Capacity building ................................................................ 4
   1.2 Context: Togo and Benin ............................................................... 5
      1.2.1 History of colonial education in Africa ............................. 6
      1.2.2 Sociolinguistic background: Togo ...................................... 7
      1.2.3 Sociolinguistic background: Benin .................................... 8
   1.3 Research questions ...................................................................... 10
   1.4 Methodology ............................................................................... 10
2 The Ifè ............................................................................................... 15
   2.1 Ifè language development program ........................................... 18
      2.1.1 Ifè orthography history ..................................................... 19
      2.1.2 Literacy program overview ............................................... 20
   2.2 History of the local literacy associations ................................... 22
      2.2.1 AVID .................................................................................. 22
      2.2.2 AMADPENI ....................................................................... 24

    2.2.3 AMIADA..................................................................................25
    2.2.4 ADCIBA..................................................................................27
    2.2.5 AVADI....................................................................................29
    2.2.6 The association *"Espoir pour l'Avenir"*..................................30
  2.3 ACATBLI's role ...............................................................................31
  2.4 Summary..........................................................................................33

## 3 *Représentations sociales*: What does Common Sense Say?.................. 35
  3.1 A brief history of the theory...........................................................36
  3.2 Characteristics and types of social representations .....................37
  3.3 Functions of a social representation..............................................38
  3.4 Related concepts .............................................................................39
  3.5 Rationale for using social representations in this study............. 41

## 4 Leadership: How Do You Identify a Good Leader? ......................... 43
  4.1 Leadership theories ........................................................................44
    4.1.1 Traits theory ..........................................................................45
    4.1.2 Skills model............................................................................46
    4.1.3 Situational theory ..................................................................48
    4.1.4 Path-goal theory.....................................................................49
    4.1.5 Transformational leadership ................................................51
  4.2 Leadership in nonprofit and human development
      organizations...................................................................................53
  4.3 African notions of leadership .........................................................55
  4.4 Discussion........................................................................................59

## 5 Literacy and Development: The Chicken or the Egg? ..................... 63
  5.1 Literacy ............................................................................................64
    5.1.1 Literacy as a skill set..............................................................64
    5.1.2 Literacy as power...................................................................65
    5.1.3 Literacy as social practice......................................................66
    5.1.4 Discussion of views on literacy.............................................67
  5.2 Development....................................................................................68
    5.2.1 Brief history of development history and trends.....................70
    5.2.2 Issues in development...........................................................72
    5.2.3 Development summary ........................................................76
  5.3 Discussion of the relationship between literacy and
      development.....................................................................................77
  5.4 Literacy, development, and social representations......................81

## 6 Ifè Representations of Leadership................................................ 83
  6.1 Social representations of a leader...................................................84
    6.1.1 Patience ..................................................................................86
    6.1.2 Faithfulness............................................................................91

    6.1.3 Exemplary ................................................................... 93
    6.1.4 Competent in work ....................................................... 97
    6.1.5 Does not dictate .......................................................... 100
    6.1.6 Some secondary features............................................ 103
  6.2 Features specific to literacy program leaders ..................... 115
    6.2.1 Qualities of literacy program heads ............................ 119
    6.2.2 Qualities of board members ........................................ 128
  6.3 Representations of subordinates ......................................... 134
    6.3.1 Willingness and obedience .......................................... 136
    6.3.2 Collaboration ............................................................... 137
    6.3.3 Attention and respect .................................................. 139
    6.3.4 Harmony and loyalty ................................................... 139
    6.3.5 Report giver ................................................................. 141
  6.4 Summary and discussion ..................................................... 144

# 7 Motivations of Literacy Workers: Representations Related to Literacy .................................................................... 147
  7.1 Representations of illiterates ............................................... 149
    7.1.1 Handicapped ................................................................ 150
    7.1.2 In darkness and ignorance ........................................... 151
    7.1.3 Distrustful .................................................................... 155
    7.1.4 Blocks to development ................................................ 156
  7.2 Representations of literacy and language ........................... 159
    7.2.1 Literacy as openness and development ...................... 160
    7.2.2 Mother tongue literacy as preservation and
          transmission of cultural knowledge and identity .... 166
    7.2.3 Literacy as full participation in society ....................... 172
    7.2.4 Ifè literacy as language maintenance and
          development ............................................................ 175
    7.2.5 French as a more difficult language than Ifè ............. 178
    7.2.6 Biliteracy as responsibility .......................................... 182
    7.2.7 Literacy as access to another language ..................... 188
    7.2.8 Ifè literacy as a qualification ....................................... 192
  7.3 Summary and discussion ..................................................... 193

# 8 Enhancing Capacity ................................................................. 197
  8.1 At the personnel level .......................................................... 199
  8.2 At the organizational level ................................................... 204
  8.3 At the community level ........................................................ 214
  8.4 Discussion .............................................................................. 223

# 9 Conclusion ................................................................................ 231
  9.1 Summary of findings ............................................................ 233

  9.1.1 Representations of leadership ................................................. 233
  9.1.2 Representations of literacy, illiterates, and language ...................... 235
  9.1.3 Capacity building and representations ................................... 236
 9.2 Contributions to theory ................................................................ 238
 9.3 Implications and recommendations ............................................... 240
  9.3.1 Recommendations for associations of the Ifè program ............................................................................. 241
  9.3.2 Implications of lessons learned for other literacy programs ............................................................................. 242
  9.3.3 Recommendations for external partner organizations ...................................................................... 243
  9.3.4 Recommendations for government policy makers ................ 245
 9.4 Limitations of the research .......................................................... 245
 9.5 Directions for further research ..................................................... 247
 9.6 Closing comments ...................................................................... 248

**Appendix A: Interview protocols** ............................................................. 249

**Appendix B: Interview excerpts** ............................................................... 257

**References** ........................................................................................... 329

**Index** ................................................................................................... 341

# Acronyms and Abbreviations

| | |
|---|---|
| ACA | *ACATBLI coopérative agricole* |
| | ACATBLI Agricultural Cooperative |
| ACATBLI | *Association chrétienne pour l'alphabétisation et la traduction biblique en langue ifè* |
| | Christian Association for Literacy and Bible Translation in the Ifè Language |
| ADCIBA | *Association pour le développement de la communauté ifè du Benin par l'alphabétisation* |
| | Association for the Development of the Ifè Community in Benin through Literacy |
| AMADPENI | *Association des moniteurs pour l'alphabétisation, le développement et la protection de l'environnement en milieu ifè* |
| | Association of Instructors for Literacy, Development, and the Protection of the Environment in the Ifè Area |
| AMI | *Association des moniteurs ifè* |
| | Association of Ifè Instructors |
| AMIADA | *Association des moniteurs ifè pour l'alphabétisation et le développement des adultes* |
| | Association of Ifè Instructors for Adult Literacy and Development |

| | |
|---|---|
| AVADI | *Association des volontaires pour l'alphabétisation et le développement des Ifè* |
| | Association of Volunteers for Literacy and the Development of the Ifè |
| AVID | *Association des volontaires ifè pour le développement* |
| | Association of Ifè Volunteers for Development |
| CEG | *Collège d'enseignement général* |
| | (first four years of secondary school) |
| CENALA | *Centre national de la linguistique appliquée* |
| | National Center of Applied Linguistics, Benin |
| CNL | *Commission nationale linguistique* |
| | National Linguistic Commission, Benin |
| CRPI | *Comité régional pour la promotion de la langue ifè* |
| | Regional Committee for the Promotion of the Ifè Language |
| DED | *Deutscher Entwicklungsdienst* |
| | German Development Service |
| DNAEA | *Direction nationale de l'alphabétisation et l'éducation des adultes* |
| | National Office of Literacy and Adult Education, Benin |
| EFA | Education for All |
| HDI | Human Development Index |
| IGA | income-generating activity |
| IMF | International Monetary Fund |
| NGO | nongovernmental organization |
| REFLECT | REgenerated Freirian Literacy through Empowering Community Techniques |
| SOTOCO | *Société togolaise de coton* |
| | Togolese Cotton Company |
| SR | social representation |

# Transcription Conventions

The following symbols are used to indicate nuances in the interview transcriptions of audio-recorded interviews in French and Ifè. The majority of these transcription conventions are based on Cavalli et al. (2003).

| Symbol | Meaning |
|---|---|
| **Symbol** | **Meaning** |
| xx | incomprehensible passage |
| . or .. or ... | pauses of various durations |
| word, | short pause with prosodic intonation |
| : | lengthened syllable |
| = | false start |
| CAPITALS | emphasis (with the exception of acronyms such as the names of the associations, government departments, or political parties) |
| la-la-la | separate enunciation of each syllable in a word |
| [ ] | overlapping words/phrases |
| { } | comment on the transcription |
| ↑ ↓ | rising or falling intonation (marked) |
| * | nonstandard word |

# Preface

Literacy workers around the globe aim to develop literacy programs that are effective—programs from which people not only pass a final exam and "graduate," but from which they go on to regularly use their newly-acquired literacy and numeracy skills for tasks that improve their lives and lead to sustainable development in their communities. Additionally, we want these programs to be durable, able to function as long as the need for them exists, which implies a certain level of capacity building, both of personnel and of the organization overseeing the program. During my nearly six years as the literacy coordinator for SIL International (SIL) in Togo and Benin, I had the privilege of getting to know and work with a number of dedicated Africans working for the betterment of their people through literacy. Some of their programs seemed to be more effective than others, however. The Ifè program was one of the more effective ones. So when it came time for me to choose a topic for my doctoral research in educational leadership, I thought of their program: *Why* has the Ifè program been so effective?

I began with the assumption that the program leadership was a major component of the effectiveness of the Ifè program, but I wanted to understand what elements of this leadership were the most significant in capacity building of teachers, learners, the organization, and the community. In part, this was because I wanted to see what could be transferred to other programs as, through literacy, these programs strive to strengthen abilities and competencies and, where necessary, adjust attitudes—all those things normally encompassed by the term "capacity building."

One significant finding—which rather surprised me—was that much of the capacity building at the personnel and organizational levels is based on decisions made by technical advisors and/or funders. On the other hand, the community-level capacity enhancement has definitely benefitted from the decisions made by the Ifè literacy team. One important facet of this team's effectiveness was that its members exemplify two of the leadership qualities that the Ifè people consider most important: patience and faithfulness—two qualities which are rarely mentioned in the literature on leadership. Another unexpected finding was the importance of the team's representations of literacy in making and keeping them motivated to work in this often-discouraging field of service.

Although the bulk of my research was carried out in 2009 for the needs of my dissertation, this book reflects the many changes that have taken place in Togo, Benin, and the Ifè literacy program between 2009 and mid-2014. It is my hope that this work will be of use to all those working in the fields of literacy and development. A number of lessons learned from the Ifè program are included in the final chapter of this book, among them the importance of capacity building that meets the needs of the beneficiaries, not first of all of those sponsoring such activity, and the importance of culturally important leadership styles, which may not fit the "molds" of leadership promoted by leadership-training models based on Western theories of leadership and organizations. Both of these issues require research among the people for which a literacy and development program is intended. The final lesson that I wish to emphasize here is that capacity building is a process and cannot be hurried; the time taken to research questions of felt needs and representations of leadership is important to that process. Patience is not only a virtue but a necessity for all of us seeking a better world.

With regard to the style of presentation, I have striven to keep this work readable but found it necessary to include some technical vocabulary, in particular from the theory of *représentations sociales* (social representations). This theory, which formed the basis of my analysis, allows the researcher to discern the framework generated by those speaking and thus obtain the insider's point of view of a topic. I found this theory invaluable to an understanding of the framework used by the Ifè literacy leaders. My subsequent research in another literacy program has confirmed the usefulness of this theory for cross-cultural workers attempting to understand why things are the way they are in relation to a particular situation.

Credit is due Agbémadon Akoété as photographer of photos used in chapters one, five, and seven. I was the photographer for the cover photo, and those used for chapters two, three, four, six, and eight.

The book is organized as follows: In the first chapter I give the reasons for this research project, an overview of pertinent concepts, and background to the study. This background contains a brief description of the political, historical, and environmental context of the Ifè people in Togo and in Benin. The

*Preface*                                                                                               XV

research questions and a brief overview of the methodology used are then presented. At the end of this chapter (and a number of other chapters), recommendations for further reading on selected topics are given.

The second chapter describes a little of the history and physical and social context of the Ifè before explaining the development of the Ifè language program. As part of the rich description essential for a case study, the history of each local association has been delineated. The current and projected role for ACATBLI, the umbrella organization of the local literacy associations, is also outlined.

Chapters 3 through 5 describe the theoretical foundations of this work. The dominant theories underlying this research are the theory of *représentations sociales,* theories of leadership, and theories of literacy and development. The theory of social representations, absolutely fundamental to my analysis of the research data, comes from French scholarship, while theories of leadership arise primarily from North American research; the two theoretical areas have not been discussed together before. Various issues in development as well as a discussion of the relationship between literacy and development are also presented.

In the sixth chapter I examine the representations of leadership among the Ifè. Most of the data in this section come from interviews with the leaders of the associations studied, but an interview with some community members is also taken into consideration in the analysis. In an effort to separate EMIC (in-group) from ETIC (outsider) perspectives, the (emic) representations that emerged were identified on the basis of the actual words of the participants. (These statements are found in Appendix A, with the English translation in the main text.) The etic perspective is found in the discussion of the findings, which concludes the chapter.

The seventh chapter discusses representations that motivate the leaders of these associations to invest their time and energies in the literacy program. These representations relating to literacy also respond in part to questions about which capacities have been or need to be reinforced, as they exert a strong influence on the leaders in the management of their programs. The etic and emic perspectives are handled in the same way as in chapter 6.

In the eighth chapter I show how the representations of leadership and of literacy have influenced and are influencing the development of the literacy program and local associations among the Ifè and their activities in the community. The capacities they have built or reinforced, as well as felt needs in this domain, are described. Additionally, I scrutinize the question of who chooses which capacities to reinforce, and draw some conclusions regarding the factors influencing the long-term sustainability of the local associations.

In the final chapter I summarize my findings and present the implications for theory, policy, and practice. Additionally, I note several of the limitations of this research project and propose directions for further research.

Many people supported my dissertation research and writing process, and several others walked with me through the editing process that led to this publication. I thank them all. I particularly wish to single out for thanks the leaders of the Ifè program: particularly Agbémadon Akoété and Setodji Kodjo, as well as all seven local association coordinators. They consented to my intrusion into their lives, giving of their time and sharing their experiences. They patiently answered questions not only during the interviews, but later as I sought to clarify the information I obtained in 2009 and to understand the changes that have taken place since then. These leaders exemplify the practice of patience, for which I am grateful.

# 1

# Introduction

*Nous marquons beaucoup d'impact positif de l'alphabétisation au milieu ifè. C'est un milieu enclavé. Il y avait PAS d'église. Il y avait PAS d'écoles. Et {consonne roulée bilabiale} ... tous est dans la faim et ils vivent misérablement. Et grâce à cette alphabétisation, qu'il y a, comme il a dit, un petit chantier, pour que les gens puissent voir que ah, notre état n'est pas bon, et nous pouvons changer notre état.*

We are showing much positive impact of literacy in the Ifè social environment. It's a closed environment. There were *no* churches. There were *no* schools. And {rolled bilabial consonant}...all are hungry and live miserably. Thanks to this literacy, that there is—as he said—a small working example, so that the people can see that, ah, our state is not good, and we can change our state. (Akoété Agbémadon, Head of Ifè literacy program, February 16, 2009)

## 1.1 Perspectives and concepts

According to UNESCO's 2010 Education for All Global Monitoring Report, illiteracy is among the greatest challenges in the fight against poverty in the twenty-first century, largely because it closes the doors of opportunity for hundreds of thousands of people. One-fifth of the world's preliterate people live in sub-Saharan Africa, which is also where countries having a low score on the Human Development Index (HDI) abound. The nations of Togo and Benin, where this study was carried out, are among the countries that have relatively low literacy rates (although both have made notable strides in the past fifteen years) and that are listed among the world's least developed nations.

Through UNESCO's Education for All (EFA) initiative, illiteracy is being attacked from two fronts: prevention through increased school enrollment levels, and remediation through adult and youth literacy classes. This latter strategy usually involves nonformal education programs run by nongovernmental organizations (NGOs) in relationship with the government of the land.

One such international NGO is SIL International (SIL—formerly the Summer Institute of Linguistics), which has formal consultative status with UNESCO. In 1998 I arrived in Togo to work as a literacy specialist with SIL Togo-Benin, a branch of SIL International. Among other activities, SIL develops and assists mother tongue literacy programs in partnership with local language communities. The support provided includes training in program management, as well as in literacy activities and theory. In 1999 I accepted the position of branch literacy coordinator. This role allowed me to learn about and be involved in the planning of numerous literacy programs, including the Ifè program that is the subject of this work.

This program is particularly interesting because of the strategy developed by its Ifè leaders to serve the entire Ifè population with literacy classes. The essence of this strategy is the creation of local literacy associations to take on the responsibility of running a literacy program in the villages of their immediate areas. One purpose of this book, then, is to describe the

## 1.1 Perspectives and concepts

program in such a way that other populous, widely dispersed ethnolinguistic groups with low literacy levels may replicate or adapt this strategy for their people.

In addition, this study provides perspectives on leadership in NGOs from francophone West Africa, an area neglected in much of the literature on leadership. These viewpoints are expressed here by Togolese and Beninese participants themselves. A better understanding of these West African perceptions of leadership may help inform the content and strategies of programs that aim to improve the capacity of literacy and development organizations in that area of the world.

### 1.1.1 Leadership

One important aspect of this strategy is the leadership involved in its development and implementation. The creation of local organizations implies the development of local leadership and of the capacities these leaders need to carry out their tasks effectively. For this reason, understanding their representations of leadership and of literacy, and how these influence capacity building in local associations, is key to leadership development and is the main focus of this case study.

Leadership development requires a clear idea of what a leader is and/or does. Most definitions of leadership indicate that it involves the ability to influence people and organizations, whether to make a particular decision, to go a certain direction during an activity, or to change opinions. Mintzberg (1973) indicates that the role of a leader entails integrating the needs of individuals with the goals of the organization in order to achieve a greater cooperation among the organization's units. Jones (2003) says that good leadership is evidenced by how well the organization's mission is communicated and moved forward. These definitions all come from North American perspectives.

Given the location of this research project, however, the views of African scholars are perhaps more pertinent here. One perspective from Africa suggests that an important indicator of good leadership is the organization's survival or durability (Ugwuegbu 2001). An additional African viewpoint states that effective leadership is able to transform ordinary people into ones who are capable of extraordinary achievements (Edoho 1998). Another take on leadership from sub-Saharan Africa emphasizes the necessity of the leader to collaboratively develop a common vision with his or her subordinates (Aire 1990). Yet another point of view, in contrasting management with leadership, states, "Leadership is of the spirit, compounded by personality and vision" (Anantharaman 1990:208). Leadership will be further discussed in chapter 4, when various theories and issues of leadership are described and discussed, before the perspective of the Ifè is presented in chapter 6.

Organizations working to improve literacy[1] rates in Africa must have leaders who can motivate and influence others, such as literacy workers and potential and current learners, as well as other community members whose support is the key to the success of any literacy program. As these motivated people work and learn, they will indeed accomplish extraordinary things in their communities. The scale of the lack of reading and writing ability among adults, combined with the current lack of universal primary school education in many countries of sub-Saharan Africa also means that these organizations must have long life spans. This need for continuing service often requires that these organizations and their leaders receive various types of support, which are generally subsumed under the heading of capacity building.

### 1.1.2 Capacity building

Capacity building has been a hot topic in the international development community for nearly two decades. The grounds for this attention is that while NGOs generally are believed to be more efficacious than governments in attaining development goals, largely because of a perceived greater sensitivity to local needs and conditions, the durability of their programs is too often dependent on outside funding and other support. As a consequence, international organizations have decided that increased attention to capacity building of national NGOs and other instruments of civil society is essential as a long-term solution to development challenges.

The term "capacity building," however, has been used in a variety of ways. As Eade (1997:206) notes, the French and Spanish equivalents, respectively, *renforcer les capacités* and *fortalecer las capacidades,* imply a

---

[1]Literacy and illiteracy statistics are generally based on the skills-based definition of literacy. A more complete discussion of what literacy can mean is found in chapter 5, section 5.1.

pre-existing capacity; one only needs to strengthen abilities or structures. On the other hand, Dym and Hutson (2005:55) observe that building capacity "is current code for becoming more businesslike." For nearly everyone, at least if one looks at what has been labeled capacity building on the ground, it implies training of some sort. Sometimes the focus of the training targets the skills and knowledge of project personnel, while at other times it is directed at organizational issues of mission, structure, and procedures (Johnson and Thomas 2007). However, both Eade (2007) and Gubbels and Koss (2000) explicitly state that training that increases skills or knowledge is insufficient to increase capacity; attitudes and behavior must also change in order for the desired transformation to take place. This last perspective requires the perception of capacity enhancement as a long-term process, a view essentially supported by this book.

The point of view taken on the various aspects of capacity building affects decisions made in this domain. If one believes that having capable personnel is essential, the accent will be put on training of individuals, which has been the case of SIL in Togo and Benin as it has supported literacy work among the Ifè and other ethnolinguistic groups. If one perceives that it is the structures, vision, and strategies that are most important to the success of the organization, not to mention its long-term sustainability, then work is focused on helping the association develop these elements, which is what the principal donor of the local associations studied in this research project has done. These issues will be further discussed in chapter 8, when the capacity-building choices made throughout the life of the Ifè literacy program are described.

## 1.2 Context: Togo and Benin

The beneficiaries of the Ifè literacy program live in Togo and Benin. In Togo forty-two African languages are currently spoken, and in Benin, fifty-five (Lewis, Simons, and Fennig 2016). Since, however, the boundaries of African territories were fixed by the European powers during the Berlin Congress of 1884–1885 without taking into account either linguistic frontiers or migration patterns (Bane 1956; Hargreaves 1974; Reader 1998), many ethnolinguistic groups, including the Ifè, found themselves politically divided by an international boundary (Webster 1974). Given that a number of these groups are found on both sides of the boundary between Togo and Benin, the total number of African languages spoken in this region is seventy-nine, not ninety-nine. (Lewis, Simons, and Fennig 2016). As we shall see, French is the language of power for both countries, since it is the official language of both, as well as the language of formal education.

### 1.2.1 History of colonial education in Africa

Throughout sub-Saharan Africa, schools were first established by Christian missionaries, even before European countries imposed formal control over the region. This was the case both in the former Togoland (forerunner of Togo) and in Dahomey (now Benin). These schools were established in order to spread both Christianity and (European) civilization. Most of the Protestant mission schools preferred to use a local language for instruction, at least for the first grades, in order to better communicate the gospel. The Catholic mission schools had the additional goal of training catechists, so although they generally accepted local customs, the majority of teaching was given in the colonial language of the land.

Each colonial power had its own educational policy that, in turn, influenced the linguistic policy in the schools. The British had two goals for education: the training of civil servants and technicians, who would need English; and the creation of a population that would be able to contribute to the economy of the British Empire. The latter only required primary and vocational education, which could therefore be in the local language. The goal of France, Portugal, and Spain was cultural assimilation of the Africans, with the result that in their colonies, education was only available in the language of the colonial master. The Belgians, however, chose to educate the entire population instead of creating an elite as the policies of the other European countries were doing. Therefore, they opted to use local languages for education; as a result, at independence, Congo had the highest literacy rate in Africa, at sixty-two percent. Nevertheless, this policy led to a serious shortage of people who had acquired sufficient education and experience to lead the country after the Belgians left. The Germans were not interested in assimilating the Africans. However, they did want to deal with only one language when communicating with villagers, so they required that the mission schools use only one dialect for basic education (the Anlo dialect of Éwé was chosen in Togoland) and German for secondary education.

### 1.2.2 Sociolinguistic background: Togo

During the colonial era, Togoland was controlled first by Germany. Schools were run by both British and German missions. During this period, therefore, the mission schools used Éwé for primary education and added English and/or German at the secondary level.

After World War I (WWI) Germany forfeited its colonies. In 1922 the League of Nations officially divided control of Togoland (as a "protectorate") between France and the United Kingdom, both of which had occupied it since 1914 (Gayibor 1997). British Togoland, the territory controlled by the U.K., was united with the British colony of the Gold Coast in 1956 to create Ghana while French Togoland, the section administered by France between 1919 and 1960, became Togo. Because the colonial policy of France favored assimilation, after WWI ended in 1919, French became the sole language of education in its part of Togoland.

At independence in 1960, the new Togolese government chose to keep French as the official language and as the language of education. In maintaining this use of the colonial language, the government followed the practice of the elites of most African nations during the era of independence. Continuation of the role of the colonial language consolidated their position in the new nation and ensured communication with European and North American powers.

However, during the 1970s, while Africa was seeking to establish its unique identity through an authenticity movement, two indigenous languages, Éwé and Kabiyè, were designated as national languages. These languages are used in the media (television, radio, and official newspaper). Also, they are each, in principle, taught as an elective during the third and fourth years of secondary school. Specifically, Éwé is supposed to be taught in Southern Togo, where it is a language of wider communication, while Kabiyè is supposed to be taught in Northern Togo, the location of the home area of the Kabiyè, the largest ethnic group in the country. However, this policy is not consistently carried out due to a lack of both trained teachers who have mastered the standardized written forms of these languages, and of materials. Instead these languages, where offered, are optional subjects. These two languages have also been authorized for primary school instruction, but again, the lack of trained teachers combined with a lack of materials, has meant they are not used at that level, with very rare exceptions.

At the same time that Éwé and Kabiyè were authorized for use in formal education, they were also designated for use in adult literacy courses in the regions (the largest political divisions in Togo) where they are spoken, although not necessarily by all peoples living in those regions. The two other languages that also had over 100,000 speakers at the time, Tem and Moba, were also chosen for use in government-directed literacy programs aimed at youth and adults. Where the local population did not speak these designated languages, literacy was offered in French. Later, the use of other languages for literacy instruction was permitted, as long as these languages had a written form, a lexical study or dictionary, trained literacy personnel, appropriate educational materials, and a body of published literature.

The linguistic policy that insisted on French-only education has been an important factor in low rates of school attendance, and thus, low literacy levels. In Togo the global illiteracy rate is estimated to be 40 percent (UNESCO 2014). Many organizations are attempting to better this state of affairs. The most important are the Ministry of Primary, Secondary, and Technical Instruction and Professional Training, and the Ministry of Social Action (the first was responsible for adult literacy from 2007 to 2014; the second is the current overseer). Until 2007 the para-governmental organization SOTOCO (the Togolese Cotton Company, now the New Cotton Company of Togo) also did much literacy work through its local cotton grower groups. Nongovernmental organizations working in literacy and education include both international NGOs and numerous local NGOs and associations. Where available, they often cooperate with networks of NGOs in their working region.

### 1.2.3 Sociolinguistic background: Benin

France took control of the former Dahomey kingdom in 1894, incorporating it in French West Africa in 1895. French became first the colony's administrative language, and then its language of education. It continues to maintain this privileged position. However, in 1972 Benin declared that all its languages were national languages. The National Linguistic Commission (*Commission nationale de linguistique,* or CNL) was created in that year to coordinate linguistic research and to establish orthographies for each one of these languages, as well as to study indigenous literature for incorporation into schools. Between 1975 and 1980, a series of seminars was organized by the CNL to help each then-identified language group establish a local linguistic commission, an alphabet, and principles for the transcription of its language.

The next step was to write and publish primers for each of the national languages. Many of these government-sponsored primers, designed during the period of the Marxist government, are still in use. They are based on the approach developed by Paolo Freire, by which he sought to make the inhabitants of Brazilian slums aware of their condition in order to empower them to improve it (Freire 1970). In 2009 the Beninese government decided to continue with its version of the Freire method as it launched the *"faire faire"* strategy, whereby the state delegates authority to private operators to run literacy programs with government funds (*Groupe Technique du Travail de Ministère de la Culture, de L'alphabétisation et de la Promotion des Langues Nationales,* or

MCAPLN 2009). This was done in the framework of the UN's Fast-Track Initiative. In 2012, however, the Beninese government switched to an approach called "pedagogy of the text," which is similar to the Freire method in its goals and focus on local conditions but bases discussions and problem solving on authentic texts.

In spite of Benin's reputation as the "Latin Quarter of French West Africa," the illiteracy rate is approximately seventy-one percent (UNESCO 2014). Nearly eighty percent of the population cannot read even one of the national languages (MCAPLN 2009). However, these figures are still far better than those of the 1970s, when the illiteracy rate was estimated at 95.4 percent (*Commission Nationale Pour la Réforme Scolaire,* or National Commission for Scholastic Reform, May 1973). This improvement is largely due to the efforts of the National Office of Literacy and Adult Education (DNAEA), supported technically and financially by the Swiss Agency for Development and Cooperation, which has assisted the Beninese government in this domain since 1983. Several other international organizations also support efforts to raise levels of literacy by running classes, offering technical support and/or publishing materials in the national languages. National organizations, including several literacy worker associations and the local language committees of the CNL, are also involved in the battle against illiteracy.

## 1.3 Research questions

During my years as literacy coordinator for SIL Togo-Benin, I became interested in lessons to be learned from the Ifè literacy program and its strategy of developing local literacy associations. My hope is that this research will provide direction to literacy practitioners, policy makers, and partner organizations offering technical and/or financial support to literacy programs, and inform researchers looking into issues of leadership, particularly in African literacy programs.

The basic questions that I sought to address are as follows:
- What are the representations of leadership constructed by literacy leaders in the Ifè literacy program and by the Ifè people, and how do these play into capacity building?
- What representations of literacy and related concepts are present among the literacy leaders, and how do these affect capacity-building choices?
- According to research participants, what capacities have been, or should be, developed in or by the local associations?
- What factors contribute to, or hinder, the development of multiple, sustainable local literacy and development associations in order to serve adequately a widely dispersed population?

## 1.4 Methodology

The methodology chosen for this research was the case study in which a detailed description of the research subject and environment is developed through the use of a variety of methods. It is valuable for its ability to avoid generalizations that miss significant points of differences, as happens too often when discussing a society. The case study also has the advantage of allowing a portrayal of the EMIC, or in-group, perspective. As I am not

## 1.4 Methodology

African, the dangers of imposing a North American understanding on the data are quite strong, in spite of my more than ten years on the continent. The development of a rich description through the methods used facilitates an accurate rendering of the emic viewpoint of leadership and capacity building in nonformal education organizations.

The research for the original case study took place over a six month time period of direct contact with a substantial number of participants. Most of the research participants are Ifè speakers who are involved in the literacy program in some way. In total, forty-one Ifè people—Togolese and Beninese, men and women, leaders and subordinates, literacy workers and others—participated directly in the research project through group interviews. Others participated indirectly through their presence at classes, meetings, and workshops that I observed. Follow-up contact by e-mail was possible with some of those interviewed in order to fill in small details and to confirm findings. Additionally, I have been able to update the information for chapters 1, 2, and 8 through direct personal contacts with a number of the association literacy coordinators as well as the ACATBLI literacy personnel, since returning to Togo. This updating was necessary due to changes in the sociopolitical environment and to evolution in the program since I completed my research in 2009.

The majority of findings presented were obtained through group interviews for each association. I interviewed representatives of the board of each local association twice (while the entire board of each association was invited, not all came). The focus of the first interview for each was organizational history, while that of the second was representations of leadership (see chapter 3 for the notion of *representations,* and chapter 6 for Ifè representations of leadership). During the second set of board interviews, I included a printed list of five statements in French (with an Ifè translation) about organizational functioning, and asked each participant to choose one about which he or she felt strongly and to explain why. I also interviewed the literacy leaders of ACATBLI together regarding their history and experiences with the literacy program.

A control group verified that the representations of leadership that emerged were not held just by the leaders. This group was composed of people who attended the teachers' meeting in Itséré, which included not only the teachers but the local residents, including literacy learners. (See

Appendix A for the interview protocols.) In addition to these series of interviews, data were collected through documents, both published and unpublished, and through personal observation of classes, workshops, and meetings. This use of multiple sources, including different interview groups, provides triangulation of data, which is essential in validating qualitative research.

Finally, ethical considerations carried special weight in the research design because of the cross-cultural nature of this research project. Particularly pertinent were issues of relationships and research positioning; cross-cultural differences in behavior and expectations; and involvement of community members in research design and implementation.

The language of research was another major issue, both ethical and methodological. Most of the research was carried out in French, which is neither my dominant language nor that of the research participants. This has the potential to skew the information received and my interpretation of it. Additionally, one or more participants in each interview had difficulty in understanding and/or responding to questions asked in French, so the use of an interpreter (between Ifè and French) was required for the interviews. The interpreter also transcribed and translated certain of the Ifè discourses. Adding a third language, English, to the mix in order to report results has the potential to cause further deviation from the original intention of the speakers.

Although Ifè and English were thus necessarily involved in the research, French was the basis for all analysis, and, as the actual voice of most of the participants, is the authoritative text. Discourses in Ifè were translated on the spot into French and later verified for accuracy. The decision to transcribe these discourses was made halfway through the research phase of the project. Thus, due to the limited amount of time with the translator, not all were transcribed; those that were not are noted by "interp." The interviews, as transcribed in French and Ifè, are given in Appendix B. These were the texts used as the basis for analysis. An English translation based on the French (and Ifè) may not reflect the intent of the speaker with complete accuracy, and should be read with this in mind. However, to aid in a natural flow of the text in English, it is the English translation that is given in the main text.

*For further reading*

Afeli, Kossi Antoine. 1996. Influence des politiques linguistiques coloniales allemande et française sur la gestion in vitro du plurilinguisme dans le Togo indépendant [The influence of German and French colonial linguistic policies on the in vitro management of plurilingualism in independent Togo]. In C. Juillard and L. Calvet (eds.), *Les politiques linguistiques, mythes et réalités : Premières journées scientifiques du réseau thématique de recherche sociolinguistique et dynamique des langues*, 7–13. Beirut and Montreal: FMA / AUPELF-UREF.

Alidou, Hassana. 2004. Medium of instruction in post-colonial Africa. In J. W. Tollefson and A. B. M. Tsui (eds.), *Medium of instruction policies: Which agenda? whose agenda?*, 195–214. Mahwah, NJ and London: Lawrence Erlbaum.

Bamgboṣe, Ayo, ed. 1976. *Mother tongue education: The West African experience.* London and Paris: Hodder and Stoughton, and UNESCO Press.

Chambers, Robert. 2005. *Ideas for development.* London, and Sterling, VA: Earthscan.

Meredith, Martin. 2005. *The fate of Africa: A history of fifty years of independence.* New York: PublicAffairs.

# 2

# The Ifè

The Ifè, the people targeted by the literacy program examined here, have a population of around 200,000 speakers distributed between Togo (two-thirds) and Benin (one-third) (Lewis, Simons, and Fennig 2013). They are sometimes known by the Éwé name for them, Ana. The geographical area covered by this group extends approximately 150 kilometers from south to north and 80 kilometers from east to west. Road travel is difficult, as most roads are neither paved nor well-maintained. During the two annual rainy seasons, extending approximately from mid-February through March and from May to September, reaching the rural zones becomes extremely difficult and virtually impossible by car.

Those who live in Togo often know some Éwé, the language of wider communication of southern Togo, while some of those who live in Benin understand Yoruba, a related language which is also a language of wider communication of that region. Since 1975 Yoruba has been the language officially designated for literacy work in that prefecture of Benin, although literacy classes in Ifè are held under the auspices of one of the local associations described later in this chapter.

The Ifè people, of Yoruba origin, emigrated from Nigeria around the eighteenth century as they fled violent conflict in the area. A series of wars among other clans of the Yoruba, and later with the Fon, the Akposso, and the Bago, caused the Ifè to become closed to outsiders. Their experiences under colonialism reinforced this distrust, as violence was used against the disobedient.

One of the results of this feeling was a marked reluctance to send children to school. The subsequent lack of schools in the area—an estimate in the late 1980s was one primary school per seven or eight villages—led to a very high illiteracy rate among the Ifè. By 1990 the estimated literacy rate among the Ifè, in any language, was between five and fifteen percent (Lewis, Simons, and Fennig 2013). Whole villages were unable to read any language spoken in the region. Although a breakdown in gender statistics is not available specifically for the Ifè, most parents saw no point in sending their daughters to school, even when one was available. One study of the entire prefecture indicated that in 1996, after a ten-year explosion in the growth of school enrollment, girls accounted for approximately 38 percent of primary school students, 26 percent of lower secondary school (CEG) students, and thirteen percent of upper secondary school (lycée) students (Awokou 1997).

# Ifè Territory

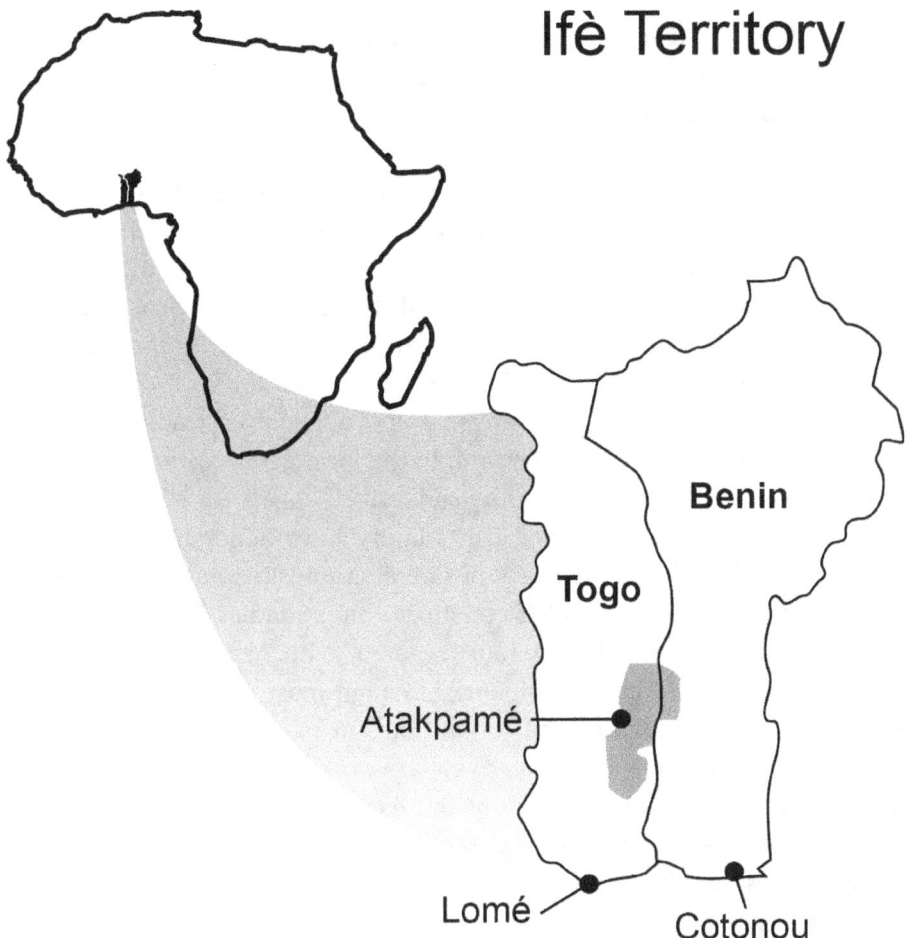

Source: Created by the author, this map is a composite from several sources, including Lewis 2009. Used with permission.

Life was—and is—physically demanding for most Ifè. The poor infrastructure in the area makes access to markets and modern health care difficult. Few communities have clinics. Access to clean water is another challenge; in the early 1990s, even where wells had been put in, often the pumps were broken. The weak economy in West Africa, even prior to the recent global economic crisis, made finding paid employment difficult even for those few who did obtain an education. One result of these difficulties that compounds the overall difficulty of the situation is the subsequent exodus of young men to points south in Togo and Benin or to Nigeria in search of paid work. A recent improvement in the infrastructure is the growth of the cell phone network; few areas are now beyond the reach of the telephone.

The majority of the Ifè follow their traditional religion, which involves worship of ancestral gods who personally take care of individual clans and occupations (Affala n.d.; Kossi-Titrikou 1997). Participating in this worship is seen not only as a privilege, but as a fulfillment of the responsibilities of a citizen. The spiritual chief, known as *iba,* is responsible for the transmission of beliefs and practices in the community, and for performing ritual sacrifices. According to Affala, anyone who offends the traditional chief also offends the gods. A common faith in the local gods has been the traditional means of building community solidarity.

Nevertheless, both Islam and Christianity have adherents among the Ifè. The Muslim Ifè are members of one clan and live mostly in a small part of the eastern portion of Ifè territory that straddles Togo and Benin. Christians are scattered throughout the area, with Assembly of God and Baptist churches being predominant. Although most of the leaders in the ACATBLI literacy program and its affiliates are Christian, it has been a major concern of these leaders to avoid creating a religious split based on literateness, particularly because of the early opposition to the program due to its ties to the spread of Christianity. They have therefore emphasized the usefulness of Ifè literacy for all Ifè and see literacy as a new basis for Ifè solidarity.

## 2.1 Ifè language development program

An SIL team composed of two European women began a linguistic research program on the Ifè language in 1981. The goals of this research were to provide a basis for Bible translation and literacy work. In order to learn to speak the language and begin linguistic and cultural research, the women lived in an Ifè village not far from Atakpamé, a large town at the western edge of the Ifè territory and the cultural center of the Ifè. While there, they met and hired Mr. Akoété Agbémadon as a part-time language-learning helper; he later became the head of the literacy program.

## 2.1.1 Ifè orthography history

The first fruit of the SIL linguistic research was a proposal for the alphabet, which was presented to around twenty influential Ifè from several towns and villages during a meeting in 1982. At this meeting, a language committee was elected to discuss questions of how to indicate tone and nasalization, as well as to determine the sociolinguistic basis of the alphabet. The committee decided that the system chosen would be based on Éwé in order to facilitate transfer to this language, as the majority of Ifè live in Togo. The SIL team developed a few materials and used them to test the acceptability of the committee's decisions. In 1984 another meeting was held to present these propositions and the results of the tests. Around 100 Ifè representing the entire region and all dialects attended this meeting and collectively approved the standard orthography. Since several important members of the first language committee had died, a second language committee was elected to discuss outstanding questions for the orthography; this committee operated until 1988. Subsequently, primers using this orthography were written and then tested with adults in each of the three dialectical regions. A third language committee was organized at the initiative of a member of the second committee; this committee supported the literacy work and sent representatives to the diploma ceremonies until it too ceased to function.

About fifteen years later, after the National Center for Applied Linguistics (*le Centre national de la linguistique appliquée,* or CENALA) in Benin had recognized Ifè as being a distinct language and not just a dialect of Yoruba, a Beninese literacy worker began to publish a rural newsletter in Ifè. Since he was not aware of the origins of the writing system, he changed several graphemes to make it more like Yoruba. Another change he made accounted for a dialectical variation. This literacy worker also reworked the primers, formatting them to be like the three-volume government series and incorporating the aforementioned orthographic changes in the process.

As the Ifè literacy program had just been implemented in Benin, its program directors quickly reacted against these changes. They organized a conference on the Ifè orthography, held in Doumé (in Benin) in December of 2003. During this meeting, the history of the development of the Ifè orthography and of the primers was presented, along with reasons for writing choices. The conference participants decided to confirm the standard orthography for use in Benin. I was one of the presenters, explaining why and how other linguistic groups in Togo and Benin had developed pan-dialectical orthographies. Additionally, prior to the conference, I had asked the DNAEA if a three-volume format was required for primers in Benin. Since the response was that the format wasn't as important as having content that was functional, the Beninese literacy workers decided to continue using the primers in five volumes furnished by their Togo-based counterparts.

### 2.1.2 Literacy program overview

The literacy program that gave birth to the associations to be described in this case study began just after the primers were tested in 1988–1989. Mr. Agbémadon, who had been working for the SIL team, was hired and trained on the job to supervise the program. A second supervisor was hired in 1996.

During the first six years, the literacy books only covered reading and writing in Ifè, which targets adult illiterate Ifè. Mathematics was introduced in 1995, but it quickly became evident that this lengthened the course to the point that it interfered with the agricultural cycle. As a result, in 1996 mathematics was made part of a second-year course, which also includes a post-literacy book and writing manual. A third-year course of learning oral and written French was piloted in 2009 and has been further developed since then; to maintain interest in reading the mother tongue, an Ifè post-literacy book forms part of the curriculum. From 1998 to 2004, the first-year course had two versions, one for church-based literacy (with Bible verses for reading material) and one for community-based literacy (with proverbs for reading material). However, use of the church-based series of primers was discontinued, except in the urban area of Atakpamé, in order to promote community unity. A further addition to the program, starting in 2010, was the inclusion, of participative discussions on current topics of interest to the community. Although it was planned for only the first-year course, it has been so popular that it is now a feature of every level in the program, which also satisfies current requirements of the Togolese government's literacy curriculum requirements.

Literature production is an important, but often overlooked and underfunded, component of literacy work. At first, the project was able to meet its printing needs with a stencil burner and duplicator. In 1995 the program hired a man to be a part-time project printer. He was gradually trained by one of the expatriates in layout, printing, book assembly, and finally in management of the print shop. The program requested funds for a copy-printer, which it subsequently purchased, in 1995. For the next eleven years, the print shop not only printed and stocked Ifè books, but also was available to print material for other literacy programs at cost. When the copy-printer needed to be replaced, gifts were received from abroad to buy a Risograph; that same year the printer became a full-time employee of the project. Several years later, however, he developed a chronic disability, so an assistant printer had to be hired and trained in book assembly and printing. The senior printer continues to handle finances, maintenance, and repair of equipment. Currently, because there are so many Ifè literacy classes needing materials, the print shop is able to meet the printing needs only of ACATBLI, serving both the translation and the literacy work.

The living conditions of the Ifè had an immediate impact on the program. First, the poor state of the roads made travel difficult. Motorcycles are more practical than cars. During the rainy season, any larger vehicle needs to be one with four-wheel drive. While also using motorcycles, the program has indeed had a four-wheel drive vehicle off and on over the life of the project, since it makes it easier for the central team to travel together to visit classes, and it enables the team to transport literature to the area more easily. However, operating and maintaining a vehicle has been expensive; after a certain point, it must be sold to prevent unreasonable drains on project resources, and funds found to purchase a replacement.

Then, early on in the program as the dry season progressed, class attendance started falling. When inquiries were made, the team learned that since the pumps in the village wells were not working and the villagers could not afford to repair them, the female students had to walk up to twenty kilometers to find water. As a result they had neither the time nor the energy to attend classes. In order to address this problem, the team got a count of the broken pumps and an estimate of repair costs. With this information in hand, the expatriate member of the team found funds to pay for the repairs and someone to do the work. Currently, villages are encouraged to form a committee, take up a collection for a bank account, and then contact Togo's water company to request a new or repaired well and pump. At least one church denomination in the area also has a fund to help communities construct wells.

The sparse financial resources of the project in its first sixteen years of existence, coupled with the low literacy rate in the population and the desire of the Ifè members of the literacy team to reach all their fellow Ifè with literacy, pushed the team early in its work to envision a strategy that was unique in Togo. The team decided not to try to establish a literacy program that would cover the entire Ifè region at the same time. Instead, they divided the territory into seven zones, with five in Togo and two in Benin according to the major travel routes. The three-phase plan was to concentrate on one zone at a time, opening literacy centers and facilitating the creation of a local association that would oversee literacy work in that zone. At the end of three or so years of capacity building, the responsibility for the literacy program in that zone would be completely transferred to the local association, and the team would begin work in another zone.

## 2.2 History of the local literacy associations

This strategy was followed for sixteen years, with some success. By the end of that time, two associations had become autonomous, but later had severe financial difficulties that effectively halted the literacy work. Two other associations, one of which encompassed two zones, were nearly ready to become independent. Work had been attempted in two other zones, but interest in literacy during this time was weak to nonexistent. This section chronologically traces the history of each of the six literacy associations, noting its distinctive characteristics and the challenges it has faced.

### 2.2.1 AVID

The first local association to take shape was the Association of Ifè Instructors (*Association des moniteurs ifè,* or AMI) in 1990. This association, which was composed of all the first literacy teachers in the Akparé zone in Togo, became autonomous in 1996 after having found, with the help of the SIL-Ifè team, funding through the German development organization DED. In 1999 AMI began a grain storage project to generate additional revenue. Shortly before this time, following the abrupt departure of its second president, it also changed its name to Association of Ifè Volunteers for Development (*Association des volontaires ifè pour le développement,* or AVID).

AVID aims to help the Ifè community develop via education, starting with literacy, but going further to the establishment of groups that will be involved in income-generating activities (IGA). Unfortunately, the association had to suspend its activities in 2001 when the grain storage IGA failed; the economy was particularly bad in that year, so AVID held on to its beans longer than planned, hoping the price would rise. However, when the granaries were opened, association leaders discovered that a weevil infestation had spoiled the beans so badly that it was impossible to sell any of them. External funding from DED had ended just a few months before this catastrophe. Nevertheless, the board submitted the documentation necessary for obtaining legal status in 2002, however, it did not receive an official response. AVID's supervisor, who later held the post of president, continued to be involved in Ifè literacy work through his technical support of the program run by SOTOCO, the Togolese Cotton Company, and in consequence continued to be invited to SIL training courses.

AVID was revitalized with the infusion of money from Swedish funders in 2006 through ACATBLI. However, this revitalization came with the cost of a loss of AVID's autonomy. A dedicated female supervisor was chosen as the literacy coordinator by the ACATBLI team leaders, the first time a woman had held this position. In addition, the association has resubmitted its paperwork for legalization twice. AVID's president identified a lack of contacts in the appropriate ministry as a reason for the difficulties in gaining formal recognition. The formal membership of AVID has also declined; according to one teacher in this zone, many of his colleagues in the Akparé area have decided not to join due to a perceived lack of energy in the board. This deprives the association of income from membership dues and may have long-term consequences for its sustainability. This will be further discussed in chapter 8.

AVID's president at the time of my interviews in 2009 stepped down after his third term in order to pursue additional training in the field of development/income-generation, as he perceived this to be the organization's greatest lack. He has subsequently worked with AVID and AVADI in several projects, including training women's groups to set up internal loan systems.

## 2.2.2 AMADPENI

AMADPENI, the Association of Instructors for Literacy, Development, and the Protection of the Environment in the Ifè Area *(l'Association des moniteurs pour l'alphabétisation, le développement et la protection de l'environnement en milieu ifè)* is the current association working in the Est-Mono region of Togo. It grew out of the work done by the association *"Jésus le Chemin"* (Jesus the Way). As the bulk of the research took place before the formation of AMADPENI, an overview of the goals and history of literacy under *Jésus le Chemin* is discussed briefly here.

*Jésus le Chemin* (which has since split into four separate organizations) was begun in 1987 as a collaboration of churches and pastors in the Baptist Convention and of Baptist missionaries. Its headquarters was in Morétan, where the Baptist training center is also based. Initially, literacy work was not included among its activities; the literacy work was begun by SIL in 1989. Although the SIL team had attempted to begin an Est-Mono chapter of AMI, this effort failed, so the literacy work was handed over to *Jésus le Chemin* after two years of work in the region.

The goal of *Jésus le Chemin* was twofold. First, it sought to bring all Ifè to the knowledge of God through Jesus Christ. Secondly, it aspired to the development of the entire person, through meeting physical needs. The latter goal was considered to be a support for the former. Literacy was regarded as a form of development and until 2006 was administered under the association's development department. Other departments included those for evangelism, men, youth, schools, projects and missions, music, the women's missionary union, and church development.

From 1991 onwards, literacy classes were undertaken by *Jésus le Chemin* with financial and practical support from the Baptist Mission and, until 1995, advice and occasional practical help from SIL literacy workers. When the Baptist missionaries abruptly left in 1999, literacy work, as well as much of the other evangelistic and development work of the association, slowed to a crawl due to a lack of funds. The few classes that took place over the next six years were taught by previously trained volunteer teachers.

In 2006 *Jésus le Chemin* created a literacy department and became a member organization under ACATBLI, when the latter received funds from a Swedish NGO to develop local community-based literacy organizations.

Swedish government funds, even when channeled through a faith-based NGO as in this case, could only be used to support the literacy component of *Jésus le Chemin*'s work; the remainder of *Jésus le Chemin*'s activities was supported by a fund created by tithes and offerings from member churches. The only aspect of the literacy work that received a contribution from this fund was the maintenance of the literacy coordinator's motorcycle; this was bought with Swedish funds through ACATBLI.

Literacy work has always intentionally been done as much as possible in collaboration with people of all faiths, with the focus being cultural and linguistic solidarity, since the leaders of *Jésus le Chemin* desired to see all Ifè able to read and write their own language. However, in part because of the funding issue, and in part because of the desire to ensure that literacy work is seen as nonconfessional, AMADPENI was formed in 2012.

AMADPENI retained the goal of development through meeting the physical and other needs of people, and added the goal of developing the environment. Thus, it continues with literacy classes and the reforestation project and plans to add other development activities. All literacy teachers are expected to be members of the association and pay annual dues.

### 2.2.3 AMIADA

Literacy work in Oké began during the 1997–1998 literacy campaign year. In line with phase two in the SIL-Ifè project strategy, the Association of Ifè Instructors for Adult Literacy and Development (*Association des moniteurs ifè pour l'alphabétisation et le développement des adultes,* or AMIADA) was created in 2000. Shortly thereafter, local authorities selected land just outside the town of Oké-Adogbénou and gave two hectares to the local association. In 2004 SIL bought those two hectares to hold for the association, plus an additional eight. When AMIADA received official recognition in 2014, it got its two hectares back. One use of this property is for teacher training and other meetings, which until this land was obtained were held in churches. Once the property was acquired, these activities were held in a temporary structure on the site, but in 2006 the SIL-Ifè project found funds to build on its portion of the land a cement block meeting hall, a small dormitory, and washrooms, which together host all training events and meetings. The property also has a small two-room building built in 2004–2005 that houses a caretaker and can host the ACATBLI leaders when they come for training or meetings.

The primary goal of AMIADA is for all Ifè in its zone to become literate. Its secondary goal is to improve life economically and spiritually for the residents of its region. The strategies for reaching this latter goal incorporate elements of the literacy program, including supplemental reading books which describe, in story form, ways to improve agricultural techniques and to manage a family harmoniously, and the mathematics program which allows small businessmen and -women *(petit[e]s commerçant[e]s)* to keep accounts and avoid being cheated. As with all the associations, local people are invited to monthly teachers' meetings in order to learn from the practical teaching given at those times. AMIADA has also been involved in encouraging literacy learners to buy fruit-tree seedlings, which ACATBLI then distributes towards the beginning of the long rainy season each year. In addition, Oké has been the home of two of ACATBLI's income-generating activities, beekeeping and sheep raising (both now discontinued; see chapter 8). These, as well as AMIADA's own projects described in the next paragraph, have inspired individuals to try to increase their incomes by these means.

AMIADA's own income-generating projects are also agriculture-based. The first IGA, begun in 2001, was storage of peppers *(piment),* although grains have been stocked in other years. In this type of IGA, commodities are bought when prices are low and resold during the natural cycle of price increases during the year. As is true of most storage projects, the success of this has fluctuated with market prices and randomly imposed government controls, as well as natural disasters such as insect infestations. In 2004 the association planted and harvested a crop of soybeans that was then sold. In addition to managing grain and pepper storage projects, AMIADA owns two hectares of land, one of which was planted with teak in 2008 as an income-generating activity. Plans for a chicken-raising project to generate funds are also in process. Another development project it would like to establish is a health center on or near its property, as there are none in the vicinity; such a facility would be helpful when participants fall ill during training sessions.

All literacy teachers are automatically members of AMIADA. They elect the board at their yearly general assembly. AMIADA members pay annual dues, which have helped to provide seed money for income-generating projects of the association and are also used for purchasing such things as benches for training courses. In 2008 AMIADA opened a bank account as a step towards self-sufficiency.

According to the original strategy, AMIADA should have become autonomous by 2002 or 2003. However, it was not ready for this step at that time. As a consequence, funding was sought and received for the period of 2004–2005 to build capacity towards independence for AMIADA. However, when ACATBLI received funding to expand the project in 2006, all existing Ifè literacy organizations that agreed to place themselves under ACATBLI in order to receive funds and training were placed on the same footing. This was done to maintain a sense of equality, with the intention of preventing feelings of jealousy. See section 8.2 for the current status of AMIADA as well as the other local associations.

### 2.2.4 ADCIBA

In Benin the Ifè people have been considered part of the Nago language group. Several related ethnic groups were placed in this group: Yoruba, Idaasha, Ica, and Cabe, as well as Ifè. Literacy was thus provided in Yoruba, the presumed common language of this group. However, as ADCIBA's president, Mr. Koumondjo, explained, *"L'alphabétisation en yorouba ne reste pas dans la tête de nos apprenants"* ("Literacy in Yoruba doesn't stay in the heads of our students").

Around 1995 an Ifè man from Doumé teaching in Benin's government literacy program for Yoruba learned about the SIL literacy work in Togo. Frustrated with the difficulties of his non-Yoruba-speaking Ifè students with learning to read, he visited the team in Atakpamé and in 1996 received training to teach Ifè literacy. For several years, he continued to receive training from the government program in Yoruba, but taught in Ifè. Meanwhile, he worked to establish a National Linguistic Commission for Ifè (discontinued after 2003, although efforts to restart it have been underway) and maintained contact with the SIL-Ifè program in Atakpamé.

Although they were unaware of what was happening in Doumé, literacy teachers in Tchetti were experiencing the same frustrations with the lack of progress in their students. In 1998 a man who had taught in the Ifè program in Oké came to Tchetti and raised awareness for mother tongue literacy and teacher training. Three years later, the Tchetti teachers were put in touch with the SIL-Ifè project thanks to another man who had been living in Oké but then returned to live in Tchetti. In 2001 SIL began classes in the area. Two years later, the Tchetti teachers formed the Regional Committee for the Promotion of the Ifè Language (*Comité régional pour la promotion de la langue ifè,* or CRPI). However, this organization did not function well and soon ceased to exist.

In 2002 the group in Doumé and the one in Tchetti became aware of each other. In 2006, after the failure of the CRPI, the two decided to unite. This decision was made primarily to present a united front to the Beninese government and literacy department as they sought recognition for Ifè as a language distinct from Yoruba and other related languages. Their chosen name, Association for the Development of the Ifè Community of Benin through Literacy (*l'Association pour le développement de la communauté ifè du Bénin par l'alphabétisation,* or ADCIBA), reflects their primary distinction from the other associations: it is located in Benin, not Togo. In 2007 their application for registration as an association was submitted and accepted. While I was there in 2009, they petitioned the DNAEA to request the recognition of Ifè as the official language of literacy for their area; this had not been granted as of 2014. As a result, they have not met the eligibility requirements for participation in the *"faire-faire"* strategy that Benin initiated in 2011 at the urging of UNESCO and the World Bank. Efforts continue to acquire the official acknowledgment of Ifè as the language of literacy in their community.

Membership in ADCIBA is open to all. Among those present at the first general assembly were literacy workers at all levels, traditional chiefs, local political authorities, heads of the majority Ifè *arrondissements* (the smallest administrative district in Benin) and local resource people from each village. This group elected the board, with each of the six Ifè *arrondissements* being allowed two representatives to the board, except for the more populous Doumé, which was permitted a third representative. For a time, the sixth *arrondissment* was not interested in belonging, and another *arrondissement* had no representatives on the board because of a lack of commitment on the part of those elected, but these situations no longer exist. The founding members of ADCIBA contribute a special sum, *la part sociale,* each year, while all members pay annual dues. The *part sociale* has been used for the constitutive assembly expenses as well as for registration fees during the legalization process.

The primary goal of ADCIBA is to achieve the development of the Ifè people through literacy. It seeks collaboration with the many development organizations who work in Benin, and it desires to translate and publish as much development information as possible. In this vein, it published a few issues of an official newsletter until the death of the editor (and owner of the computer) in 2010. It also hopes to provide support for those learners who want to start IGAs, and already does so for those who have begun to raise chickens. Another focus is reforestation through education and participation in ACATBLI's tree-planting program, as well as through planting teak on its own property.

ADCIBA owns land in each zone, on which it pursues agricultural development activities such as crops, tree plantations, or animal husbandry. It had already tried to raise chickens on part of its land, but ran into difficulties and stopped that activity, opting instead to have a communal field. The Tchetti zone is the site of five hectares. ADCIBA started with two, but since their members were not permitted to plant on that parcel, three more hectares were acquired in order to have a site for future income generation through the teak plantation and other agricultural activities. The Doumé zone contains a small piece of property in town where ADCIBA hopes to build a training center. It also has three other hectares of land, one of which is planted in teak for future income.

### 2.2.5 AVADI

SIL first attempted to establish literacy work in the Buko region in 1993. However, the people were very reluctant to accept classes, and the few classes begun did not finish. In 2002 an Ifè Assembly of God pastor was assigned to the area. He reflected on the poverty of the area and began conversations with a number of people on what could be done to fight this condition. The outcome of these conversations was the establishment of the Association of Volunteers for Literacy and the Development of the Ifè (*l'Association des volontaires pour l'alphabétisation et le développement des Ifè,* or AVADI) in 2006. Deciding that the first step in its fight against poverty was literacy, it held meetings to raise awareness of the need for literacy and invited ACATBLI to come and start literacy classes, which it did in late 2006.

The goal of AVADI is to develop the Buko region economically, culturally, and educationally. Its theme, in line with one heard in the international development community, is to fight poverty. AVADI leaders desire to see every Ifè able to read and write, whether in Ifè through the literacy program or in French through the formal education program. Another concern is the health domain, as most villages in their area lack latrines and organizations for maintaining village cleanliness. Yet another area where they hope to develop the region is through the establishment of cultural centers, where folktales can be transmitted and other cultural activities occur.

So far they have worked through the literacy classes to accomplish their goals. Students in the classes are encouraged to organize themselves to pursue IGAs and other development projects. For example, one class took up a collection to buy corn for a grain storage project. Additionally, many literacy class graduates have organized local schools for their children. As mentioned earlier, they also benefited recently from training in setting up internal loan systems for women's groups.

Membership in AVADI is open to the community. Teachers are encouraged but not required to be members; so far, all have joined. Collections have been taken, but to this point, the association has minimal financial resources outside of what ACATBLI and its financial partners have been able to provide. It has, however, twice submitted the documents needed to obtain legalization.

### 2.2.6 The association *"Espoir pour l'Avenir"*

SIL attempted to start literacy work in the Datcha-Glei region, to the south of Atakpamé, from 1995 to 1999. However, because many members of the local population were concerned that the classes were merely a mask for evangelization, the SIL-Ifè program had minimal success in establishing classes, much less a local association. The literacy team finally decided to put its resources elsewhere until the time seemed right to try again.

Literacy work was restarted in this area in 2008, with the help of an Ifè pastor committed to promoting literacy. By this time, people had heard from other areas that the literacy classes were for all Ifè and

## 2.3 ACATBLI's role

not a place of evangelism. ACATBLI asked the pastor to be the literacy coordinator for this zone. With the agreement of his denominational leaders, he accepted. The association *"Espoir pour l'Avenir"* (Hope for the Future) was not yet formally organized by 2009. For this reason, it did not form part of my research project. However, it did have its constitutive assembly in May 2010, an essential step in forming a viable, formally recognized association in Togo. The association's board was established that same year.

The sequence of development of the associations discussed so far is summarized in the timeline shown in figure 2.1.

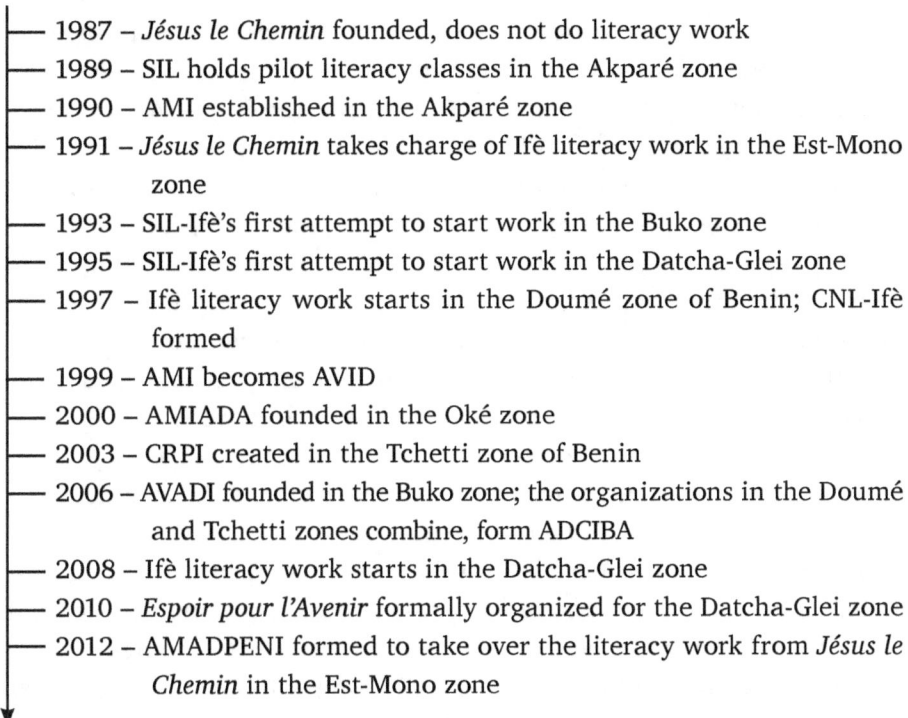

- 1987 – *Jésus le Chemin* founded, does not do literacy work
- 1989 – SIL holds pilot literacy classes in the Akparé zone
- 1990 – AMI established in the Akparé zone
- 1991 – *Jésus le Chemin* takes charge of Ifè literacy work in the Est-Mono zone
- 1993 – SIL-Ifè's first attempt to start work in the Buko zone
- 1995 – SIL-Ifè's first attempt to start work in the Datcha-Glei zone
- 1997 – Ifè literacy work starts in the Doumé zone of Benin; CNL-Ifè formed
- 1999 – AMI becomes AVID
- 2000 – AMIADA founded in the Oké zone
- 2003 – CRPI created in the Tchetti zone of Benin
- 2006 – AVADI founded in the Buko zone; the organizations in the Doumé and Tchetti zones combine, form ADCIBA
- 2008 – Ifè literacy work starts in the Datcha-Glei zone
- 2010 – *Espoir pour l'Avenir* formally organized for the Datcha-Glei zone
- 2012 – AMADPENI formed to take over the literacy work from *Jésus le Chemin* in the Est-Mono zone

Figure 2.1. Association development timeline.

## 2.3 ACATBLI's role

ACATBLI was created in 2007 and legalized in 2008 in order to ensure continuity of the literacy and translation work after the departure of the expatriates in the program. It is the umbrella organization for the local associations discussed in the previous sections. In addition, the local associations are collectively represented on ACATBLI's board by three people, elected by all six associations. Other members of ACATBLI's board include the association's employees and various community members. At this point in time, its literacy workers are still heavily involved in carrying out certain responsibilities that will be handed over to the various local associations when their leaders are ready to work independently (see table 8.1).

Once the associations become autonomous, the ACATBLI leaders foresee a shift in their role. They expect, first of all, to continue to organize and supervise literacy classes, but only in Atakpamé. The city is technically part of AVID's zone of responsibility, but AVID's zone covers three cantons, and thus their leaders will welcome ACATBLI's help in the city. ACATBLI, therefore, intends to supplement AVID's efforts in the city to ensure that all Ifè have the opportunity to read their mother tongue. In addition, ACATBLI's literacy personnel plan to focus on literature production, since they are well aware of the need to develop a literate environment and to provide ample reading material, both to build fluency among new literates and to motivate Ifè to learn to read their mother tongue. They also desire to ensure that materials that support development efforts—economic, cultural, social, and religious—are available to their people. However, due to various factors, including their currently heavy workload in overseeing the local associations as well as managing external funds, they have not been able to do much in this area for some time.

One relatively recent development has been the hiring of an administrator, of an accountant, and of an agro-engineer. The administrator and the accountant have helped to lighten the workload of the head of the literacy program. The agro-engineer is working with current and former literacy classes to form *groupements* that then join a cooperative, known as ACATBLI's Agricultural Cooperative (*ACATBLI coopérative agricole*, or ACA). The goals of this cooperative are to support functional literacy through the development of income-generating activities with newly literate Ifè (all graduates of the Ifè literacy program are included) and to establish a durable source of income for ACATBLI's activities. A number of activities have begun, including the purchase of fertilizer in bulk for distribution to participants and training in organic farming techniques. Others are planned, including the drilling of wells and installation of community solar panels. So far, this project has been well received and is meeting its goals.

## 2.4 Summary

The Ifè people live on both sides of the Togo-Benin border. Historical reasons led to the Ifè becoming closed to outsiders, with the results of low school attendance and subsequent low literacy rates. The infrastructure throughout most of their area is underdeveloped, with the recent exception of the cell phone network. Most Ifè follow their traditional religion, although there are some Muslim Ifè and the Christian church is growing among the Ifè.

Language development work began in 1981. The writing system was established by 1989 and literacy classes begun. The poor infrastructure in the area forced the team from the start of the literacy program to implement certain development activities in order to ensure literacy class success. In the effort to reach the entire Ifè population, a strategy to form local literacy and development associations was devised by the Ifè members of the SIL team. By 2008 a total of six local associations had been established, and the Ifè literacy and translation workers had established an umbrella organization for these associations.

# 3

# *Représentations sociales:* What does Common Sense Say?

The theory of représentations sociales came out of social psychology but is now used throughout the social sciences. It forms the basis for my analysis of leadership in the Ifè culture and literacy organizations and its influence on what happens in those organizations. This theory also sheds light on the motivations of mother tongue literacy program leaders and the choices they make in training and in program management.

## 3.1 A brief history of the theory

The notion of *représentations sociales,* or SOCIAL REPRESENTATIONS (SR), was developed in the French-speaking academic community. Most of what has been written on this theory was written in French and has not yet been translated into English (Duveen 2000). The genesis of this theory is generally attributed to the sociologist Émile Durkheim (Bonardi and Roussiau 1999). He first posited the notion of COLLECTIVE REPRESENTATIONS, stating that societies consist of people in relationship; as individuals act and react within that societal relationship, their personal representations merge with others and in the process are transformed, becoming collective representations. These representations then take on a life of their own, able to influence the members and institutions of the society (Durkheim 1898). These collective understandings, such as those found in myths, religion, and moral law, form a system and are very stable. They also constrain members of that group in their ways of acting and thinking, in essence regulating social life. However, the fairly exclusive application of this concept to explanations of traditional ("other") societies led to its marginalization in the field of psychology (Moscovici 1989).

This view of representations as socially constructed was then taken up by social psychologist Serge Moscovici in the early 1960s as he studied how French society constructed representations of the relatively new practice of psychoanalysis. His application of the notion to modern, diversified societies with a fast pace of change expanded the concept to include a wide range of ideas and knowledge that have a collective origin, thereby producing the theory of SRs (Moscovici 1989). Whereas for Durkheim, it was the substrata of collective life—the group—that was significant in the construction of a collective representation, for Moscovici, it was the interactions among individuals that were essential to the construction of SRs. Since that time, the notion of SR has been recognized as an important theoretical tool and applied throughout the social sciences as researchers strive to better understand communication as well as social practices and thought (Dagenais and Jacquet 2008; Doise 1986).

## 3.2 Characteristics and types of social representations

The diversity of domains of application has led to a wide range of understandings of the character of an SR. Essentially, the theory of social representations seeks to explain how meaning is constructed and spread throughout a group (Py 2003). SRs are viewed as both a social process and a cognitive one (Abric 2001; Bonardi and Roussiau 1999). An SR, then, is seen as a socially generated, interpretive framework (Py 2003) or "microtheory" (Moore and Py 2008), often perceived by those who share it as "common sense" (Jodelet 1989). It is constructed through experience, through group and individual interaction, and by portrayals of the object in the media (Py 2004), generally from a common reference point, also known as a "social anchor" (Gajo 2000). However, just because a person recognizes an SR does not mean he or she agrees with it; thus discourses and behaviors that seem to contradict the SR may be in evidence within the group (Gajo 2000; Py 2004).

Two types of representations are recognized by researchers coming from a linguistic approach, which is the approach I have taken. For each type of SR, three terms are in use, each of which highlights a particular aspect of the type. The first type is one that is widely recognized in a given group, and fairly stable. Gajo (2000) calls these PRECONSTRUCTED REPRESENTATIONS *(représentations préconstruites),* while Py (2003, 2004) refers to them as REFERENCE REPRESENTATIONS *(représentations de référence).* Cavalli and Coletta (2003:62), however, label them as FUNDAMENTAL FEATURES of an SR. Py notes that these representations usually are decontextualized and often emerge as set phrases, such as expressions of stereotypes, proverbs, maxims, and other sayings and clichés. Cavalli and Coletta add that they are not tied to social or professional roles.

The second type of representation is one whose meaning has been proposed and negotiated in the particular discursive context in which it was expressed, thus rendering this type of representation very flexible. The negotiated aspect of this type of representation has led Gajo to label them CO-CONSTRUCTED REPRESENTATIONS *(représentations co-construites).* Py and Cavalli and Coletta, however, highlight the link to context by their use, respectively, of the terms EMPLOYED REPRESENTATION *(représentation d'usage)* and CONTEXTUAL FEATURE. These elements of an SR are very strongly linked to the social roles and behaviors of those expressing them (Cavalli and Coletta 2003:82).

In a given situation, the distinction between the two varieties is not necessarily sharp. The categorization of a representation is meant to help in an analysis, but generalizations and categories tend to break down (Py 2004). In a given discourse, both may be present and even mixed, as is true for the data gathered for this study. In fact, Moore (2001:18) identifies their relationship in the construction of a representation as

> taking the preconstructed representations and adapting them to a new situation, in context, by the strengthening or dilution of certain features, and by the selection of elements that will convey the content of the representation in a more pertinent manner. (My translation.)
>
> *(prendre en charge les préconstruits et de les adapter à une nouvelle situation, en contexte, par le renforcement ou la dilution de certains traits, et par la sélection des éléments qui vont porter de manière plus saillante le contenu de la représentation.)*

So, as participants in a discourse speak, choosing terms, reformulating expressions and clarifying statements, fundamental features are adapted to the specific context of the communication. In any case, the communal vigor of an SR is shown by the expression of both stable and contextual elements (Gajo 2000).

## 3.3 Functions of a social representation

Researchers across traditions, while holding different opinions on the character of an SR, agree that it has several functions. First, it gives meaning to social realities or "social objects," such as education or HIV-AIDS, helping individuals to orient themselves in relation to these realities. Part of this orientation involves the social positioning of those interacting with or communicating about the object (Cavalli and Coletta 2003; Moore and Py 2008). Further, an SR also allows a person to know how to behave in a socially accepted manner in relationship to that object (Bonardi and Roussiau 1999; Jodelet 1989). An SR also allows people to justify their practices, beliefs, and behaviors (Bonardi and Roussiau 1999; Moliner et al. 2002). These various functions of an SR—of mutual understanding, of identification, of orientation, and of justification—make this theory valuable to this case study, as I seek to understand how Ifè literacy leaders understand leadership and literacy, orient themselves in relationship to these social objects, and use SRs to explain their practices as leaders and the choices they have made in the literacy program.

## 3.4 Related concepts

Several concepts are closely tied to the notion of social representations, and their relationships to it have been widely discussed. A stereotype is a particular, well-known type of representation (Py 2003), one that is simplified, fixed, and stable, allowing discourse participants to quickly identify and categorize the object of the stereotype (Boyer 2003). Beliefs and opinions are generally, but not universally, considered to be components of a representation (Abric 2003; Moliner et al. 2002). Opinions may also be seen as precursors to representations (Py 2000; cited in Boyer 2003), the result of someone asking about beliefs (Py 2004), or as a discourse theme that reveals a representation (Negura 2006). I included beliefs and opinions among the features of representations that emerged during the course of my research.

Attitudes, however, are considered by some to be a component of SRs, but by others to be related to, yet not a part of, representations. It should be noted that "attitude" in English and *attitude* in French do not quite have the same semantic content. The French word has much stronger connotations of behavior than does the American English word, which in its most common sense generally refers to a mental state reflecting feelings or opinions. This may be why some French researchers insist that attitudes are integral components of a representation (Abric 2003; Cavalli and Coletta 2003). In discourse, however, an attitude is not observable but must be inferred (Moore 2001). So for other researchers, an attitude is not, then, part of a representation, but related to representations through its evaluative character, which shows up as reasons or motives for holding a particular representation. Accordingly, attitudes are seen as influencing the development of representations and vice versa (Moore and Py 2008). I did not distinguish between opinions and attitudes in my analysis of the data, because for me, both have evaluative connotations, whether or not behaviors are implied.

Thus attitudes, particularly towards those unable to read and/or to read and write in Ifè, may be found among the features of the representations described in chapters 6 and 7.

Although most literature concerning SRs is found in traditions of French scholarship, similar notions have arisen in other academic traditions. In English, the social linguist James Gee proposed the notion of DISCOURSES with a capital D; these are *"saying(writing)-doing-being-valuing-believing combinations"* (1996:127, italics in the original). This conception is probably the closest in English-language scholarship to the notion of social representations (Kramsch 2008). Like an SR, a Discourse displays both an identity and a membership in a particular social group "through words, actions, values, and beliefs" (Gee 1996:128). However, a Discourse is also tied to ideologies and can either empower or disempower self and others.

The idea of a CULTURAL NARRATIVE as used by Dym and Hutson also has much in common with the theory of social representations. These authors indicate that a cultural narrative is "the sum of a particular society's ideas about how people are supposed to behave, think, and feel [and] is more than just a perspective. It is the means by which a culture puts forth, promotes, and imposes its standards on members" (2005:48). The main differences here seem to be that a cultural narrative applies to a much wider group (a whole society) than those described by works on SRs generally do, and is communicated more by stories than through ordinary discourse.

It must be noted that the translation of the French term for social representations does not completely correspond to what is generally understood by that term in English. In English, the usual meaning of "social representation" is a strictly cognitive phenomenon describing schemata or other mental structures (Duveen 2000);[1] it does not include behaviors. In French, however, the term covers not just attitudes, beliefs, and ideas but social norms, actions, and practices that result from and construct those mental states and structures (Kramsch 2008). In this study, the term "social representation" will be used strictly in the sense of the French term *représentation sociale,* that is, the interpretive framework around a social object, generated by a distinct social group, that encompasses "thought and action, knowledge and practice, the saying and the doing" (Kramsch 2008:321).

---

[1] Schemata are systems "of cognitive structures stored in memory that are abstract representations of events, objects, and relationships in the world" (Harris and Hodges 1995:227).

## 3.5 Rationale for using social representations in this study

In the context of my research, I became interested in the theory of social representations for its power to explain African social practices and thought, in this case in relation to leadership in literacy associations, from an insider's perspective. As a cross-cultural worker, sometimes I do not understand the actions or reactions of African friends and colleagues (and I am certain that, at times, they are confused by mine). This theory offers a means to access the interpretive framework of my African colleagues that is the basis of their "common sense." This study, therefore, is only a starting point, since I work closely with many Africans who are not Ifè; I will need to explore the representations of other groups. Such research can lay the groundwork for adjusting the content of capacity-building courses and workshops currently based on Western resources and knowledge, to content more in line with local realities.

As has been stated, an SR motivates and justifies behavior. The SRs circulating in a group profoundly influence the interaction among group members and with other groups. The SRs of leadership determine both what a leader expects and is expected to do, and also what is expected of his or her subordinates. This in turn influences the type of decision-making, authority structures, and activities developed and accepted by the group. To facilitate better understanding of the training the Ifè leaders have had, as well as the organizational and cultural environment in which they work, pertinent theories and models of leadership are discussed in the next chapter.

### For further reading

Flament, C. 2001. Structure, dynamiques et transformation des *représentations sociales* [The structure, dynamics, and transformation of social representations]. In J.-C. Abric (ed.), *Pratiques sociales et représentations* [Social practices and representations], 37–58. Third edition. Paris: Presses Universitaires de France.

Moliner, Pascal. 1996. *Images et représentations sociales : De la théorie des représentations à l'étude des images sociales* [Images and social representations: From the theory of representations to the study of social images]. Grenoble: Presses Universitaires de Grenoble.

# 4

# Leadership: How Do You Identify a Good Leader?

During my more than ten years of living in Africa and working in a nongovernmental organization in the area of mother tongue literacy program development, I have had several opportunities to observe clashes between African and Western leadership and management styles, particularly in the handling of financial issues and of conflicts. Nevertheless, the program management courses offered by our organization and others have been based on Western models of business leadership, largely due to the lack of an alternative African model, although a number of authors have noted this mismatch between Western management and leadership models and African styles of leadership. While various studies have analyzed the leadership traits of African business managers and African bureaucrats, particularly in English-speaking Africa, studies of leadership of African nongovernmental organizations, of African organizations that depend on volunteers, or of organizations that are situated in French-speaking Africa, are much less common. One aim of this study is to contribute to the development of an African model of leadership through the description and study of the essence of what Africans believe about and expect from leadership: their *représentations sociales* of leadership. In this way, training in the area of organizational capacity building can be better adapted to the African context.

Leadership theories and models have generally been built around experiences with Euro-American businesses and politics. However, a growing body of literature about leadership in nonprofit organizations and in sub-Saharan Africa does exist. Although leadership theories that fully account for cultural variations have not yet been developed, attempts have been made to do so, most notably in the GLOBE study of middle managers in sixty-two countries (Chhokar, Brodbeck, and House 2007); their findings on African leadership are described in section 4.3. In this chapter I briefly discuss some of the leadership theories most relevant to the methods and objectives of this study and then look at leadership of nonprofit (volunteer) and development organizations, as these are the types of organizations described in this case study. Finally, I examine the literature for information on African leadership models before concluding with a discussion of the pertinence of these various views and expectations of leadership.

## 4.1 Leadership theories

A number of leadership theories and approaches have been developed in the past 100 years or so. As Burke (2007) points out, many of them were conceived in light of the shifts in expectations of leaders as the pace of cultural shifts and economic change has accelerated. In addition, emphases

## 4.1 Leadership theories

shift according to each theory's views of the relative importance of leaders, followers, and context in a situation calling for leadership. Another major point of differentiation is the attention given or not given to motivational factors in each theory. All are useful for understanding leadership, but all also have weaknesses, particularly when applied to non-American cultures. A comprehensive review is beyond the scope of this book; the focus is on those theories that are relevant to the project in focus here, to African modes of leadership, and to capacity-building models promoted by NGOs.

### 4.1.1 Traits theory

The traits theory of leadership, sometimes known as the "great leader theory" (since early versions focused on identifying the character traits of great leaders), has been around the longest, having been developed early in the twentieth century (Northouse 2007; St-Germain 2002). This theory is based on the idea that people are born with the traits that make them leaders. This idea is often revealed when what is emphasized in a discourse are a leader's character qualities. The core traits identified by Western scholarship include intelligence, self-confidence, good communication skills, eagerness to accept responsibility, and trustworthiness, among others (Dym and Hutson 2005; Northouse 2007).

Although many theories have since been developed to challenge this theory, it continues in popularity. Nevertheless, it has had a number of different theoretical and practical emphases, the most current being a focus on the role of traits in effective leadership. Part of its popularity stems from its intuitive appeal and the fact that most people, when asked what makes a great leader, will come up with a list of character traits. *In Essays on Leadership* (1998), for example, both former Secretary-General of the UN Boutros Boutros-Ghali and Archbishop Desmond Tutu framed their descriptions of leadership in terms of qualities or attributes such as vision, credibility, eloquence, a spirit of cooperation, and courage. This listing of characteristics occurred during this research project as well. However, the list generated from the research participants, while overlapping somewhat with the lists produced by American research, contains many significant elements rarely, if ever, mentioned in leadership literature, such as patience and faithfulness. These will be discussed in chapter 6. Since one of the criticisms of the traits theory is that most of the core traits are culturally biased towards Western cultures, this study may be a valuable contribution to researchers seeking to redress this imbalance.

In response to the earliest emphasis of the traits theory, that great leaders were born that way, an opposing belief arose that leaders were not just naturally occurring; they could—and should—be made. The following theories are based on this idea: that leadership does not depend solely on the traits of the leader, but also on his or her behavior, on the abilities, expectations and/or motivation of the followers, and/or on the situation. Since leadership development is a component of many capacity-building efforts, these models are quite relevant to this study.

### 4.1.2 Skills model

The skills approach looks at the capabilities a leader needs in order to function effectively in his or her organization (Mumford, Zaccaro, Harding et al. 2000). According to Northouse (2007), Robert L. Katz's early model (1955) of this approach identified the three areas of skills as those relating to ideas, people, and things, which are needed in differing proportions according to rank in an organization. Mumford and his colleagues, however, focus on the knowledge and skills needed by leaders, and particularly those related to problem solving and the development of appropriate solutions in a socially effective manner. These are presumed to be the result of a combination of traits and career experience. In this view, effective leadership requires three areas of knowledge: of people, of the organization, and of the problem and related variables. The importance of problem solving and social skills to performance is also stressed in this model.

While, in contrast with most current theories, the modern skills model de-emphasizes the follower, which is a weakness, it does acknowledge the important role that environmental influences, including the capabilities of subordinates, have both on the leader and on the problem-solving and implementation processes. Other environmental influences include organizational culture, and time and financial limitations (Mumford, Zaccaro, Harding et al. 2000).

Thus, leadership development under this model assumes that while leaders have some inherent traits, such as intelligence, their capabilities can be improved through mentoring, training, experiences in and exposure to complex, ill-defined problems, and practice in problem solving. In addition, knowledge of the organizational culture and the people with whom a leader works can be learned and will affect performance.

This model is of interest to our understanding of SRs of leadership among the Ifè, because the skills and experiences of the Ifè literacy leaders were explored during the interviews, as were the opinions of the subordinates (e.g., teachers) regarding their training. The results of my research generally seem to support this model, although I did not attempt to evaluate such areas as intelligence, personality, or specific problem-solving skills.

However, this model is open to several criticisms. Mumford, Zaccaro, Connelly, and Marks (2000) note that the influence of leaders' beliefs and values on their performance needs to be examined, as do variables in skill and knowledge application to a problem. Northouse (2007) agrees with this latter critique, and additionally sees its inclusion of traits as a weakness. In fact, Northouse considers the theory too broad, as it appeals to other domains such as conflict management, motivational theory, and personality theory in its construction. However, I disagree with this criticism since motivational theory is considered to be very important to leadership in the literature on volunteer and nonprofit organizations, and is one of those on which path-goal theory is based (House 1996).

This theory, as is, also can be criticized for the narrowness of its cultural viewpoint. Among the cognitive abilities Mumford, Zaccaro, Harding et al. (2000) say a leader requires is a high degree of literacy (reading and writing) skills. Oral cultures also have leaders; it would be more accurate to say that the cognitive abilities required include all the communication skills necessary for the context. Another problem with the model is the explicit limitation of experience to career experiences (ibid.). I would argue that all life experiences influence the development of personality, abilities, and problem-solving skills. For example, social skills such as persuasion, negotiation, and the ability to adapt to the needs and expectations of others are initially learned in childhood through interaction with families, peers, and communities. An additional critique is that performance evaluation is based on the effectiveness of the leader in carrying out his duties (Northouse 2007); but while in many organizations, effectiveness can be determined by others in the organization's hierarchy, in service organizations, the best evaluator is the client, whose input is nevertheless rarely sought in such evaluations (Edmunds 1978). In fact, another weakness of this model is its overall focus on the individual leader; the synergy available in team leadership situations is not addressed. Finally, while this model does note the influence of organizational culture, the following theories better take into account the wider situation.

### 4.1.3 Situational theory

In contrast to the two preceding theories, situational theory, frequently regarded as a contingency theory, focuses on the behavior a leader should adopt according to the level of understanding and experience his or her subordinates have for a particular task (Graeff 1983). The primary four behavior-based styles are given as directing, coaching, supporting, and delegating. These are based on two continua: supportive behavior and directive behavior. Supportive behavior involves affective issues around confidence and good working relationships with coworkers. Directive behavior focuses on getting the job done by setting goals and evaluation criteria and by identifying who should be doing what at which point. A subordinate's development level is contingent on his competence as well as his dedication to the task (Northouse 2007). A subordinate working on a task completely new to him will need his leader to be very directive but may not need him to be supportive; he just needs to follow directions to get the job done. On the other hand, a subordinate who understands what to do and how to do it may work independently; the leader only needs to delegate the task in order for it to be accomplished well.

This is the model most often used in leadership training programs (Northouse 2007), and in fact has been used in SIL program management training in Africa since the mid-1990s; however, most of the trainers, myself included, did not fully understand the theory behind the leadership styles we presented, and so the contingent nature of the styles has frequently not been taught. Yet according to Graeff (1983), this focus on adaptation of behavior to accommodate the needs of the subordinate is one of the main contributions of situational theory to the study of leadership. Nevertheless, this section of the SIL program management course received highly positive reviews from participants when it was taught in 2004, largely, I suspect, because it helped the participants recognize that there are various valid ways to lead, even though we did not help them understand that these styles were follower-focused.

In spite of its popularity, situational leadership is vulnerable to several criticisms. Northouse (2007) points out the lack of a large corpus of published research that would validate it. The follower component of the model can also be criticized. In the first place, the model does not make clear the reason a subordinate's development resides in competence and commitment (Graeff 1983). Secondly, it does not recognize the fact that other factors, such as affective needs or rational needs, play into whether or not a follower chooses to cooperate with a leader (Dym and Hutson 2005; Ugwuegbu 2001). Another major criticism of this model, and particularly pertinent to this research project, is that it does not take cultural factors into account as it describes reactions to styles of leadership (Burke 2007; Northouse 2007). Related to that criticism is a lack of attention to organizational culture and its influence (Bess and Goldman 2001). Yet another criticism levied against this model is that it does not address leadership of groups; in a group setting, subordinate development levels are unlikely to be identical, but the theory does not speak to the issue of what a leader should do in a situation where various levels are represented (Bess and Goldman 2001; Northouse 2007).

Nevertheless, because of its attention to the needs of the situation and of the subordinate, situational theory is likely to remain a favored basis for development of the capacities of leaders. However, motivational factors are poorly addressed in this model; it is for that reason that path-goal theory may provide insights on the capacity building being done in volunteer programs, such as the Ifè literacy program.

### 4.1.4 Path-goal theory

The path-goal theory states that effective leadership depends on the ability to motivate followers, using whichever of the eight to ten styles that will accomplish it best (House 1996). A leader motivates subordinates by making sure they see how their actions will accomplish their goals, and ensuring that they have all the necessary resources to do so. The 1996 version of the theory adds that the leader will show or model appropriate task behavior and facilitate the development of collegial relationships within the work-unit as well as between work-units in the organization. In addition, he or she will empower subordinates and increase their satisfaction and effectiveness, both individually and as a work-unit. It must be noted, however, that Robert J. House, the primary developer of this theory, considers it to be more of a theory of supervision, addressing as it does a superior and his subordinates in a work-unit, and explicitly not leadership of an organization.

The emphasis on motivational factors is what makes this theory of interest to leaders of volunteer organizations. While the original version of this theory was based primarily on the motivational theory of Victor Vroom (1964), theories such as David McClelland's are more strongly emphasized in the more recent version. Vroom's expectancy theory states that the effort people put into a task is linked both to their belief that their activity will lead to a desired end and to how much they want that end (Droar 2006). McClelland's "three needs" theory, on the other hand, posits that people are motivated by one of three needs: for achievement, for power, or for affiliation (McClelland 1976). Path-goal theory focuses on the need for achievement as being a major leader characteristic. It also addresses the questions of which needs may motivate followers and thus affect the leader's behavior. These are important questions for organizations using volunteers such as those in this case study.

Path-goal theory shares some of the criticisms of situational leadership, particularly the lack of substantial empirical support (Bess and Goldman 2001; Northouse 2007). In addition, Northouse says the theory is difficult to apply practically, whether in training or in practice, both because of its complexity and because descriptions of specific behaviors that ensure the motivation of subordinates, compelling them to act as desired, are not clearly explicated. On the other hand, Bess and Goldman's study of American universities and of K–12 institutions notes that a major problem in applying this theory to the domain of formal education lies in the situational constraints, including educational policies and practices, that restrict the leader's power to remove obstacles to goal achievement, and that may or may not motivate subordinates. Actually, this lack of attention to context outside the organization and its work-units, including culture as well as policies, is a general drawback of the theory. A further weakness in the theory is identified by House himself, who notes that in a group situation, a leader cannot be all things to all followers, so leaders will generally engage in the behavior they are most comfortable with; in addition, the theory does not attempt to provide a complete list of leader behaviors. A final major criticism is that the focus is so strongly on the leader that the responsibilities of the subordinate in the relationship are ignored (Northouse 2007). This last point is an accurate criticism of the original theory, which focused very strongly on the dyadic leader-follower relationship. However, the updated theory includes a focus on the responsibilities of all members of the work-unit.

One of the legacies of the original path-goal theory as noted by House (1996) is its contribution to the development of the charismatic theory of leadership. This particular theory is occasionally seen as a version of trait theory, but more often as one of the versions of transformational leadership, which is the final theory to be discussed here.

### 4.1.5 Transformational leadership

Transformational leadership, one of the most popular current approaches to leadership, aims to change people as it inspires and empowers them. In doing so, transformational leadership also involves notions of attitudes, values, ethics, and morality, unlike most other theories (Manning 2003; Northouse 2007). In essence, transformational leaders are those who have a relationship with their followers through which they either motivate them to put their own desires after the needs of the larger group, or use the followers' own values to motivate them to accomplish more than they believed themselves capable of achieving (Dym and Hutson 2005; Northouse 2007).

A number of models of transformational leadership exist. Bess's model (Bess and Goldman 2001) identifies four dominant factors of transformational leadership. The first is charisma: followers respect and desire to imitate those who possess this characteristic. The second is the ability to motivate followers through symbolism and emotional appeals to strive for extraordinary goals. Next is the ability to inspire and support creativity, innovation, and critical thinking. The final factor is demonstrating concern for and working toward the development of followers to their full potential. However, a transformational leader may not manifest all these qualities.

Another model is that of Bennis and Nanus (2005, cited in Northouse 2007). In this model, the strategic elements of vision creation, mobilization, trust, and self-awareness are the key to leadership that transforms. Bennis (2007) later added the abilities to develop others as leaders and to get results. These elements overlap with the model elaborated by Kouzes and Posner, although their focus was practices, not strategies. These practices include modeling, inspiring vision, questioning the status quo, collaborating with others, and rewarding others (Kouzes and Posner 1987). These strategies and practices are all generally regarded as important for leadership in volunteer organizations, as will be discussed further in the next section.

Transformational leadership is generally regarded as being the most effective style of leadership, as well as the one most suited to human services organizations. But it has also been criticized. One frequent criticism is the degree of attention paid to leader traits, with the concurrent implication that some people are born to be leaders, others followers. However, others disagree with this view, believing that transformational leaders encourage the emergence of leadership in others (Bennis 2007; Manning 2003). Those who acknowledge the validity of this criticism call for research that would show how to develop transformational leaders, generally thought to occur through experiences that would influence people's values (Russell and Kuhnert 1992).

Another criticism is that, although most models stress the relationship leaders have with followers, in this model, the leader is still seen as the sole catalyst for change (Burke 2007; Northouse 2007). An additional limitation seems to be that transformational leadership requires an atmosphere of trust and collaboration. Where opportunities to build those prerequisites are limited, as can happen in strongly hierarchical organizations where authority is firmly linked to position, transformational leadership rarely flourishes (Bess and Goldman 2001).

But the strongest criticism of transformational theory in the light of this study comes from Blunt and Jones (1997). They note that many of its underlying values, such as the importance of equality, a willingness to confront differences of opinion and personality openly, and a high tolerance for ambiguity and uncertainty are not common in most non-Western cultures. Africans, for example, typically seek to resolve conflicts through a third party, as I have experienced many times in my years on the continent. Blunt and Jones also note that transformational leadership encourages the taking of initiative by subordinates once overall goals are set. However, studies in East Africa (e.g., Littrell and Baguma 2005) have shown that subordinates are generally expected only to carry out explicit directives. Other authors also note that, while transformational theory at least attempts to take culture into account, it, like the other theories discussed here, still falls short of being a universal, cross-cultural leadership theory usable for leadership development in non-Western contexts (Burke 2007).

## 4.2 Leadership in nonprofit and human development organizations

Since leadership theories tend to be developed based on studies of business or political leaders, the issues raised focus on how leaders can be most effective, generally meaning how efficiently they meet the goals of their organizations or nations. As the theories discussed above show, it is assumed that the answer lies in their relationship with their subordinates, the nature of the subordinates themselves, the power inherent in the leaders' positions or roles, the approach they take to management, and/or the influence of situational factors, including the characteristics of tasks to be carried out, which may or may not be under the control of the leaders (Dym and Hutson 2005; Northouse 2007). While many of these are relevant to leadership and management of nonprofit organizations using volunteers in the domains of education and the development industry, certain issues are more likely to arise in human development organizations than in businesses or politics.

One of the most important issues for leadership in volunteer organizations is motivation. Leadership that is unable to motivate people to volunteer and then to keep them engaged will not have the work force to carry out the organization's primary function(s) and thus ensure its survival (Pell 1972). Any model of leadership intended to apply to volunteer organizations must therefore address motivations of subordinates, that is, the factors related to social identity that cause volunteers to invest their time and energy in the organization (Norton 2000).

One of the more effective ways this has been accomplished is through the vision of the organization. Volunteers who are convinced that their efforts contribute to meeting the visionary goals of the organization, especially when they have similar or related goals, are more likely to continue to work for the organization. Thus perhaps the most important task of any leader of volunteers is to develop and promote a vision for the organization. In this light, in order to inspire volunteers, it is important that leaders themselves be seen to be personally engaged in bringing that vision to pass (Brudney 2005; Drucker 1990).

Leaders have other ways to maintain volunteer motivation in addition to vision. First, volunteers are more likely to continue their contribution if their work empowers them, not only in this domain but in their personal and professional lives (Brudney 2005). One way to ensure that is to offer continuous learning opportunities. Another way to maintain the motivation of volunteers is for them to participate in decision-making (Ilsley 1990). Both continual training opportunities and opportunities for participation in decision-making and governance feature in the associations studied in this paper and will be discussed in chapter 8.

Leaders of nonprofit and human development organizations also must pay attention to ethical issues in the organization and in its relationships with the communities they serve. To do this, they should first be aware of their own values. They must also regularly reflect on organizational practices (Fisher and Cole 1993). Some of the foundational ethical practices that ought to be observed are the promotion of the well-being of their staff and of the population they serve, the choice of evaluation measures that reflect the values of the organization (Manning 2003), and the avoidance of hidden agendas (Viltard 2008). Above all, a human service organization must offer moral leadership; it must have leaders and other personnel who are respected in the community, because they exemplify the moral values held by that community (Manning 2003). This view of leadership is found in transformational leadership theory.

One important aspect of ethical leadership is accountability, which is a factor in relationships not only between a leader and his or her subordinates, but also between the organization and its other stakeholders. The leader of an organization is responsible for ensuring accountability to stakeholders. Accountability consists of being held responsible for one's actions, both in finances and in the impact of one's strategies. For nonprofit leaders, the former is often important for financial survival of their organization, as otherwise donors cease to give. However, since the mission of a nonprofit and human development organization depends on the impact of its strategies, the latter point is generally a more crucial issue for their leadership. In addition, Drucker (1990) underlines the importance of a leader of volunteers being accountable to them so that they will want to follow him or her.

This issue of accountability to multiple parties leads to one of the major challenges for leaders of nonprofit organizations, which is tied to the situational context: they must be able to balance fundraising activities with core activities. Far too often, instead of the mission driving the form of core activities, these become constructed in order to meet the demands of donors; that is, dependency on funding allows the desires of donors to outweigh the felt needs of program beneficiaries (Eade 2007; Lacey and Ilcan 2006; Robichaud 1998). Leaders of nonprofits thus need to maintain a strong sense of mission and to communicate well, using their powers of persuasion with donors, staff (including volunteers), and the target population, as well as any other stakeholders in order to ensure that core activities are not neglected (Lacey and Ilcan 2006). Current models of leadership do not account for leadership in such a complex, sensitive situation.

The effectiveness of leaders in nonprofit and human development organizations depends on a number of factors often not present in the business world where leadership models are developed. Subordinates, more often than not, are volunteers, who have more freedom to walk away from the organization than employees. A nonprofit organization is usually, although not always, dependent on outside funding, which is a significant contextual factor for leadership. Finally, the number of stakeholders and the necessity of maintaining healthy relationships with each and every one in order to pursue the vision of the organization introduce a high level of complexity in accountability and communication. All of these indicate a need for leaders with high moral and ethical standards, able to motivate volunteers and attract donors in order to attain organizational goals.

## 4.3 African notions of leadership

As was stated earlier, during my years in Africa working with SIL in the domain of mother tongue literacy program development, several dissonances between Western and African leadership and management styles became evident, most notably in two areas: in the handling of finances and of conflicts. Nevertheless, training in program management presented styles of leadership based on the theories discussed earlier. This section will discuss the ideas of African leadership as found in the literature, written both by researchers and by internationally recognized African leaders themselves.

It is somewhat misleading to talk of "African leadership," since Africa, even just sub-Saharan African, covers a large territory with a nonhomogenous population. These differences must be taken into account in any discussion. This discussion will highlight the issues and characteristics that have been identified by research and leaders across the continent.

The GLOBE project mentioned earlier included mid-level managers from seven different sub-Saharan African nations in its study, and came to certain conclusions about leadership in Africa. These were that Africans were "charismatic/value based," "team oriented," and "participative," as well as "humane-oriented" (Chhokar et al. 2007:1065–1066). Overall, Africans appeared to prefer leaders who are caring and compassionate, competent and modest. However, although purporting to represent all of black Africa (white South Africans were included in another regional grouping), this project only studied countries in English-speaking Africa. In addition, although it noted that subcultures were present in countries with multiple languages and that it attempted to sample the one "in which there was the greatest amount of commercial activity" (Chhokar et al. 2007:21), none of the specific subcultures in the seven African countries, four of which are neighbors, were named, which makes it difficult to evaluate how broadly applicable the results might be. Silverthorne (2005) does note that a research project in the Gambia gives different values than the GLOBE results.

Other researchers examining African leadership in Southern Africa, Eastern Africa, and Nigeria, have identified a number of characteristics of good leadership. Those common to all these areas include the ability to maintain good relationships, a knowledge of patterns and methods of communication proper to the local culture and expertise in using them, respect for others, courage, and the ability to implement decisions that were reached by consensus. A leader is generally expected to be the spokesperson for the group as well, as Littrell and Baguma's (2005) study of Ugandan educators and my personal experience have shown.

## 4.3 African notions of leadership

Authors writing from a Bantu perspective often discuss leadership in the context of *ubuntu,* a philosophy emphasizing solidarity, interdependence, and African humanism. Mbigi says the exact meaning of the word, which derives from the proto-Bantu word meaning "man," is "I am because we are; I can only be a person through others" (2007:4). Writers from Eastern and Southern Africa also tend to claim that the values of *ubuntu* are pan-African.

However, one of the common claims these writers make is the importance of participatory democracy in all African cultures. Silverthorne (2005) does note its presence in the Gambia. I myself have seen that in action among the Pagabete (a Bantu group of the Democratic Republic of Congo), and it is important among the Ifè, as will be seen in chapter 6. Yet it is not universal. For example, among the Éwé of Togo and Ghana, their king has absolute authority over his subjects. Another example is the Akan society of Ghana, whose paramount chief with his council, although elected by elders, wielded substantial power prior to the colonial era (Woronoff 1972). Other examples from Ghana of resistance to participatory forms of government have also been noted. However, chiefs in many West African societies, including the Ifè, can be "destooled" in the case of abuse of power or bad administration (Koba 1996; Woronoff 1972). According to Woronoff, this custom has been used as a justification for coups deposing modern presidents.

In addition to the above studies, several African leaders have written books and articles in which they identified significant characteristics of leaders and/or African leadership. Nelson Rolihlahla Mandela and Julius Kambarage Nyerere, two of sub-Saharan Africa's great leaders of the past sixty years, both came from Bantu groups, so it is perhaps not surprising that they identified the key elements of leadership as being decision-making where everyone is heard, good communication, consensus making, and leadership by example (Mandela 1994; Nyerere 1967, 1973). Both also noted the importance of a humble attitude and of taking responsibility for followers and their actions.

Several of these elements are echoed by Desmond Tutu, a leader in the religious domain who also has a Bantu heritage. His list of attributes of good leadership, based on a reflection on the characters of Mandela, the Dalai Lama, and Mother Theresa, include goodness, credibility, a readiness to suffer, solidarity with one's followers, humility, altruism, and intuition (Tutu 1998). His biographer notes that Tutu himself exemplifies several of these and related qualities, notably a readiness to suffer, a humble attitude, integrity, a desire to mentor others, and a strong tendency to follow his intuition (Allen 2006).

Wangari Maathai, a member of a different Bantu ethnicity and Nobel Peace Prize recipient who led an African NGO and who was a member of the Kenyan parliament, explicitly linked leadership to values: "Leadership is an expression of a set of values; its presence, or the lack of it, determines the direction of a society, and affects not only the actions but the motivations and visions of the individuals and communities that make up that society" (Maahai 2009:25). In her view, a good leader is honest, transparent, humble, a model for others, and willing to make personal sacrifices. As did the other African leaders already discussed in this section, she believed that the qualities of "fairness, justice, deliberation, and representation" (ibid., 218) are inherent to traditional African life and leadership, and that they must be taught to future generations in order for Africa to have the leaders—and followers—it needs. In addition, accountability must be reintegrated into societal values, as it was in her Kikuyu tradition, in order to prevent corruption and the abuses of power for which many African governments have become known.

While much less has been written about non-Bantu leaders, in those a number of similarities are found. For example, Léopold S. Senghor, Senegal's first president and a Christian in a predominately Muslim country, created unity and loyalty through his respect for others, both traditional and religious authorities as well as more humble Senegalese; he was an excellent communicator and persuader who recognized the value of language use and the media; and he listened well, whether in person or through listening to radio call-in programs, in order to understand the concerns of rural Senegalese (Bourges 2006).

Felix Houphouët-Boigny, the first president of Côte d'Ivoire who held onto power until his death in 1993, was able to do so in part, because, at least during his first decade in power, he actively sought to build national unity through cooperation and reconciliation with many (although not all) of his opponents. Additionally, he maintained open communication with his support base, frequently seeking out village-level farmers and talking with them. He also motivated donations by wealthy Ivoirians to development and other projects through his personal example of generosity (Woronoff 1972).

Kwame Nkrumah, Ghana's first president, on the other hand, was a charismatic leader who used speeches and written works to spread his ideologies, gaining for himself a following around the continent. However, neither consensus making nor an exemplary life were features of either Houphouët-Boigny's or Nkrumah's rule. Nkrumah in particular did not take responsibility for his actions and those of his followers, always blaming policy failures on others, and especially on other countries (Woronoff 1972). Yet both of these men did seek the welfare of those under them, Nkrumah limiting this to the members of his political party, while Houphouët-Boigny worked to raise the standard of living of all Ivoirians.

Leadership representations in Africa vary according to ethnic group, but some widely held representations do exist. Foremost is the importance of good communication skills. A degree of respect for others, as well as at least some inclusion of others in decision-making, is also characteristic of African leadership. A certain level of paternalism is also accepted, and even expected, from African leaders (Blunt and Jones 1997; Littrell and Baguma 2005; Nyerere 1967). In addition, the ability to implement decisions made with the input of others is required. However, while consensus building and an exemplary life are seen as important for many, they are not universal values across the continent and have been lacking in several key political leaders.

## 4.4 Discussion

Current leadership theories have generally ignored or inadequately incorporated the influence of culture on leadership in their models. While some studies, such as the GLOBE study, have attempted to identify cultural factors of leadership, they do not seem to have succeeded in constructing a theory that accounts for all the dynamics of leadership. Furthermore, many of these theories have been based on studies of business, political and/or military leadership, and so also have not accounted for the dynamics found in leadership of nonprofit organizations, a particular type of organizational subculture that often relies on a volunteer workforce and that is represented in this case study.

Leadership theories and models are relevant to practice only insofar as they take into account the elements found in SRs of leadership and followership. The traits and skills theories acknowledge some aspects of these SRs, but exclude the motivations, actions, and expectations of leaders and their subordinates. Situational theory and path-goal theory seem to do better in accounting for contextual variations in a work situation and motivation, but do not go far enough, being limited strictly to the situation between a single leader and his or her follower or work-unit even though leadership occurs primarily in groups. Transformational theory, while giving central place to the relationship between leaders and their followers, still places all responsibility for leadership choices within leaders themselves and has underlying values that are not universal across cultures; yet it still is valuable in understanding how leaders interact with their followers to inspire them, both to follow and to become leaders themselves.

A theory that accounts for preferred leader characteristics, follower motivations, expectations, group dynamics, contextual factors (including organizational culture, infrastructure, and governmental policies), and cultural variations is still needed. Such a theory, to be of value to volunteer-based organizations, also should consider all the parties to whom a leader is accountable. This dynamic, which is an important element of the SR of the leader of a volunteer, nonprofit organization, is not present in any of the leadership theories I have examined. The theory of social representations is a tool that may help construct such a theory of leadership.

Such a theory would be most useful to those of us working in cross-cultural situations where we may be assisting or facilitating the development of community-based institutions and their leadership. It would help current and developing leaders understand what they must do, what they can do, and what they cannot do in order to be effective, however that is defined (e.g., profits, number of people impacted, change occurring). This understanding is particularly important in the domains of literacy and development, which are the subject of the next chapter, in countries where illiteracy rates are high and standards of living overall are low.

*For further reading*

Langlois, L., and C. Lapointe. 2002. Le concept de leadership éducationnel : Origines et évolution [The concept of educational leadership: Origins and evolution]. In L. Langlois and C. Lapointe (eds.), *Le leadership en éducation : Plusieurs regards, une même passion,* 1–9. Montreal: Chenelière/McGraw-Hill.

McSweeney, P., and D. Alexander. 1996. *Managing volunteers effectively.* Aldershot, UK: Arena.

Moemeka, A. 1996. Interpersonal communication in communalistic societies in Africa. In W. B. Gudykunst, S. Ting-Toomey, and T. Nishida (eds.), *Communication in personal relationships across cultures*, 197–214. Thousand Oaks, Calif.: Sage.

Pearce, J. L. 1982. Leading and following volunteers: Implications for a changing society. *The Journal of Applied Behavioral Science* 18:385–394.

Willis, G. 2000. Managing a good cause. *CMA Management* 74(10):18–24.

# 5

# Literacy and Development: The Chicken or the Egg?

Literacy and development are often found in the same discourse. One school of thought, seen quite clearly in the Education for All (EFA) initiative, as well as in other places, believes that literacy leads to development (Kingsbury 2004; Rassool 2009). Another field of thought claims that true development will ceate a demand for literacy (Mutaka and Attia 2008; Tadadjeu 2008). It is probably most accurate to see the relationship as recursive: progress or lack thereof in one influences the state of the other (Doronila 1996; Windham 1999).

As noted in chapter 2, the members of the local associations studied in this project see their organizations as literacy *and* development associations; their representations that underlie this conception will be discussed in chapter 7. However, a framework for understanding the literacy discourses that surround them, in which they are immersed, and that are influencing them is useful in understanding that discussion, and thus is presented here.

## 5.1 Literacy

The representation of literacy is one of those areas—along with notions of community, responsibility, the role of volunteerism, and others—where the basic conception affects the shape of a literacy program and of the organization in charge of it. However, literacy has divergent representations in the academic community, as well as in the world of practitioners. The focus may be on skills acquisition, on the use of literacy to empower people, or on the various uses of literacy—this last emphasis particularly as applied to multilingual societies.

### 5.1.1 Literacy as a skill set

Traditionally, literacy has been viewed as a set of technical skills covering reading and writing, generally acquired by an individual as opposed to a culture or society. It emerged from the research traditions of experimental psychology and psycholinguistics (Rassool 2009). In this view, acquisition activities may be decontextualized; it is for the individuals to decide how they will use their new skills, since literacy itself is autonomous (Street 1990; UNESCO 2006). This is the view behind the widely quoted 1958 definition of literacy from UNESCO, "[A literate person is one] who can with understanding both read and write a short simple statement on his everyday life."

This view of literacy has been strongly criticized, however. It has been labeled a deficit model, implying that people without skills in reading and writing are less than complete (Rogers 2001; D. M. Smith 1986). Instead, it

*5.1 Literacy* 65

is argued, literacy and orality should be viewed as a continuum (Finnegan 1999; Street 1990). Another criticism is that programs with this view tend to overlook the cultural changes that happen with the introduction of literacy into a society (Street 1995). In addition, I would say that this view of literacy overlooks, or even denies, the influence of material designers in promoting a particular ideology as they choose what the learners will read or write about.

### 5.1.2 Literacy as power

As ethnographers and sociolinguists began to study the uses of literacy and the dimensions of power around literacy, other models developed to challenge the traditional, skills-based model. One of the earliest and best known is that developed by Paulo Freire, the Brazilian educator. In the 1960s, he reconceptualized the acquisition of literacy skills as only a part of the true goal of a literacy program, which is for participants to learn to "read the world" through conscientization, which occurs through dialogue (Freire 1970). The skills acquired are only valuable insofar as they permit the poor and disenfranchised, working as a community group, to improve their situation by challenging established power bases (Finnegan 1999). This model, also known as literacy for social transformation, has often been used to promote particular ideologies, as when it was adopted by Benin in the mid-1970s to promote the political and social agenda of the Marxist regime then in power. It has since been adapted by ActionAid as the basis of the REFLECT (REgenerated Freirian Literacy through Empowering Community Techniques) method to promote economic as well as societal development (Archer and Cottingham 2007) and is used by a number of NGOs in the developing world, including *Aide et Action* in Togo.

This conception of literacy also has its critics. First, literacy for social transformation is censured for the underlying ideology that believes the illiterate person is helpless and can only be an object, not an agent (Rogers 2001), that is, the belief that an illiterate person is incapable of effecting changes in his or her society. In addition, like the traditional model, it also introduces literacy practices that are new to the culture instead of building on what is already present (Maddox 2001). It should also be noted that while some governments have adopted it as their preferred model, others have seen it as a threat because of the method's focus on encouraging the newly literate to transform their world, often by challenging current power structures. On a more practical note, Freire's method has been difficult to implement as conceived because it requires well-educated teachers, like the college students who were Freire's first recruits, instead of those who did not complete high school who, as in the Ifè program, are most often those willing and available to teach their fellow community members.

### 5.1.3 Literacy as social practice

The final major current conceptualization places literacy firmly in its sociocultural context, having drawn from social anthropology, sociology, critical linguistics, and discourse theory in its development (Rassool 2009). This approach, epitomized by the New Literacy Studies, states that literacy is never unchanging and cannot be defined apart from the specific culture in which it occurs (Ferdman 1999; Street 1995). It is intimately tied to the uses and the contexts of literacy and may even include oral practices (Gee 1996). Furthermore, it includes the examination of power relations and so is sometimes referred to as an ideological model of literacy (Street 2001:1–17). In this view, the language used for literacy becomes very significant, as literacy practices may—and frequently do—vary according to the language in use (Martin-Jones 2000).

This view of literacy is also not without critics. Two major criticisms are discussed in Fraenkel and Mbodj 2010. First, the ethnographic approach favored by researchers examining the social practices of literacy usually results in a very narrow view of literacy, with only the immediately visible contexts of literacy being foregrounded. This distances literacy from its roots in institutions and individuals who have promoted it. The second criticism that has been made is tied to examinations of power inherent in different literacies. By focusing on descriptions of different literacies, the inequalities resulting from the lack of access to reading and writing skills, and the consequences thereof, are hidden from view.

However, Angélil-Carter (1997) uses an approach that answers at least one of the above criticisms. She applies Norton's (1997, 2000) theory of investment, which explicitly links power dynamics to the acquisition of languages and identity in a social and historical context, to the acquisition

## 5.1 Literacy

of literacies, or discourses, showing how investments in these literacies are also historically and socially constructed.[1] This type of approach would help to ensure that the roots of literacy with their power bases and their influence on individuals, the development of the identities of these individuals, and their acquisition of literacy skills are revealed.

In any case, literacy as conceived by researchers in the New Literacy Studies has much in common with the theory of *représentations sociales*. For example, in their discussion of literacy practices, Barton and Hamilton say that these are "general cultural ways of utilising written language...based on actions, values, attitudes, feelings and social relationships." Literacy practices also involve "people's awareness of literacy, constructions of literacy and discourses of literacy, how people talk about and make sense of literacy" (1999:7). In addition, they "are more usefully understood as existing in the relations between people, within groups and communities, rather than as a set of properties residing in individuals" (ibid., 8). All these are also elements describing the concept and construction of social representations, which as noted earlier, are socially constructed (through discourse, whether orally or in print) interpretive frameworks that allow people to think about and act in relation to particular social objects, one of which is literacy.

### 5.1.4 Discussion of views on literacy

Functional literacy is the currently favored approach of both the Togolese and Beninese governments. It is a melding of the skills view with development activities, but can also be seen as a social practice (Doronila 1996). It generally has to do with the belief that a person must be able to handle the reading and writing tasks considered normal for his or her culture. A functional approach attempts to make the literacy skills being learned immediately applicable to the lives of learners, by using content that teaches skills, whether improved agricultural techniques, hygiene practices, or marketing, and thus promoting self-sufficiency.

---

[1] Angélil-Carter prefers the term discourses when discussing forms of writing or speaking, using the definition of Kress ["systematically organized sets of statements which give expression to the meanings and values of an institution...in that it provides descriptions, rules, permissions and prohibitions of social and individual actions" (1985:7)]. She thereby links her work to prior research on discourses, such as by Bourdieu (1991), Fairclough (1992), Gee (1990), and others.

It is important to realize that, from the viewpoint of those interested in the practicalities of teaching someone to read and write, all of the above perceptions of literacy are valuable and useful. Those of us working in literacy are, for the most part, interested in helping people acquire competences that will be useful to them in their daily lives, whether to reinforce or to develop an identity (ethnicity, nationality, or adherence to a religion), to empower them to take charge of their lives, and/or to open doors to improved health or economic status. Literacy workers in areas where the reading and writing of text is a new technology are also interested in questions of how text literacy becomes integrated into a society, and how to facilitate the development of cultural literacy practices that will enable a community to make decisions about its future in the face of modernization and globalization (Davis 2004; Tadadjeu 2008). These are all issues that are linked to the development domain, which is the topic of the next section. Issues common to literacy and development will be explored in the final section of this chapter.

## 5.2 Development

"Development" is a problematic term—any precise definition is closely tied to the ideologies of those using it (Kingsbury 2004; Willis 2005). It implies, first of all, a mind-set of change (Droz and Lavigne 2006): a belief that things can and should be different from what they are. Beyond that, it can refer to a process, a vision of a desired state, purposive behavior (Johnson and Thomas 2004) or an ideological project (Coquery-Vidrovitch, Hemery, and Piel [1988] 2007).

Those who see development as a process place it in a historical context of change (ibid). Kambhampati (2004:12) identifies it as "a multi-dimensional process, one that changes the economy, polity and society of the countries in which it occurs." Tadjedeu (2008) perceives development in Africa as the process of transformation from a pre-industrial society to an industrial society, which will require an adaptation of its economic, political, cultural, and educational systems, but not of its values, to new realities. On the other hand, Hope and Timmel see development as "an awakening process—a way in which people see themselves awaken to their right to live as human beings" (1995:27). One aspect of that awakening is an increase in the choices

## 5.2 Development

available to individuals that can lead to an improvement in their overall well-being (Vernières 2008). As far as local communities are concerned, development involves the process of reducing susceptibilities to harmful events and building the capacity to solve problems (Eade 1997), preferably to the point of being able to do so with their own resources (Schanely 1983).

Of course, many of the above processes occur without outside intervention. But the term development as it is used today frequently refers to deliberate actions to bring about a state of change (D. Lewis 2001). This is most often seen when development is used as an adjective, as in the phrases DEVELOPMENT ACTIVITY or DEVELOPMENT PROJECT. This brings up the issue, to be discussed below, of who is initiating and controlling the direction of these deliberate actions.

Whether development is a process or a deliberate action, it is generally moving towards a vision of a preferred state of affairs. Generally, development in this sense refers to an improved standard of living and well-being. This includes an adequate income, good nutrition, and access to education for all. However, it can also refer to empowerment (Kingsbury 2004), a just distribution of resources (Latouche [1988] 2007; Vernières 2003), a culture of peace and social justice (Busia 1968; Mutaka and Attia 2008), or maintenance and development of local cultural resources (Mutaka and Attia 2008). It may also mean having a standard of living equivalent to that found in rich countries, with the accompanying status accorded to their governments (Latouche [1988] 2007). This plethora of meanings has led one Togolese development agent to observe that the very fact that "development" is such an ill-defined term prevents its application and thereby its ability to obtain tangible results (Lamboni 2008).

In addition to this criticism, it is important to remember what Tanzania's first president, Julius Nyerere, said in 1968: "For the truth is that development means the development of *people*. Roads, buildings, the increases of crop output, and other things of this nature, are not development; they are only the tools of development" (Nyerere 1973:59). He went on to say, in the same speech, "Development brings freedom, provided it is development of *people*. But people cannot be developed; they can only develop themselves" (1973:60). Many development programs and activities focus on building infrastructure and improving the economy, on empowering people and especially women, or on capacity building for sustainable development.

Nonetheless, it is essential to keep in mind that all such activity has meaning only insofar as the target population has input into all aspects of the decision-making and implementation processes. This has not always been the case, as the remainder of this chapter will show.

### 5.2.1 Brief history of development history and trends

The concept of development goes back to the Enlightenment and its notion of progress (Latouche [1988] 2007). In the minds of Europeans, this notion, augmented by the theory of evolution applied to societies, justified their domination of those lacking a European heritage, whom they perceived as "backwards," not having the trappings of civilization recognized by the Europeans. Thus, many of the actions taken by Europeans arriving in Africa were with the aim of civilizing the Africans as well as serving the political and economic goals of the Europeans. This was principally done through the schools, whether church-run or government-run, to the detriment of African societies.

After World War II, economic recovery and reconstruction were the focus of development efforts throughout the world. Overall, however, development during this period aimed to improve economic growth as much for the North as for the South. Economic development continues to dominate the field, as most measures of successful projects focus on the economic impacts, although measures that also include other dimensions have arisen in the past twenty years, most notably the UN's Human Development Index (HDI), which was developed in 1990. However, even when overtly the development program is, say, to improve education, it generally is with the long-term goal of improving the economic contribution and situation of the people. Classical, neo-liberal, and Marxist theories espoused this view; however, classical and neo-liberal theories identified the market as the key to development, whereas Marxist-based theories focused on the need for the state to have active control over all processes that lead to modernization.

Socialist theories came into favor in Africa as part of the movement to decolonize Africa, that is, to throw off not only the political domination of Europe, but also the cultural and social domination of the North. These theories took two forms: African, or populist, socialism, the approach taken by Tanzania under Nyerere as well as other countries; and Afro-Marxism, or Marxist-Leninism, the approach adopted by Senegal under Senghor, as well as by Benin, and other countries in the 1970s. In African socialism, Nyerere and others sought to motivate people towards collective ownership and work through an ideology that drew on ideas of African society prior to the arrival of the Europeans; this ideology is known as *ujamaa* (Nyerere 1973), which means "familyhood" (Nyerere 1967). Where necessary, the Tanzanian state intervened to ensure that collective villages were established (Kambhampati 2004). However, the dream of Tanzanians working first for the group and afterwards for themselves was not realized.

In Afro-Marxism, the state plans all activity and owns important industries (Willis 2005). Unlike Marxism as practiced in Europe, however, Afro-Marxism acknowledged the important role of African spirituality in society (Bourges 2006). However, this approach was no more successful in achieving development goals than classical approaches. As a result, most African countries have now adopted capitalist policies. However, during the period between independence and the abandonment of socialist policies, many had also acquired large amounts of international debt which, it became evident, they were not going to be able to repay. These enduring problems led to the next two—incompatible—development theory emphases: structuralism and grassroots approaches.

From the 1980s to the mid-1990s, structuralism came into prominence. This theory stated that the main problem with developing countries was that their governments were neither structured nor managed efficiently, and that a lack of accountability was hindering development. As a result, the World Bank and the International Monetary Fund (IMF) imposed structural adjustment policies on countries seeking loans, with devastating results to the education and health care systems of many of these countries, as these, being areas of high expenditure, were prime targets for being "adjusted," that is, having expenses reduced, including the salaries of teachers and health workers (Moulton et al. 2002).

In contrast to these extremely top-down policies, grassroots approaches emphasize the participation of the local community. Although these theories began to be formulated in the 1970s, they gained wide-spread popularity in the 1990s. In a grassroots approach, local communities are asked, at a minimum, to participate in the prioritization of needs and in discussions on how to address them, and at best, to be actively involved in every phase of the planning, implementation, and evaluation of the development projects. One important manifestation of this conception of how to accomplish development is the rise in importance of nongovernmental organizations and other members of civil society to development efforts (Eade 1997; Planche 2004).

In conjunction with grassroots approaches, theories about what would make development sustainable over the long term gained popularity, largely as "developed" nations began to realize what their own drive towards progress had done to their environment. Although definitions of what makes development sustainable vary, generally these approaches center around development that is economically feasible, socially acceptable, and ecologically friendly to the environment. This conception, however, has been criticized for being very Western since its emphasis is on the needs of future generations, de-emphasizing or even excluding those of past and present ones (Helame 2009). Through this and the rise of postmodernist philosophy in the North, the idea that perhaps there are alternate paths to development began to gain popularity. At the same time, the influence of globalization became more evident, resulting in a concern for regional-level development initiatives, such as NEPAD (New Partnership for Africa's Development), an initiative of the African Union. Another effect of globalization is the coordination of multiple actors to address economic growth in the fight against poverty, one of the current themes in the world development scene (Bellier 2008; Droz and Lavigne 2006).

All of these theories and approaches, however, have had limited success in Africa. According to the 2013 HDI report, thirty-three countries of sub-Saharan Africa were among those designated as having "low human development"; none were rated as having either "high" or "very high human development." This index bases its conclusion on three factors: health, education, and income. Of particular interest to this study are the rankings of Togo and of Benin: respectively, 166th and 165th out of 187 countries (UNDP 2013).

The failure of so many theories and policies to effect durable, positive change has led many analysts to identify issues that contribute to continuing unacceptable levels of poverty and social ill-being. These are the focus of the next section.

### 5.2.2 Issues in development

Among the forefront of development issues is the question of power. Who holds the power to decide—governments? local communities? funders? multilateral organizations on behalf of "the international community"? A number of authors have observed that too often, the peoples being affected by interventions have not had input into the decision-making processes; or, even in grassroots projects, that local concerns are overridden by the agenda of those funding the projects, whether the national government, a donor nation, an NGO, or a United Nations agency. Bellier (2008) and Kingsbury (2004) both note that one of the things that indigenous peoples want is not only the right to be consulted, but the right to consent to or to refuse development projects in their localities.

Other potential problems with grassroots approaches include an oversimplification of structures, difficulty in integrating local development efforts into national or regional plans, and a lack of overall efficiency (Landy 2008). In addition, it can be difficult to ensure the participation of every stakeholder in the local community (Ajulu 2001). Finally, no matter how inclusive the process is, experience in Ghana, at least, has shown that the key factor in project sustainability is local leadership (Nkasa and Chapman 2006).

While some of these concerns are eliminated when the national or regional government is making the decisions or coordinating the actions, development directed by this level carries its own concerns. Poor or corrupt national-level leadership has been identified as a major reason Africa has not made the progress other continents have in improving life for its people (Aire 1990; Maathai 2009). In addition, national governments often have difficulty in fairly balancing the needs of all in the country. Therefore, difficulties with grassroots approaches notwithstanding, the local community must be involved at the early stages of development projects in order to ensure that the needs of the community are actually met.

This is particularly important in light of the fact that areas in which Northern and multilateral organizations tend to impose their own agendas include development priorities, project timetables, and the definitions of what makes for good practice and adequate standards (Droz and Lavigne 2006; Planche 2004). For instance, clean water provision is currently a major funding thrust. However, I know of a number of communities in Togo where an outside organization came in, dug wells for the community or protected the community's water supply, and then left. After several years, the wells were filled in and the pumps, due to a lack of maintenance, were broken; there was neither interest in nor resources for repairing them.

Having clean, protected water sources was (and is) not a high priority for those communities. Also of concern to beneficiaries are donor timetables, which are frequently set with little or no regard for local realities, and too much concern with "efficiency" (Eade 2007; Landy 2008; Nkasa and Chapman 2006). The insistence on certain forms of reporting or management structures not known in the culture is another area where Northern organizations often impose their will on Southern organizations and communities (Eade 1997).

In reaction to these insensitivities to local felt needs, an emphasis on partnership has arisen. Besides increasing the participation of beneficiaries in the development process, partnerships are also seen as a way to be more efficient in the use of resources and to facilitate institutional sustainability (D. Lewis 2001). However, partnerships are not a panacea; the notion of partnership in an environment where partners are not equal in terms of resources is inherently flawed (Bellier 2008). It is too easy for the partnership not to be of mutual benefit, leading to the dependence of beneficiaries on the wealthier partner(s) (D. Lewis 2001; Maathai 2009). A major concern for local communities is ensuring that the allocation of resources and the means of their participation are protected regardless of who is in power, as well as balancing the roles between modern and traditional authorities (Bellier 2008).

In order to meet these concerns, accountability must be mutual, with donors examining what they can learn from those whom they are helping as well as evaluating the impacts of their aid (Eade 2007; Planche 2004). As the former president of Senegal, Léopold S. Senghor, said in his call for partnerships, Africans seek *"un partenariat humaniste où les intérêts immédiats sauront céder la place à une véritable symbiose des cœurs et des esprits"* ("a humanistic partnership where immediate interests will give way to a true symbiosis of hearts and spirits"; from a speech given in May 2000 at the Colloque *"Africanité, universalité,"* University of Paris XIII, quoted in Bourges 2006:117). The goal of partnership, based on shared values, should truly be one of working together in every sense of the word (Planche 2004).

Yet even when partnerships seem to be working well, disadvantages exist. These include extra organizational costs for communication and travel, additional responsibility for program personnel, new obligations to share information with other organizations (D. Lewis 2001), and significant time

## 5.2 Development

spent in maintaining these relationships (L. D. Wagner 2003). In addition, the focus or emphases of one partner may influence the direction of the other in ways potentially detrimental to the original mission of the less powerful organization (Eade 1997; D. Lewis 2001) and/or to organizational sustainability (Kingsbury 2004; Planche 2004). For these reasons, partnerships must be carefully monitored for costs and benefits to all involved and reworked as necessary (D. Lewis 2001). More powerful partners need to examine the impacts they are having, both intended and unintended, and be sensitive to and willing to learn from the concerns of and points of view expressed by their partners (Eade 2007; Planche 2004).

Cultural diversity, although currently getting lip service on the international scene, comes into conflict with globalization and is therefore often disregarded by development organizations (Helame 2009). One area in which outsiders often err is not respecting or seeking to understand local communication patterns, although these affect decision-making (Ansu-Kyeremeh 2005; Cosway and Anankum 1996). Oftentimes, the best response to community needs may be an indigenous solution. Yet frequently, technology and other solutions developed in Europe or North America are promoted as being the best (L. T. Smith 1999). For instance, soils were depleted from overcultivation due to the high population density in the area of Northern Togo where I lived for several years. The Kabiyè traditionally prepared a compost for their fields, using a pit where goats were kept and grasses and organic waste were thrown. However, this practice has greatly diminished in favor of imported fertilizers. These are expensive and must be applied at the proper time in relation to rainfall, which is becoming erratic due to climate change. As a result, several literacy programs in the area now promote composting, whether through the traditional technique or through one not using animal waste, as a better though more labor-intensive way to enrich poor soils.

One aspect of globalization is a supposed consensus on "internationally recognized" values, such as democracy, gender equality, environmental safe-keeping and sharing of knowledge (D. Lewis 2001; Viltard 2008). These often conflict with local values and structures (Mabogunje 1990). For instance, gender equality has been at or near the top of the international development agenda for some time (Willis 2005). But when this value has been imposed on communities, unintended consequences are known to occur, negative as well as positive (Kingsbury 2004). Linda Tuhiwai Smith (1999) identifies this as a type of cultural arrogance that threatens marginalized ethnic groups. At least one African researcher has gone further and stated that the Western social development goals are destroying recent advancements made by Africans (Abdi 2006). Another African professor, Esoh Helame (2009), has noted that the Western concepts of such things as sustainable development do not take into account the African notions of the importance of past as well as of future generations. In fact, he says, development actors, because they are not fully dedicated to cultural diversity, tend to foist Western beliefs of the way things should be on other civilizations instead of looking for ways by which cultures can enrich each other in the process of development.

Several authors have noted, in fact, that development agents must be sensitive to local contexts and avoid assuming that others have or need the same structures, ways of thinking, or conceptions of time and space (Droz and Lavigne 2006; Matemba 2007; Warren et al. 1996). They must be cognizant that local people are more knowledgeable about possible constraints to new techniques (Schanely 1983). They must also be aware of how new techniques may disrupt the social order (Mabogunje 1990). When the local context is fully taken into consideration, innovations will endure, as happened in one project combating water-borne diseases in Ghana (Cosway and Anankum 1996). The consequence of disregarding this cultural diversity, however, is that that which is called development may become more destructive than constructive (Droz and Lavigne 2006).

### 5.2.3 Development summary

Development is a term with a wide range of meanings and can refer to a process, a vision of the way things "should" be, or intentional behavior. Economic development, which leads to a better standard of living, is probably the most dominant understanding; but social development, which improves quality of life, is also frequently invoked, particularly in terms of health and education. Another form of development is cultural, which generally seeks to maintain a group's heritage, but may also seek to help it adapt to modern life. Ideology and, more recently, globalization are factors that influence the direction of all of these.

However, the history of development efforts shows that decisions about what should be done—whether economically, socially, or culturally—are closely tied to ideology and power. All too often, decisions have been made with the interests of the industrial nations or of the elite of the "developing" world in the forefront. However, none of the major top-down strategies, whether driven by capitalist or Marxist ideologies, has had significant, lasting positive results.

In response, grassroots approaches and the creation of "partnerships" have become popular. These, however, are not without their problems. Among the difficulties of grassroots approaches are those of involving all the members of a community in the decision making, whether from cultural factors or time constraints, and of ensuring that the communities' participation continues from initial planning through final evaluation. Too often, the external partners in this process impose their own agendas, standards, timetables, and evaluation tools. Since they are usually the main source of finances for the project, they cannot be refused without the danger of having funds withdrawn. Another concern about external partnerships is that too often, local wisdom for solutions is overlooked in favor of imported, technological solutions. What appears to be a sustainable practice from the outside may not be so, due to unknown (to the outsiders) or misunderstood factors in the cultural, regional, or national context (Matemba 2007; Schanely 1983). It is, therefore, important for all development agents to be sensitive to local priorities and knowledge, even while seeking to further the aims of national development or to align with the social goals of the international community. This may mean choosing not to pursue certain national or international objectives unless or until a majority of the local community desires them (Bellier 2008). Otherwise, any progress towards these objectives is unlikely to be permanent (Droz and Lavigne 2006).

## 5.3 Discussion of the relationship between literacy and development

The precise relationship between literacy and development, whether economic, social, or cultural, is not well understood. Although many assume widespread literacy is a prerequisite to improving the standards of living, literacy can only be shown to correlate with certain changes such as an improvement in maternal health; it cannot be shown as a cause for this change or any other development target (Eade 1997; Rogers 2001). Conversely, neither an improved standard or quality of life nor development projects will necessarily motivate people to learn to read and write, as I and my colleagues have seen repeatedly.

Carrington and Luke (1997) explain this noncorrelation through an application of Bourdieu and Passeron's (1970) notion of CAPITAL. Capital is a form of relative social power, any form of which must be recognized as such in a particular group or domain for it to have power. Economic and cultural capital, according to Bourdieu and Spire (2002), are the two principal modes of domination. CULTURAL CAPITAL consists of knowledge, skills, practices, material cultural objects, and acknowledgment of qualifications by recognized social institutions (Carrington and Luke 1997). Literateness is one potential form of cultural capital. In order for it to provide the benefits attributed to it by folk theories of literacy, three things must be in place: other capital must also be available to literates, the literate practices they control must be needed for what they want to do, and literacy must be recognized as valuable capital by the appropriate institutions (ibid.). So according to this view, literacy acquisition will only benefit development if other factors are in place to make that so; and development will only lead to literacy if literate practices are valued as a form of capital.

However, activities in the two domains do have the capacity to reinforce one another, and thus strategies that combine the two are more effective than those that focus on only one or the other (Kingsbury 2004). Literacy enables access to written materials, which may teach new information or reinforce oral teaching, as has been noted in the literature on African development (Tadadjeu 2008) and pointed out in the interviews (see chapter 7). It also allows citizens of a country to communicate appropriately with their authorities, such as when legal documents need to be obtained or rights claimed (Davis 2004). Furthermore, development activities may provide uses for literacy and numeracy that are not present in a strictly oral culture, as happened among the Machiguenga (Matsigenka) of Peru (ibid.). The introduction of income-generating activities and health clinics in their area, for example, created uses for literacy in bookkeeping and inventory, which then kept the former viable. This mutual effect is one motivation for functional literacy programs.

Literacy and development agents, however, must be sensitive to ethical concerns. Principles of social change such as those proposed by Appel (1990, cited in Kingsbury 2004) or Wallace (1956, cited in Davis 2004) indicate that all change in a culture—such as that induced by the introduction of literacy or other changes in social practice—involves destruction of something, replacement of something, and stress; thus those who introduce such change must be sensitive to the consequences of their actions and work to mitigate negative side effects. For instance, education oriented away from agriculture has resulted in a labor shortage in rural Nigeria, as schooled youth leave the countryside, placing the burden of agricultural production on women, who often do not have land rights. Policy makers and development agents should therefore develop strategies to address these concerns (Mabogunje 1990).

One of the most important ethical issues in both literacy and development activities is participation in the decision-making process (Eade 2007; Kingsbury 2004; Rogers 2001). Who, for instance, is making the decisions about what literacy methodology and ideology are used in a community? Frequently it is the government. For example, it was the choice of the Beninese government to use Freirean methodology during their Marxist period, and later to emphasize functional literacy. In both cases, it was and is with the goal of promoting national social and economic development. In other instances, it is the NGO running the program that makes such decisions. For instance, SIL has developed several different methods in its years of serving minority language communities; but it has generally been an expatriate facilitating the start of the program who chooses which method is used. In Togo and Benin, the Gudschinsky method, an analytic-synthetic method, has been the preferred choice and is the basis of the Ifè primers. The content of the reading material in these primers, however, has been an area where local people have had significant input as well as authorship, although government preferences for functional literacy are taken into consideration as well.

Another area of ethical concern is changes in the balances of power present, whether locally or nationally. These will be influenced by both literacy and development activities (Kingsbury 2004), as these change the cultural capital of those participating in those activities. For instance, when these target the younger population of a community, traditional structures that grant authority and respect to those who have gained wisdom through the experience of age are often disturbed (Maathai 2009). Another area that impacts power balances is the language of literacy and the social capital it provides (Bourdieu and Passeron 1970). Mother tongue literacy may grant people enough cultural self-esteem that they are willing to challenge the status quo, but generally has limited use outside the language area (Baker 1998; Mutaka and Attia 2008). In order to interact with the national or even the regional government, literacy in the official language is usually required of at least some individuals in the community, often those who have attended school long enough to acquire that language. Adult literacy programs often are unable to compensate for the power imbalances that exist between the schooled and the newly literate adult (Kingsbury 2004). While the newly literate may feel (or even be) empowered to take control of various aspects of their lives, the potential arises for resentment and even conflict with those who have had power through their control of the language(s) of literacy (ibid.).

A final area to address is how the links between literacy and development are presented. I have attended several regional International Literacy Day commemorations and other literacy awareness-raising events that promote the benefits of literacy through skits. Too often, the situations depicted are more issues of the language of literacy than of literacy itself (e.g., not being able to read "do not urinate here" signs, which I have only seen in French, or not being able to read usage and dosage instructions for a medication, which are only available in French, English, and, for dosage, symbols). At other times, literacy is presented as being a way to improve one's economic status or to enable travel to other countries. While some individuals may realize these benefits (see section 7.2 for some examples of the former), it cannot be taken for granted (Davison 2008). Literacy and development agents must be careful, therefore, as to how they present the benefits of being literate in order not to raise false expectations.

Finally, literacy and development programs do not happen in an environmental vacuum. The physical infrastructure available in an area will affect what is possible to do as well as indicate potential areas of intervention. Transportation and communication links are the most significant of those areas, although access to electricity, or the lack thereof, also plays a major role in shaping programs. Although the main work of infrastructure development rests in the hands of governments, development projects may occasionally address some of these issues, such as the provision of solar power or wind-generated local systems. Local communities frequently maintain roads and bridges in their immediate neighborhoods in order to prevent being cut off completely from the outside. For instance, a small bridge on a road I took to one of the interview sites was being fixed—at least temporarily—by the inhabitants of the nearest village. Regardless of how it occurs, without attention to infrastructure, development work will not endure, and those who live in rural areas will continue to be marginalized (Landy 2008), whether or not they are literate.

## 5.4 Literacy, development, and social representations

Social representations of literacy, including its relationship to development and to language use, influence what is expected of a literacy program and situate it in the community. Literacy program leaders who are aware of these SRs are able to use them in program development, thereby motivating not only volunteers but also potential and current students. Additionally, appropriate responses to the SRs circulating in the community will increase the impact of the program, beyond teachers and students to the whole community, as has happened in the Ifè program and is described in chapter 8.

However, the very act of introducing change in a community, whether in the form of increased levels of literacy, of alternative sources of income, or of new ways of doing things, changes the social representations circulating in a community. Thus, good program leaders need to be listening to and dialoguing with community members and then adapting program goals, strategies, and activities to changes in expectations as well as to changes in the environment. The remainder of this case study will examine the Ifè representations of leadership and of literacy, and look at how the program leaders have created and adapted the program in such a way as to positively impact the development of the Ifè people.

### For further reading

Dubin, F. 1989. Situating literacy within traditions of communicative competence. *Applied Linguistics* 10:171–181. doi:10.1093/applin/10.2.171.

Klugman, J. 2010. *The real wealth of nations: Pathways to human development* (Human Development Report 2010). New York: United Nations Development Program.

Nettle, D., and S. Romaine. 2000. *Vanishing voices: The extinction of the world's languages.* New York: Oxford University Press.

# 6

# Ifè Representations of Leadership

As was discussed in chapter 3, social representations are frameworks for viewing the world. SRs of leadership do not convey solely an individual's point of view, even though the components of these representations have been expressed by individuals. Representations are recognized as "social," whether convergent or not, when they appear several times in a group interview, are discussed by several participants, and/or arise in several interviews. When a majority of participants share the same attitude towards a particular quality—be it a trait, a skill, a virtue or other attribute—it is considered to be a fundamental component of the representation (Cavalli and Coletta 2003), particularly if one or more people make explicit that it is a very important quality, or even essential to their definition of the object.

In order to arrive at an understanding of Ifè representations of leadership, I asked each of the five association boards interviewed to define or give a description of a leader *(chef)*, of a literacy program head *(responsable d'alphabétisation)*, and of an association's board *(bureau exécutif;* see Appendix A). In context, this last type of leader was generally understood to be a member of a literacy and development association's board; whenever participants manifested uncertainty, I said, *"C'est vous"* ("It's you"). Because there was a notable lack of discussion during the first interview when these questions were asked, starting with *Jésus le Chemin,* I added the question "What are his (or her) three or four most important qualities?" in most future interviews. Additionally, I asked for a description of a problem that the board had had to resolve in order to discern what these leaders do in reality, for the purpose of seeing if reported behavior was consistent with what they had verbally expressed about leadership.

I also asked for the qualities of a subordinate, since every leader has subordinates toward whom he or she has a responsibility. In fact, most current models of leadership incorporate the role of follower into the model. As will be seen in several sections of this chapter, this link between leadership and "followership" (Blunt and Jones 1997) was apparently quite strong for several of the interview participants, since for three groups, the discussion on the qualities or responsibilities of a subordinate returned to the qualities and expectations of a leader.

In an effort to separate in-group from outsider perspectives, the representations which emerged are described in this study using the words of the participants as much as possible. The original French and Ifè, the languages of the interviews, are found in Appendix B while the English translations are given here in the text. The outsider perspective is found in the discussion of the findings, which concludes each of these chapters.

## 6.1 Social representations of a leader

The French word *chef,* which can be translated into English as leader, tribal chief, head (of a family or of state), director (of an institution), superior, boss, foreman, or captain, was used without clarification on my part in

## 6.1 Social representations of a leader

order to ascertain the reference point of the SR for leader. In Ifè, the word corresponding to *chef, ólú,* includes all the meanings of the French word. In addition, there is a word, *ɔgá,* which is limited to the manager or head of a group or association *(chef de service/groupe/association).* However, it can also be used when speaking of the head of the household.

I had expected to find that the reference point of the SR would be a traditional chief, but several groups based their examples on other leaders, particularly the head of a family or of an association. The moderator of *Jésus le Chemin,* though, began with a truly broad definition, saying that a *chef* is *"le premier responsable dans un cercle donné"* ("the main person in charge in a given circle"). The only times the characteristics of traditional chiefs were mentioned, in fact, were when I specifically asked if a characteristic or part of a definition applied also to traditional chiefs.

Analogies comparing the head of an association with his group and a father with his family emerged in two interviews (AVID's first one and AMIADA's second one). According to Moliner et al. (2002), these analogies are a manifestation of the psychological embeddedness of a representation. This supposition is supported by the work of anthropologist Schatzberg (1993:451), who notes that in many African cultures notions of legitimate authority and governance are derived from an "idealised vision of patterns of authority and behaviour within the family." This foundational model generates the expectation that a leader will take care of and protect his people just as a father does his family, which accords with the notions of African leadership expressed in chapter 4. Another such expectation is that there will come a time when he needs to relinquish authority, transferring it to his "children." This view also emerged in the interviews.

Interview responses were sorted according to the following list:
- the qualities possessed by a leader,
- what he or she is,
- what he or she is not,
- what he or she should do,
- what he or she should not do.

These headings are in line with the definition of an SR, which includes notions of behavior linked with the social object as well as ideas and beliefs about it.

I began with the hypothesis that those qualities recognized as important or essential for a majority of the groups are fundamental to the SR, especially if they appeared in discussions for each type of leader (unspecified leader, literacy program head, or board member). Thus, the fundamental qualities of leadership for the participants of this study are patience, faithfulness, an exemplary life, competence in group management, and avoidance of dictating. Each of these primary elements in turn gives rise to other elements of the representation.

Other themes were also indicated as being important, but by a minority of groups, so that they appear to be less fundamental to the SR: caring, making decisions as a group, and forgiveness. Nevertheless, as the president of AMIADA remarked, all these qualities are interdependent and form a whole.

### 6.1.1 Patience

Only one feature was mentioned in every interview: patience. This quality was important for every type of leader. In addition, four groups indicated that it was essential for any leader. Furthermore, the ACATBLI leaders defined it, not as a trait, inherent in a person's character, but as a competence necessary for every literacy leader. Moreover, Mr. Agbémadon emphasized the importance of this quality, saying that a leader "is always patient," and then elaborating that a leader listens attentively to reactions while accepting criticisms, and makes decisions after analysis has been done. He and his colleague also brought up the importance of patience in leadership during their last interview, pointing out that patience "disarms" those who are being difficult. (See Appendix B for an explanation on how the following interview excerpts are tagged; and see page xiii for the interview transcription conventions.)

A.3.SK 30m There where I will say again, there where the Lord has blessed us a lot, for our strengths, it's that truly he has given us patience.. Otherwise, if we didn't have this strength, (laughs) we wouldn't be able to continue= we couldn't do the work. Because the instructors aren't easy, eh? It has been very hard but, God has helped us to acquire, this skill of patience, and

*6.1 Social representations of a leader* 87

|  |  |
|---|---|
|  | from time to time, they themselves say, that: truly, when they come with decisions, they are involved, they have meetings, to prepare themselves, when they bring, but just when talking {tongue click} |
| A.3.AgbA ff. | They are disarmed [{laughs}] |
| A.3.SK ff. | [They are disarmed!] {both laugh} |

AMIADA participants identified it as one of the most important qualities for a literacy program head, since the ability to control anger is important.

C.3.AmA 9m  Well, in the case of literacy, in order to elect a head {of a literacy program}, the most necessary or important qualities, first I see the most important quality, it's patience. He must be very patient before becoming a leader. So, when a leader doesn't have enough patience, it is necessary that the= his patience dominates his anger . that he be slow to anger. That is a prime quality that is. First quality it's patience.
C.3.MK 13m  since it's literacy, they are IMPORTANT people, they are even going to do something even there are people who are going to ask you, parents who are going to .. to hurl insults at you you aren't PATIENT, you canNOT receive but you must be patient.

When they were deciding what the three or four most important qualities for a literacy leader were, this statement was made:

C.3.AmA 20m  If you are chief your patience must be great, really.
C.3.All ff.   Indeed!

Later in their interview, they also affirmed that patience is an important quality for a village chief.

C.3.AmA 29m  If . it's about a village . chief, before electing a chief . in a village, I see that these qualities are also important . to a village chief. First the chief must also {be} patient. If a chief isn't patient, we cannot elect him, because . people will say well,

> our chief here . he is not patient can he still reign over us, he can lead this village, he even has money, he has thus and such but, he ha= he is impatient. Thus, if the chief is not patient in my opinion, it's not the smart thing to do.

During *Jésus le Chemin*'s interview, the reason patience is essential for the leader of a literacy program was explained in terms of the time necessary to truly understand the students.

C.5.OK 6m   If he is not patient with the adults .. that won't work. It's why I say .. it's the most important quality for the head of a literacy program. {a request from JR to speak more loudly} I said that, the most important quality for a literacy program head, it's patience. He ought to have a lot of patience towards adults . because it takes time to understand them . given that possibly you are literate, certain behaviors you will find to be bizarre .. truly, you must accept them just as they are, to be able to go xx I suggest patience to manage such a group.

One participant remarked that patience is also a very important quality for subordinates, as mischief-makers may otherwise turn subordinates against their leader.

C.4.ANA 34m   Sometimes they can even go as far as to say to you, ah you don't see how your boss is in the process of evolving nevertheless he himself is improving at your expense it's that which he should give you and he isn't giving it to you and he's in the process of building something and well he's in the process of buying all this, so, go on you must go on strike against him, you must reclaim this right, you must do this, you must do that, yes, that happens often and if you the subordinate you are not .. patient, you won't be able to analyze correctly, these agitators you risk your well-being or block the work, that is to say what he expects of you.

Thus, patience is an essential attribute, not only for the leader of a group, but for all the members of a group. A leader should listen to and receive all that

## 6.1 Social representations of a leader

is said to him and seek the common good. These beliefs were not only stated frequently during the interviews, but were also seen in the descriptions of actions taken by the associations' leaders. When each group gave an example of a situation where the members had to resolve a problem, all spoke of meeting to discuss the problem. While they themselves were always present during these meetings, usually others involved in the situation were also present, whether supervisors, teachers, students, or village members, including village chiefs. According to these data, it seems that the resolution of a problem among the Ifè is a process. This process frequently involves several meetings and much time in listening to every person and in discussing the issue before arriving at a solution together. This process requires, therefore, a superior level of patience.

*Problem with a supervisor*

C.1.NK 17m   And .. through questioning, we knew that the supervisor had such a problem. Now, when we called him in in into [YMA: the office] to the office, he acknowledged the facts.

*Problem at village level with teachers*

C.2.VA1 32m   So, it was after everything we met with the other instructors who had proposed themselves, and in the association, and we said well here is the problem, what do you think? They said fine okay, and the others who were instructors, we heard their ideas,

*Problem with the functioning of a literacy class*

C.2.VA1 34m   So, then, we go out from time to time to regulate such problems meet with the learners AND the instructors, discuss things with them and restart the class.

*Problem at a subzone level with a supervisor and the teachers under him*

C.3.AmA 49m   And at the end of the 2002 campaign now, we met here and we have, we decided that well as we work together with the brothers, the supervisors, the supervisor who is on the other side, the instructors, and {work there} had to be suspended, so we'll revisit this issue. And we called a meeting and we went to them. And we .. we met, and each one said what is wrong.

*Problem with ACATBLI among the literacy coordinators*

C.4.JR 47m    So, this understanding it came about during a meeting such as the gen[eral assembly, during]
C.4.ANA ff.            [yes, many meetings ourselves] we had many meetings to discuss this.

*Problem at the local association level*

C.4.GÐ 54m    (interpreted by ANA) we debated these issues, this dragged on for almost a month before we were able to elect the board. We discussed from here to there that really, if we aren't careful, we risk . having a still-born association.

*Problem with teachers*

C.4.GÐ 59m    (interpreted by ANA) So, it was resolved, it was resolved, we coordinators, supervisors, first coordinators we really explained it to the supervisors and together with the supervisors we had meetings about the complaints with the experienced instructors to really bring them to see reason, to tell them .. what was needed so that they can continue to work.

*Problem at association level with member churches*

C.5.OK 21m    So, it was through through negotiation on several occasions by this means we were able . to bring back many, some of whom are still wavering.

These examples show that patience is an essential factor in group management and problem solving among the Ifè. Other, secondary

6.1 Social representations of a leader    91

elements of the representation emerged during the discussions of patience and the management of problems: decision-making in groups and love or compassion for everyone. These will be discussed later in this chapter. However, first let us consider other fundamental components of the SR of leaders.

### 6.1.2 Faithfulness

Faithfulness *(la fidélité)* is another very important quality in an Ifè leader. Participants in four interviews placed it among the most important qualities for a leader and/or a literacy program head. This quality was also mentioned by the ACATBLI literacy directors during my 2007 research project on leaders and literacy program heads. It is interesting to note that, as Mr. N'tchou, president of AVID, said, *"La fidélité englobe beaucoup de choses,"* 'faithfulness covers many things'. Other people also specified several actions and attitudes that are included in this concept, thereby showing the fundamentality of this feature of the representation and how central qualities generate others.

AgbA 10 Oct 07   He is faithful. He correctly manages monies, he is impartial, open to development innovations. (explanation of the importance of this quality for a leader) To know how to manage personnel, teaching material, stock of the office and program funds. Have sound accounting practices to gain the confidence of donors.

SK 10 Oct 07   (explanation of the importance of this quality for a leader) He is impartial so that the villagers trust him. He enjoys assuming his responsibility. (and for a literacy program head) Know how to manage personnel and program funds. Have sound accounting practices.

From the above extracts, it seems a major component of faithfulness is conscientiousness, although the French equivalent never appeared in the interviews. However, one translation of conscientiousness is *honnêteté*, or honesty. Although this word also was not used, the importance of truthfulness as a part of fidelity did appear in one interview.

C.1.NK 4m   Faithfulness in his actions first, faithfulness in management ... of the enterprise, faithfulness also in word you cannot say one thing and the next day say another . or what you are going to say, perhaps you put into place an action that you have all .. uh . discussed, decided on then, to be faithful also in his supervision in his accomplishment. That's how it is.

Another quality one person tentatively identified as linked to faithfulness was soundness of reasoning *(justesse)*.

C.2.VA2 11m   Or as well soundness of reasoning enters into faithfulness, I don't know,

However, consensus on the components of faithfulness does not always exist, as this extract from AVID's second interview shows. One person claimed that one needs to care about everyone, but another disagreed.

C.1.YMA 3m   If you are faithful, if you are faithful, you will care about everyone.
C.1.AgA ff.   You can be faithful without caring about everyone.
C.1.YMA ff.   Then in that case you aren't faithful.

Some indications of the motivations for the inclusion of this quality appear in the extracts above. Nevertheless, the principal reason a leader should be faithful is clear: so that the work can succeed.

C.2.VA3 6m   Faithfulness is very important, if you are the leader, and you don't practice faithfulness, it is bad.
C.2.VA1 ff.   That's right. It destroys the association.
C.3.AmA 25m   You see, it is necessary that, if someone is a leader, but not possessing the spirit of faithfulness, the work will not go well.
C.5.EK 13m   If there isn't faithfulness, well, we'll fail in the work.

This concern for the smooth functioning of the group surfaced in another area of AMIADA's interview. They linked the quality of being dynamic or active to the healthy functioning of a group. The lead-in to this quality in

## 6.1 Social representations of a leader

AMIADA's interview was a saying ("When the head is sick, the whole body doesn't feel well") followed by a family analogy before the conclusion that a leader must be dynamic.

C.3.SY 8m  (interpreted) The leader, he's the head. And when the head is sick, the whole body doesn't feel well. For example, the father of a family who is slack, not alert, who doesn't arouse who doesn't make his children work well, the children are behind him, when papa speaks, they act, he doesn't speak, they stay put. So, a group leader, of any group, he should be someone who is truly dynamic and helps the group to move.

This quality of being dynamic or active may be one generated by fidelity. AVID's participants put the two together as they began their identification of the qualities of board members.

C.1.NK 10m  So, these committee members, that committee, should also be a committee who is .. ho .. faithful.
C.1.YMA ff.  active
C.1.NK ff.  active .. and … faithful active,

We see then that faithfulness is truly a fundamental aspect of leadership for the Ifè. It is important in order to gain the trust of collaborators and to do one's work well. These extracts also show that impartiality and righteousness, as well as possibly caring and dynamism, are a few of the features generated by faithfulness.

### 6.1.3 Exemplary

An Ifè leader should also live an exemplary life. This accords with descriptions of African leadership in general as related in chapter 4, section 4.3. The president of AVID, in fact, began his description of a leader by saying that a leader should have good behavior and be an example. The Ifè want to be able to trust their leaders in all things. The village women in Interview D put this quality among the most important ones, in contrast to the men of their area. These latter had, however, included exemplary in their list of desired characteristics of a leader, defined by them as "he does things correctly" *("il fait des choses justes")* and irreproachable, defined as "he does not do things for which he can be reproached" *("il ne fait pas des choses qu'on peut lui reprocher")*. Two groups stated that a leader should be a good model or a good example to others.

C.1.AgA 3m   Be a model for others also.
C.2.VA2 3m   If I may add, I want to say, that which he just said, he should be exemplary, as he {VA3} said.

Other groups specified the manner in which a leader is a model. Both the general qualities of good behavior and/or good morality were given as well as specific behaviors to do or to avoid.

C.4.ANA 3m   And it's also necessary that he have good behavior, good morality, .. since it's he who must be an example to others, good leadership should show how to act and not dictate what one must do.
C.4.GĐ 20m   He should know right from wrong, avoid rumors of debt around him, whether elsewhere or in the association. The president, the secretary and the treasurer must have the same positive conduct, be united, so their words do not differ from each other.

AVADI participants explained the reason that good behavior is particularly important for a literacy program leader in this way:

C.2.VA2 14m   So uh well, our work here, if you: .. well: your behavior . is ho is not .. gentle, to attract others, you will have many problems. So, you must be exemplary, and: going from there, well, you can even so attract people and easily pass on . ho: your = that is to say .. the message like.
C.2.VA1 ff.   He should also have a share of a healthy moral life.
C.2.VA2 ff.   Mmm. Yes, xx
C.2.VA1 ff.   That is, I see that as important .. his life . in the area . plays an important role. So uh he should even so . adopt certain behaviors, as was just said, that they are going:

|  | that they aren't, don't become an obstacle . to the literacy program. |
|---|---|
| C.2.VA2 ff. | That's right. |

I asked the ADCIBA participants to specify what they understood by the phrases of "good behavior" and "good morality," since the norms for behavior and morality vary from culture to culture. The response of the treasurer (and a literacy coordinator) included a list of things a person should avoid doing, such as adultery, theft, arrogance, aggressive behavior, and drunkenness, and he explained why.[1]

|  |  |
|---|---|
| C.4.ANA 4m | With us here, especially in Africa, it must not be someone who commits adultery, it must not be someone who steals. Theft= .. it isn't anyone who is too arrogant, who .. is aggressive and who really who quarrels with a lot of people, it must not be someone who is a= a drunkard. Someone who gets drunk and says things without realizing it, which I say is not good. Especially the first element there, it's, let's say, well .. this here category, the African especially on the standard of adultery, the African is extremely strict about that. And it's because it takes TOO much time to be able to get past it. You commit adultery . this year and in twenty years, the families aren't going to let it go. That's why we DISTRUST THAT A LOT. |

In describing the qualities desired in a board member, another ADCIBA member repeated that he should avoid committing adultery, especially taking the wife of another. He used a proverb to emphasize his point that such a situation would have lasting repercussions: it was like a bottle in the ground, which will never decay.

|  |  |
|---|---|
| C.4.GÐ 22m | (interpreted) It is necessary that in .. in the heart of the board or the executive board that there be love between the members, also to avoid adultery as the other one said and |

---

[1] Adultery is defined in the Ifè culture as a man sleeping with another man's wife, as well as a woman who sleeps with a man not her husband (A. Agbémadon and K. Sétodji, personal communication, September 24, 2010).

to avoid taking the wife of another. When that there that gets in the group it can never work. It's as our elders say, it's like a bottle in the ground, which never rots. {several people chuckle}. That's why, then, we must do everything to avoid this situation.

Most of the behaviors to avoid were also named by other groups. An AVADI participant specified that a person who commits adultery or who steals should not have any responsibilities in a literacy program. An AMIADA member agreed that aggression is not a desirable quality in a leader.

C.2.VA2 17m   Well, as he said the reason, well I, myself, normally, for a man like that, he isn't literate, who is going to try to run after the wives of others or someone well who knows well .. who who steals, for example. If you have this character, thus, you are not well placed for this work.
C.3.AmA 1m   it also must not be that he is a fairly violent leader.

The opposite of arrogance, humility, was a quality that was named by three groups: AVADI, *Jésus le Chemin,* and the men in the general village interview. These last listed it as a quality for a literacy program head, whereas the participants in the AVADI and *Jésus le Chemin* interviews identified it as a necessary characteristic for two types of different leaders. Those in AVADI gave it for all leaders as well as for board members; *Jésus le Chemin*'s members presented it for a literacy program leader in addition to board members. The latter group explained why they saw it as an important quality.

C.2.VA2 5m   Yes! It is necessary that he do this also, good behavior, well, a good reputation, with a good, that there, a good reputation isn't it?
C.2.VA1 ff.   A good reputation. Yes, that he be someone who is humble. All that should enter into {it}, absolutely, .. because if there's someone and if he says something, he wants, without a doubt, that that be done, so that's that.

6.1 Social representations of a leader								97

C.2.VA1 21m  They should be humble, they should listen to others, they should not deliver their opinions as though they were ... were perfect and know everything, who want to do everything as they please.

C.5.ĐO 9m  (interpreted) Such a program head should avoid pride and .. instead show humility. In this humility, that would make it so that all whom he leads, they are truly going to want to approach him at all times and learn from him. Otherwise, by giving the impression that it's only he who knows anything, it's he who is the head, that causes people to withdraw.

C.5.OK 11m  because here .. in the midst of a group that they lead, if they aren't patient, are not humble, if they aren't moderate, uh, if they aren't open, they cannot lead the group .. over which they are put.

In summary, the Ifè require that their leaders lead exemplary lives. They want them to be humble and not aggressive. They should not steal or commit adultery. Essentially, this model life is necessary to ensure that their subordinates will submit to them and that the work will succeed. This element of the representation was raised by many participants regardless of their roles in society, so it is regarded as a fundamental feature of leadership.

### 6.1.4 Competent in work

Another fundamental, normative element in the SR of leadership for the Ifè is competence. Two people referred to this quality when they defined a leader. Another cited it when describing an association's board.

C.3.AmA 1m  When one says that someone is a leader in an association, or that he is the head of an association, first, he should have . uh competence in his work. Does this person, the responsibility which is being entrusted to him, is he competent in it? Does he have the competency? That is the first quality in my opinion.

C.5.BK 2m  So, the leader is he who is supposed to .. have the competence, the maturity and the spirit of coordination, to have .. a way of directing through group consensus, so, he himself he takes the

|          | ideas and = he works with them in order to have a product to bring good to the group over which he is established as leader. |
|---|---|
| C.1.NK 9m | Well, the qualities, I myself see the board .. is the organ which is capable, that is to say who who has all the: ... possible qualities to direct. |

Mr. Agbémadon, during my 2007 research project on leader representations, stated that competence should be a characteristic of literacy program heads. He explained, "He should really know his work, be capable to direct, to be able to plan activities." This point is very important for the analysis of capacity building done in and by ACATBLI; I will return to it in chapter 8.

A leader is expected to be competent in several domains. The most important is competence in group management, that which should be done *"par concert"* ('in concert'; C.5.BK 2m). To do that well, the leader needs to have several abilities, such as skills in decision-making, meeting management, problem solving, and public speaking. Even though decisions may be made by consensus, the final responsibility for the decision apparently rests with the leader.

|  |  |
|---|---|
| AgbA 10 Oct 07 | A leader is wise. He knows how to make decisions, he has professional capabilities (knows how to direct, coordinate activities, has a feel for the organization). |
| C.1.NK 0m13s | Okay. I would say that that leader well he should know how to listen to his associates, he should be able to ensure that each person has a chance to speak, he should also, as the lady said, forgive, know how to forgive . and also know how to lead meetings in the sense can each one . put forth his ideas and now he should also know how to BEHAVE, behave in such a way that, if someone gives his ideas perhaps, he should not reject them xxly as if they have no basis. So he should accept EVERYTHING and together analyze that idea first. |

This concern that a leader listens to his or her colleagues or subordinates was expressed by several people, as only in that way can a leader correctly administer the group.

## 6.1 Social representations of a leader

C.3.SY 6m (interpreted) Thus, he receives many things, that is to say from left to right, he himself receives he now knows how to administer it so that this can go forward.

C.5.ĐO 4m (interpreted) everybody comes to make a proposal, good or bad, and he receives it. And, it's to the leader now to differentiate between all that he's received and choose what is good.

Another skill needed by leaders for group management is public speaking. This includes not just confidence but also the ability to maintain a calm demeanor even when difficult issues are argued.

C.4.GĐ 2m A good leader should have the courage to speak before people without fear. He should also know how to address people, know how to speak, not to speak with arrogance when responding to questions but with wisdom and gentleness even when the question {was given in} a hard or loud tone.

C.4.ANA 6m it is absolutely necessary to have a head . who manages to manage well all that happens, and under difficult circumstances, that when there are difficulties, that is to say in the course of the execution of . of a program, when a difficulty enters in. That is when a difficult situation comes up, this person must be able to direct, to direct that, in such a manner that the association will not be blocked. It's very important for leadership.

These extracts also show that the idea of competence generates several other elements of the representation, such as discernment, wisdom, and knowledge of administration, management, and supervision. It is also important for leaders to listen well to their subordinates and to accept all that they say without being defensive. They should equally know how to speak in public and calm down or persuade their audience when necessary. As Mr. Saanya (of AMIADA) and Mr. Affonféré (of ADCIBA) noted, without competence and all the qualities linked to it, the work would be blocked and nothing would be accomplished.

### 6.1.5 Does not dictate

Distaste for dictatorship is very strong among the Ifè. For them, it is absolutely essential for a leader to make decisions in harmony with the group's thinking. This accords well with the writings on African leadership discussed in chapter 4 that indicate the importance of consensus and the presence of notions of participatory leadership in sub-Saharan regions.

C.1.NK 1m  Thus he should accept EVERYTHING and together analyze that idea first. So, he should not be a dictator. He should not be a dictator.

C.2.VA2 36m  They {adults} do not want for only one person decide that well, today we should do this and so on like that. An adult doesn't like such a situation.

Again, the importance of listening to others emerges as a significant factor in making decisions that will advance the group or the work.

C.5.EK 5m  He also should not decide about something by himself, by just himself, let's say that I am the leader, so I'm going to act how I want. He should call his members and and ask the question, describe the situation and together they will discuss and find the best solution.

Speakers in two groups brought up the point that ignoring or refusing to hear the advice of subordinates is a way of mistreating them that will discourage them and prevent the work from being accomplished.

C.3.AmA 43m  that is to say the leader should consider the subordinates, the leader must not make decisions alone. The leader must not be a dictatorial leader. He alone is going to make decisions like that, that's what I want us to do .. without having the opinion of the subordinates, without gathering their information, their ideas . so, if it's like that, if the subordinates are mistreated, the work cannot advance.

## 6.1 Social representations of a leader

C.5.ÐO 32m  (interpreted) Well, in a group or in an association, the leader is there, and when he brings a problem, he should desire to receive the opinion of each person. And gather ideas, debate together in order to make a decision. And without that, the association can't improve. And when the subordinates or his coworkers will finish by discovering that no, our leader, our boss is in the process of doing .. he makes his own proclamations, or he decides by himself what he wants, in the end, they will desist or be discouraged, withdraw and the work can no longer go forward. There must be collaboration.

In addition, among the affirmations of what makes for a healthy organization, seven people chose the proposition "A literacy program will best succeed when all its members can give their opinion when decisions are being made." These seven people represent four different associations, which seems to imply that the skill of decision-making in groups is a shared component of the representation of leadership.

Tied very closely to the idea that leaders must not dictate is that they need to have a realistic view of their position in the group, and not an overly proud one.

C.5.EK 30m  it is that if a group wants to do something, well the leader of this group, it must not be that he sees himself already .. too high, he says it is I who am the leader, so, I am going to make only, just my decision to direct the work, that won't work. He needs to call the members and sit you down and each one give his opinion, and on that basis, we cut out what is not good, and those which those which are good, we add them, and it's together that the group can evolve.

As noted in section 6.1.3 on exemplary qualities expected of leaders, lack of pride *(orgueil)* or presence of humility was expressly stated as a desirable characteristic by several groups. This included the men in the Itséré interview, who listed it as necessary for a literacy program leader. AVADI participants framed these notions of humility and listening to others in terms of submitting to others.

C.2.VA2 4m  He should submit, so that the thing goes well and at the right time, it's still for him to act.
C.2.VA1 ff.  He should also have the quality of listening to others. He should, as our brother just= the president just said, he should always be available to listen to others and to analyze others' ideas and have how one can even so .. use some ideas that others have brought.

They went on to link all these qualities, along with a good reputation, with the notion of a servant leader.

C.2.VA1 5m  He should submit, become the servant of others.
C.2.VA2 ff.  He becomes a servant, yes.
C.2.VA1 ff.  It's what God himself tells us. He who is the head, he must be the servant of others, yes!
C.2.VA2 ff.  He must truly be a servant, yes! That's it, to submit. Heh! He must also do something too, good behavior, well, a good name, with good, that there, a good name, right?
C.2.VA1 ff.  A good name. Yes, that he be one who humbles himself. All that must enter into {it} for sure .. because if there is someone and if he says something, of course he wants for it to be done, so there.

Finally, as the last part of the extract above shows, discussion of the characteristic of not dictating also returns to the idea that a leader should model appropriate behavior.

C.4.ANA 4m  a good leadership should show how to do and not dictate what one should do.

The fundamental characteristics of leadership among the Ifè thus reveal the importance of patience, faithfulness, competence, and high moral standards in intragroup interactions between leaders and followers. In addition, leaders ought to make decisions with the group, demonstrating humility. Without these qualities, relationships—and thus the work—are damaged. Secondary characteristics of the shared representation of leadership are

## 6.1 Social representations of a leader

also important in the maintenance of good relations and the accomplishment of the work; these are discussed next.

### 6.1.6 Some secondary features

Certain elements evoked by the fundamental features of the representation were identified above. In this section those themes raised by three or four groups will be discussed, as well as ones that, while cited by only two groups, were identified as highly important by one of them. These elements are considered secondary, less fundamental—although still important—components of the representation of leadership: caring, forgiving, literate, serious, and available.

#### 6.1.6.1 Caring

Three French words were used in the interviews that I have combined under the term "caring": *amour, aimer (tout le monde)* and *\*compassionner*. These qualities were identified as most important during the AVID, AMIADA, and Itséré interviews. Both leaders in general and literacy leaders should care about their subordinates as well as the work itself.

C.3.MK 3m   it is necessary that the person {leader}, first of all, have compassion on everyone.

C.3.AmA 10m   The second quality, it is necessary that it be also love he must love the= it is necessary that he it is necessary that the person {head} love first the work which is before him he must also care about him= that that which he wants to govern, those who he wants to guide, he must care about them. Thus, he cannot work without caring. That is the second quality.

Discussion of this quality in Ifè was lively during both AVID's and AMIADA's interviews, as some participants saw this characteristic as an element of other qualities.

C.1.AgA 3m   The third, to be he who likes everyone.

C.1.YMA ff.   If you are faithful, if you are faithful, you will care about everyone.
C.1.AgA ff.   You can be faithful without caring about everyone.
C.1.YMA ff.   Then you are not faithful.

From this extract we see that faithfulness and caring are closely related concepts for some Ifè. The following extract shows that caring has a tie to patience as well.

C.3.AmA 20m  And finally, caring.
C.3.MK ff.    I want to know, between patience and caring …
C.3.AmA ff.   Never, it's different.
C.3.SY ff.    For patience, you can care about someone and not have patience.
C.3.AmA ff.   Right!
C.3.SY ff.    Do you understand now? You can, you can, you yourself you get to know someone who cares about you, but if it's a question of work, this one becomes haughty. It is he who sees himself at the top, so if you advance an idea, he doesn't accept it.

The Itséré male interviewees listed the quality of caring for both chiefs and for literacy program heads. When they explained why it was so important for chiefs, they indicated it would help them carry out one of their responsibilities without prejudice.

D.Rep.men 16s And also if he cares about everyone, even if his enemies come, he will judge well.

The ADCIBA vice-president also insisted that board members should care about each other in order for the association to succeed.

C.4.GÐ 21m   Love is very indispensable between members of the board, without that, the association will not succeed.

He continued his explanation a little later, showing exactly how the lack of caring, as demonstrated by a lack of listening to others, can bring about failure of the association:

## 6.1 Social representations of a leader

C.4.GĐ 22m   Another thing to note, if one of the board members doesn't care about isn't in the habit of understanding listening to the members of the association, this neutralizes the efforts of the others and there is division. They become divided because of this person then they are no longer able to continue life in the association.

Actually, as is typical with SRs, people do know of cases where the expectations set up by the representation are not met (Serra 2000). This knowledge was made explicit in AMIADA's discussion of the four most important qualities of a leader. When I asked these interviewees if the four most important qualities they had listed were equally true for a traditional chief, one person said no but another said yes, although he recognized that there are traditional chiefs who do not possess them. When I then asked the first person if he would have responded differently if I had asked for the qualities of a good leader, he affirmed that he would have.

C.3.MK 27m   Well, it would be different. {discussion of other qualities} So, there it is necessary .. firstly, there are chiefs in the area who don't have love.

C.3.AmA 29m   I myself am going a bit . in the other direction from what the brother just said. If . it concerns a village chief, before electing a chief . in a village, I see that these qualities also are important for a village chief. {discussion re: patience} {tongue click} I myself want to say automatically as far as I'm concerned, in my humble opinion that, this step= these three= these four qualities here . are also important for a village chief, in my opinion. But in contrast, we see the opposite side . of chiefs . in our villages. So, normally, these qualities have to be in our chief.

C.3.JR ff.   So, if I had asked for the qualities of a GOOD chief, would that have changed your..

C.3.MK ff.   Yes, if you had said a good chief, then, automatically, those are the qualities. But if you say CHIEF, that's vague. th= so a good chief, automatically, that's it.

When I asked what the other two participants in AMIADA's interview thought about this issue, they agreed: a good leader should have the attributes discussed, including caring, but examples of leaders in the area who do not practice these qualities are well-known.

C.5.OKD 30m   I want to add, a leader should have these qualities. The four xx a good leader should have those. Even if it's a village chief, he does these four qualities xx, and it's over.

C.3.SY 32m   (interpreted) He says that, what the brothers said, that it's true and often these qualities are found in the heads of administrative departments. And often they try to put them into practice so that all the personnel can work well. But on the other hand, when we see our chiefs today, they only do the opposite.

The ACATBLI leaders provide practical examples of caring for subordinates. During one of the interviews, Mr. Agbémadon indicated that he was currently hosting a former literacy teacher in order to help him deposit some money in a bank account. This emerged during a discussion of their self-perceived strengths, one of which is a lack of pride or haughtiness.

A.3.AgbA 34m   Uh . our strength, as I said that . there is no pride, that it that is seen when they approach us .. and they even come to present their household problems to us. So, there is a . trust which is there, that he can bring his household problem with his wife, his children, well, often we try to . guide them a bit. [That's it.]

A.3.SK ff.   [That's what] I say even as currently with our instructors, we are no longer .. to say their bosses, but we've become brothers. We have become brothers, whoever comes now to Atakpamé, wants to see uh go see Akoété, go see Kodjo, or Akpovi. We've even become like brothers. We're very close.

A.3.AgbA ff.   There is a former instructor who's been at my house for three days now [SK: See] today he's going to leave.

A.3.SK ff.   Yes then, truly.

6.1 Social representations of a leader                                   107

A.3.AgbA ff.   He came I helped him to deposit his money in one in one of the small banks here. So, this morning he's going to leave.

In summary, the quality of caring is seen as important, even though it is not practiced by every leader. Caring has links to other leadership attributes, notably patience and faithfulness, as well as lack of pride or haughtiness. Leaders who care about their subordinates and colleagues will listen well, judge fairly, and give practical help. This is consistent with other research highlighting the importance of maintaining good relationships in Africa, even between leaders or managers and their subordinates (Maranz 2001; Theimann 2007).

### 6.1.6.2 Forgiving

Another area that manifests this overall societal importance of maintaining harmonious relationships typical in Africa is the importance of forgiveness on the part of leaders. Three groups listed this as important for leaders in general: the men and women in Itséré, and AVID, although none listed it as essential. The first person in AVID's interview to mention this quality did so while the recorder was not working, so her comments are lost. However, another person did bring it up later.

C.1.NK 0m25s   He should also be, as the woman said, forgiving, know how to forgive.

AVID members later gave the example of their management of a problem with a literacy supervisor. The fact that they in essence forgave him the problems that he had caused them with the police by not suspending him reveals the importance of this quality in their representation of leadership.

### 6.1.6.3 Literate

Since the context of the interviews was in meetings with literacy personnel, with even the village interview taking place after a literacy teacher meeting, it is perhaps not surprising that being literate came out as a desired characteristic for leaders. Interestingly, while being literate was given as an important quality for both leaders in general and for board members, it was not specifically listed as one for a literacy program head. This is likely because it is so essential to the role that no discussion is needed (Chhokar et al. 2007).

The importance of "knowing paper" is seen as very important in the modern world, and since leaders in this world must communicate with others, literateness is necessary according to ADCIBA members, the Itséré men, and the ACATBLI literacy leaders.

C.4.ANA 9m   Well, also, a very important skill, that is for this new world, he should be literate {laughs}. But if not, he cannot advance. He must be literate, it's obligatory.

One of the Beninese men noted, during a discussion of why literacy in the local language is important, that literateness is becoming a skill that outweighs other, usually more fundamental characteristics in the selection of leaders; an illiterate person is frequently no longer seriously considered for leadership positions even when he possessess the other qualities generally considered essential for a leader. It is particularly significant that this view was stated by one of the men who became literate through the literacy program, not through school.

C.4.KÐ 1h12m (interpreted) It's true, today a leader, someone can have these qualities and for a start lead a group, but he has the lack of not having learned to read, or he isn't literate. So, people think that this person, he can do it, but then he's blocked at this level he isn't literate, he doesn't know paper. The one who we see who cannot even, who does not have these qualities but who knows paper, it's him that we can give the post to.

The Itséré men specified the reason that a leader should be literate: in order to write reports after a decision has been made.

D.Rep.men 22s If he is literate, everything he judges, he is going to make his reports.

## 6.1 Social representations of a leader

The ACATBLI literacy coordinator listed other reasons for a leader to be literate, which included being informed about laws and about new ideas for the development of the community.

SK 10 Oct. 07   He should be literate to be better informed, able to assist at meetings, to have access to readings on development, be able to record innovations, to read documents on legislation.

While being literate is important, however, the level of literacy required for a board member is not necessarily a very high one. The coordinator of the Doumé zone explained why: too often, highly literate people seem to have no time to help others in their village.

C.4.ANA 25m   So, that is why it is now necessary, after the changes in the world, it's truly necessary that that trio, president, treasurer, secretary, all these three, know how to read and write, at least. We aren't requiring someone with a diploma or at a high level, since we don't often have the luck especially in villages or rural areas to find people who who are truly literate, that is to say who have a high level, and who will give of themselves to cause change in others, that is to help others. Often, they are people who are just thinking how to build fancy houses how to buy a nice car, and those no longer have the time to help others. Yeah, so those folks also think especially of having a big salary, so, they don't have the time to cope with the evolution of their locale, you see. So it's often the people who barely have the primary . uh . level or barely, well, barely the secondary level for example to the third year or more, it's it's often these people, among these people that one finds the people who give of themselves for the development of their community.

In fact, the AMIADA coordinator noted that many literacy program graduates have taken on leadership positions, in the church and in the community at large.

B.3.AmA 1h11m  What I see now, thanks to literacy and thanks to .. to this work that we do of lit= in the domain of literacy, I have seen that .. uh many people fill minor, minor positions minor positions minor positions minor positions. That is to say that, for example, he {indicating SY}, he is a deacon now in his church. He was not converted when we began the work. But, he saw that this work it is good. And he converted. Now, he has become a deacon in ou= in his church. And he is also .. also a scheduled preacher. He preaches properly and others interpret into other languages. That is one fruit. And he isn't the only one. There are other examples. There are also other people more than, we can't name them all. The other that you see back there {indicating someone seated at the back of the hall}. Him, he's a supervisor. He's at Affolé, he's at the border {with Benin}. When there's a project .. which concerns development, when the project arrives, they have to get in touch with him first. And it's he who welcomes strangers. It's he, when one says we want to change, we want we want .. uh .. we want to work on development at the school, we want to have such a vision, such a vision on the plan.

Among the posts acquired by literacy program graduates are literacy supervisor and board member. Two such graduates testified to the advantages of being literate, such as acquiring self-assurance and the abilities to figure out how to sound out French and to do math.

B.3.SY 43m  (interpreted) He wants, it's still the same point on the good that literacy has produced in his life, really. Well, in times past, people knew him as nonliterate, unable to read, but through Ifè literacy, he is able now to read and to write, and figure out some French words. He can read certain words, but maybe not understand them well. That is already one point. And it's by the grace today, of God today, he's starting to be able to read French smoothly in front of people. All those who turned back, who withdrew, this can make them

6.1 Social representations of a leader                                111

> come back. So, it's truly a great step, so today being a supervisor, starting from zero achieving supervisor it's a great step.

C.5.Ðo 48m (interpreted) He says that literacy is very important from the moment where, he himself he is foremost a testimony because he was completely, he was nonliterate, at the arrival of literacy he got involved and so here today he can do many things and which he is in the process of doing for that matter. Thus, that helped him a lot, that got him out of of many things of ignorance, but today he can today calculate, if it's money, ten million, thirty million, he can do it. He can stop at the bank, when the teller does poorly, does a calculation, he can say to him that no, he needs to start over, because he's sure of what he is doing in front of him.

Board positions held by literacy program graduates include vice-president and advisor. These require the ability to read and write reports. The fact that these men are also living witnesses that it is possible to learn to read and write even as an older adult is perhaps an additional factor in their selections to these leadership posts.

### 6.1.6.4 Serious

Three groups stated a leader should be serious *(sérieux)*. This representational feature was given by both AVID members and the men of Itséré for leaders in general, and by AVADI participants for literacy association presidents. *Sérieux* has several possible translations (for examples, see www.wordreference.com/fren/serieux); it seems that the way it was used during the interviews was taking one's work seriously, or being reliable. Because of an equipment malfunction, the reason why AVID's leaders included this attribute was lost. The men of Itséré, however, explained that this quality precludes corruption.

D.Rep. men 11s if he is reliable, he is not going to accept money from someone to misjudge cases.

The reason literacy association presidents should be serious emerged in the discussion of what characteristics make a literacy organization function best.

C.2.VA4 39m   Well, precisely, the president of the association ought to supervise classes well. {3 second pause} Well, he should rise up whi= that he work a lot, to him who brings everyone to understand about all the work. So, he should be, first of all, serious and watch over the adult classes.

It appears, therefore, that seriousness, or reliability, is a leadership attribute appreciated for the contribution it makes to the quality of a leader's work. Having this characteristic ensures that the leader gives the work the attention it should have.

### 6.1.6.5 Available

Availability *(disponibilité)* was considered to be an important quality for two groups, AVADI and AMIADA, and was also mentioned during ADCIBA's interview. This quality, like many others, is seen as crucial for the functioning of the group.

The president of AVADI, who is also a village chief, indicated that the attitude of the chief towards meetings affects the attitudes of his followers.

C.2.VA3 3m   A leader should be available since if anyone calls a meeting it's the leader, and if the leader says he's busy, then who's going to come? So, the leader should also be available.

The discussion among AMIADA members regarding availability led into a discussion about caring about the work and its relationship to availability, or making the time to participate in work activities.

C.3.AmA 21m   Let's suppose, as we are here today, excuse me, that one says that that guy didn't come, the other time also, he wasn't there. When a meeting is called, he doesn't go there, so, how can anyone entrust you with a task to do?

## 6.1 Social representations of a leader

| | |
|---|---|
| C.3.MK ff. | That's what is important. |
| C.3.SY ff. | That's what it is to like the work. |
| C.3.AmA ff. | No, liking the work, that goes with having time, for that which concerns availability. It's having the time, to have time for the work. Can someone care about the work and not have time to come to it? |
| C.3.SY ff. | That's why I say that one must love the work. If, truly, you care about the work, anytime, this prevents, that can never stop you from working. To care about the work, that's different from having love for the work. To have love for the work, it's collective on one hand, but, if individually you care about the work, even being alone, you are going to go there, "I haven't seen my second-in-command" won't enter into it. |
| C.3.AmA ff. | Yes, speak. |
| C.3.MK ff. | What I understand in |
| C.3.AmA ff. | Speak up, speak up! |
| C.3.MK ff. | What you have, what I understand in what he said now. You can care about the work, and the work before which you are left you must have time for it, because there where you go, it's the work that you are going to do. |
| C.3.AmA ff. | You should also care about the people. |
| C.3.MK ff. | Exactly, that's what we've said, isn't it? You see, have time for the work. If you care about the work, then you learn that there is another job elsewhere and you leave, and if people come in your absence, can one say then that you care about the work? You don't care about the work. Thus, what is there, that's having time available for the work. That's what the brothers said, finding time for the work, that's the fourth {point}. Availability is included, all the others are within it. |

In both groups the point was made that if a leader did not make the time to participate in the work of the group, such as a meeting, his behavior would discourage others from participating. It seems, therefore, that availability is part of being an example to others, as leaders should model the conduct they desire from their followers.

ADCIBA's participants, on the other hand, emphasized the importance of this quality in order to see that the work is carried out, and went on to link availability to the willingness to make sacrifices for the group.

C.4.KÐ 11m    (interpreted) this program head should be available at all times. If there is news, a job to do, he should give of himself heart and soul so that this opportunity that presents itself not be .. how to say it? lost. He should do all in his power to bring about good things for the association. And still more, {if} he asks for a service, or a sacrifice, he should give of himself to do it, he shouldn't wait, saying so-and-so isn't here, the other one isn't here either, so I'm going to wait, until they are here, we'll start the work together, no. A program head should give of himself and should make sacrifices to do the work in order to, so that the association or the program may work well.

This point of making sacrifices, also mentioned by AMIADA, was taken up by one of the ADCIBA board members.

C.4.KÐ 12m    (interpreted) A program head should give of himself and should sacrifice himself to do the work so that, in order for the association or the program to be able to work well.

In fact, ADCIBA had decided years earlier that availability and self-sacrificing commitment needed to be qualifications for election to the board. They realized this when the first board president chosen was later elected to a political position. After a long debate, they came to the conclusion that anyone who was chosen to be on the board must be available and committed to literacy work. Otherwise, the association would be stillborn.

C.4.GÐ 51m    (interpreted by ANA) we debated these . problems, it dragged out for {smile heard in his voice} nearly a month before being able to elect the board. We discussed it here and back that really, if we didn't pay attention, we risked . having a stillborn

> association. Since when we elect the leading officers, who aren't first of all available , and who aren't going to want to invest themselves heart and soul like those there will be others who are in the process of investing themselves heart and soul, and if those first are more interested in profi = profiting, or to .. to do what they think with the association, that won't work. So, we swore that really . we are obliged to elect those who already are investing themselves those in whom we sense ZEAL .. to really make literacy work otherwise, we'll create a stillborn association.

Availability thus has to do with making time for the group, but also with listening to others and being willing to make sacrifices. All this has to do with the smooth functioning of the group, both in relationships and in the attainment of goals, as do all the other fundamental and secondary features of the representation, with the possible exception of literateness.

## 6.2 Features specific to literacy program leaders

Certain qualities and expectations were brought up for only one type of leader, that is, either a person with program responsibilities (executive, coordinator, or supervisor; *un responsable*) or a board member. Those that concern a *responsable* were rarely shared among the groups interviewed. On the other hand, four qualities or expectations were shared for board members among two or more groups.

One quality, however, was shared by four groups for all literacy program leaders, whether board members or coordinators, supervisors or program executives: creativity, or innovation. This has been identified also by Western research on leadership as an important characteristic of leaders (Duluc 2008; Dym and Hutson 2005). It first emerged in discussions of the type of qualities needed by a board, one function of which is to bring in new ideas.

> C.2.VA1 23m The board should be people who have vision and above all who bring new things so that the association can live and all

this when they have vision when they have new things, they should return to the source, discuss with the association, before knowing how one can carry out this plan of action as the brother just said.

Later, when participants were asked to choose among five statements about how organizations should function, five people in two groups chose the statement "The continuity of the life of organizations relies on the creative action of human beings" (Morgan 1999:66 see Appendix A for all five statements and the original French). The explanations of these board members as to why they chose this statement reveal that it is an important element in their representation of a leader in a literacy association.

C.2.VA1 36m  He says, the continuity of the LIFE .. of organizations depends on the creative action .. of human beings. That's true, you can start something today. And↑. you can not have good results .. if there aren't ideas .. that are new which enter into the program .. new ideas. So, I, I choose that because today, .. in a literacy program, we have .. xx in our region we have begun. So, years go by. In order for the program to last, so it can last, there must be people who bring in other ideas, who create yet other other things to always strengthen this program that we started a while ago. And may continuity exist there . because it's important. If there aren't other things, .. than . to know how to read and write, they'll ask what good is it to know how to read and write . if there aren't other things that we'll do .. on the basis of knowing how to read and write. When we learn to read and to write, what are we going to do with it? So, there must be ideas, there must be creativity, there must be things which can demonstrate that really, if it hadn't started from the basis of reading and writing, we wouldn't have gotten here.

C.2.JR ff.  Okay. Thank you. {I look at the next person.}

C.2.VA3 ff.  Well, it's the fifth one here that I've chosen like the pastor did. For example, in our association, we have teachers' meetings .. which help us a lot. Well I'm going to say as we

## 6.2 *Features specific to literacy program leaders*

haven't yet done . this year, that is stopping us quite a bit . since . certain meeting places for all the instructors, and, and what you have as a problem in your class, you are going to explain to in= before all the instructors, and everyone .. will help you through their thoughts, how he's dealt with it in his village and it works well. So this here, one has= .. we have asked that everyone give his contribution for development, so, I see that number five interests me a lot. You must have all the thoughts of everyone so that you too can make progress.

Both the above extract from AVADI's discussion and the following one from ADCIBA's show how this creativity is particularly important not only for the development of the program, but also to bring economic and social development to their people.

C.4.ANA 1h1m  Well, this idea, I have for that . I agree with that, because truly I have felt that ... in an association . above all to bring that is to say to pull . adults along to a change in behavior, or, to go forward or to come out of .. to get out of a difficult situation. When you, leadership, that is to say the guide ... you aren= you haven't really= you are not moved by a creative spirit, you will not be able to successfully complete .. the program. Since man, given that he is .. he always changes ... uh I don't know really, man changes quickly. Man changes every moment, faced with each situation, man changes. So, you the guide, if truly there is . uh . faced with a difficulty maybe which wants to block .. uh .. the evolution or, which really sidetracks . your objective or the primary goal of the association, really when you don't have .. you don't have .. a creative spirit, when you are not moved by creative ideas, really, you won't be able to overcome. You can't really succeed .. in .. your objective, or else the goal, which you are= which has been fixed. So, it's this idea here that I really agree with. That that that interests me a lot {smile in his voice} since I have I have really some some cases like that, {laughter}I have seen that only the creativity of of of certain, of of certain ideas have saved me. {laughter}

Mr. Kpondza of ADCIBA waxed philosophical about the need for creativity in order to evolve along with the rest of the world. His comments were followed by one of his colleagues who gave a very specific example of a change their association was in the process of introducing in order to attract students.

C.4.KÐ 1h07m (interpreted) So, in such a way that all that man does if we see the world in the beginning, since creation, he isn't = the world is no longer at this stage. The world evolves. We also should seek to evolve. We must cultivate, we must seek out new ideas, to enlarge the field, and how to bring man to grow up, that is to say how to broaden our understanding, our knowledge. If we must stay always in the xx it's what we have done for some time, it's like THAT that we do. When people are going to know that well, when it's like that, today, we do the same thing↓ tomorrow it's the same thing↓ . what else am I going to seek. But when there are new ideas, others are going to seek to come see to discover what is new. So, that's why he also has chosen the fifth formula.

C.4.JR ff. Okay. Anything to add?

C.4.KL ff. Myself, I will only, repeat what the others said. Otherwise, to do that, in our association we are in the process of . of creating .. well . uh the raising of of chickens now, according, there thus, to reinvigorate especially those who are . a bit bored, those who are . in, those who were in a long time ago and there wasn't any change so, we brought them this to awaken them again from their sleep. Also to . please others . who aren't yet here, that if they will come, they can discover other things.

One of the ACATBLI leaders had listed creativity on the questionnaire of my previous research in this domain and mentioned it later as an asset of their team. In the questionnaire, he identified being open to innovations for development as a component of being faithful. In the interview, he claimed the sharing of such innovations as one of the strengths of the ACATBLI literacy team.

*6.2 Features specific to literacy program leaders* 119

A.3.AgbA 28m   Well, I think that . {he taps the table} that's it, it's our strength, and ... means that if= we also have .. well that enters in when we have innovations .. new ideas, we share {them} always with the others.

His colleague picked up this idea in his continuation of the discussion, specifying areas where such creativity is important.

A.3.SK 29m   I will say again that the true strength, it's that . we are really thirsty for the Ifè people for them to succeed. That means that, day and night, we are thinking about . what we can do, how we can pass . to be able to make the people come out so, from time to time, that's why he just spoke of innovations, we have innovations of encouragement, ideas to . to encourage our instructors, our s= the villages to be able to continue the work.

His example echoed the reason given above by one of the ADCIBA coordinators, that it was only through creative solutions to problems that the literacy program has been able to continue, regardless of the area involved. Thus for these four groups, creativity or new ideas are essential for the effective functioning of the literacy program as well as of the associations, so that teachers, literacy learners, and other people are motivated to participate in the effort to bring literacy and development to the Ifè.

### 6.2.1 Qualities of literacy program heads

While no qualities specific to a literacy program head were shared, all of the important qualities for this role also were considered important for any leader. Six groups agreed that patience was the single most important quality for a literacy leader. Three named faithfulness, caring about everyone, and respectful of work and of time as qualities expected for a literacy leader. Two thought that humility and listening skills were important. Thirty-two other characteristics and behaviors were named, but each by only one group and just nine of those were unique to literacy program staff. However, among the qualities shared by another leader type, two were deemed essential to literacy program leaders by at least one group: availability and enjoying the work. The unique qualities are a mix of basic personality traits and of skills or attitudes about the work itself.

Social representations normally circulate around a social object (Jodelet 1989). The fact that there was little to no convergence of qualities for a *responsable d'un programme d'alphabétisation* other than those for any leader strongly suggests that this type of leader is not perceived as a social object. Given the relative newness of this position and its embodiment in just a few persons, this is not particularly surprising, although among the members of these literacy associations, I had expected more consensus.

### 6.2.1.1 *Respectful of work and of time*

Although this quality was not exclusive to literacy leaders, being respectful of the work and of the time of others in the execution of duties still was specifically mentioned by three groups for those holding positions of responsibility in a literacy program, and only once for any other leader. While punctuality is not often a high value in Africa, its presence here is likely because it is emphasized in literacy teacher and supervisor training.

The AMIADA advisor explained that when a leader respects his program and does what he said he would do, it brings joy to all members of the association, as they know they can trust his word.

C.3.SY 15m    (interpreted) When a leader is there, he has established a program, he should respect it, he should complete it as is, that will make all the association, all the group, joyful . because they will say that no, our leader, if he says something, he does it.

Nevertheless, this quality elicited a heated discussion, in Ifè, among AMIADA board members when they were establishing the top four qualities for the head of a literacy program. It did not make their final list, but

## 6.2 Features specific to literacy program leaders 121

the discussion was lively and involved all participants. The main point of argument revolved around the difference between respect (for the work) and availability.

| | |
|---|---|
| C.3.OKD 24m | Respect can take the place of availability. |
| C.3.SY ff. | It's having respect for the work, right? |
| C.3.All ff. | Yes! |
| C.3.OKD ff. | Know that that can take the place of this, then this will disappear and respect also becomes more important than everything else. |
| C.3.AmA ff. | That cannot cause availability to lose its place, availability, it's separate, it's time, it's time for work, that's it the time for work. The time for work can be separate. |
| C.3.OKD ff. | xx{speaks softly} |
| C.3.AmA ff. | Do you understand me now? |
| C.3.OKD ff. | Listen to what I also say, if you respect the time, that means that you're going to go to work on time. If I don't respect today for example, I would not come, and it's that I don't have time for work, but I have respect for what had been said, for the hour set, and I'm there, do you see? |
| C.3.AmA ff. | Yes! I'm not rejecting what you say. You see, it is necessary that, if someone is the leader, not having a spirit of faithfulness, the work won't make progress. |
| C.3.OKD ff. | For that which concerns faithfulness, I don't disagree. |
| C.3.MK ff. | Yes, put that there. All that you say, you understand? |
| C.3.AmA ff. | That which you brought up will be for the fifth heading. |
| C.3.MK ff. | All that which you are in the process of saying. All that you say is within it. |
| C.3.AmA ff. | One can find it, it's a whole. All is combined. It's an interdependence. |

The above discussion concludes with the observation that all the qualities AMIADA members have discussed for literacy leaders are interrelated: patience, fidelity, caring, availability, and respect. This interrelatedness also appeared during the discussion among AVID members of the qualities of a literacy program leader, when they included working hard and caring about the work for the third most important quality for a literacy leader.

C.1.AgA 5m It should be someone, if he wants to work, will not become lazy. In other words, he should value his work at all times.
C.1.NK ff. Yes!
C.1.YMA ff. Because it isn't everyone who is a teacher and who cares about the work.
C.1.AgA ff. He should care about the work.

Two members of AVADI also listed respect as a quality of literacy leaders, emphasizing the respect for punctuality. The second person who did so explained the importance of this attitude when teaching adults.

C.2.VA3 18m since our learners are adults. To respect the hours that have been set for teaching. So, if someone is already older than you if he arrives for class at the set time and you yourself haven't arrived, he sees you, he is your student but he sees that you are even late. So, he ought to be fair regarding to the day
C.2.VA1 ff. of the time
C.2.VA3 ff. and to the hours to the days of the students and also to the set time.

Respect for seniors thus plays a part in establishing this characteristic among those important for a literacy leader. This respect for those older than oneself is well attested in African societies (Allen 2006).

ADCIBA's president also explained why he saw this quality as essential for a literacy leader. As indicated earlier, leaders need to provide good examples.

C.4.KL 17m But, firstly a head should be on time when we speak of a meeting. He should be on time to give a good example to the other members.

## 6.2 Features specific to literacy program leaders

It is clear that respecting work, which includes being on time in this domain, is linked closely with many other representational features already discussed. In effect, it seems that respecting the work and time is a way of manifesting the qualities of being a good example to others, patience, fidelity, caring, and availability. Again, this has a high likelihood of being a learned quality. Its justification as a leader quality is created by tying it to other elements in the fundamental representation of leadership.

### 6.2.1.2 Teachable and able to teach

Not surprisingly for organizations involved in nonformal education, among the competencies identified as important for literacy program leaders were the ability to teach as well as a willingness to learn. Most, if not all, of the coordinators and many supervisors are regularly involved in teacher training, as I observed during the teacher-training session I attended. Moreover, the involvement of ACATBLI personnel as well as that of coordinators and supervisors in regular training sessions was discussed in several interviews.

AVID's participants, in fact, listed the ability to teach among the top three qualities of a literacy program leader and linked it to specific content: knowing the rules for a good teacher, including how to teach a literacy lesson.

C.1.NK 5m   He should know the conditions/rules of a good instructor. And he should know how to teach anyone
C.1.YMA ff.  should know how to present a lesson.
C.1.NK ff.   should know how to present a lesson. To know the rules of a good instructor, he should know how to present a lesson.

This is not abstract knowledge for a program leader, or just something a coordinator or supervisor has to know in order to teach others. For example, the AMIADA coordinator mentioned that he was the teacher for the transition to French class in his village.

C.3.AmA 1h15m The time= yesterday there was a brother who came {his voice lowers} he is at boarding school it's he who did all this on the chalkboard {the chalkboard is covered with mathematical formulas} and this morning I, I taught our students, that is those who make up the third level here at Adogbenou here, I'm the one who teaches them.

However, the ability to teach is also tied to the transfer of competencies in order to provide a succession of leadership. This was a topic at a literacy forum in Kara in 2008, and so impressed the AMIADA coordinator that he now makes a point of having the supervisors in this program take on some of the training responsibilities.

C.3.AmA 41m So, when I returned from Kara that day, I said to myself, Ah, okay I ought to transfer my skills to others, I must share the work with them. Often when we go to teachers' meetings, well, the coordinator gives a practical lesson. So, from that day on, when we say there is a meeting of in this month, there is a teachers' meeting in the next month, I say Ah, you, prepare yourself, prepare a practical teaching that you will present. You, the month after, prepare a practical teaching that you will present and I no longer do everything. {chuckles}

The above extract was actually part of the response to a question about the responsibilities of subordinates. Teachability is thus a characteristic of leaders and of those who may become leaders. The AVADI coordinator noted that the development of professional competences requires continuous training.

C.2.VA1 18m It's someone even so .. well, I don't know if we want to go there. There will always be needs for training because certain things are also necessary so that this program can evolve. Well, for example, in the area of management, of .. of people or management of finances, .. this literacy program head should be trained in this area. He should have these professional skills, in the area of management of people and management of materials, of management of finances.

## 6.2 Features specific to literacy program leaders

The ADCIBA vice-president, when explaining how he became qualified for his position, indicated, in fact, his desire to learn more, and used a proverb to reinforce his statement: "Lots of meat doesn't ruin the sauce."

| | |
|---|---|
| B.4.GÐ 14m | (interpreted) His own experience, it's that he began at the level {of the church} he was elected president |
| B.4.ANA ff. | president of a local .. church |
| B.4.GÐ ff. | A local . church, so that allowed him also to have some experience and to come out of certain {ordeals} and more, since then they've chosen him to be a member of this committee of the literacy association {gap ad}ministration, that has also helped him a lot, and really, as the elders have said, lots of meat doesn't ruin the sauce. {laughter of all} So, if he can also have the chance to [have] |
| B.4.ANA ff. | [complete] |
| B.4.GÐ ff. | (interp.) complete, that would be great for him. |

Training of leaders and by leaders is part of capacity building. This training adds to and reinforces the competencies required for leadership and management. These and other areas where capacity has been and is being built in the Ifè associations will be further discussed in chapter 8.

### 6.2.1.3 Other qualities

Among the unique qualities listed, a few deserve discussion as they are not often found in the literature on leadership. These are a cooperative spirit, being ready to provide for the program needs from one's own funds, and knowing the personalities of those for whom one is responsible.

The association members with whom I spoke were very much aware that they themselves needed the help of others. They primarily look to ACATBLI, but most are also seeking to collaborate with other organizations for additional training, particularly in the areas of income generation, financial aid, and health. The AMIADA vice-president specified that a program head should have a cooperative spirit in order to help the work expand.

C.3.SY 15m (interpreted) a leader should have a spirit of . a cooperative spirit he should have relationships with other associations and that would make his work blossom.

Even though no one else named this as a necessary quality, the idea of collaboration with other organizations was a theme in certain interviews. For example, as ADCIBA's treasurer/co-coordinator clearly expressed, its members are in a position to help other NGOs through their knowledge of Ifè culture and orthography. In fact, they strongly desire that other development organizations collaborate with them, so that they can reinforce what has been taught and produce development-related materials in Ifè.

C.4.ANA 1h44m a few rare times others come of of other ethnic groups or from other locales or from from other lands . to come to speak to us of things, after their departure, we forget everything. Since there isn't an organization who puts that, who translates that .. in texts. Like that there, that which we've heard orally, HOW many days how many months can that . the memory can keep it for how long? {chuckle} You know that the capacity of the memory is limited .{chuckle} and when someone talks a lot, you forget lots of things you keep a little. So, if truly those who come, like the NGOs also the governmental organizations even, who truly want to train .. the people about certain agricultural . practices or that it be . uh a change in behavior all that, they should involve us we .. literacy actors so that if possible if they can explain that to us more deeply so that it will be easy for us to translate to write it down, and it would now be maintained this training will be maintained eternally .. since a training in which you have . booklets, or brochures which speak of that which the training is explaining, it's become immortal this training will last forever.

AVID's members also discussed the importance of collaboration. The president noted his intention to collaborate with development NGOs in order to meet AVID's goal of creating cooperative groups *(groupements)* that will engage in income-generating activities.

## 6.2 Features specific to literacy program leaders

B.1.NK afl 10m  So, we know that, IF we manage to organize a class, for example, into a mutual aid group, so for us since we don't have the ability, we are now going to ask for technical support from NGOs who will now step in to our program to be able to help them, to now help this mutual aid group.

The above extract mentions the lack of certain technical capacities. The lack of financial resources was another theme. ADCIBA's participants, therefore, identified the need for literacy program heads to be ready to put their own funds at the disposal of the organization in order to make sure certain activities are carried out.

C.4.KĐ 12m  (interpreted by ANA) sometimes moments arrive where the head, or else the leader in the xx literacy program puts his own FUNDS in it. While perhaps waiting to see if the community or the members are going to help him, going to pay their contributions so that he can replace them {the funds}. If he doesn't want to put his own interests for the benefit of the group, it won't work. There are some who really don't want to take their own money to help the group, no. Someone like that cannot direct a literacy program since moments arrive truly, if you don't like to take money out of your pocket, that that risks hindering the program, it hinders it, this it must be someone who really has the idea of pushing this program forward cost cost cost {i.e., whatever the cost}

As has already been stated, relationships are a strong value in most of Africa. The above can be seen as an example of the outworking of the value on group solidarity, which will be discussed further in section 6.2.2.1. Relationships are based on more than feelings of solidarity, however; the final quality given as important for literacy program leaders is that of knowing association members well in order to know how best to relate to them.

C.5.EK 8m  So, I myself would say that he should also make an effort to know the situation of his .. of his members. Well, for example, in a given group, you must know, who is this, well, what does he like, what does he dislike, how do you need to approach him to be able to get him to come to you or be able to make him understand well what is going to happen, so, .. those are the qualities he should take on, a literacy group leader.

Although the qualities of a cooperative spirit, being ready to provide for program needs from one's own funds, and knowing personally and well the members of one's organization are not found in most literature on leadership, they are congruent with African emphases on the value of relationships and group solidarity (Maathai 2009; Theimann and April 2007). Research participants also identified them as elements that will promote the smooth functioning of the literacy program and its development arm. As such, their importance to the representation of literacy program leadership among the Ifè should not be underestimated.

### 6.2.2 Qualities of board members

Board members are expected to share many of the characteristics of leaders in general: patience, faithfulness, humility, looking out for group interests, and listening well. However, a few characteristics were listed only for board members. Those that were mentioned by at least two groups were solidarity, discretion, and the characteristic of not reacting to a situation immediately.

#### *6.2.2.1 Solidarity and discretion*

Solidarity is frequently accorded a high value in African societies (Maathai 2009; Maranz 2001). It is so among the Ifè; according to Affala (n.d.:24), *"Dans cette communauté ifè, l'unité est ressenti comme un gage de sécurité et d'efficacité dans un système où la solidarité était l'unique couverture sociale devant les inconnus de l'existence"* ("In this Ifè community, unity is felt to be a guarantee of security and effectiveness in a system where solidarity was the sole social protection in the face of the unknown.")

Although it emerged without prompting in the second set of board interviews, I had explicitly introduced the notion in the first interview set. Literature on organizational theory refers to the use of ritual and

## 6.2 Features specific to literacy program leaders 129

ceremonies in order to create and maintain organizational unity and/or loyalty (Bolman and Deal 1996). I had therefore planned a question asking about rites or ceremonies in the organization (see Appendix A), but the first group of interviewees denied that there were any such things on the organizational level. So in the next interview, I modified the question, introducing the idea of group cohesion by "How do you promote the solidarity of your association? Do you have rites or ceremonies?" It seemed to me that the question of rites or ceremonies still was not well understood, so in subsequent interviews I merely asked how solidarity was constructed in the association. That may have influenced responses to the question about the qualities of board members in the second set of interviews. However, in the first set of interviews, the question was referring to the solidarity of the association; in the second, nearly all responses discussed solidarity among board members.

The primary reason given for the need of solidarity among board members is to be regarded well by the regular members of the association and in the community as a whole, in order to be able to make decisions, and otherwise do their work correctly. In fact, solidarity is closely tied to the qualities of exemplary behavior and caring for each other, as the following extracts show.

C.4.GĐ 20m    The president, the secretary and the treasurer must behave in the same positive way, be united, their words not differing from each other's. They should not allow the president's words to be different from those of the secretary, from those of the treasurer this will be very bad. When those who are simply members learn of these things, they say that there is jealousy or dissension between the leaders according to their analysis.

In fact, *Jésus le Chemin* committee members, in describing a situation that they were in the midst of resolving, noted that unity through the culture is what keeps the association strong.

C.5.OK 22m    Because we want as we said last time, to safeguard unity through the culture and all that which unites us. And especially in this manner we are stronger than being divided .

because our association as we indicated last time, it is what truly makes our strength, it's that which knits us together, that we share together and it's good to preserve that.

This problem of divisive elements that rupture solidarity or unity was raised several times. As expressed earlier by ADCIBA's vice-president (see 6.1.6.1, excerpt C.4.GĐ 22m), as well as in the following extract from AVADI's interview, mutual understanding, an important component of solidarity, is essential for the good of the association. When it is lacking, divisions result and decisions made by the association cannot be successfully implemented. This counteracts the good work that has been done by the association and its members.

C.2.VA2 22m  and .. how, how to say, {they must be} united and ho have the idea also to listen to ho the association, the members like of the association and well to put into practice these things ho their decisions and well, well they must put into practice what they've made as decisions in well in the association is what I want to say. And briefly, I will say that it is necessary also to have someone as was said, who understands others, who doesn't cause friction and so on like.

Another quality that seems to be closely tied with solidarity is that of discretion, or the ability to keep confidences. This is supported by Maranz (2001), who observes that Africans will avoid publicly shaming others, and especially family members, as a show of solidarity. This is true even when corrupt or scandalous behavior is involved, as this extract from AMIADA's interview shows.

C.3.AmA 36m  the executive board should also have the attribute of solidarity. The board must have the solidarity of work because when we work here, that which .. that which we lack, or is th= many things which enter here where leaks happen to influen= for there where come the leaks to hinder the evolution of the work aspects of scandal, to be able to to to overcome them

## 6.2 Features specific to literacy program leaders

it is essential that we be united. May the spirit of solidarity be in us, there, if there is solidarity, the work it will go peacefully there won't be so many problems.

This quality of discretion or keeping confidences was important for two other groups as well. For *Jésus le Chemin* participants, the need to keep confidences is the reason board members need to be moderate in all their actions, which was one of the qualities they also gave for a literacy program leader.

C.5.BK 12m   On the other hand, they should deal with {situations} in confidence, where sobriety, confidence, the files of of the group, it should be confidential. Insomuch if we deal with a subject concerning .. a church a third person that that does not serve as an occasion to reveal the idea we have constructed together. Thus, it is necessary that they be, they confidentially manage the files which were submitted to them. In order to not create prejudices.

Solidarity thus is needed for the board to function effectively. A major source of board solidarity is the culture. The notion of solidarity includes the idea that board members must listen to each other and reach a mutual understanding before taking decisions collectively. They also must not reveal confidences that would harm or discredit others. Above all, their behavior must not divide the association, making it unable to perform the tasks for which it exists.

### 6.2.2.2 Study a situation before reacting

Another quality prized in boards is deliberation in making decisions. Whether discussion is oriented towards planning or towards problem solving, decisions should not be made hastily.

C.2.VA1 20m   the executive {board} now should have the time to study certain ideas before putting them into action.

Later in the same discourse:

> They should always rely on . the will of the people. That which the others want, and that's what they should look at . to, uh know what to do to lead to . what they themSELVES have said.

As the ADCIBA vice-president noted, one reason for studying the problem carefully is to discern between truth and falsehood.

C.4.GĐ 18m  Before a president calls a meeting about an affair, he should be sure and carefully study the problem in advance. Because in an association, there is a little of everything, lies as well as truth.

When groups are faced with a problem, avoiding hasty reactions is particularly valued. During the explanations of how associations had dealt with specific issues, many references were made to taking time to gather information and to listen well to all those affected by the decision. Only after this process were decisions made. These actions all correlate also with the quality of patience, so necessary for Ifè leaders. While the relevant quotes are found in section 6.1.1, the problems and actions are summarized here, since a social representation is composed not only of the ideas about an object, but the behavior in relation to it as well (Kramsch 2008).

AVID's participants discussed a problem with a supervisor who had not carried out his financial responsibilities. They learned this when he stopped supervising his classes. The first thing they did was to investigate why, and they learned that the supervisor had not deposited the students' registration fees with the association. Next they called him in and gave him a chance to explain. Recognizing his fault, he agreed to repay the money.

AVADI's board gave two examples. The first concerned a conflict regarding the choice of teachers in a village, when villagers wanted to deprive two successful teachers, who were Ifè but not originally of that village, of their positions since the villagers had learned there was some reimbursement involved. The first step the AVADI board members took was to see if the village leaders could resolve it. They met with the chief and others in the village to explain their point of view. The next step was to meet with all the proposed teachers of that village; after listening to everyone,

## 6.2 Features specific to literacy program leaders 133

a solution was found and implemented. The coordinator summed it up like this:

C.2.VA1 32m  And there it was, well, that's what we did, and sometimes we were on hand to see the situation to listen to others and that through themselves we tried to find solutions to this problem which was born.

As the above extract shows, part of the action of studying a situation before reacting includes giving others the chance to come up with solutions. The second example given by AVADI participants is one common in literacy programs: either students or teachers do not show up for class. When the board is made aware of a problem, the board members go to talk to the class and try to determine what is really going on before restarting the class.

The AMIADA and ADCIBA boards both mentioned conflict occurring over use of the association-provided transportation. In both cases, meetings to discuss the problem and to give everyone a chance to present his or her point of view were held. The leaders were then able to explain why things were as they were, and hold out hope that additional transportation might be forthcoming in the next budget cycle, which calmed everyone down. A similar procedure was followed for another conflict ADCIBA experienced over per diems during teacher training.

The resolution of *Jésus le Chemin*'s problem with some of their zones that sought greater autonomy also required negotiation. This occurred over the course of many meetings. During these meetings, documents establishing the scope of authority ascribed to their regional zones were reviewed and presented to the members of the areas who were making decisions that went beyond their mandates. They noted that the original texts delimiting authority had been voted upon by all the membership, which gave them additional weight in the discussions. In addition, not only during these meetings but any time there is a problem, *Jésus le Chemin* leaders use the Bible to encourage a unified understanding of the principle under discussion.

To summarize, in the thinking of Ifè literacy leaders, a board should always study a situation before reacting. This ensures that all people have been heard and allows time for any underlying issues to emerge. Doing so facilitates the choice of a response acceptable to all, which in turn promotes solidarity in the association.

## 6.3 Representations of subordinates

As was mentioned during the discussion of leadership in chapter 4, followership can be considered a component of leadership. In fact, models developed from the perspective of contingency theories (see sections 4.1.3 and 4.1.4) take into account the characteristics and needs of subordinates. For this reason, the representations of subordinates that emerged from the interviews are examined here.

However, it should be noted that the meaning of the question translated as "What are the responsibilities of a subordinate or collaborator?" required an explanation. Only AMIADA's board members did not require such clarification; however, their responses also tended to focus on the responsibilities of leaders towards their subordinates more often than the responses from the other associations, in the process showing the interrelatedness of the roles. My interpreter explained the term, in Ifè, to both *Jésus le Chemin*'s and AVADI's boards. In ADCIBA's interview, one man asked who the subordinate in question was; one of the coordinators gave him a concrete example from the program.

C.4.GĐ 30m    The subordinate we're talking about, is he a member of the board or what?

C.4.ANA ff.    Let's suppose, just as you are with Labité for example, he is coordinator and supervisor, what are your duties as a subordinate to Labité? In the literacy domain, it's you, for example who are after the leader, so there what should you do and what should you not do?

In contrast, AVID's president and I worked together to make the meaning clear to the other participants.

C.1.YMA 13m    The advisor.

C.1.NK ff.    No! Subordinate, that's to say .. let's say I am the head, you, you are my subordinates, what duties fall to you?

## 6.3 Representations of subordinates

C.1.JR ff.    The other members of the association
C.1.NK ff.    of the asso[ciation]
C.1.JR ff.                   [what a]re, what are their responsibilities.
C.1.YMA ff.   There, {in Ifè, not transcribed}
C.1.JR ff.    Or, you all as members of a village, and you are under a chief I suppose, what are the responsibilities [of someone who]
C.1.NK ff.                                                [You see,] on this subject, we've already been initiated.

The president then went on to list some of the responsibilities of a subordinate.

A subordinate was generally understood by the participants to be someone directly under the authority of another. The person closest in the hierarchy to the head of a group often plays the role of a mediator, a role not uncommon in Africa, but not generally recognized in most North American cultures. Two members of ADCIBA's board brought up this point. Mr. Kpondza of ADCIBA likened a subordinate to an ear.

C.4.KÐ 37m   (interpreted) the top leader should listen to, should respect highly his subordinate. In another sense, the subordinate is like his ear, because, here in the .. in the black race or in Africa often people don't like to approach the top leader. It's his subordinate that you push, if there is something, it's to the subordinate that you say it.

However, perhaps the strongest indication that the leader needs the group came from the discussion among ADCIBA's board members, when they were condemning leaders who were not open about their activities. An Ifè proverb closed the argument: "One person is close to death, but the group never dies from a single blow."

C.4.ANA 39m  if the leader .. doesn't like for his subordinates to know his activities, to know what he's involved in, or else, one person alone, we say in in in among ourselves, that one person is: often .. it's someone who can die: or that is to say it's someone who is close to death. But if we say the group, the group never dies from a single blow.

Eight themes for subordinates were found among more than one group, but never in more than three. Those found in the discourses of three groups were closely related: being willing to do what is asked, obeying, and collaborating. Those identified by two groups were listening to, respecting, giving a good report to, being in harmony with, and being attached to one's superior.

### 6.3.1 Willingness and obedience

Willingness and obedience were closely related in the interviews, the one generally being followed in the discourse by the other. Willingness seems to be the general attitude expected of a subordinate, while obedience is the outward expression of that attitude. As *Jésus le Chemin*'s moderator indicated, this is not always easy.

C.5.BK 16m  Yes, the: the subordinate or: him over whom one is established should display his will in all things. He should be willing . to .. to be a MEMber . with uh . all that: all that which it requires of him = all that which one expects of him to accomplish in . in the work which we have all signed on to. So, he must be willing. It's his cheerful acquiescence which will predispose him to do to fulfill his responsibility. So, it is not easy to be a subordinate but, if one displays one's will, the WHOLE will, we we'll be able to get down to it.

As Mr. Bassan's colleague indicated, a prerequisite to this attitude is the recognition that someone has authority over oneself; and then one must assume the tasks requested by this superior.

C.5.EK 17m  the subordinate he should also recognize that . he has a a superior. He should recognize that he has a superior, and the whole task that the superior gives to him, he should take on.

The link between attitude and action was explicitly brought out by AMIADA's vice-president.

6.3 *Representations of subordinates* 137

C.3.SY 45m (interpreted) a subordinate should be available to receive from the leader, and after having received, he must execute it, he emphasizes that which he's received.

AVADI's board also associated attitudes with action.

C.2.VA4 26m He must obey him who is established as a leader over him. He should at all times grant a great importance to his work.
C.2.VA2 ff. He should have a high regard for his work in the association.

Submission to the wishes of the leader was a theme in the interview with AVID members. The president had listed it among the responsibilities of a subordinate. The coordinator added it a little later as she made her contribution to the discussion.

C.1.AgA 14m that it was our leader, if he says something, we must= we must submit,

Subordinates, therefore, should have a willing, positive attitude towards the work they are asked to do by the leader. The attitude is not enough, however; they must also submit to the leader, obeying him or her.

### 6.3.2 Collaboration

Nevertheless, the transactions between a leader and his or her subordinates in Ifè culture are not just one way. This was captured through the notion of collaboration that came out several times, usually speaking of the responsibility of both parties to collaborate. As AVADI's coordinator indicated, not only should the leader be willing to collaborate, but also the subordinates must accept that collaboration in order to meet their common goal.

C.2.VA1 26m As he says the leader or the head should be someone who collaborates, the subject must also accept this collaboration and that he also collaborates with the head and that their ideas be the same to carry out the same fight cause the success of the project which they've put into place.

The same ideas emerged during the interview with *Jésus le Chemin*'s committee. However, the advisor's comments were related to the theme that Ifè leaders should not dictate.

C.5.ÐO 32m  (interpreted) And when the subordinates or his coworkers will finish by discovering that no, our leader, our boss is in the process of doing .. he makes his own proclamations, or he decides by himself what he wants, in the end, they will desist or be discouraged, withdraw and the work can no longer go forward. There must be collaboration.

Collaboration, however, requires a certain level of understanding. One of ADCIBA's coordinators pointed out that in order for a subordinate to be able to work towards goals in the absence of the leader, that leader must be willing to share information with and even delegate tasks to those under him. This practice is not always found in African cultures.

C.4.ANA 38m  uh: it would be that really there must be a good understanding between the subordinates . and: the leader. Especially in a manner that the chef . may know that . that which he who is under him that also {register rises} should understand, if even possible, to even know what he himself is in the process of doing. How does he do it? Since when he isn't there then, it's his subordinate who ought to continue the work . that he has even so the will to hand . uh over the task to: to his subordinate.

The theme of collaboration, then, links representations of leaders with those of subordinates. Subordinates as well as leaders should be willing to collaborate in order to accomplish goals. It is also important that leaders be open to sharing information with their subordinates, so that when they are not present, the work may continue.

6.3 *Representations of subordinates* 139

### 6.3.3 Attention and respect

Understanding is also a component of another theme that emerged: attention, or listening *(écouter)*. This quality was named without elaboration in the interviews with AVID's and AVADI's boards in conjunction with respecting (implicitly understood as obeying) one's leader. Understanding emerged immediately after these two qualities were identified by AVADI's participants as important responsibilities of a subordinate.

C.2.VA3 25m  He should listen to his leader.
C.2.VA1 ff.  He should respect (obey) what he told him to do.
C.2.VA2 ff.  They must have understanding in the association.

AVID's president, with the explicit agreement of the others, placed these qualities together with obedience and service.

C.1.NK 14m  The subordinate . also listens to .. his leader, the subordinate also .. uh . respects .. his = the head, and .. submit to him . his ideas, he submits, he respects, he listens to, and he renders service to him.

Being a subordinate involves listening to, respecting, and understanding one's leader in order to serve him or her well. These are connected to the following interrelated themes: being in harmony with, and loyal to one's superior.

### 6.3.4 Harmony and loyalty

As has been noted before, relationships are key in sub-Saharan Africa to accomplishing almost anything. The relationship between a subordinate and his or her leader or boss is no exception. For this reason, being in harmony with one's superior in an organization is important for achieving the project's or group's goals. This thought was expressed in two interviews by three people.

C.2.VA1 27m  So, the responsibility it's .. it's to to be in harmony with the executive or with the head whom they are under. So, the member

|              |                                                                                                                                                                                                                                                    |
|--------------|----------------------------------------------------------------------------------------------------------------------------------------------------------------------------------------------------------------------------------------------------|
|              | should be in harmony with him, he should share the same ideas as the others so that the project may succeed.                                                                                                                                       |
| C.2.JR ff.   | Other things to complete that, to add to it?                                                                                                                                                                                                       |
| C.2.VA2 ff.  | Otherwise, ho, harmony, if there is harmony, then the work will evolve well. So, the decisions taken, may they be in harmony and in the ho to have a same idea so that can cause the group to advance and so on.                                   |
| C.4.KĐ 37m   | (interpreted) Thus, if there isn't harmony between the head leader and his subordinate, the work will go on with difficulty.                                                                                                                       |

It is not enough to be simply in harmony with one's superior. Subordinates should also care about their leaders and truly be attached to them for their own good. Mr. Saanya began by citing a Bible verse to provide an example of the importance of being dependent on the leader.

|            |                                                                                                                                                                                                                                                                                                                                                                                    |
|------------|------------------------------------------------------------------------------------------------------------------------------------------------------------------------------------------------------------------------------------------------------------------------------------------------------------------------------------------------------------------------------------|
| C.3.SY 45m | (interpreted) There, it's there where he gives the example of the gospel according to John, chapter 15, and one gives an example there that, all branches which are not attached to the vine cannot bear fruit. So, if he wants to stay independent, he's going to drown. So, the subordinates also must be attached to the boss in order to benefit from the good which= which the boss has, or the leader has and so they also can evolve. |

In the discourse among AMIADA members, the connection between caring about one's leader and advancing the work was made explicit. The importance of this caring and loyalty was described in a situation where the leader was the subject of gossip.

|            |                                                                                                                                                                                                                                                                                                                                                          |
|------------|----------------------------------------------------------------------------------------------------------------------------------------------------------------------------------------------------------------------------------------------------------------------------------------------------------------------------------------------------------|
| C.4.GĐ 33m | (interpreted) He should care about his hea=. his top leader, he should also care about the work which has been entrusted to him and be the friend of the head. By caring about the fir= when the top leader and the subordinate care about the top leader, truly the work can advance. |

## 6.3 Representations of subordinates

C.4.Interpr. ff.   And I think that that is what I remembered, if I've forgotten one side, you must tell me.

C.4.ANA ff.   I, myself see that it's a very important connection because when you are under someone people try to break the bond which is between you the subordinate and the head. Sometimes they can even go as far as to say to you, ah you don't see how your boss is in the process of evolving nevertheless he himself is improving at your expense it's that which he should give you and he isn't giving it to you and he's in the process of building something and well he's in the process of buying all this, so, go on you must go on strike against him, you must reclaim this right, you must do this, you must do that, yes, that happens often and if you the subordinate you are not .. patient, you won't be able to analyze correctly, these agitators you risk your well-being or block the work, that is to say what he expects of you. Truly that, it's why it's necessary that it requires a, a love and truly, a good understanding between the leader and the subordinate or he who is under him.

The above discourse also returns to the idea that understanding between a leader and his or her subordinate is necessary. Note also that the theme of patience, so important to the Ifè representation of leadership, also resurfaces. It seems to play a role here in facilitating the defense of one's leader. Such loyalty, which arises from positive emotions about the leader, and harmony between a subordinate and his or her leader ensures that the group's work will continue.

### 6.3.5 Report giver

A subordinate also has the responsibility of reporting back to the leader on what has been done. This point was raised by a number of people in two interviews. In that with *Jésus le Chemin*'s committee, it was named by the coordinator and agreed upon by the director of projects and of missions.

C.5.EK 17m   He gives a good report to his superior.

| | |
|---|---|
| C.5.OK ff. | That's right. That's what I was going to add. He has the responsibility to render an account. |
| C.5.EK ff. | That's it. |
| C.5.OK ff. | to render an account |

One of ADCIBA's coordinators linked reporting to the representation of a leader as being able to teach. When a subordinate completes an activity, the leader should take the opportunity to instruct or correct as necessary. This leads back to the theme of collaboration.

| | |
|---|---|
| C.4.ANA 40m | So, like that he must truly TEACH his subordinate HOW it must be done. And even, start them on doing it, and you the head now, you correct . in the case where it's done badly. Like that, they also, they are more = they are mo = they are more light-hearted in approaching you the head . since you have entrusted them . a an activity session to do, {higher register} after having finished he should take heed of it, and like that you bring him . the additional things or: the corrections which he himself also knows. Ah, I also I know a little of what the leader does. So he also, that that that will make him grow, and like that, frank collaboration can exist. |

However, returning to the idea that a subordinate is also a mediator between a leader and the larger group, the subordinate also should be able to report to the leader on what has been going on in the group.

| | |
|---|---|
| C.4.KÐ 37m | (interp.) It's his subordinate that he pushes, if there is something, it's to the subordinate that one says it. With the intention that it's he who can convey it, who [xx] |
| C.4.ANA ff. | [xx] |
| C.4.KÐ ff. | (interp.) who can give an account of what it's what was done. |

This is particularly important when rumors are going around, as a leader who is informed can better prepare to respond to criticisms.

## 6.3 Representations of subordinates

C.4.GĐ 32 (interp.) In this sense that, when there is a problem, or one has spoken to about the head for example the masses don't like to go directly to the head, the top leader to accuse him. These are rumors. And the subordinate he who is under the head, he is closer to the masses. So, being alert, he can also listen to the masses, and there, he can collect information. This information now, it's forj him to evaluate them, to analyze them and to know how to present them to the leader and how by his subordinate the leader will also be prepared.

Still, the role of mediator goes both ways. A subordinate also should be able to answer questions from that larger membership about the activities undertaken by the leader.

C.4.KL 35m So, he should be alert and follow all that happens. And will also be in a position to respond when there are questions and .. by the members who are not on the board.

Thus, reporting is an important responsibility of a subordinate. It allows the leader to know what has been happening in the group and to respond to rumors. It also lets the leader know how well the subordinate is carrying out his or her activities and permits correction or further instruction of the subordinate. However, reporting also goes the other direction, as through the subordinate, the leader keeps the rest of the group informed about what is happening.

In summary, a subordinate is willing to do whatever the leader asks of him or her. The role of mediator played by subordinates in this culture, and indeed in much of Africa, requires an understanding of the leader's thoughts that allows collaboration. Subordinates who understand their leaders also respect, listen to, and care for those leaders. This establishes harmony between them and develops loyalty. With these attitudes in place, subordinates are able to report freely to their leaders and accurately explain to the larger group membership the actions and thoughts of their leader.

## 6.4 Summary and discussion

The social representation of the Ifè concerning their leaders revolves around the following points. Good leaders need to be competent in their work. They should live exemplary lives by manifesting patience, faithfulness, and humility. In addition, they should care about *(aimer)* everyone, receive all that is said to them, and choose the best idea among those proposed by the group. Above all, they should never impose their own wills, but make all decisions with the group. This representation agrees with ideas of African leadership found in the literature, especially a participatory style of leadership based on respect for the other person and the maintenance of harmonious relationships (Malunga 2006; Mandela 1994).

The representations of subordinates support this view of relational leadership. Subordinates are supposed to listen well to and respect their leaders, being willing to do whatever is asked of them. However, in line with the theme that leaders should not dictate, a spirit of harmonious collaboration is expected between a leader and his or her subordinates. This is facilitated when the leader shares his or her thoughts, even teaching the subordinates, giving them insight and understanding regarding the leader and his or her plans. In this way, subordinates can better mediate between the leader and the wider group membership, communicating to each what the other is thinking or saying.

Nevertheless, the SR of a leader is a representation in transition. Globalization and the introduction of writing and of reading, whether it is in French, Ifè, or another language in this traditionally oral society, have brought several people to believe that today it is essential that a chief be literate. It is also possible that the introduction of Christianity and the training of pastors at Bible schools may be in the process of changing the conception of a leader, more precisely to include the notion of a "servant leader," which one pastor insisted upon in his group's definition of a leader. However, I would have had to identify the religion of each participant (at least one non-Christian participated in the interviews) and ensure the representation of all religions currently practiced among the Ifè in order to verify this hypothesis.

Many researchers believe that social representations are best studied by comparing and contrasting groups and their opinions. In this study, the villagers of Itséré and Cycle 3 teachers from AVID and AVADI's zones were

## 6.4 Summary and discussion 145

used to check how SR among the Ifè may shift according to group membership. The groups in this case involved those in leadership positions in a literacy and development association versus teachers, ordinary villagers, and class participants. Differences between the two groups do indeed exist regarding the representations of a leader and of a literacy leader, yet patience and faithfulness are fundamental to the SR of all groups. All other qualities mentioned by the villagers in Itséré (used as a control group to verify that the representations of leadership of leaders were not limited to those in positions of leadership) were given as well by at least one board, although not necessarily for the same type of leader. Nevertheless, the general leadership characteristics of caring, good behavior, managing one's family well, and being literate seem to be held in common by most groups, including the control group.

While the priorities given to the qualities for leaders *(chefs)* were strikingly different between the men and women of Itséré (see table 6.1), it is not possible to generalize those results as typical differences between men and women. In part, this is because village dynamics that may have produced those differences are unknown; in part because the sample size was so small in any case; and in part because the only other female participant in the interviews, AVID's literacy coordinator, was present at the Itséré meeting and acted as the interpreter for the women during the interview, although AVID's board had not yet responded to those questions. Gender-based differences in the representations of leadership are therefore an area for further research.

Table 6.1. Qualities important for a leader *(chef)*: Itséré villagers

| **Men (7)** | **Women (6)** |
|---|---|
| *Serious | *Faithful |
| *Cares about everyone | Forgives everyone |
| *Literate | |
| Exemplary | *Good behavior |
| Irreproachable | *Patient |
| Leader of his home | |
| Forgives everyone | |

*Ranked as the top three most important qualities by the group

ACATBLI and *Jésus le Chemin* are overtly Christian organizations, as are most of the research participants, with the AVADI coordinator being the pastor of the other board members in that association. Therefore, another question could be whether or not typical Christian values such as love for all or forgiveness influenced the responses. All the same, it should be noted that most of the references to God or the Lord in the interviews were thanking Him or attributing to Him responses to requested needs. However, the importance of relationships to African societies has already been noted, and caring for others is generally recognized as fundamental to healthy relationships. Furthermore, the importance of the capacity to forgive in leaders has been noted by other researchers of leadership in Africa (Blunt and Jones 1997). In fact, one ethnolinguistic group of northern Togo, the Moba, considers knowing how to forgive as a fundamental moral value and an essential qualification for leadership. Indeed, B. J. Koabike, former member of the Moba New Testament translation team, told me that, traditionally, no one would be chosen to lead a group unless that person had demonstrated, from a young age, the ability to be exacting while also being able to forgive when necessary. Therefore, it seems unlikely that Christianity influenced the naming of forgiving or caring as a leadership quality in these interviews. In any case, a control group of non-Christians was not included in the research design, which makes answering the question of the degree of Christian influence problematical. This would be another possible area for further research.

# 7

# Motivations of Literacy Workers: Representations Related to Literacy

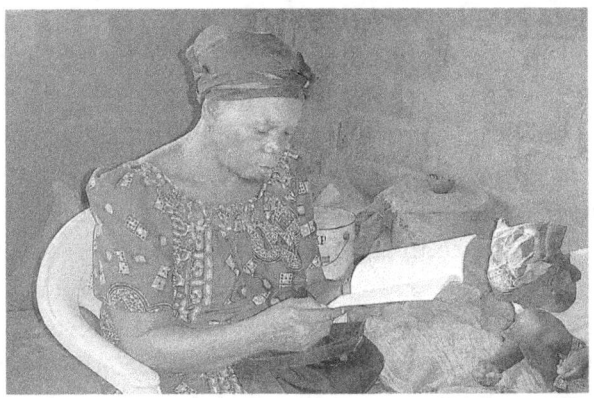

Nongovernmental organizations invest considerable resources in the training of people capable of managing an association and a literacy program, but my experience and that of peers working in other NGOs show that often, these leaders leave the literacy association when they have enough training to take a better-paid position. Mr. Agbémadon of ACATBLI indicated, in fact, that he had had such an opportunity after he had been involved in the program for three or four years. The impact this has on organizational capacity building indicates that it is therefore important to look at the motivations of those who stay with literacy programs and learn what gives them passion for the work.

The representations of literacy and language held by Ifè literacy leaders seem to be a major influence directing their personal investment in this work, although several leaders are also involved for spiritual reasons. Norton (1997, 2000) theorizes that individuals are motivated, not because of an intrinsic personal trait, but from investment in their identity, which has been constructed over time by their social environment. This notion resonates with the strength of the representations presented in this chapter that involve the importance of literacy in Ifè to maintaining a unique cultural and linguistic identity, and the importance of being literate in any language. This latter representation is particularly significant in the light of the number of participants who are newly literate themselves. An investment in a particular type of work is also an investment in social identity, in this case, that of literacy worker *(alphabétiseur)*. Hence, it can be argued that the representations expressed here also justify the time, energy, and sometimes, scarce financial resources these literacy leaders expend in providing literacy and development services to their communities.

Another reason these representations of literacy and language are significant to the purposes of this case study is the effect they have on the decisions about program direction, including capacity building. It is in this dual framework of importance to capacity building and to motivation through investment in identity, therefore, that representations of illiterates, literacy, and language held by literacy program leaders are explored in this chapter.

It appears that the primary reason that the associations' leaders believe in the importance of local language literacy comes from changes in the environment. According to several interviewees, these changes are essentially the results of modernization and of globalization.

C.1.NK 31m   The importance of doing literacy work in local languages . it's that today, we: = everyone, whatever the social rung of each community, that, the life of our old ones, of our ancestors, that which they led is different than that which we have today. As usual we say that there is globalization and all that, so everything is changed.

Faced with these changes, several people stated that today, most members of the local communities recognize the importance of becoming literate.

C.1.NK 32m  So, we cannot live .. without knowing reading and writing now, even our parents or the= . the Ifè community with whom we work today, recognizes, they see now the importance of becoming literate,
B.2.VA2 13m  since everyone wants, can xx know uh know how to write his language and speak fluently . and read, that's it.

In this chapter the discussion is focused on the representations held of illiterates, literacy, and language as they emerged from the interviews. Certain representations seem to be socially constructed, as they are shared by nearly all the sources. Other representations have a much more limited distribution, expressed by only a few individuals. Regardless of how widespread the representations are, these are the ones that motivate these literacy leaders to continue to invest in this work, even when there is or has been strong community opposition.

## 7.1 Representations of illiterates

Although no questions were asked specifically about people who could not read in any language, representations of illiterates *(analphabètes)* were repeatedly evoked during the interviews. The majority of these were expressed when respondents were explaining why developing literacy in the local language was important, but others emerged when they were explaining their personal motivations for being involved in literacy work or listing the qualifications of leaders. Some came out during other parts of the interviews. As such, these representations can be seen as contextual features of the representation of literacy. Many of the views held are echoes of the positions held in countries with long traditions of textual literacy, and most likely tied to the belief stated earlier, that literacy is needed for the modern world.

Although many generations of people around the world have lived happy, productive lives without needing to read and write, today the illiterate is frequently viewed with pity or scorn by the literate. The research participants expressed the view that an illiterate is handicapped, without an understanding of the modern world, fearful, and even a block to development. However, these beliefs have not generally been expressed by illiterates themselves in other places in West Africa, as in Cheffy's (2006) research on the conceptions of literacy in northern Cameroon. Nevertheless, these beliefs about those who cannot read and write have motivated not only the international community, as seen by the Education for All initiative, but also individuals in the local communities to address this perceived lack of an essential skill.

## 7.1.1 Handicapped

A common view, expressed not only during these interviews but also during the research of others (see, e.g., Cheffy 2006; Doronila 1996), is that an illiterate person is handicapped, incapable of doing what he or she should or needs to do.

C.2.VA2 40m  In the first place, I myself I will say that: it's important because: uh the: someone . the adult . who: well .. he is handicapped . because he isn't acquainted with . writing and reading.

One way in which people unable to read or write are seen to be handicapped is that they are perceived as being unable to manage their affairs and as a result, are incapable of being self-sufficient.

A.2.AgbA 9m  So, the most important, it's literacy.. When the person isn't literate, you can give him a million francs, he'll squander it.
C.2.VA1 43m  Someone who doesn't know how to read and write, CANNOT be self-sufficient. He cannot be self-sufficient.

This type of handicap is often expressed as blindness or deafness. Cheffy's Cameroonian interviewees used the same two metaphors. One AMIADA member clearly stated that his behavior is motivated by his compassion for these people whom he perceives as being blind, deaf, and in a tunnel not of their choosing.

## 7.1 Representations of illiterates

C.3.MK 13m   but it is necessary to be patient and have compassion on these people, since they're like the blind, they are deaf also they don't know anything. That's it, why I myself always care about the compassion on these people and who= the person is going to see that the people that they don't know anything and it's him, it's for him to bring them out of the tunnels where they are.

Another perceived type of handicap is the inability to be an informed participant in democratic processes. In Benin, where a democratic national government has been established for a generation, one coordinator expressed how the illiterate, nearly all of whom do not understand French, are effectively shut out of the accompanying processes and unable to truly receive the benefits of democracy.

C.4.ANA 1h20m   How can he who is not lettered .. find himself .. in: . can= can recognize HIS SHARE {intensely but softly} . in the fruit of democracy? Here it that he doesn't know how to read the texts... Even the electoral texts . they don't understand anything of that.

This view of those who cannot comprehend or create text as handicapped, whether blind, deaf, or simply incapable, is common to several people. The basis of this notion seems to be a perception that they are incapable of doing things that would allow them to function in the modern world and to join those who are improving their lives. This idea, as shown by the examples given, most likely arose from the experiences they and their family members have had as they negotiate life in modern Togo and Benin, but may also have been fostered through literacy awareness-raising *(sensibilisation)* efforts run by their governments that reinforce this stereotype. This is true also for the following representations of illiterates.

### 7.1.2 In darkness and ignorance

A related idea to that of illiterates as handicapped, and particularly the perception that they are blind, is that they live in darkness and ignorance. The fact that the metaphors of darkness and light are also found in Christianity might suggest that these are derived from contact with this religion. However, in Togo and Benin most church denominations (with one major exception in Benin) have had little direct involvement in promoting literacy, in contrast to other areas of Africa where a number of denominations have literature and literacy departments, with some even requiring literacy for church membership. It is unlikely, therefore, that Christianity is the source of these metaphors in relation to illiteracy and illiterates, especially since it is only in the past twenty years that Christianity has become the majority religion among the Ifè.

In Cheffy's interviews in rural Cameroon, blindness and darkness were more often explicitly linked than in my interviews. However, in my interviews the view of illiterates as living in darkness and ignorance was clearly tied to life in a literate world.

C.1.NK 33m  Thus, people are now aware of being able to read and write, even knowing how to calculate now to manage their own farms, their own business, and now, to no longer be in darkness . in this lettered world.

A little later, this speaker continued on the same theme and identified the media as one source of this particular view of illiterates being in darkness.

C.1.NK 34m  even at the level of the media, all that they say now in awareness-raising, all that is said that everybody should come out of darkness and be now open now, to this lettered world which is calling out to everyone. That's it.

Another man testified how he was being mocked for spending his time trying to teach the illiterates of his village. One day, another man came to him and encouraged him to continue, as by teaching them, he was helping to bring them out of darkness.

C.4.KL 1h15m  So, today he came to encourage me to continue, that I would awa= that I myself I am going to bring them out now . uh . from the darkness.

This encouragement gave him the strength to continue. Another person gave this as his group's reason for engaging in literacy work—in today's

## 7.1 Representations of illiterates

world, those who cannot read (literally, "do not know paper") are inferior to those who can.

C.5.EK 41m   Well, today for example, if we are going to see our reasons for example, those who are acquainted with paper .. are not the same as those who do not know paper.

In fact, another participant in the same interview went further, expressing the view that only literate people are civilized. This is a direct echo of the colonialist discourse mentioned in the development history section in chapter 5, where Europeans justified their colonization of Africa on the basis of the perceived lack of civilization on that continent, and "offered" schooling to redress that lack.

C.5.BK 43m   I can say that literacy is in the interest of of civilization. A literate man is the same as a civilized man. What that means is, he has left, he has broken through the local barriers and now can be in contact with the exterior. For the the the reason which the brother explained. So, when he receives something from the outside and is able to manage that himself, he is civilized.

This view of illiterates as being inferior to others also emerged in another interview. One of the ADCIBA board members who became literate through the Ifè program described how illiterates are treated as though they are nothing but slaves or beasts, with few or no rights when they are cheated.

C.4.GÐ 1h10m (interp.) So, they were also like slaves . or I would say even beasts, execution (or implementation) before protests. Were there even protests, even
C.4.ANA ff.   no, you don't understand anything
C.4.GÐ ff.    (interp.) for you before someone who is lettered, when he speaks, it's so you can say yes. And you carry it out, that which is good or bad, it's he who said if it's true or not, that which he said, you don't see anything.

This board member later concluded his discourse by saying that this is why he does all he can to see that the program continues.

C.4.GÐ 1h11m (interpreted) And that's why, day and night, he struggles so that this program may continue.

The view that illiterates are in bondage is also seen in a *Togo Presse* article. The government's regional head of literacy was quoted as thanking SIL for promoting local languages, "thus aiding the government to realize its program of emancipating the Togolese" (my translation; ATOP, Nov. 27, 2007:7).

Yet another participant who sees illiterates as being in the darkness perceives part of that as a disorder in their thinking processes. When literacy enters their lives, they are able to reason more clearly and to take advantage of training opportunities in development.

C.5.BK 44m So, literacy is going to bring the learners to be enlightened. They can read, write, transmit all they want in a methodical manner, logically and methodically. Before, without literacy, their reasoning was .. unclear, but by= uh with the arrival of literacy, they who have applied themselves, they've be able to exploit this training.

Others also claim that the illiterate are unable to benefit fully from training. One example was given describing ignorance as the old norm and crediting literacy with opening eyes, thus evoking the view of illiterates being blind.

C.3.SY 1h21m (interpreted) From the moment where before, in the past, we were .. all the people were in ignorance. All that we could do, in an interval of time, a little time to gain something we used so much energy and we didn't gain anything. But on the basis of literacy, eyes are open, people have understood,

Ignorance was also identified as the state of the illiterate by one of the *Jésus le Chemin* board members who became literate through the program.

*7.1 Representations of illiterates* 155

C.5.ÐO 48m (interpreted) because he was completely, he was nonliterate, when literacy arrived he got involved and so here today he can do many things and he is doing them besides. So, that helped him a lot, that got him out of of many things from ignorance,

The perception of those who cannot read and write as being in darkness and ignorance is a powerful motivator for literacy workers. They desire to help their parents, siblings, and cousins improve their lives through coming out of this ignorance into the light of knowledge and reason. This view is fostered at least in part through the media. The role of the media in the construction and dissemination of the representations of literacy and illiterates will be discussed in the final section of this chapter.

### 7.1.3 Distrustful

Another view of illiterates is that they are, with reason, distrustful of others, particularly literates. This belief emerged in the discussions of why literacy was important. However, the distinction between literacy and language was blurred; in fact, it seems to be the schooled literates, who use French, not all literates, whom the illiterate mistrust. Not only is this indicated by the following extract from AVID's interview, but by numerous testimonies I heard during my years in Central and West Africa. Note the link again to the idea that those unable to read and write are in darkness.

C.1.YMA 30mI myself see the importance if: there is literacy . and: our: parents are going to come out of darkness .. if they are nonliterate . this teaches, and from there, they don't have mistrust. If I speak of mistrust, if I, a literate person, if I read my book to choose one of these= well, and if an nonliterate, an unlettered person is with me here, he .. he will ask himself what I'm saying. Am I speaking about him. But if I say Ɛgbɛ́-kã̀= Ɛgbɛ́-kã̀ yèé then, she, he will also understand in consequence what I wanted to say. So, that's why I speak of mistrust. There will not be any= any mistrust.

It was the ADCIBA interviewees who supplied a reason for this distrust: illiterates are not infrequently cheated by others. During the first interview with the ADCIBA board, an example of the program's impacts was given of a seamstress who was consistently cheated by people who claimed they owed less on their accounts than she remembered. Since nothing was written, she could not take them to court to get her money. Once she went through both levels of literacy classes, she was able to keep her accounts and prove what her customers owed her. Another ADCIBA participant and adult neoliterate made the following observation during his second interview:

C.4.GĐ 1h10m (interpreted) truly literacy is very important . from the time where, they had been so cheated when they were nonliterate, in the past, when they didn't know paper, they were cheated . and their interests were really ridiculed.

The perception that illiterates are distrustful is another motivator for these literacy leaders. Reasons for the distrust have to do both with the experiences of being cheated as well as with non-comprehension of French and the uncertainty that that brings. Literacy and numeracy are seen as providing tools to combat deception and to develop self-confidence.

### 7.1.4 Blocks to development

In the interviews, the idea that development is not possible without literate people emerged frequently. Furthermore, it is held by the ACATBLI literacy heads, who undoubtedly influence the others.

A.2.AgbA 8m the foremost idea is: all development is only possible when .. the person is lettered.
A.2.SK ff. That's right. Everyone should be lettered.

Development itself is seen as evolution and movement. So those who are not learning to read and write are standing in the way of such change and advancement.

C.2.VA2 42m and going from there as well, he knows that, well if one doesn't learn, one cannot change.

## 7.1 Representations of illiterates

B.1.NK af1 29m   it's at the start .. like that made that the number of nonliterate Ifè is very very very high in our area. Even today. So, that has put the brakes on many things. You know, some .. people don't understa= when you aren't literate, that means that you don't understand the importance of of your child, that you must introduce him to formal schooling.

One graphic picture of illiterates, also linked to ignorance, is that they are at the bottom of a ladder *(échelle),* which, it is implied, they may mount as life improves through the knowledge of reading and writing.

C.2.VA1 45m   And I can say .. in the framework of .. of thi= our our parents, as we said, since we are within our .. framework . of literacy, they have= they had worked a lot, but not knowing how to improve .. the techniques to: make the most of it, they had always been .. uh stuck at the bottom of the ladder.

One ADCIBA coordinator believed that the responsibility for these blocks to development actually lies with his government, because it has not sufficiently addressed the problems of illiteracy, and it communicates important information too often only in the official language.

C.4.ANA 1h18m   But if ... a government really wants . that development be real .. harmonious . and that the good, that is to say the fruit of the effort of a government be shared .. correctly, .. rationally, . with all the citizens, that government must THINK . first of literacy. {5 second pause} ALL the leaders . who hold meetings before the population, they EITHER speak to them in their language, OR else they look for a representative, or an interpreter, .. to be able to translate. Even . {chuckle} and then, things published, on the radio↓ . in the newspapers↓ .. the populations are not involved—that is to say the populations don't find their portion within↑. They cannot read . in the newspapers, they don't listen to French they don't understand the French which is spoken . on the

|              |                                                                                                                                                                                                      |
|--------------|------------------------------------------------------------------------------------------------------------------------------------------------------------------------------------------------------|
|              | radio .. Does the information of this government GET to the great majority of people? No to the small minority of people. {3 second pause}                                                          |
| C.4.JR ff.   | So                                                                                                                                                                                                   |
| C.4.ANA ff.  | SO, WITHOUT really .. a government . attaching any importance . to literacy, the development they talk about, we'll always talk about it, but it won't be rea= realistic. That's what I myself have understood. |

This same person had stated in the first interview set that those who are unable to read and write often are unable to take advantage of learning opportunities fully, because when they participate in such events, they can neither note down what is being said, nor read the handouts if given. As a result, they generally forget important details of the development teachings. Since most of what he said had been lost due to an equipment malfunction, during a supplemental interview I asked him and his co-coordinator to fill in what they could, based on what had been recorded.

|                   |                                                                                                                                                                                                                                                                                                                                                                                                                               |
|-------------------|-------------------------------------------------------------------------------------------------------------------------------------------------------------------------------------------------------------------------------------------------------------------------------------------------------------------------------------------------------------------------------------------------------------------------------|
| B.4.ANA si2 5m    | There are NGOs who have really attempted to to help, to come to the aid of rural populations. And because of non-literacy, since the people don't know how to write, they have practically: thrown their money away because .. the training that they: will have given doesn't= . isn't to their . uh motivation that is to say they cannot really . uh maintain this training and put it into practice [KL: yes] purely as it should be so that they can benefit . [JR: Mmhm] from it. |
| B.4.JR si2 ff.    | Okay. Okay ..                                                                                                                                                                                                                                                                                                                                                                                                                 |
| B.4.KL si2 ff.    | They invested they [did the training but,]                                                                                                                                                                                                                                                                                                                                                                                    |
| B.4.ANA si2 ff.   |                                    [They invested they did the training]                                                                                                                                                                              |
| B.4.KL si2 ff.    | the training wasn't received and put into practice.                                                                                                                                                                                                                                                                                                                                                                           |

Mr. Affonféré repeated this idea in the next ADCIBA board interview.

|                 |                                                                                                          |
|-----------------|----------------------------------------------------------------------------------------------------------|
| C.4.ANA 1h21m   | AS the cultural space is reduced from day to day, we have to change our behavior. And the change of this= of these |

behaviors, UNLESS man cannot read . on paper, or note them on paper, he cannot follow them exactly. To be able to gain, you have a small parcel . to be able to cultivate. You don't have the money to buy a large area. How now to maintain the richness of this space to be able to give you uh a good result, a good return .. I see that, when someone tells you how orally, in practice, you're going to forget some things and instead of increasing your return you are going to .. diminish even worse the return that you had had.

One of the main issues in the oral vs. literate culture debates has been the question of memory (Diagne 2005; Furniss 2004). The above extract, supported by evidence from Cameroon (Tadadjeu 2008), indicates that verbatim memorization of material heard, or at least of new material, is indeed difficult even for illiterates from an oral culture. As a result, the lack of reading and writing skills is seen as a block to development. Participants remarked that the high rate of illiteracy in their own Ifè culture is one factor that has slowed their progress relative to the other ethnicities around them. The Beninese participants stated their belief that their government should do more to tackle high illiteracy rates. However, sometimes the lack of effective communication of new information is not due to a lack of lieracy skills, but to the lack of comprehension of the language in which the information is conveyed.

## 7.2 Representations of literacy and language

In this section various themes relating to representations of literacy, including those in relationship to language, are discussed. These themes were revealed both in the interviews and in articles about the Ifè literacy program from the official national newspaper, *Togo Presse*. The most fundamental representations are those that perceive literacy as openness and development, and mother tongue literacy as a way to preserve and transmit cultural knowledge and identity. Other dominant themes see literacy as the door to full participation in society and mother tongue literacy as language maintenance and development. Two secondary themes, each shared by half the groups, concerned language: French as more difficult than Ifè and biliteracy as a responsibility. Two other themes were developed by only one or two groups: literacy as access to another language and literacy as a qualification. All these representations not only motivate the leaders to work, but also influence their choice of program activities, including the ones designed to enhance capacity.

The distinction between oral and written language was apparently not important to most research participants; frequently, examples purporting to demonstrate why literacy was important actually showed the importance of communicating in Ifè, whether orally or in writing. The reason for this may be, in the words of one participant, *"Puisque écrire aussi c'est parler"* ("because to write is also to speak"; C.4.ANA). In other words, writing is an extension of the communication that occurs through spoken language. This lack of differentiation is not unique to the Ifè or even to Africans. I once asked a Korean-American student of mine during an introductory sociolinguistics course, who I knew spoke Korean, if she could also write Korean. Her response, surprising me at the time, was, "Yes, I am fully bilingual."

The Ifè have much contact with other language groups, but for the participants of this research project, the majority of whom spoke French from having attended school, their own language holds a privileged position in the maintenance of their culture and identity. When speaking of the Ifè language, the participants used either a possessive pronoun with *"propre langue"* (e.g., 'my own language, his/her own language') or the term *"langue maternelle"* 'mother tongue'. I will follow the same usage in the discussion that follows.

### 7.2.1 Literacy as openness and development

During a discussion towards the end of a seminar on literacy and development that I was leading for SIL, I first heard the idea that literacy leads to openness; a Kabiyè participant noted that while literacy did not automatically reduce poverty, the newly literate were more open to new ideas than they had been. The conception of literacy as openness is found elsewhere in Africa as well. The participants in Ian Cheffy's research in Cameroon also used this metaphor. Cheffy additionally noted that openness is perceived to be related to the "modern way of life" (p. 2006:125), namely, acceptance of technological innovations and a scientific view of illness and mishaps.

From almost the beginning, development-style activities have been a part of this program's activities. This was largely due to the problem

## 7.2 Representations of literacy and language

of water supply that interfered with the running of classes, because the teachers and learners had to go long distances to obtain water for their household needs, especially during the dry season. In order to ensure the smooth functioning of the classes, the program leaders facilitated classes on the repair and/or construction of pumps and wells in those villages. It is therefore not surprising that literacy is so closely tied to development in the eyes of many people. In fact, a number of the literacy workers recognize that they are considered development agents.

B.1.NK af2 16m    However, we are = they say that we are development agents. Social . development and economic development. That's what matters. That, that sticks in my heart.

In addition, several leaders indicated that their motivation was based on their desire to see improvement in the well-being of their people. One was AVID's coordinator:

B.1.AgA 15m  But myself . I SEEK the well-being of my brothers.

When the ADCIBA participants were discussing how they chose board members and literacy leaders, they were very firm about what these people had to want, having gone through the experience of having a board with members not having this desire: people who were committed to work through literacy for the development of their communities.

B.4.KL si1 10m  Now this last board that we have taken now, we said, it's THOSE . WHO . WANT . to do the work, so those who are .. fit for the work that we took.
C.4.ANA 27m  So, it must truly be people .. who are really going to devote themselves . who are going to leave behind their own evolution in some way, and want the evolution of the group, or else of the commu = of the whole community.
C.4.GÐ 55m  (interpreted by ANA) So, we swore that really . we are obliged to elect those who are already investing themselves . those in whom we sense ZEAL .. to really make literacy work.

Literacy is seen as a way to open minds and permit both personal and cultural development. This development is not limited to economic development, but also includes moral and spiritual development, that is, a "holistic development of the environment" (my translation; ATOP no. 7910, Nov. 13, 2008). In fact, a number of people, including this next speaker, believed that reading and writing are the basis for development:

B.1.NK af1 6m and we, the objective aimed for normally, it's first, we know that all development relies on .. on certain knowledge. So, someone who is in ignorance, ... in ignorance in a global .. sense, but↑ specific, we know that in our Ifè area, especially in the villages, the remote villages, they have not been to school. So, this .. literacy, firstly, is the foremost base of development, that's what we've understood.

Not only are reading and writing seen as the basis for development, but also as a requirement for a measure of self-sufficiency and even discipline that will help people escape poverty.

C.2.VA1 43m I myself often say that ... reading and writing .. make the basis of a development . of an individual, of an association, or of a community because it's very important to know how to read and write. That's the basis. Someone who doesn't know how to read and write, cannot be self-sufficient. He cannot be self-sufficient. We have the means, but because we, we don't know them, we don't use them, and poverty always gains ground.

A board member who became literate through the program in his area specifically noted that literacy helps people to manage their goods and money better.

C.3.SY 1h21m (interpreted) All that we could do, in an interval of time, a little time to gain something we used so much energy and we didn't gain anything. But on the basis of literacy, eyes are open, people have understood, consciences are awakened,

## 7.2 Representations of literacy and language 163

people have begun to understand something and discipline has arrived.

Two village teachers at the Itséré meeting also stated that because of literacy and the teachings given, they were enlightened and eyes were opened. One teacher noted that he himself was unconvinced at first of the value of mother tongue literacy but finally decided to become involved in the program and now recognizes how much he has learned.

D.H4 6m   Myself, I have seen that through Ifè literacy which they have brought us, it has so opened our eyes, that has opened our eyes a lot. The reason for which this has opened our eyes so much is that like me I also inserted, the first year when they brought literacy to us here, I myself said to myself, really, well, it's our language, it's our own language, it's for us ourselves really, I'm going to do this school so that it will take me where? But, now in our time, I see that I learn enough things through this.

One concrete example of how literacy can lead to development was given by the literacy coordinator of *Jésus le Chemin*. He testified that several market women, having become literate in Cycle 1 and therefore eligible to attend the math class (in Cycle 2), are now able to calculate prices and profits.

C.5.EK 43m   And one thing more, business, for example, there are some women who gave me testimonies last time, who .. on the basis of literacy now, they are in the classes of level 2. But today they are able to calculate. They are able to calculate. When they are going to thing, the market now, if they sell something, it's they themselves who calculate, they no longer need to go find someone, come help me calculate this which I've sold or another thing. So, now, they have found that it's good to be literate. So, on that basis, literacy can develop us.

Another participant in the same interview reiterated the view that those who cannot read and write cannot engage with the modern world. He also expressed his hopes that literacy would permit the Ifè people to "emerge," just as the Chinese have, to influence the world.

C.5.BK 39m   By our actions, by the the literacy classes which are going to allow them to be in contact with the= uh the modern life, by reading, and: by the ability to write. So, all this will allow the Ifè people to emerge, as other people who in the past . uh: saw themselves left behind. We can notice the Chinese people, in the years of the sixteenth century who were a people, one of the least people on the earth and who by the effort of . of applying themselves, of studying their own language, have emerged and today influence the whole world. So, we hope to see that, the Ifè people will emerge and according to what God will want, from here on out.

This representation of literacy as development is widely found. International and multilateral organizations such as UNESCO also promote this vision of literacy, where economic development still dominates, but a concern for social and political development also exists (Doronila 1996; UNESCO 2006). This discourse is found also at the government level in Togo and Benin, with the preference that literacy programs be functionally based, that is, lead towards economic and social development.

In line with that policy, one member of the ACATBLI leadership team identified their program as being a functional program.

A.1.SK afl 44m   I see that really .. literacy among the Ifè is functional. That is to say there are skills in the reading, in the writing, in the math, and then also to have enough reflection, that is to say that literacy brings the Ifè now to better reflect on their life situation to be able to manage it . and there is a lot of knowledge, that is, we want to see the integral application of of literacy in the life of the Ifè . among the Ifè people.

## 7.2 Representations of literacy and language

This view is supported by the articles found in *Togo Presse* about the Ifè literacy program. In 2000 one article covering a teacher-training session stated that "Discussions were also held with the participants on functional literacy and the environment, beekeeping, improved goat raising, sheep raising, bodily hygiene, and African medicinal plants" (my translation, ATOP, Dec. 6, 2000, Prefectures page). The AVID president also identified the media as one source of this message that literacy leads to development.

C.1.NK 32m   so it's better now to benefit so that . they may also be open now and to the literate . society . so, everyone can be open now to this literate society so that all that they think, they can write. All that they hear, they can write. All that they see, they can read, and this will change many things in their conduct .. ho of each day, in the program in their activities, in the I don't know what so there are many things which surround this this this phenomenon. Thus, people are now aware of being able to read and write, even knowing how to calculate now to manage their own farms, their own business, and now, to no longer be in darkness . in this lettered world. So, it's close to, according to the testimonies, what we see on the ground which testifies the manifest will now of .. of the nonliterate people who want to now be new literates to now be open to this lettered world . to benefit from many things, through posters now, there are many things done even at the level of the media, all that they say now in awareness-raising, all that is said that everybody should come out of darkness and be now open now, to this lettered world which is calling out to everyone. That's it.

Indeed, the ACATBLI coordinator identified education as being the base of development.

A.3.SK 9m   That means that, the basis of development is education. So, we should say development, it's education.

Literacy as openness and development seems to be a widely held representation. This view is related to life in the modern world, encompassing social, cultural, and spiritual domains as well as the more frequently considered economic field. The program leaders recognize that they are seen as agents of development. The program itself incorporates various activities and teachings in these areas, making it a functional literacy program. In this way, these participants hope to improve the lives of their people.

### 7.2.2 Mother tongue literacy as preservation and transmission of cultural knowledge and identity

One theme that frequently emerged was that Ifè literacy is essential to the preservation and transmission of cultural knowledge, which in its turn helps maintain cultural identity. Part of the reason for this is found in the belief among the research participants that cultural riches are found in the language, and to maintain them, the language must be written. This is in line with the often-cited saying "when an elder dies, a library dies with him." The conditions in which cultural knowledge was handed down in the past—initiation ceremonies and regular evening gatherings of multiple generations around a fire while folktales and history were recounted—are disappearing in many areas. When this traditionally orally-transmitted information is not written down, it disappears; this "cultural wealth" vanishes. This was a recurring theme, particularly for ADCIBA's members, but other participants also noted this challenge to the maintenance of their culture.

> C.2.VA1 49m  So, I myself see that it's important because above all there are also things .. cultural ... riches .. in EACH local language, which are expressed . in certain books.

In fact, one ADCIBA person linked the lack of writing to the reduction of that cultural wealth.

> C.4.ANA 1h31m  And the other thing, it's that↑ . cultural riches are hidden in the language SPOKEN by that community .. WITHOUT having

> learned this language, you cannot maintain . these cultural riches ... You cannot even use them ... If there isn't writing in a language for an ethnic group .. the cultural riches of this ethnic group diminish from day to day ... That's it.

His thinking behind this was explained earlier in the interview.

C.4.ANA 1h22m   There is always intermingling now of ethnicities . of peoples. And those, our behavior, they come to live among you, all that, WHAT is: their original behavior? You, you, yourself you have an original behavior, as an Ifè man for example, or as a Fon man, as a Kabiyè man, what do you have the habit of doing, what do you not= don't you do in your ethnicity? No one has written these things down anywhere. That diminishes and that means that . each one does as he wants nowadays.

The saving of customs and other cultural information is a strong motivation both for literacy workers and literacy learners. This was explicitly stated during AVID's second interview.

C.1.NK 37m   people are interested because they want to keep their customs.

One of the main ways literacy helps to save cultural knowledge is in enabling people to write down things for the following generations.

C.2.VA3 47m   So, I myself can also say that . others . today who can write things down .. when they are old for the children .. for like the sharing of heritage like that.. And they can write them in Ifè. It's already a: blessing for them.

One area in which this is happening is in religious beliefs. Because churches have often been established in the wake of literacy classes, many villages were reluctant to initiate literacy classes until it was understood that being literate in Ifè had nothing to do with which religion one followed.

This was a direct result of awareness-raising campaigns. Both ACATBLI and AMIADA leaders testified to this.

A.2.AgbA 0m   When we were in the villages, we saw the chief, and we approached to tell him that we were there to .. uh .. do awareness-raising, opening of literacy CLASSES in their village. He said, you are welcome. But I want to warn you. Here, in my village, we don't even have . the question of a church. Us, we're pagans, we are ido= idol-worshipers, we will not hear of a church. And if ever I hear that, I will put you out. Oh: that is, there was someone who came to evangelize the village, but subsequently, he died. And I told him, Chief, thank you for this warning. But I have come to speak to you of the Ifè language and not of Christianity. And here, I came to speak to you how we can de= develop ourselves, how we can develop our village. Given that I myself, I am the child of= of a parent .. who worships idols, I am telling you that, before becoming a witch doctor, you follow a training course. And a witch doctor's training means that you stay there at least three months, and you will receive instruction. And, I explained to him ALL what goes on there, and I told him it's in the same manner that people learn to read and write because, with the witch doctors, they have their writing which is only lines, and with the . l= mm . let's say .. the .. literacy, we have lines, but they are well prepared .. and .. prettier. And I explained to him, he says Ah, so, if it's only that, okay.

In Mr. Agbémadon's discussion above with the village chief, he highlighted the traditional notation system of the leaders of the traditional religion and drew an analogy with Ifè literacy. AMIADA's coordinator stated that when their members build literacy awareness in the communities, they point out that in the modern education system, it is being literate that counts, not one's religion.

B.3.AmA 26m   Well, that really had an effect on the work at the start, but with time, they themselves have understood that Ah being literate isn't the business of religion. We rework the aware-

## 7.2 Representations of literacy and language 169

ness-raising, again we asked them do=. when you send your children to school, does the State or the teachers ask your enrolled children if they are Christians or not? If he isn't religious, is it that that is the goal of the teachers. Their goal, it's that, if you are religious or not, you must be literate. That's what brings us together.

During AVID's board interview, the example one person gave led to another one, both having to do with *féticheurs* 'those who work with fetishes', that is, local leaders in the Ifè traditional religion. In that second example, the work the literacy workers do in raising awareness is evident. The entire sequence follows:

C.1.AgA 34m And the day before yesterday, a fetishist told me . how: .. he he knows how to write and read now, he is going to make . a legacy to keep for the fetish. If someone comes . he is going to look at the fetish there if someone wants to kill, uh . a chicken . a rooster, you see= you do like this, like this this this this before killing it. You must pray you must pray like this like this like this before doing it that's what he is going to write in its entirety and keep under {laughter} the fetish before leaving. That's why he is in the process of . of attending.

C.1.NK ff.     a a testimony
C.1.AgA ff.     a testimony [it's a testimony]
C.1.NK ff.                   [because] .. this brings me to say also one, one day I was in a village, and it's: a: fetishist who asked me the question if we want to bring them . the word of God . {AgA laughs} and I said to him, even if we= we are going to bring you the word of God, that's not a bad thing. You, you are presently: the follower of this fetish. Is, the origin of this fetish, do you know it? He says no Why don't you know it? His ancestors didn't . write leave something about: the origin of this fetish is thus and such. He says Ahan. How do you pray? The= your ancestors prayed to the fetish and do you know how now He says no, Do you have any idea who had= who left to look for

the fetish No That's why we have brought literacy. So that, from now on uh, that which you know, you mark it down . like that, the day when you are no longer he who will come to succeed you will know that Ah that's how my ancestor prayed, it's like that that he did things, the ceremonies, until such . a moment, such a moment, I must do this at this time I must do this. So, it's like that. He says Ahan. Truly, if it's that, that interests them now. Ahan. So, there are many things unh that the Ifè community understands now about the importance of literacy [JR: unhun] .. in their local language.

So although it is true that one of ACATBLI's goals is to "help the churches to use Ifè well in reading, preaching, and Bible studies" (my translation, ATOP, May 13, 2008:9), it and the local associations promote the use of literacy in all domains for the preservation of cultural knowledge. In fact, AVADI's coordinator noted that one of their long-term goals is to establish cultural centers.

B.2.VA1 10m   Thus, for the moment, we have tried, we have ideas on uh health, on uh . even cultural development, because .. before, in the time of our ancestors, they assembled the children to tell them folk stories:, to do things with them:, and had bef= today, that doesn't happen any more. So, we said to ourselves, if we could help each village, or each .. burg have a cultural center, where people could come and express themselves.

The decline of customs such as elders gathering children to tell folktales and relate other knowledge has left a void that literacy may fill. In addition, ADCIBA's co-coordinator noted that these folktales teach things that promote the development of the Ifè.

C.4.ANA 1h35m   It's why we write books booklets, whatsit of ideas of whatever whatever whatever, histories folktales, all that. There are stories today .. which translate in a manner as one can do to develop a community. And which the the ancestors told orally. If we can simply write them . in, in the language, we

## 7.2 Representations of literacy and language

can= since there are so many . literate people now, they can also read and understand that Ah that's how we can do to really develop our area, our locality. That's it.

Being able to read in Ifè is also a source of pride and ethnic identity for the literacy workers. In AVADI's board interview, this emerged after the activity with the organizational statements was done.

C.2.VA3 53m  I myself I took the paper it's the Ifè I read right away . and I didn't read the French since I know that I am an Ifè instructor,

However, numerous villages in the AVADI territory are shared with Fon and Kabiyè peoples. Later in that same interview, the coordinator related a concern some Fon individuals have expressed, that they would be "converted" to Ifè.

C.2.VA1 54m  And well, even today, even some, some Fon say Ah, we will be converted into Ifè later because well they speak Ifè today: they xx in Ifè, and then they write in Ifè

The elevated status of French means that some Ifè see no value in being able to read their own language. However, the AMIADA coordinator has fought that attitude by drawing attention to the fact that the French have to learn to read their own language, and so the Ifè should too.

B.3.AmA 37m  And we take the notes= we take the paper now, we write sentences in Ifè, we ask them to read and it's difficult for them, and we tell them, unhuh, it's like that, the whites they are born they express themselves in French but they go to school, there are people also who are old there but who have never gone to school, when you bring them notes, they call the little children, and read to them. Unhuh.

In other places, those who are literate in French have become aware that they are missing out by not knowing how to read and write their own language.

C.1.NK 36m  It's that people want .. to read and to write in their own language. Even when you know a foreign language, and you don't know your own language, you'll miss many things. That's why in our centers in our classes, you are going to see that people who have done French classes and they are enrolled now TO learn to read {in their own language}.

In contrast with this reinforcement of identity through literacy, the Beninese noted at the time of our interviews that although five *arrondissements* were represented in their association, there are actually six *arrondissements* that are historically Ifè. The link between language and ethnic identity is apparently a factor in the distancing from the other five, of this sixth *arrondissement,* whose dialect is more similar to Ica.

B.4.KL si1 1m   But, there is a sixth which does not want to behave as Ifè.
B.4.JR si1 ff.  Unhuh.
B.4.KL si1 ff.  in Savalo.
B.4.JR si1 ff.  Unhun {in a surprised tone of voice}.
B.4.KL si1 ff.  Yes, in the commune of Savalo there is another *arrondissement.* It's: . Pataba.
B.4.JR si1 ff.  Mmhm. Okay.
B.4.KL si1 ff.  Yes. They speak an Ifè close to .. what's it called? Ica.
B.4.JR si1 ff.  Mmhm.
B.4.KL si1 ff.  Yes, their Ifè is close to Ica, so they don't want to behave as or accept Ifè, properly speaking.

Language is seen as a guardian of a rich cultural heritage, and literacy as a means of preserving that heritage for future generations. The knowledge implicit in that heritage can cover any domain, from personal reminiscences to traditional values to religious knowledge. In preserving their cultural heritage, their pride in being Ifè is reinforced.

### 7.2.3 Literacy as full participation in society

One benefit of literacy that is frequently mentioned in the literature is that newly literate people often gain self-confidence and are more likely to offer their

## 7.2 Representations of literacy and language

opinions in group settings (Doronila 1996; UNESCO 2006). In African settings it is generally quite important that during group discussions, all points of view are expressed and discussed until consensus is reached. However, when people feel that they are on society's margins, they are much less likely to speak up, even when they have the right to make their voices heard. So this aspect of becoming literate was quite important to the interviewees, several of whom mentioned it.

C.2.VA2 41m   Well: together, well, of of= in the course of of a meeting, he may speak even if it's his local language, since he knows . what he want to say. He knows the imp= THERE IS {intensely but softly}, he learned, an idea thus of the importance of things, he has learned that, through: through through education. And so, he is no longer = he is no longer afraid of the population. He = the fact of staying together also learning all these ideas going to the chalkboard: and so on all that, it's good .. [we can say that]
C.2.VA1 ff.                                                                                                                   [He isn't afraid]
of others.
C.2.VA2 ff.   He isn't afraid of others, like. So, THAT is an advantage,

One man who became literate through the Ifè literacy program, when explaining why he thought literacy was important, gave a concrete example of what would often happen during meetings as far as illiterates are concerned, and how that can change once they learn to read and write.

C.3.SY 1h22m (interpreted) So, today, those who are literate, they can take notes, they can be in contact with documents, and read themselves know and have the message that is the content of the message. At a meeting for example, people, when they= someone is going to call them together, they no longer have to sit with their arms crossed to wait for someone else to come and give a report they themselves they can take a pen take notes of what is said, listen to the meeting.

Another testimony of how literacy enables people to do things they could not do before for the good of their community came from the husband of a graduate of the literacy program.

C.5.BK 45m  So I, to testify, my wife hadn't had the chance to to be instructed at the secular school. But with literacy as the wife of the pastor, she is able to minister by visits with the reading of translated portions of James which she has, with that, she encourages the women, the sick, and many others as well. In my absence, or if I am, if I= if I am prevented from doing the ministry, it's enough to indicate to her do this do this, she's able to do it in an efficient .. uh manner. So, it's truly good what this does for society.

Another board member who became literate through the Ifè literacy program described how his newly found self-confidence helps him at the bank.

C.5.ÐO 48m  (interpreted) He can stop at the bank today, when the teller makes a mistake, makes a calculation, he can tell him no, he needs to redo it, because he is sure of what is happening before him.

One concrete example, which also addressed the issue of the language of literacy, came from one of the activities of the research process itself, when I gave them a set of statements which they were to read and then choose one on which to comment.

C.5.ÐO 50m  (interpreted) And the sheet of of the questionnaire that you just gave out then, the part above it was, it's in French. He said that if what was there hadn't been translated on the other side, he would have been completely in the dark. So, on the basis of that, he too was able to respond to the question.

In addition, literacy opens doors to participation in society that were otherwise closed, namely, certain positions. One African educationist, in fact, expressed the view that illiterates cannot fully participate in "the social and civic life of contemporary Africa" (Busia 1968). He also agreed with the point of view expressed in chapter 6, namely, that village chiefs and other elected officials must be literate. The Beninese gave examples of how literacy enables people to obtain positions of community responsibility in their areas.

## 7.2 Representations of literacy and language 175

B.4.ANA si2 12m  Oh, yes, yes, I would say that .. uh that .. lit= thanks to literacy, we now have people . who have gotten into politics, and who are: uh elected, who have now become elected either they are counselors in their village, or they are counselors in the commune, or they are counselors in the *arrondissement* that is village chiefs in their village they are chiefs of their village et cetera. There is someone who is the *arrondissement* chief now, in my *arrondissement* of Doumé even.

Another position that is open to the newly literate is that of development agent.

C.4.ANA 1h43m  we have already translated many books on medicine, history .. which can truly help people . in changing behavior so that people really, we can strengthen the abilities of the newly literate, in order to be able to increase the level of active people in community development . since we need right now people active in the development of our community.

Finally, being literate in Ifè also means one can obtain a position within the literacy program itself. This is a source of considerable pride, as Mr. Saanya testified.

B.3.SY 43m  (interpreted) So, it's already a big step, so today being a supervisor, starting from zero attaining supervisor it's a big step.

So a number of community roles are open only to those who are literate, regardless of the language of literacy. Neoliterates are also seen to acquire influence as they gain the confidence to speak up at community meetings. In addition, they can read Scripture portions to encourage others. As such they are able to participate in all aspects of society.

### 7.2.4 Ifè literacy as language maintenance and development

One of the goals of ACATBLI is to promote and enhance the value of the Ifè language through literacy and Bible translation. Not only did Mr. Agbémadon of ACATBLI identify the promotion of the language as a common goal of all the associations that helps unite the Ifè people, but he also gave it as one of his personal motivations to work in literacy.

A.1.AgbA af1 2m   And later, I had seen clearly that, it's more a call for me . to do this work, because I have at heart .. my ethnic group.. Someone must develop . the language. Someone must be a pioneer so that the language may be recognized nationally or, have its weight.

In addition, he saw this common goal as a great asset for the associations.

A.3.AgbA 24s   It's .. to cause the Ifè language to evolve. So, and they have seen that, to e= cause the Ifè language to evolve, they cannot be scattered all over the place, they must come together . in association . to develop that. And it's that which has made .. the= this motivation, or the prestige of the language, has made that . we know . now .. we have forgotten our differences .. whether you are Muslim, whether you are pagan, whether you are Christian, whether you are: Buddhist I don't know, {brief laugh} whether you are a polit= a politician or not, whether you are a member of the RPT or of the RPFC . no, it's Ifè that brings us together. And it's that, it's a great asset . for the success of these associations. And, and going from there, all: the other Ifè who are not of ... of the team here, all expect from us . to do= do something to develop the language. And they are ready at least to support us even if they don't have money. And they encourage us . to evolve. To the point that, when an Ifè speaks Ifè, and someone hears a foreign word in it he says, no↑, that isn't Ifè, you must speak Ifè.. That's it. So they encourage us to [search {the doorbell rings}]
A.3.SK ff.           [do research]
A.3.AgbA ff.   even words, even words, search out these words even if we must create them, we must create, so they may be Ifè. That it's it's. it's an asset.

He noted that others expect them not just to rediscover, but in case of need, to create words. During one of the interviews, I learned that one

## 7.2 Representations of literacy and language

example of a modern object that currently has two Ifè names, according to dialect, is the cell phone. In one dialect, the Ifè term means 'telephone without a wire' *(ókpákù àtapforífo)*, while in another dialect the phrase used means 'telephone in the air' *(ókpákù kpimi)*.

The theme of literacy leading to the revival of the language and to the rediscovery of unused words emerged also in the second interview with the ADCIBA board.

C.4.KƉ 1h29m (interpreted) truly literacy, it's a, I would say, a sign of revival. It has really awakened the people or it's that which continues to revive us. Why he says, he says that, because, there are certain . certain expressions, certain words. in Ifè which are there which our former parents, our ancestors used. Today, whether one is nonliterate or has gone to school, we no longer arrive at these these these expressions or these nouns are no longer retained. All is forgotten. But through literacy, people have done research to rediscover these words, rediscover these expressions, and they have brought them to us today so he who integ= enrolls in literacy, he is automatically, he is going to rediscover these expressions and these terms and that means that the life which he is, even the source, he returns to the source, and the language would be kept on the level.
C.4.ANA ff. original
Interpreter ff. (interp.) original—or primordial—if it must be said.

In another interview, the theme of promotion of the language helping to unite distant groups of Ifè emerged. AMIADA's treasurer reported how the Ifè living near the frontier with Benin were brought to cooperate with the group at Oké, in spite of the distances involved.

B.3.MK 14m where I can add a little, it's that before, the instructors were far from us here. And to have their bicycles to reach them, we left the seat of the association to meet them to rea= to reach them quickly, right in the middle, there it's called Patala. Then at that time, as they didn't they didn't uh . obey, they weren't uh .. or, to know what we wanted to do there, they= when you are going to say to come by then, it can be difficult to travel right then .. then we came near to them, and then it was in the middle, and they came quickly. They, since we approach them, they come, they give us ideas and tools they are interested, that so our own language it won't fail so we are going to evolve.

Literacy in the mother tongue plays a significant role in unifying different groups among the Ifè. The program explicitly works to develop the language through the didactic reading materials and other literature. In addition, Ifè literacy is also a means for reviving old terms and spreading newly minted ones. In so doing, it maintains the distinctiveness of the Ifè language.

### 7.2.5 French as a more difficult language than Ifè

A persistent theme in several interviews was that Ifè literacy is needed because French is a difficult language and a barrier to communication. However, as noted earlier, the examples were often drawn from oral situations, as in the following quote.

C.1.AgA 29m  If we express ourselves in our languages, we understand . well, better than, in other languages. If I speak Ifè now . uh . to an Ifè person, insomuch as I am speaking to an Ifè person, she will understand better . than reading .. or than than spea= speaking another language.. They also, if we write in Ifè, well .. that suits us, we read well. But in French to explain besides, that French, m?m. It's phrased like that, so phrased like that but it says to us the same thing .. and in other languages too it's like that if it's in Ifè, it's in Ifè if we say now in Ifè *tsaka tsaka,* it's *tsaka tsaka* it hasn't changed. If we say *okpa,* it's *okpa.*

A number of people compared Ifè and French. Several of these comments came as an unintended result of the activity earlier in the second board interview, when participants were asked to read five statements about

## 7.2 Representations of literacy and language 179

organizational life and choose one on which to comment. The five statements had been translated into Ifè, and each participant was handed a sheet that had the French statements on the top half and the Ifè equivalents on the bottom half. When later asked about the importance of Ifè literacy or about the importance of French literates learning to read their own language, four participants referred to this activity.

A common theme was that Ifè is comprehensible, unlike French. One man who does not speak French observed that he understood the Ifè, which allowed him to participate in the activity.

C.3.SY 1h21m (interpreted) In our time, he for example, the document which you just gave us, the sheet of information, before that, it's one part in French, the other in Ifè, but he left the French part he read what was in Ifè he understood and he also was able to give his opinion about what had been asked.

Three of the AVADI participants commented on their participation in the activity and the effect the language they read had on their contribution. The first person's remarks correspond with the theme of comprehension. He said the French ones were hard to understand, but the Ifè was clear.

C.2.VA1 48m because↑ .. right away when you showed us this paper . the French is written above, I read these five . statements in French, and I was not able to immediately understand . the meaning . of all that you want= one wants to say in each sentence. And at the same time I descended to the bottom. I read in Ifè, and, automatically, I understood everything. And it's a= here then it's of this that it's speaking here. And then you are going to see in French it took up nearly: . one line only, but in Ifè it's up to three lines↓ which means . that it wants to explain many things. And I understood at the same time.

The next person to speak was sorry he had based his answer on what he had read in French. He brought out the point that often, those who can read French do not understand it as well as they think they do.

C.2.VA2 51m  Frankly: well as I too I took the paper, I myself read only in French. Since: it failed five, and I had read the fifth, I'm sorry to have chosen the second {laughter of all} because if I had read that in Ifè, truly it was =. it is very clear and I see that it's really . important. And of the two . if you know someone . who thinks he is lettered hunh↑ .. he says well I already know French why learn my local language again even if someone writes me I can read. He's wrong. Not to say: frankly me: . well: I said that, that well, if I take: well Fre = Ifè I can read. And I read, I have difficulties, in fact even↑. if I don't understand the language I cannot read. So, if I read that it doesn't sound right so it's like that it should be phrased, and I have = I = before the phrase, I try hard, and it sounds. So I didn't know that, so the arrows there are going to say this, {someone snorts softly with laughter} say like that and so on {soft snort of laughter}. But I have not written. however, really as he just said, there are certain people, who can read are strong in mathematics and it's like that↓ but they don't have easy verbs. Because they don't have thousands they don't have . many verbs. But in our local language, we have easy verbs, so expression is easy, so we can even write down the remark . it allows us well, we say now well, if the Ifè well . we will have many things. Since when in the past said xx easily comes out in your: local language. Otherwise it's very important if even, the best even, the lettered are better placed than even: . well I want to say that . that the: those who don't understand . don't have the importance of paper.

The third participant, continuing the theme of better comprehension in Ifè, added that being able to read and fully understand what was read is a source of joy for him.

C.2.VA3 53m  there is nothing which can to me = I will read if it asked again for the interpretation, I read, I understood . and: . it's a joy for me since there are things that I'm going to read in French here and I'm not able .. {chuckle} to: understand the words well.

## 7.2 Representations of literacy and language

The AVADI coordinator has to work with French extensively in his other role as a pastor. Nevertheless, he had quite a bit to say about the difficulties he has in reading and writing that language. He began by discussing his sermon preparation and how it helps if the Scripture portion he plans to use exists in Ifè.

C.2.VA1 48m  There are certain: uh. nevertheless .. portions of the Bible already translated into Ifè↑ . and that when I want to prepare my sermon↓ I myself am a pastor↑ . I read in French, and, it helps me a lot if there is this portion in Ifè.
C.2.VA2 ff.  in Ifè yes
C.2.VA1 ff.  When I take it in Ifè and I READ .. uh = uh = truly, it's it's .. it directs me to many things.

He referred to portions of the Bible because the Ifè New Testament was not distributed until six months after our interview, having been published that year. A bit later in the interview, he focused on the general difficulties of reading comprehension in French, as a reason why those who can read French should learn to read in their own language.

C.2.VA1 49m  and when: you = I know how to read only French, and when I don't know how to read = you cannot read my mother tongue, I LOSE {softly but with emphasis}. I lose because in reading the mother tongue, you understand . at the same time . what you are reading, and in French you also need dictionaries↑, you have to look for them↑, you need = cer = certain words have: for the first time come and then, you are embarrassed and some sentences are formed in many ways . in the French language .. a sole = one sole sentence is formed in many ways ↑and you will read the same sentence and one will write in another way that you cannot understand . that it's the same thing that you wanted to say. Whereas in Ifè, there isn't anything telling you you can change anything, as you read, you understand.

Finally, he highlighted the difficulties of writing in French, comparing it with the ease of expressing his thoughts in Ifè.

C.2.VA1 50m   and above all .. and= and when I want to write for example a TEXT .. I write it . in French, but:↑ I put my ideas in Ifè. And sometimes↑ . what I THINK I'm not able even to exp= put on paper, because I lack words↓ . I lack expressions↓ . to express what I think whereas if it were in Ifè, I would transmit them at the same time directly and that, those who want to read could understand me at the same time.

The representations in this section deal with the comparison of Ifè language and literacy with French. Ifè is perceived as being far easier to comprehend, whether orally or in writing. It is also easier to write since all the vocabulary and grammar is already well-known by Ifè speakers. French, on the other hand, is seen as difficult, requiring research to learn the meaning of words read or heard, or to find the right expression when writing. Even then, the meaning of a French discourse, oral or written, is difficult to grasp. The participants here seem to think that this is true for all literates who learned French in school, and thus a reason for these people to learn to read and write in their mother tongue.

### 7.2.6 Biliteracy as responsibility

Another reason that those who have learned to read and write in French should learn to read and write Ifè is that they have responsibilities that they cannot carry out if they fail to learn Ifè literacy skills. One participant used a proverb to make his point that those who are literate in French ought to learn to read and write their mother tongue.

C.4.ANA 1h31m   I myself say that it's even obligatory that he know how to read and write his own language . because on one hand, we say that, if you don't know how . to clean your own household, that is to say your house, you mustn't try to go sweep the street. {interpreter laughs} Mm↑. You who don't know how . to read . to write . in your own language and you act as a pedant in another language, .. you are hurting yourself first of all.

## 7.2 Representations of literacy and language

This view that the educated have a responsibility towards their own people is congruent with the African notions of solidarity discussed in chapter 4. It is important to note that here, educated Ifè are perceived as hurting themselves when they do not know how to read and write their own language, even when they express themselves well, perhaps even teach, in another language. This indicates that becoming biliterate may be a responsibility they have towards themselves.

Another speaker observed that one consequence of people not being able to read their own language even though they speak it is that, when they make errors in interpretation, people will think and speak badly of them.

C.3.AmA 1h26m   So, it is important for him who already knows French to know also how to read in his own language. We hear about this problem especially= this problem, we see it often in the churches. In the churches it's difficult. There is the pastor who speaks French. If uh: . the interpreter is Ifè, he doesn't know how to read Ifè, it's difficult it doesn't pass on the information well. The information, it doesn't feel= it it doesn't penetrate the members. When the the interpreter interprets badly, there are murmurings, there are curse words, people xx oh no no no, he isn't interpreting well what the pastor said to him. So, when this person who knows already how to read French he should get some fresh ideas in Ifè . to be able to .. pass on well his message or pass on well what he received, like. It's necessary, it's very necessary.

Yet another consequence of those who can read French but not communicate in Ifè is that they cannot share their ideas effectively and thus are prevented from helping their people develop. This theme, which has strong links to the fundamental representation of literacy as openness and development, emerged in multiple interviews. This view applied both to the literates who have stayed close to their home communities and those who have left. Mr. Saanya of AMIADA pointed out that oral messages given in French will not help the community; they must be given in Ifè.

C.3.SY 1h28m (interpreted) Whatever the level of your French, you have your high school diploma, your master's or whatever it may be, people today are there they have mastered French well, they come, they give, they give a presentation, they can make the presentation in French, someone asks them to transmit the message in their mother tongue, they are blocked. They cannot do it. There, it's a gap. So, at this time, it is important for every person, whatever her level of knowledge of the French language, she must return to study her own language, to master it and to give messages in it and it's more penetrating like.

Another participant observed that people who want to help by providing reports of meetings, whether they are held in French or in Ifè, in the other language, are prevented from doing a good job if they cannot read and write Ifè. This view ties in with the representation of literacy as language maintenance.

C.4.GĐ 1h27m (interpreted) Why, for example there are certain nouns in Ifè . that, if someone= if you indicate something to someone for example in Ifè and who wants to go report on .. this name, if the person knows the name in Ifè he can make a good report. For example someone who has only learned and who knows French, he speaks the language a little, but when you speak to him, you give him this name .. in Ifè getting to now, when he wants to make the report in French or he takes the report in French arriving he wants to report on that in Ifè, at that level there he is blocked. He doesn't know the name. That's why it is important that, whatever his= your level, in French or any other language, you must return to the origin . to study his mother tongue, to read and to write, like that it will help even to have the original terms. That's its importance.

According to several participants, one of the responsibilities of biliterates, especially those who have left the area, is to provide books and their translations for their brothers in the villages.

*7.2 Representations of literacy and language* 185

C.5.ÐO 49m   (interpreted) So, he asks, he wishes, that the brothers who are ahead provide more effort to bring books other books in other languages, to translate them into Ifè, and as there are good things in them, they may also benefit.

This was, in fact, a dominant theme for ADCIBA's coordinators.

C.4.ANA 1h32m   Now they say that there are .. new agricultural techniques.. There are books already published either in English or in French. There are books which deal with = which speak of many illnesses in English, in French.. You now .. who understand well . English, even you have evolved you understand two languages like that English French. You want . to help . your population. You want to help your people.. How can you do it.. Your people are well = well and truly literate yet here you yourself you don't know how to write . this language. You don't know how to read it. Can you do a translation? I say no.

After going on to give the example of how the Bible translation project would never have proceeded without Ifè people willing and able to read and write in both French and Ifè, he continued with his plea for the educated to help. Not only did he appeal to ethnic solidarity, but he chided those who need interpreters even to talk with their parents.

C.4.ANA 1h33m   So I myself I see that it's even more important for those who . already know . French or English or other foreign languages . to QUICKLY catch up. Those should quickly catch up so that truly we can come together to aid . our population or else our community. It's those who find . how things go elsewhere, often. It's they who have had the opportunity to evolve perhaps in the lands of others but, whether or in France in the United States, or who have had the chance to travel a lot where they found new ideas, new practices, new behaviors, who are now going to want to write it in their language to spread it throughout their community, and when you don't know how to write your language, it would be a fiasco you

> can't do it. You can well and truly have the will to help your people but, you cannot.. That YOU . NAtive . of an ethnic group or of a people .. of a language and that you still find an interpreter, I myself find that it's {tongue click} .. it's really bad on his side {laughter} that you find that you look for an interpreter in order to be able to go . speak with your parents, really that isn't good.

He went on to say that the educated should be able to communicate new ideas in such a way that they seem less strange for the community. He also emphasized that literacy work will be blocked if the educated abdicate their responsibility to learn to read and write their language, on a very practical, personal level: they will be unable to directly communicate with their parents and therefore give their own families any advantages.

C.4.ANA 1h35m   And it's often some people who have had the opportunity to understand other languages, it's those folks, if they find an idea they can quickly develop it. They can develop . that idea, the small idea that the old ones are going to say, those others can develop that and make it more .. uh: ordinary .. a↑ . since it's easier to use= to be used for others according to the world of today, according to the evolution of the world. So, unless . our brothers who know how to read and write in another language return .. to learn their own language, truly literacy would be blocked ↑in such a way that, if your parent wants to write to you . but here he doesn't understand French, he will be obliged to go see someone else that, of whom he wouldn't want that he .. he know what he wants to tell you. Even if he writes to you in his language= in your language you can't read it . there where you are in France perhaps or in the United States. Whereas it's he who put you in the world, you don't understand his language . when it's a question of writing, but that, it's *gauche!* {chuckle} If you yourself want to write to your dad or to your mom .. who understand your own language, you will have to write in French .. And it's another, {snaps fingers twice} the son of another man or another

## 7.2 Representations of literacy and language 187

> woman but who is going to read it, who is going to understand what you are in the process of teaching your mom or your parents, and who perhaps . says something else, translates something else and goes to put it into practice in his own family first. And your family will be obliged to cheat with him. Isn't, that isn't hurting oneself? I see really see that and I am in the process of exhorting our brothers our big brothers who know how to read in other languages to come help us. Those who should help us, and if they don't learn the language they cannot help us.

The other ADCIBA co-coordinator called attention to the fact that the literacy program can only go so far in developing the community. They need the help of those who are better educated in order to progress. Furthermore, he expressed the desire that they help develop the language itself to the point where it could be used as an administrative language in their areas.

C.4.KL 1h37m   For me, those who know how to read .. French already, those who .. uh those who know paper already, and: . it is very important for them also to return . to learn to write and read their own language. Otherwise, we who are doing literacy today↓ we do BASIC literacy. But, IF THOSE who have progressed in studies don't return to learn again the language with us, we can no longer progress in our steps, we can no longer change more than we are today we will be always like this. But those others they have already studied they have already gone to a high level. So, like this, if they also learn to read and to write, they can also CAUSE our language to develop, so that we too we may progress and even . work .. do all that those others do in a foreign language also in our language.

C.4.JR ff.   Mmhm

C.4.KL ff.   Yes, so that's why it is s= it is very important that those others return to learn .. uh to read and to write the language. Yes. Otherwise well, we now who are actors today, we= we think, we dream

C.4.ANA ff.   Mhmm

| | |
|---|---|
| C.4.KL ff | that our language may be an administrative .. language .. |
| C.4.ANA ff. | in our [community at least] |
| C.4.KL ff. | [in our communi]ty at least. So, IF uh: those who have progressed do= well, here, we we don't have a high level, so, it's those who have a lo= well studied who can return, translate uh: |
| C.4.ANA ff. | documents |
| C.4.KL ff. | documents, and we too we can progress. |

In the view of these participants, and especially the Beninese, those who are literate in French and perhaps even in English have a responsibility to learn to read and write their mother tongue. This will enable these literates to function well in the domains of church service interpretation, meeting reports, communication with family, and translation of development-oriented ideas and materials. In this way, they will demonstrate solidarity with their people and their desire to help their home communities develop.

### 7.2.7 Literacy as access to another language

One of the most common reasons for participation in a literacy class heard by those of us who work in literacy in West Africa is to gain access to another, usually the official, language. Over the years, I have heard various anecdotes about people who, once literate in their mother tongues, figured out on their own how to read another language. As one coordinator pointed out, when one knows the letter and sound correspondence for the writing system of one language, one can often decipher the writing system for another, when the same graphemes are involved.

| | |
|---|---|
| C.5.EK 52m | Well, if we take now, that thing in the local Ifè language, if we take . the letter a. So, in the language, we say aa. Already this a is in French. So we see that it's the same . letter. Someone who has done uh literacy, in seeing in French already the letter a, recognizes at the same time that it's the letter a and he can read. So, if we see in the letters, well, there are many |

## 7.2 Representations of literacy and language

> letters . which are . well, which are the same. For example, the letter b also, well . many in the= in literacy. Yes. So, I know truly that there is a relationship . in some . other languages also.

One of AMIADA's board members even testified that once he became literate in Ifè, he was able to decode French, reading in public even though he does not always understand what he is reading. This has motivated others to reconsider the value of taking Ifè literacy classes.

B.3.SY 43m (interpreted) Well, in times past, people knew him as nonliterate, unable to read, but through Ifè literacy, he is able now to read and to write, and figure out some French words. He can read certain words, but maybe not understand them well. That is already one point. And it's by the grace today, of God today, he's starting to be able to read French smoothly in front of people. All those who turned back, who withdrew, this can make them come back.

However, it is more common for the newly literate to take a course for learning—and learning to read—the official language. The French course for newly literate Ifè was being piloted during my research. Courses were being held in three districts at the time, once the first four classes had successfully made progress. As the AMIADA coordinator said, this third-level course met a desire of their students.

B.3.AmA 6m And today now, it was last week that we started a third cycle because those who have learned to read and write Ifè, and also to do math and writing, those who are a bit perfect in the course, they hoped that we would have a third cycle to be able to help us to xx a bit in French. And it was that the desire of our learners.

Interestingly, this course has not only helped the students, but also the teachers. This is related to the earlier theme of French being difficult to understand and is probably a reflection on the quality of teaching available in the typical African village located far from the large towns.

C.3.AmA 1h14m   The reports which I've gathered . on the third cycle {tongue click}, that the course= the French course which we just started {tongue click}, it's giving enough light .. first of all .. to the instructors .. who: did formal classes they say that, it's just now that they understand . the meaning of the grammar, the vocabulary, the spelling .. the sound, the sense of the words its spelling vocabulary well they have they have lots of light on this course . in comparison with what they learned on the bench. The time= yesterday there was a brother who came {his voice lowers} he is in boarding school it's he who did all this here on the chalkboard {the chalkboard is covered with mathematical formulas} {then explanatory aside about how he teaches the third cycle class there} He has much .. he really appreciated the documents saying, it's now that, {tongue click} it seems that, it's we who are .. on the real study like. That, the document, it's okay, it's okay, it it is clearer, more accessible than in in comparison with what one teaches . at the formal .. school . and we we principally, we who represent↓ we who are instructors to teach the the people for the third cycle, really that has brought us a lot of light. We can't even express how much. {chuckle} It helps us.

One of the very practical reasons people want to make the transfer to French is for contact with outsiders, and particularly the soldiers who guard the border, who generally do not know Ifè. Indeed, this reason has even been a draw for former literacy teachers to attend the course.

B.3.AmA 31m   There are even former instructors, who worked a lot in the beginning, and they withdrew, left, and when this third cycle arrived now, they say ah how they have wished for a third cycle for a long time but it hadn't succeeded, that's why when they go, they are going to travel, they travel, they get to the border, the soldiers ask them questions in French there, they are not able to express themselves there, it's that which

## 7.2 Representations of literacy and language 191

caused them to no longer be able to continue to work with us as such. So, happily since the third cycle is here, that will help them a bit.

A sub-theme that emerged in the AMIADA board interviews was that of teaching children to read and write in Ifè. The topic of multilingual education had been discussed at the previous year's literacy forum in Kara. The AMIADA coordinator summarized what had been taught and revealed the impact it had on him.

B.3.AmA 52m   When I arrived = my child is four years old I said when he is five years old, he's going to go to formal school sometimes, when I find a little time, I I have I I initiate him a bit into {literacy in} the mother tongue. For both of them, when he arrives at school, it will go quickly like.

This coordinator was the only person who talked about teaching his children mother tongue literacy to improve their learning once in school, but others had also observed the negative impact of French schooling on their children. The AMIADA vice-president had already stated his hopes that ACATBLI leaders would help them embed the teaching of Ifè literacy in schools and explained why he believes it is necessary to do so.

B.3.SY 49m   (interpreted) It will require the engagement of literacy workers in the formal schools in order to support the students, so that children from a young age start by studying the language they already know how to speak. Like that to write it. And arriving, in evolving, they will no longer be blocked. Because they have noticed today that, when children start with French, at a certain moment, the idea comes back when they ask them to go do additional research on their birth, they are blocked at this time, so, if they had done that from a young age, they would not be blocked at this level. We must make these children, these children of men made from a young age because, already at six years old, the child starts formal school, and Ifè firstly isn't yet he isn't anchored in it, and with French school, or formal school, they change, they don't understand Ifè well, nor French and they're between a vise and, how does it go, a rock and a hard place {literally, an anvil and a hammer}, and no longer know what to do. When you ask them to return to the Ifè way, you say certain words to them, they are unable to understand, but then they also have difficulties one day so a good foundation is essential for the building to be built well.

So whether one is an adult or a child, Ifè literacy is seen as a good place to start in order to obtain access to a second language, usually French. The new French class for new literates is greatly appreciated for its role in helping Ifè acquire this language. It also has helped those with some knowledge of the language to understand it better, besides motivating some teachers and students who had left the program to return.

### 7.2.8 Ifè literacy as a qualification

AMIADA participants seem to have a final representation of literacy, that of qualification. They have used lack of literateness in Ifè as a barrier to those who wish to take positions in the program that might earn them some money, but who otherwise have not shown any interest in learning to read and write Ifè. The first position they mentioned was related to the income-generating project of beekeeping.

B.3.AmA 38m  Now, people have learned in the villages, they are specialist in raising in beekeeping but they haven't learned to read and write in Ifè. And they come to us to ask us to involve them in the committee we tell them NO, unhun, it's an example, like. Well, others too, when for example, the project asked can you hire a shepherd. Here came people from right and left, say it's they who are going to follow the shepherd, excuse me, the sheepfold so that if there is

### 7.3 Summary and discussion 193

> a small allowance that they would take that monthly. We told them no, we brought you literacy here you refused, now you see, don't you?

The second role where literateness in Ifè was required was teacher for the third cycle.

> C.3.AmA 1h23m   Second point, the instructor must have completed the second cycle. Second level {Ifè} literacy cycle. Because↑ .. all that you are going to meet in French, you have to transmit that in Ifè. ↑It is necessary .. yes, he must he must transmit that to others in Ifè.

They also use literacy in Ifè as a prerequisite to participating in the Cycle 3 class, forcing those who want to participate to prove that they have passed second level first.

> B.3.AmA 41m Well, already my view the third cycle now which we just said that we just said now, there are people when they understand that it's French, ah↑ all they do is bother me. All they do is bother the supervisors and the supervisors come tell me everything. And the criterion, the bar which I myself put, is if someone doesn't have his diploma, of the second cycle, he ought not enroll in the third cycle. Out of the question. They can come with presents, it's out of the question.

So for the AMIADA coordinator, Ifè literacy is a qualification for participation in the program, whether for a paid position or to learn French. This stance has the possibility of providing those who do want to participate in these activities a reason to enroll in classes.

## 7.3 Summary and discussion

In this chapter many of the representations that motivate the participants of this study to invest their time and energy in the literacy program were discussed. These representations are largely contextual, tied to the roles of these literacy leaders and drawing on their experiences with literacy, languages, and the illiterate. In their discourses, these leaders reveal that they are motivated largely by their concern for the status and well-being of their people and their language. The most widely shared representations, found among nearly all participants, are those concerning illiterates, development through literacy, and literacy in the Ifè language.

Those who cannot read or write text in any language are seen as being handicapped, ignorant, distrustful, and blocks to development. The acquisition of literacy creates an attitude of openness that permits development. This development may be economic, social, cultural, or spiritual. Mother tongue literacy also promotes the maintenance and development of the Ifè language, and the preservation and transmission of Ifè cultural heritage and identity.

Literacy in Ifè is not the only textual literacy available, however. A number of people discussed the presence of oral French and French literacy in their environment. For the nonschooled, the use of French by those around them reinforces feelings of distrust and insecurity. To combat these feelings, the program has begun a French course for those who have passed the first two years of the regular literacy and numeracy curriculum. This has been very popular and is motivating those who have had no interest in learning their mother tongue to join Ifè classes, probably because it is seen as increasing cultural capital, since French is so valuable socially and economically in the wider society. In certain zones people who are already literate in French are considering learning to read and write in Ifè in order to be accepted as teachers of that course. This investment could provide them with a small income, at least under the funding system in place at the time of my fieldwork. Meanwhile, those who are teaching it find that their own grasp of French vocabulary and grammar has improved. Even so, those who do know French have difficulty in fully understanding what they read and in easily expressing themselves in writing.

People who have acquired competence in French are seen to have a responsibility to learn to read and write their own language. Much of this has to do with community solidarity. By becoming literate in Ifè, they proclaim their identities as Ifè and their willingness to help their ethnic group develop. According to the interviewees, the primary way in which they can do this is by supplying and/or translating works into Ifè that communicate new ideas helpful to the community. In addition to demonstrating solidarity, literateness in Ifè will allow them to communicate with family back in the village without relying on intermediaries and permit them to participate in community life through interpretation done well. This last item will prevent gossip harmful to their reputations.

For one association, lack of literateness in Ifè is used as a barrier against those who desire (remunerated) positions within the program but who have not been open to learning to read and write Ifè. In this way, the association attempts to reserve the development function of literacy for its students and graduates, ensuring that a link between literacy and development is visible. It also affirms the investment of time and effort these literacy leaders have put into learning to read and write Ifè themselves, as well as their investment in the local associations.

Many of these representations are found in public discourse such as the media. This is consistent with the theory of social representations and how these representations are formed in a society. In Togo and Benin the radio is the most widely accessible media form, because radios generally require batteries but not necessarily grid electricity, and because they do not require that their hearers be literate. More recently, radios have been incorporated in some cell phone models, increasing the availability of radio access. In addition, radio programs are more likely than other media forms to be available in languages other than French or English. However, national newspapers published in the capitals of the two countries do make their way inland and are another source of dissemination of representations. Additionally, where electricity from grids or generators is available, televisions may be found and thus also influence thinking about such things as literacy and illiterates.

All these representations of literacy not only motivate literacy program workers to persevere in the face of uncertain finances, community opposition, and program difficulties, but also affect the decisions about capacity building. The decision to initiate a third year course that teaches French has already been discussed. The influence of the representations of literacy as openness and development, and those pertaining to mother tongue literacy, also influence decisions about program activities, including curriculum development and post-literacy publications. These decisions and activities are the focus of the next chapter.

# 8

# Enhancing Capacity

In this chapter the relationship of representations of leadership and of literacy to capacity enhancement decisions will be explored. Decisions leading to improved capacity in an organization or community may seem sensible to those making them but are often also controversial, as such decisions change the way things are done. Social representations help the members of a group determine how to respond to such practical and controversial issues (Py 2003). The SRs of leadership and of literacy discussed in the previous two chapters affect the Ifè responses to such issues, providing justification for decisions made (Abric 2001; Py 2003) that enhance the capacity of the Ifè community and literacy organizations.

The principal *raison d'être* of most capacity-building efforts in nonprofit development organizations is long-term sustainability, so that an organization's or a community's goals may be achieved, positive outcomes maintained, and negative effects ameliorated. Therefore, any examination of growth in capacity must look at the sustainable attainment of this end goal. However, all discussions must also take into consideration the fact that the enhancement of capacity is a process, and a long-term one at that (Eade 1997; Imdieke 2003). The final goal of nonprofits, after all, is people whose lives have been transformed (Drucker 1990). As one aim of this study is to identify the factors that promote or hamper healthy development of community-based literacy organizations, this long-term view of capacity building is essential.

Nkasa and Chapman (2006), in their study of six Ghanaian communities involved in externally initiated educational development projects, have outlined a number of models of project sustainability. The first model focuses on economic sustainability: the project is able to continue after external funding ceases because participants are able to generate funds themselves. Another model is based on sociocultural factors: project personnel are able to continue the project because the required capacity in knowledge, skills, and structures has been developed. Yet a third model is based on sustainable development theory, focusing on ecological concerns: project needs are met in such a way as to ensure the existence of resources to future generations. The fourth model they describe is one based on innovation and diffusion: a project is sustainable when the community has embraced ownership, since the project is consistent with community values and beliefs, has participatory mechanisms, and has effective leadership. The final model they propose is a synthetic one: a project is sustainable when both management components and sociocultural components are in place. Management components include planning, transparency, leadership, and participation. Sociocultural elements include social cohesion, community skills, resources (both economic and skill-based), and a strong value for education. This last model is the one I use here to assess which factors have helped or hindered the implementation of a multiple-association strategy to ensure access to literacy throughout a large language group.

A major aim of this work is to provide insights into what drives and affects capacity-building choices and efforts. In examining the capacity-enhancement choices made in the Ifè literacy program as expressed in interviews and revealed in archival documents, it became evident that the capacity building occurring in and through this program and its associations can be divided into three levels: at the personnel level, where training leads towards greater professionalization; at the organizational level, where capacity building has focused on helping the associations become more structured and businesslike; and at the community level, where efforts aim to enhance the villagers' ability to improve their standard of living and to empower them in other areas. At each level, the influence of representations of leadership and literacy are seen in the choices made and in the management of their implementation, and can be used to identify factors for the development of sustainable organizations and of strategies capable of serving a large population. With this information, literacy practitioners, policy makers, technical advisors, and donors will be able to make more informed decisions.

## 8.1 At the personnel level

Capacity building of personnel is concerned with adding to or enhancing the knowledge and skills of people working with the organization, whether employees or volunteers (de Pree in Drucker 1990), and often includes developing certain attitudes as well (Edoho 1998). Literacy program personnel typically include literacy center teachers, supervisors, trainers, and coordinators. They may also include writers, editors, and printers. In a literacy and development-focused organization, training covers the literacy, development, and management domains.

The literacy domain includes typical educational topics tailored for the level needed. Village adult literacy teachers—who, in my experience in sub-Saharan Africa, are rarely educated beyond the third year of secondary school and usually have no more than a primary school education—are taught such things as how to write on a chalkboard and how to teach the method used in the primers during large group workshops. They are also often given practice in reading and writing their own language and in working arithmetic problems. In adult literacy programs it is also common to focus on principles of adult education, as the only experience with classrooms most teacher trainees have had is schools for children. Obviously, treating adults as one would treat children is almost guaranteed to have a negative effect on literacy class attendance. Thus, principles of adult education encourage teachers to adopt certain attitudes towards students, particularly respect. All these topics feature in the Ifè teacher training. In addition, the Ifè teacher training includes a unit on the principles of community development.

The Ifè program has also worked to develop authors through writers' workshops. These have included participation in SIL-sponsored workshops with external facilitators as well as internally run workshops with the ACATBLI literacy personnel as facilitators. Some workshops focus on creative writing, while others concentrate on translating/adapting factual material. The long-term goals are to build writing fluency in the Ifè community and to produce publishable post-literacy material. However, the exigencies of management of the enlarged program had prevented the organization of such workshops for over five years at the time of my on-site research. This was a source of dismay already in 2009 for at least one ADCIBA board member. Additionally, in the past both the ACATBLI literacy workers and the Bible translators worked on editing books, but time when both teams were free was quite limited. As a result, more recently the editing has been done by the ACATBLI literacy workers and the coordinators of the local associations, which has resulted in the publication of three documents between 2011 and 2014, with others in the pipeline. Without a dedicated editor, however, the production of documents remains slow.

While the teachers and writers generally are taught in a workshop format, much of the capacity building for leaders that has occurred in this program has been through the mentorship model, first with the men originally hired by SIL, and then with the supervisors and coordinators of the local associations. In a mentorship model, learning is primarily done first through observation, followed by doing the task under supervision, receiving feedback, and finally by doing the task unsupervised. In the Ifè associations, this type of training has been used in both the literacy and management domains. Mr. Agbémadon's first mentor was Ms. Boëthius, who taught him first how to write the initial literacy materials, then to supervise classes, and later to run the program. I also mentored Mr. Agbémadon to lead training sessions

## 8.1 At the personnel level

for supervisors and program coordinators in Kara. Mr. Sétodji was coached jointly by Ms. Boëthius and Mr. Agbémadon in his initial program-level role as supervisor. SIL members working with the Ifè project trained both men in strategic program planning.

The coordinators of the local associations, several of whom also have or had other roles on their respective boards, have been, as noted, primarily developed through mentorship in the program management domain. The mentors in these cases have been the ACATBLI literacy head, coordinator, and supervisor. The literacy program tasks that the coordinators learned in this manner range from awareness raising and class creation through teacher training, class supervision, evaluations, and leading teachers' meetings, as well as overall program coordination.

The ACATBLI literacy leaders as well as the association coordinators and a few board members have also participated in various training events organized by SIL in Togo. Since 1997 these have covered such topics as program management (including situational leadership styles), post-literacy possibilities, literacy and development, principles of adult education, basic reading theory and literacy methods, and principles of orthography development. Moreover, the head of the literacy work has participated in a variety of seminars and courses held in other countries, among them a REFLECT trainers' seminar and an English course, the latter to assist him in communicating with funders. In addition, he was part of a group that visited Ghana in 1999 to observe a literacy and development program there and to talk with the development and women's work coordinators of GILLBT (Ghanaian Institute of Linguistics, Literacy, and Bible Translation). Mr. Agbémadon also was one of a small group who attended a course on fundraising in Lomé in 2003. Both Mr. Agbémadon and Mr. Sétodji have attended one of the biennial Pan-African Conferences on Reading for All, Mr. Agbémadon (accompanying me) in 2003 and Mr. Sétodji in 2007.

The association coordinators and boards have primarily received training in the management domain. They too have benefited from targeted workshop and seminar training, mostly as part of the Swedish-funded organizational capacity-building project. The main topics of this training have been handling money and program planning. In addition, several of them were prepared for their board roles through their involvement with other associations or their churches. However, several board members expressed a desire for further training on the roles and responsibilities of board members. This was a particularly strong desire both for AVADI's and AMIADA's boards.

B.2.VA1 25m   So, that's why they have xx to ask at the same time it is necessary= we need training, we need other things to be able to situate things.
B.2.JR ff.   Does anyone want to add something? {3 second pause}
B.2.VA3 ff.   To add, we want to attend training. Or else we need some training, to manage an association we must have training. So, we need even so some training.

AMIADA's president specifically noted that although officers learned several significant things through the training they have had, it was inadequate. Therefore, one of their expectations of ACATBLI is that they will receive further training in this domain.

B.3.AmA 21m   Well, please, in 2006, ACATBLI came to train us. The role of the president . the role of the secretary, the role of the treasurer. But that training, it was good, but it was insufficient for us. And we beg, ACATBLI must return again to train us.

This willingness to learn and the willingness to teach are among the themes of the Ifè representations of leadership for literacy program leaders. Other leadership themes are also seen in this area of capacity building, such as the need for competence, developed during participation in the various workshops and seminars, and the need to be literate, acquired during both the teacher-training sessions and the writers' workshops. The mentorship model is one where certain themes in the Ifè representation of leadership, i.e., those impacting relationship quality, probably have a strong impact, notably those of patience, faithfulness, an exemplary life, being caring, forgiving, cooperative, and knowing the situation of one's subordinates.

Representations of literacy not only motivate leaders to invest their time and energy in the program, but also influence certain choices made in the program. Teacher and writer training is done in the Ifè language, thereby promoting the value of the mother tongue and enabling those who are literate in Ifè to assume respected positions in society. The aim of the writers' workshops is to develop literature that will contribute to the maintenance and development of the language and of the Ifè culture and community. Writers' workshops that have focused on the translation of development and/or religious literature are linked to the representation of literacy as openness and development, as well as demonstrating the responsibility of biliterates to their brothers and sisters who know only their own language. The addition of participatory discussions on current community issues to each level of the program is an additional example of the influence of the representation of literacy as openness and development. Finally, the establishment of Cycle 3 with the French grammar and vocabulary review afforded to the teachers of this level, as well as the occasional French to Ifè transition classes, demonstrate the representation of literacy giving access to another language.

However, in the discussion of literacy and development issues in chapter 5, the question of who is making decisions was identified as a major concern in these domains. As can be inferred from the above information, the overwhelming majority of decisions as to which capacities to develop within the program leadership were made not by local people but by expatriates, myself and the funders included. Although the topics addressed in SIL's training events in Kara are based on the expressed desires of former participants, the actual choice is made according to a combination of those desires, what we expatriates see as major needs common to the programs we serve and available expertise and resources.

Areas where the program leadership are making decisions regarding training do exist. The most important is in the area of literature development, as writers' workshops have been completely under the control of Ifè leadership in the program for several years. In addition, although the teacher and supervisor trainings were originally developed by expatriates, as areas of concern are seen, training is modified to address those concerns. Questions of timing for the training of supervisors and teachers, as well as the start of each year's classes, are also in the hands of the local leadership. Finally, while program leaders make recommendations as to the frequency and duration of classes, each literacy class chooses the days and times when it meets.

## 8.2 At the organizational level

Capacity building at the organizational level aims to develop or enhance the skills of employees and board members, to improve procedures to obtain greater efficiency, and to strengthen the organization's ability to function in general (Eade 1997; Edoho 1998). Particularly in contexts where a community-based association is developing, it also aims to promote viability and autonomy (Gubbels and Koss 2000). Most often, the focus is on strengthening structures and communication, enhancing planning and decision-making, and ensuring that all recommended management tools are in place, as occurred in the workshop series I attended during the research period. Another area of emphasis necessary to healthy functioning is the establishment of sustainable financing practices (Eade 1997). However, as Gubbels and Koss note, "Organizational capacity is a complex and context-specific phenomenon. Due to these complexities, enhancing organizational capacity takes time to achieve and requires a coherent, long-term strategy that goes far beyond tools" (2000:6). Thus, while the goal of an enduring organization is the same regardless of what or where it is, efforts at capacity building should not take a "one-size-fits-all" approach.

In nonprofit organizations relying on volunteers, the dynamics of a healthy organization may lead to a slightly different capacity-building emphasis than that which is usual for businesses. Specifically, the mission and ethos of the organization are key, as these are what attract both volunteers (Edmunds 1978; Tandon 1988) and funding (Imdieke 2003). However, growth and/or funders' requirements often create a push towards greater professionalization and a more businesslike organization (Dym and Hutson 2005; Ilsley 1990), leading to capacity-building initiatives that focus on structures and management procedures.

While training focused on the areas noted above is important, as Max de Pree states, "When you take the risk of developing people, the odds are very good that the organization will get what it needs" (Drucker 1990:38). In fact, several associations' boards identified their only abundant resource as their people. It is not just the skills of the people, however, but their relationships that are important to the health of an organization (Imdieke

## 8.2 At the organizational level

2003). ACATBLI and its affiliated associations have strong relationships within and between themselves, but several of the associations' interviewees acknowledge the need to develop additional relationships with financial and potential technical supporters. An exception to this is AMIADA, which in 2009 developed relationships with three other organizations that provided specific limited support.

The long-term survival of a community-based organization is dependent upon a number of factors. Four of the factors identified by Gubbels and Koss (2000) have to do with finances: the ability to meet core costs, the ability to continue working when external financial aid has ceased, access to a wide variety of funding sources, and effective financial management. They note, however, that a viable organization needs to be purpose-driven, not donor-driven. In addition, leaders must be able to plan strategically and develop relationships with other organizations. While Johnson and Thomas (2007) agree with these last two points, they also emphasize the importance of having an organizational culture that promotes learning, not just for individuals but for the organization itself. This relates to the key point of Kinsey and Raker (2003), which states that the organization must continually strive to improve the product or service it provides in addition to paying attention to all the points mentioned previously. ACATBLI has done this most recently through the establishment in 2012 of the agricultural cooperative (see section 2.3).

As noted in the previous section, a workshop on the roles and functioning of the board was given to the boards of several associations by ACATBLI leaders with funds from Sweden. During this workshop, the board members learned such things as the basics of operating a cash box and the role of each board member. However, AMIADA's president-coordinator rather forcefully stated his association's need for additional training in leadership roles.

B.3.AmA 1h04m   I, for example, in our association, we ought to= we want to again have training on the role of leadership. How to manage the association. How was, excuse me, the committee, the committee, train the committee, where the committee of the association should receive a training TOGETHER. And each one will know what he EXPECTS, what is NEEDED of him, which SKILLS he should HAVE, do it's the= a primary objective for me.

AVADI's coordinator also noted that their leaders needed more training on board roles and responsibilities.

B.2.VA1 26m  Uh . yes, for .. that is training above all .. very necessary. And, after this training, they must .. {chuckles} they must put us in the field on the ground floor .. and: .. make us work .. and supervise us. So, this we= we really desire it, and, trying to define ourselves .. what does the president do, and the coordinator what does he do, the secretary what is he going to do, train train the people in it and we .. again stimulate us give us again some other ideas, which can conquer, which can come to the development of the Ifè.

Training in role responsibilities was not the only felt need, however; the need for additional training in association management was also frequently expressed. When participants identified which aspect of management was most needed, they mentioned financial management. AVADI's secretary explained why: to avoid losses.

B.2.VA2 12m  Especially in management: . well it's that, we don't know how to manage, it's that we can do but sometimes: we always ha= well losses everywhere .. unhuh ... okay.

During AMIADA's first interview, its president gave a concrete example of a type of financial management knowledge, related to use of the cash box, they had not had before the first board management training they received.

B.3.AmA 58m  So, it's training on management and the role of the leadership that opened our eyes to have a cash box. We didn't know we needed to open a cash box for a bank account, and before we left the money in a bedroom we slept with the money, which isn't prudent. So when we have the money over there we're free.

ACATBLI's leadership recognized this area as one that needs strengthening and identified it as a major area to develop before each association is granted full autonomy.

## 8.2 At the organizational level

This desire for additional training in financial management was not a universally felt need, however. The officers of AVID, the oldest association, had at one time managed their own finances and felt that they still had the necessary competence to do so again. In his discourse on this point, AVID president Mr. N'tchou emphasized that without financial autonomy, no association could claim to have autonomy; essentially, that those who hold the purse strings are the true decision makers.

B.1.NK afl 46m   Well .. with uh: . this suspension, and it's that which brought us to organize ourselves with ACATBLI so that ACATBLI looks for funding, {he taps the table} and they manage the funds, {he taps the table} with the associations. So, today we are NOT autonomous. Because we don't decide anything .. What .. they decide, {softly} with our members, that's what we do .. That's it. So, we are not autonomous. Sure ACATBLI is our umbrella, it we ar= it's all like it's a network of all the associations which are again on their feet {?}. But none of the associations, which you will find today, if any of them say they are autonomous, no. When you talk about autonomy, you must first have financial autonomy. When you don't have financial autonomy, you are not autonomous. So, we don't have financial autonomy, we aren't autonomous. Even though we can= we have our our meetings within the association:, we have suggestions we make how to . do this or that. But in the area of: of management .. we aren't there.

Drucker (1990) notes that one of the main functions of a nonprofit's board is fund development. Association board members repeatedly stated that this is an area in which they need much more help and direction from ACATBLI and SIL. ADCIBA's president specified that they not only wanted to learn how to write funding proposals, but also to be assisted in finding financial partners. It is in this area that AMIADA's coordinator has been able to work with two national NGOs with ties to other organizations to find funds for construction and equipping of two literacy centers.

In 2009 the Swedish funders sponsored two weeks of capacity-building workshops for ACATBLI's board and the local associations' coordinators (three of whom are also on ACATBLI's board), with the goal of promoting organizational sustainability. This workshop series covered the topics of identifying strengths and weaknesses of their associations, the creation of an association, strategic planning, management tools, finances and budgeting, and communication techniques. The local association coordinators were expected to share this content with their own boards. An additional capacity-building seminar funded by Sweden was held in Kara for literacy associations throughout Togo and Benin later in 2009. This included the topics of conflict resolution and of transition programs to basic French, both of which had been requested by program leaders; and building teams, including legal aspects such as statutes and by-laws, as well as identification of what makes a healthy team. During the 2010 literacy forum held in Kara, a discussion on effective time management strategies addressed organizational capacity growth.

When a Swedish NGO began funding the program and the associations were all brought under ACATBLI, they were all, with the exception of the very newest association, put on the same footing, regardless of previous experience and established competence, primarily in order to prevent jealousy (although see Mr. N'tchou's quote above for the resulting resentment from one long-established group). Responsibilities have been gradually handed over to the associations, as their members demonstrate under supervision that they are capable of handling the task. Before the associations are declared to be autonomous, their officers will have learned to raise and manage their own funds. In addition, each organization will need to demonstrate its viability through its membership numbers, by having obtained legal status with the government of its country and by the establishment of at least one income-generating activity. See table 8.1 for a summary.

## 8.2 At the organizational level

Table 8.1. Steps towards associational autonomy

| Other requirements (no order) | Responsibilities to be assumed (in order) | Comments[a] |
|---|---|---|
| Legal recognition by the state | Community awareness-raising and mobilization | Already delegated |
| | Organization of classes | Already delegated |
| | Teacher training | Already delegated |
| | Supervision of classes | Already delegated |
| | Student evaluations | Already delegated |
| | Leading teachers' meetings | Delegated to all |
| | Organization of diploma ceremonies | Delegated to all |
| Establishment of viable income-generating projects | Payment of the supervisors' monthly stipends | Done by the associations' literacy coordinators |
| | Payment of the year-end stipend/bonus *(gratification)* to literacy teachers and supervisors | Done by the associations' literacy coordinators |
| | Planning and management of all activities | Planning done together; management done by the associations' literacy coordinators |
| Adequate membership numbers | Management of funds | At ACATBLI's level |
| | Fundraising | At ACATBLI's level |

[a]These were true as of July 2013.

The establishment of sustainable financing systems, while not the sole indicator of organizational sustainability, is still a critical element. Eade (1997) outlines a number of financial strategies, most of which are feasible in the Ifè situation. One is limiting administrative costs through ensuring only necessary use of equipment and services such as the telephone, and through keeping the paid staff as small as possible. Another is linked to budget creation, keeping the administrative budget and the program budget separate, but including an administrative overhead in all grant proposals. A third strategy is to generate enough income to cover administrative costs. It is important to note that Eade expects program activities to require outside funding.

So, both internal and external fund generation is important for long-term sustainability of these organizations. While it is unlikely that enough funds can be generated in the environment of the local economy to maintain current levels of service, a low level of service can be provided when an association has some activities that generate income. During the capacity-building seminar mentioned earlier, the ACATBLI leaders noted they were weak in generating funds internally through membership dues. However, over the years, various income-generating activities have been tried. The ACATBLI literacy team received training in sheep raising through a veterinarian on their board and in beekeeping through an SIL community development specialist. So for several years, projects for literacy activity support included bean and grain storage for resale and beekeeping for the sale of honey. In addition, the team was able to buy a plot of land in Oké and build a training center with a meeting room, six bedrooms, showers, and toilet facilities. When the literacy program is not using it, other organizations may rent it. Fruit trees have also been planted on this land and can be used to generate income through the sale of the fruit. They had had a sheep-raising project as well, but between problems with the area where the sheep were kept and with the hired shepherd, this IGA was discontinued. This diversification of IGAs provided a measure of protection against financial losses, which had happened from insect infestations, special government-imposed price controls on grains, fire, drought, and disease.

However, with the establishment of ACA (ACATBLI *coopérative agricole,* or ACATBLI Agricultural Cooperative) in 2010, all other IGAs except the renting of the training center and the growing of fruit and teak trees ceased. *Groupements* (as described in section 2.3) pay dues to ACATBLI, which provides a source of revenue for the project. In its first year of existence, through the training and follow-up of the proper times for hoeing and application of fertilizer, the *groupements* of ACA were able to double their usual yield, the net revenues of which were returned to the local farmer (ACA recovers its administration costs). ACA also helps members understand the procedures to obtain credit through cooperative credit agencies.

Internal funds for the local associations have two main sources: member dues and income-generating activities (IGAs), although sometimes board members put in their own personal funds to meet urgent needs. The associations benefit from development training given during teacher-training times and meetings to develop IGAs. However, three associations expressed a desire for further practical training in this area, especially in animal husbandry.

All of the associations have obtained, through purchase or gift, anywhere from one to five hectares of land. In 2008 funds were provided to purchase enough teak trees to plant one hectare in each zone (one for each association except ADCIBA, which has two zones). More recently, funds were obtained to plant an additional twenty-five hectares of teak and other commercially useful trees. This initiative gives all the associations a future source of income, as the teak can be harvested every five to twelve years. Although the longer harvesting can be put off, the greater the income realized will be. In addition, three associations have food storage projects to generate income, while another has a collective field. Other projects had been tried, including a micro-credit project, but they did not do well and were discontinued. Chicken-raising did not do well as a project for one association, but is working well for another.

Another possible source of funds is one common to many West African groups: the hometown or ethnic group association. My first experience with this type of association occurred during my orientation to living in Africa, when I lived in a Cameroonian village for three weeks. During that third week, current and former residents of that area met near the chief's compound for a day of speeches, feasting, and, most importantly, collecting donations that were then used to improve the area. Warren et al. (1996) note the importance of Nigerian hometown associations to development efforts. In the early years of the Ifè project, the Ifè association based in Lomé made a donation to the literacy work, which has from time to time been repeated. However, this potential source of funds has not been fully exploited.

One aspect of organizational capacity building that often does not receive much attention in the literature is the development of physical resources. Literacy supervisors and coordinators need some form of transportation to be able to reach all the classes for which they are responsible in a timely fashion. This need is being met in the Ifè community with motorcycles and bicycles, obtained through outside funding.

Another felt need of each local association is to have a building for offices, meetings, and training. A building gives a certain amount of credibility to an association, implying it has sufficient access to resources to be permanent and ensuring that people can find the officers. In addition, AMIADA's coordinator noted that the dormitory at the ACATBLI training center in Oké was too small to house the number of trainees at ACATBLI's sessions. However, many donors currently perceive construction more as a luxury than a necessity when it comes to organizational capacity building, although it can be appealing because it does not require a long-term commitment.

Office equipment is another area of felt need for some local associations; none owns a computer although one coordinator (now deceased) had been using his personal one for desktop publishing to benefit literacy work in his area. Given that in today's funding environment, donors expect electronic communication from their recipients, this appears to be a serious lack.

However, many aspects of useful physical infrastructure are outside the control of ACATBLI and the local associations. In chapter 2 the fact was noted that much of the Ifè area is not on the national electric grids. While most board members have cell phones, they are dependent on access to generators, batteries, or visits to towns that are on the national grids to keep them charged. Without access to an electricity grid, running a computer is problematic. Internet cafés now exist in most towns with regular electricity and phone lines, but frequent use is beyond the budget of most people in rural areas. The state of the roads continues to make travel difficult and maintenance of bicycles and motorcycles costly.

Like capacity building at the personnel level, much of the organizational capacity building that has occurred has taken place under the direction of people or organizations other than the Ifè and their associations. Nevertheless, the requests for capacity building show that representations of leadership still play a role in what is desired in this area. Foremost is competency in work; board members truly want to be able to carry out their responsibilities fully. Another is the need for literacy leaders to be creative in their ideas of how to sustain the organization and its activities; several participants said that they had ideas, but needed help from ACATBLI or others to develop or implement them. AMIADA's treasurer noted that this is an area that shows that they are developing well as an association, but noted also that they need more training.

B.3.MK 1h09m  If I may also add, it's that .. uh .. personally, we, the association, when we are going also, before, it's that our superiors are going to come to tell us do this .. to go .. supervise the instructors now to go do services have techniques the level xx who are going to

## 8.2 At the organizational level

> come lead us. Do this. Do this. So, at our level . now, we have, us too, ourselves we have ideas that .. that .. and these ideas aren't coming .. it's .. from from our .. superv={tongue click} from our superiors and ourselves who have ideas which already we are launching ahead and then doing things and the inst= the learners and the instructors see us MORE and they know that thus our association AMIADA it's that which is taking place, that which works, and then we .. we bring reports, things to know that so, also, there where we are in consequence, we are going to do some THING. Then we see well that there where we are now, it's good. What we LACK, it's that which we have already asked that to train again more more from there we are going to evolve.

The solidarity within each association is another area where representations of leadership play out. As relationships become ever stronger, these in turn strengthen the associations. One board member, when discussing solidarity in the association, used a proverb to indicate that it must be intentionally developed:

B.2.VA2 41m   Well, solidarity, well, as he said, and in fact it's us we don't do as they know us, well, they say, you must each time water the fruit and good or well, clean out .. hoe all around the fruit that= of the tree that is producing.

The leaders build their association's solidarity through caring for each other, ensuring good communication, and meeting regularly. This sense of solidarity increases as each feels responsible for the work and as all members see it bear fruit. These all relate to the representations of leadership described in chapter 6.

A final theme relating specifically to board leadership is having a spirit of cooperation. As noted above, the local associations have strong ties with ACATBLI and with each other. They cooperate with each other in various areas such as holding joint training sessions. However, this theme was not expressed by many groups, which may explain why only one group explicitly expressed a desire for cooperation with additional groups (outside of possible funders). This group desires to do so in order to fully carry out its vision of development.

The local associations do have control of a few areas of organizational capacity building. The most important is the development of each organization's vision and mission statements, which have been influenced by the representation of literacy as openness and development. The focus for each is slightly different, with some having more of an economic focus, others more of a social focus, and still others having a very holistic view of development. ADCIBA also has the challenge of representing the Ifè community to the national and regional governments of Benin. As the associations take on more responsibility in the process towards organizational autonomy, they will have increasing opportunities to exercise and develop their own leadership.

## 8.3 At the community level

Capacity building at the community level is generally concerned with equipping and empowering people, individually and collectively, to bring about the changes they desire to see in their communities (Eade and Williams 1995, quoted in Eade 1997; Imdieke 2003). It may also be seen as a means to bring about a more equitable society (Eade 1997) or to control the environment for the benefit of individuals and society (Edoho 1998). All this can be seen as leading to community development.

In the early 1990s the following three community felt needs among the Ifè were presented to the SIL team during its literacy awareness-raising campaigns: (1) health services and family planning, (2) small-scale businesses to make the Ifè less dependent on agriculture by diversifying their income, and (3) water supply in villages where it is inadequate. These are all still felt needs, so the various associations working in Ifè literacy seek to meet these needs, both directly and indirectly, through literacy and development activities, including mobilization and awareness raising. They also work to make the agricultural sector more productive. ACA was formed in response to a survey in 2010 that revealed that eighty percent of the Ifè population were involved in agriculture, but with low returns. While the local associations do not have the technical competences to intervene directly in many areas, they have been a catalyst for change in the Ifè area through literature production, teaching, and mobilization. As Carroll (1992; cited in Lewis 2001) indicates, this is one of the true evaluation indicators of the worth of the Ifè literacy program.

## 8.3 At the community level

In addition to the above means of community development, the ACATBLI literacy leaders are not infrequently asked to help with local problems. When that happens, their response is to work with the community to come up with solutions that the community can implement.

A.1.AgbA af2 40m   And what we do, often it's that, we see the problem together with them, and we give them approaches to solutions. And as we don't have any money, when they put it into practice, they can settle the problem.

Later on in the same interview, Mr. Agbémadon and Mr. Sétodji, both of ACATBLI, described a little more fully how community development most often occurs as a result of their encouragement, emphasizing how community members work together to solve their own problems.

A.2.AgbA 7m   All that is development. And: ..
A.2.SK ff.   of the community
A.2.AgbA ff.   of the community, we work in the community {laughs}. And, it's it's a work that is done *en masse,* not individually. So, uh . that means that, there are some villages, they have initiated . some= some mutual aids, five or six people meet, and they work in a group. And there are even former classes which become small mutual help groups.
A.2.SK ff.   That's right. .. Small mutual aid groups, like.
A.2.AgbA ff.   Mmm. So, it's of the community, because, THERE when there is the problem of water, they sit down together and together they discuss everyone discusses. Yes.

They are therefore following the best practices of organizations who work in community development, including participatory development strategies towards empowerment (Hope and Timmel 1995). In the process, they are also meeting Ifè expectations of leadership, showing they care by listening to all and coming to a consensus about what should be done.

The literacy leaders all identified numerous, wide-ranging impacts of the literacy program. The community development impacts most frequently noted (by six to nine individuals, some more than once) were increased agricultural production, which has meant both more to eat and more to sell; increased literacy rates; much greater openness to literacy and education with concurrent participation in nonformal and formal education; and an increase in the number of churches, along with spiritual growth by individual Christian believers as they read Scripture. Also often identified (by three to five participants) were better business practices, better familial relations, better health practices, greater attention to the ecology of the area, better quality of civic participation, growth in the number of leaders, increased access to (clean) water, and the increasing status of women. Other fruits of the program identified by some people were the formation of mutual aid groups, better relations between villages and between adherents to different faiths, more active political participation (in Benin), and increased openness to the outside world.

Income-generating activities that directly support the associations were discussed earlier, but there is also a thrust that has the more general goal of economic development in the villages. Small businessmen and -women benefit from the math lessons. However, most efforts focus primarily on the agricultural field, as they build on the knowledge and skills already present and require little to no new capital. The literacy materials used in the program include, for example, a book about a farmer who learned how best to manage his fields. This has improved the agricultural practices of many literacy teachers and graduates, leading to better yields. In addition, through teacher-training sessions and meetings during the literacy cycle, instruction is given on topics such as animal raising, preparing for old age, family management, and planning field work. When feasible, experts in these fields such as veterinarians are brought in. These meetings are open to the whole village. ACA now works with literacy classes to organize themselves into *groupements*. Not only does it provide training and demonstration fields in best agricultural practices, including organic farming, but it also uses the buying power of the cooperative to buy seed and fertilizer in bulk and to secure contracts for the harvest. It also has plans to provide village-level mills, wells, and solar panels.

Deforestation and access to water are both environmental issues in the Ifè area. As a result, program leaders decided to start a reforestation project in the early 1990s. They first educate literacy teachers on the need to plant trees both for food and for environmental benefits such as avoiding

## 8.3 At the community level

drought. The teachers pass this information on to their classes. ACATBLI personnel then take orders and money for seedlings and then buy and transport seedlings from the nurseries in the large towns to the villages (literacy teachers are given two seedlings). Many villagers are now earning some income from the sale of the fruit, and the deforestation rate has slowed. Meanwhile, communities are encouraged to do what is necessary to ask for governmental help to get wells and pumps for clean water that will be available throughout the year.

One of the most significant impacts of the Ifè program in community-level growth is in the openness to literacy and education, which has led to a growth in educational opportunities for Ifè children and youth. Several interviewees noted that as parents became literate, they became open to the idea of sending their children to school and began to actively support them in their studies.

B.2.VA1 18m  We recognize today, all has changed with ACATBLI who tries to give information, tries to give them information how to make them aware, they are going to pay all has changed. And especially the children today↑ . are more devoted to school than before. The rate of instruction in the formal schools has risen. And there are now schools that have been born recently nearly everywhere . in some villages, there are schools for children today, and the children try to go there. And the children today accept helping the children = and the parents accept today helping their children at school otherwise, before, he says no {claps hands}, that won't give us anything, the child only has to stay to go to the field. But now, they accept sending their children to school, they accept buying kerosene so that the children can learn at home. Because he has reached, certain parents have said to me, Aah pastor, I didn't know that it was (like) that! Before as my child failed at school, ooo {very high tone}, I took the stick. I say that he is lazy so when he returns from school, I say to him to do this do that I don't have him the time to learn. But even so, myself, I had been taught to read my language, I knew that, AH, if you don't learn at home, you can't succeed at school. So from now on, I will help my child to learn his lessons at the house in order for him to succeed. So, we have seen that, we are in the process we are on the right road . yes, in the Ifè region.

Both AVADI's coordinator above and AVID's president below noted that parents who send their children to school are making financial sacrifices, a point that is sometimes overlooked in the push for universal primary education. The financial investment goes beyond school fees, uniforms, and loss of help in the house and fields to such things as buying fuel for lamps and paying living expenses when youths must live in town to continue their studies.

B.1.NK af1 31m   So, this has made us say that, we have seen that, AH, people have now understood the GOOD of literacy because it does many things for them. First, for their own life, FOR the life of their children, and people ACCEPT now to send their children to school. Imagine. A woman, a woman let's say a peasant who is going to agree to bring her children here to town, and it's she herself who is going to carry the charcoal, food to bring to her child, before, the woman isn't going to do that! What will the child come to do with it. And she also suffers above all. Today it's the women themselves who really who are rallying together to look for places for their children at the school here.

Another area of impact in the community development arena is through raising the status of women and empowering them to take charge of various aspects of their lives. This is best seen in areas that have had Ifè literacy classes the longest. One way in which the literacy work increases the status of women is to encourage and accept them as literacy teachers. This in turn increases the participation and confidence of women in those classes. The visibility of Mrs. Agayi as a leader in the literacy program has also had an impact on the attitudes of women in her area.

B.1.AgA af1 37m   Now, we are proud, because our women also want to be like me too, go to the office {laughs} everywhere, everywhere,

*8.3 At the community level* 219

> they are interested .. and they too, are in the process of .. making an effort to get there. {laughter}

The president of her association made the point that it truly is her visibility that is influencing attitudes, including the acceptance of sending girls to school.

> B.1.NK af1 1h4m   Well, because . there is a change, first at the level . of the group of the base population . whom we teach literacy to. There is a change . {FA answers his cell phone} even at the level of individuals .. We spoke about how: people now really: . fight for the the the life of their children in the in the the the .. in the classical school. Whether it is girls or boys .. First, there we have really seen .. the advances that we have made. Among our instructors . there is now jostling. Menfolk fight now to be an instructor. Womenfolk fight to be an instructor. Because they knew that AH↑ women can also be instructors? Because we have seen our trainer, the supervi= . our supervisor. She is a woman like me but nevertheless she is the rider . of a bicycle, she is on the MOtorcycle↑, she came from my area I also can be one. So, already we have seen that, at least in part, we have these changes .. right.

However, few African women have leadership roles outside of women-only groups. Women in Africa have many household responsibilities, and often these take precedence over involvement in other activities. I assume this was the reason AVADI's treasurer, a woman who was expected for both interviews, did not arrive. Women who do not have the strong motivation like that of Mrs. Agayi, or who do not have the approval of their husbands are unlikely to take on leadership positions. Never-married women, however, may not have sufficient community standing to take on leadership positions. When asked why she had been chosen to be the coordinator, Mrs. Agayi, who is the sole female coordinator, said:

> B.1.AgA af1 15m   {chuckles} Because, in our association, there aren't any women, who have .. they who have their vision on literacy or working voluntarily like that. They look for what they're

going to eat today, we say, in our place, us women, but me, I seek the well-being of my brothers.

So although equality for women is often touted as a benefit of literacy, other, more profound attitudinal and cultural changes as well as economic improvement must take place before this is a reality among the Ifè, or for that matter, anywhere in sub-Saharan Africa.

Another impact identified several times during the interviews is improved relationships. The fact that some villages have shared literacy classes has helped them "sow peace" and resolve problems. The same improvement has been true for relations between Muslims and Christians. One of the supplementary reading books for the second year of the literacy program addresses family relationships. Numerous people credited this with improving the relationships within families, and even their own families.

C.3.SY 1h11m (interpreted) There is also another document which is called Ɔ̀nyaḍɔ̃ tsoko náàrìmáa dzɛnɛ̀ . that is how to manage a household. Lea = don't leave abandon her husband to other women et cetera how there should be harmony between the wife and her husband between the husband and his wife, how to avoid disorder, and he says that, on the basis of these documents, truly the households, or the life in the households are improved and there where there were difficulties, today there is harmony, there is love, there is development which has begun. So, this is how we have added a plus to the life of the Ifè people. {3 second pause with soft talking in background}

C.3.OKD ff. To add some more, xx this, on the basis of of the these documents, now, it has changed much in my life.. Before, I myself want that uh I just go around the wife. [others: hah] But as I became again an inst= became instructor now I have learned the I must have much patience, if the wife goes around now I look at her as if she doesn't know what she's saying. {others laugh softly} And so currently . in my life that that did a lot of things.

The literacy classes have enabled both men and women to improve the health of their families as well. For example, ADCIBA was able to publish

## 8.3 At the community level

some leaflets regarding infant nutrition that have helped mothers adjust their practices to better nourish their babies. Also, ACATBLI held a session during one teacher-training course on effective remedies using traditional medicine, and produced a booklet in conjunction with that, which has helped participants treat their own families for things like diarrhea without recourse to more expensive Western medicines. However, this is an area where capacities have much room to grow. AVADI's board in particular has this as a target area for community development, while AMIADA's officers would like to see the establishment of a health clinic in Oké, perhaps on their property so that people using the training center do not have to be transported to health centers in other locations when they fall sick. Easier access to reading and prescription glasses, which directly impacts literacy learners and neoliterates, and therefore the program, is an additional felt need.

Another area where the literacy program has influence is in the fostering of civic responsibility and an improved understanding of formal democratic practices. The Beninese, in particular, have worked on this area. One of ADCIBA's coordinators noted that a number of neoliterates have been elected to positions of responsibility in their communities. He went on to say that teachers, supervisors, and board members of ADCIBA have actively worked at helping class members understand their civic rights and responsibilities.

> B.4.ANA si2 13m {chuckle} So, thanks to that {literacy} also, we have understood that politics, democracy, is really becoming established. [JR: ahan] That is to say people have begun to understand we are getting there, it's an opportunity to explain to them more carefully what they need, their rights and responsibilities of citizenship like. So, they themselves also understand, even at the level of election day, what one shouldn't do what one should do, we're able to explain to them all these things.

One ADCIBA board member who became literate through the program gave an example of how politicians can improperly seek to influence others, and how the literacy program personnel were able to prevent that from happening during election time.

B.4.GÐ 39m  (interpreted) It's the remark seems that {before} people who hadn't ever set foot in school were not considered . in politics {recording gap} they wanted to make the choice for them {recording gap} of them but such sight .. when the people of authority sent certain people to be able to do certain things . they said to themselves but, these people they don't know anything, we can turn them any which way, but as the literacy workers, the coordinators and others they were really vigilant they had prepared the people in spite of the fact they hadn't had any formal schooling, they were prepared in such a way they you cannot get around them. So, they wanted to deviate towards these people who had only learned their mother tongue . maybe to fix them {to rig the elections}, but finally, they saw that they couldn't, they didn't succeed in their lies {?}.

Mr. Gudu goes on a little later to say that among new skills of neoliterates is the ability to analyze, at least somewhat, the claims of politicians.

The final area where community-level growth in capacity is experienced is in Christian churches. Although the program itself does not contain evangelistic elements, among the sixty or so books offered for sale at graduation ceremonies are the New Testament and other portions of the Bible. A number of people have become Christians after reading them and having had the chance to observe the conduct of the ACATBLI leaders and other Christian leaders in the program. This has led to the establishment of churches in communities that had never had them. In addition, believers who become literate have taken on leadership roles in their local churches.

Three representations of literacy held by program leaders have had a great impact on the community-level capacity building that has occurred through the Ifè program. The most evident is literacy as openness and development. This has guided all of the program's activities to increase the ability of the Ifè people to meet their needs economically, socially, and spiritually. The representation of mother tongue literacy as transmitting cultural knowledge is seen through the health lessons using traditional remedies, as well as in the reading material used in the literacy program, which frequently uses proverbs. Finally, literacy as full participation in society leads to the acceptance of any adult literate Ifè as a teacher in the program, not just men or people with schooling.

The impact of the literacy program in terms of social change has much to do with the degree to which Ifè representations of leadership are exemplified by the literacy leaders. In discussing factors significant to effecting change, Fullan (2003) identifies the importance of being able to trust leaders who are willing to listen to criticisms and are change agents themselves, and of the quality of knowledge being co-constructed and shared for the common good. The Ifè literacy leaders' relationships with their communities reveal faithfulness, patience, competence in the literacy domain and in management, willingness to listen and to work together with a group to find solutions, respect for others and especially traditional authorities, caring, and solidarity. They also live exemplary lives, avoiding adultery theft, arrogance, aggressiveness, drunkenness, fighting, and indebtedness. They have not only proven themselves trustworthy, but worked for the benefit of all Ifè.

## 8.4 Discussion

As the discussion of social representations in chapter 3 indicated, SRs are an interpretive framework, generated by and circulating in a group, for a social object (Py 2003). This framework not only helps a person recognize and interact with that object (Gajo 2000) but also motivates and influences the actions and attitudes of members of that group (Abric 2001; Py 2003). The literacy associations' decisions and practices related to capacity building are thus influenced, to varying degrees, by the representations of leadership and of literacy circulating among their members.

In examining the representations that have impacted capacity-building decisions, two have influenced decisions on all three levels discussed in this chapter: literacy as openness and development, and leadership as caring. The vision and mission statements of each association, as well as the associations' names, reflect the representation of literacy as openness and development. Literacy is not seen by these Ifè leaders as an end in and of itself: it leads to changed attitudes that open the door to transformation in the lives of individuals and of the community. These transformations include economic, social, and spiritual ones. Thus the monthly teachers' meetings, which are open to all community members, have become a site for practical, development-oriented lessons. Additionally, teacher-training workshops include health, agricultural, and animal husbandry topics, in addition to the expected ones concerning teaching and literacy skills.

The representation of leadership as caring has also affected capacity building in all areas. Caring enhances mentoring relationships, making that aspect of personnel training all the more effective, particularly in Africa where relationships are key to effective action (Lewis 2001; Littrell and Baguma 2005). It also is a way of building solidarity within each association as well as between the ACATBLI leaders and members of the local associations, from board officers to literacy center instructors. The caring demonstrated by Ifè literacy program leaders also is undoubtedly a factor in the acceptance of the program and its activities in local communities, which in turn has allowed the program to impact various aspects of community life that might otherwise have remained unchanged, such as attitudes towards schooling and the importance of reforestation.

Other representations have also influenced at least two areas of capacity building in the associations studied. Among these, themes found for representations of leadership in general are competence, patience, faithfulness, and living an exemplary life. These enhance capacity building both for personnel and in the community, as they facilitate the establishment of trusting relationships. These are essential for effective mentoring relationships among the Ifè and have been factors in the acceptance of the literacy work in communities that were traditionally closed to anyone not of their village.

Representations specifically pertinent to literacy leaders and boards that affect how capacities are developed include the willingness to learn and to teach, solidarity, creativity, and knowing the situation of one's subordinates. Willingness to learn encourages participation in workshops and the monthly teachers' meetings. Willingness to teach ensures staff for those workshops and mentors for new workers. Both this representation and that of literacy as openness and development motivate the opening of teachers' meetings to the whole community. Solidarity on the board as an element of organizational capacity was discussed above in connection with the theme of caring. Literacy leaders attribute creativity with helping them to have fresh ideas to strengthen the program and their association, making each more attractive to the local community even as these ideas aid in community development. Finally, knowing the

## 8.4 Discussion

situation of one's subordinates plays a role in the effectiveness of the mentorship relationship involved in teacher and supervisor training.

Three representations of literacy also play a role in capacity-building decisions on both the personnel and community levels. The representation of literacy as full participation in society ensures that participation in the literacy program—whether as a learner, a teacher, a supervisor, a coordinator, or a board member—is open to all community members, regardless of gender or religion, although in some associations, certain roles are open only to Ifè. This latter restriction seems to be linked to two other representations, that of mother tongue literacy as preservation and transmission of the culture and identity, and that of Ifè literacy as language maintenance and development. The literacy program works to promote the value of the language and culture, working towards the development and maintenance of literacy skills in Ifè both for those who cannot read or write in any language as well as for those literate in French. Another outworking of this last representation is the use of Ifè during all workshops and meetings, whether for teacher-training, board meetings, literacy awareness-raising, or practical teachings for the community.

As has been seen above, representations of leadership and of literacy have played an important role in shaping the Ifè literacy program, through the choices of goals, strategies, and activities, and through the development of relationships that strengthen the associations. The final research question to answer is what factors in the representations themselves, in the decisions and actions taken, or in the interplay between representations and decisions, have promoted local association development in such a way as will permit them to achieve the ACATBLI literacy team's vision of all Ifè being able to read and write their own language.

One important factor in local association development has been the involvement of highly motivated people. For various reasons, these leaders have chosen to invest their time, energy, and even personal financial resources in order to meet the goals of their associations. Many of these reasons relate to SRs of literacy, although spiritual reasons are key for some individuals. As Edoho (1998:251) observes, "The acid test of effective leadership is the ability…to mobilize ordinary people to accomplish extraordinary goals." The ACATBLI leadership has been able to mobilize the Ifè population to accept the value of literacy and education; to stimulate the formation of local associations to develop the work of literacy and development in their zones; and to inspire individuals to volunteer their time, energy, and ideas in order to help others. These leaders have been able to attract others, now leaders in the local associations, who have the same passion for their people and are willing to work towards the common goal of the promotion of the Ifè people and language, whether in Togo or in Benin. Thus, the leadership of the Ifè program meets Edoho's acid test for effective leadership, which is the most significant management component of Nkasa and Chapman's (2006) model for sustainability.

However, one aspect of sustainable leadership, brought up by AMIADA's president, is the matter of succession. He worked on transferring his skills and knowledge to ensure a successor and was able to step away from the role of president a few years after these interviews were done, although he continues in the role of association literacy coordinator. AVID has already undergone a major change in leadership three times. One of ADCIBA's dynamic leaders passed away after I did the initial research for this project, requiring the organization to find another coordinator and board treasurer. ACATBLI, however, has not yet had to face this issue. While the ACATBLI literacy leadership is a strong, complementary team with a tremendous amount of collective knowledge, skills, and passion, if any member of this team were suddenly to be no longer available, no obvious successor exists to fill that team spot. In addition, SIL and ACATBLI had to request that the church denomination of which two coordinators are pastors forego transferring them for several more years, as without their presence during the early stage of their associations' development, these associations would have surely failed. So attention to leadership development, including preparation for succession, is another factor to consider in ensuring the development of sustainable local associations.

Other management components are also in place, in most instances. These relate to the representation of leaders not dictating to the group they lead, but instead listening to all group members when decisions must be made. ACATBLI's board officers engage in yearly planning and self-evaluation with input from the representatives of the local associations. They then report to members on plans and activities during their annual general assembly. The planning completed to this point by the boards of the local associations, on the other hand, is generally informal. They report on their activities, however, to their general assemblies, which take place more

## 8.4 Discussion

or less on an annual basis. The Ifè culture itself values participatory decision-making, so that is a feature of the governance of all the associations.

Another major factor in local association development is the attention to financial considerations. All internally generated income is useful for ensuring continued, if limited, service to the community, in case external funding is slow in coming (as sometimes happens when financial calendars are different between organizations) or ceases. This happened to AVID in the late 1990s (see section 2.2.1). Because it only had one IGA at the time DED's support finished, when that IGA failed in a subsequent year, all activity ceased for a time. The attention ACATBLI gave during its first twenty years of existence to establishing a variety of income-generating projects in order to overcome this limitation is a model, therefore, for the local associations and is related to the literacy leadership theme of creativity. The teak plantation project, in addition to the grain storage projects already in place, should strengthen the resource base of the local associations, although the ideas some have for additional IGAs, if implemented, will provide extra insurance against failure in any one project.

However, as in most service-oriented work, external funding will likely be a constant need (Eade 1997). Thus capacity building in the area of writing grant applications and building relationships with current and potential donors is a significant need and is an expressed felt need of several of the associations' board members interviewed during this research project. The existence of, and relationships with, hometown associations is also a factor to consider when seeking funds for projects.

One major favorable factor in the development of the local literacy and development associations is the program's attention to the felt needs of the population. The program's content and activities have evolved, as needed, to encourage those unable to read and write to participate in the program as well as to meet physical needs, such as for nearby access to water, the lack of which may be hindering those with the desire to learn from attending class. Additionally, the program has put time into the creation of new literature, which both gives the newly literate something to read and provides a reason for those who cannot read their language to invest the time needed to learn to do so.

Other factors may hinder the development of sustainable local associations, however. Nkasa and Chapman's (2006) model for sustainable projects includes the sociocultural elements of social cohesion, community skills, resources (both economic and skill-based), and a strong value for education. The strength of these varies from association to association. As has been noted several times earlier, the literacy associations have actively sought to make the program a force for social cohesion by focusing on the language and ethnic identity. Furthermore, education is becoming a high value for the Ifè through the work of the program. However, several indicators of the acceptance of literacy as a community value, such as a literate environment and the establishment of literate practices beyond the church context, are weak or lacking, which indicate further need for growth in these areas. Community skills and resources are also areas in which growth is still needed, as was discussed earlier in this chapter.

Infrastructure is a factor that may help or hinder the development of multiple local literacy and development organizations. The leaders of the umbrella organization and the local associations need to be able to contact each other. The growing number of cell towers and the increased availability of cell phones in Togo and Benin have facilitated this communication for the Ifè project. However, without regular, reliable, or affordable Internet connections, those associations located in communities without such access are hindered from communicating with donors who insist on this rapid form of written contact.

Factors that seem to be essential in the development of local literacy associations are committed leadership that exercises authority and makes decisions in ways congruent with local representations of leadership, attention to issues of leadership succession, acceptance by the community of the value of education, and social cohesion or solidarity. Other factors that may help or hinder the development of sustainable local literacy associations include the degree to which community needs are met through the association's activities, the amount and content of reading material available, the existing literacy practices in the community, and infrastructure availability. However, the development of multiple local associations and concurrent capacity building takes time; it has taken the Ifè program over twenty years to reach this point in its personnel, its organizations, and its communities. So regardless of the presence of the above favorable or unfavorable factors in a given situation, a time frame that ensures the adequate mentoring of the leadership for each new association as well as the time to discover, develop, and establish locally viable income-generating activities is of primary importance.

In the case of the Ifè, what has already been done in organizational and personnel capacity building should permit literacy efforts among the Ifè to continue, given the committed leadership in each association, and assuming the attention to a variety of income-generating activities as well as the development of long-term financial partners. The continuation of the program will in turn promote economic and social improvements to the benefit of the Ifè people and of their neighbors, as well as the preservation and development of the Ife language and culture.

## For further reading

Leduc, R. F., and T. W. McAdam. 1988. The development of useful curricula for nonprofit management. In M. O'Neill and D. R. Yount (eds.), *Educating managers of nonprofit organizations,* 95–100. New York: Praeger.

# 9

# Conclusion

In my years of working in Central and West Africa, I have interacted with the leaders of at least twenty-five different literacy programs. A common challenge of large or widely dispersed language groups is providing access to mother tongue and/or transition literacy instruction to all speakers of the language without excessive—and unsustainable—dependence on outside funding. My initial motivation for undertaking this case study therefore was the hope that a clearer, more complete understanding of the Ifè literacy program's strategy of creating local associations to carry on the work of literacy and development might help other West African literacy programs develop similar strategies tailored for their particular situations.

My initial hypothesis was that the key to the success of the Ifè strategy would be found in the leadership and that therefore, a study of the social representations of leadership found among the Ifè would be beneficial for understanding how they work. As an adjunct to that facet of the study, theories of leadership were explored for what they might contribute to an understanding of the dynamics of leadership in the local associations. In addition, since the associations are engaged in literacy and development activities, theories in these domains informed my research.

The bulk of my data came from a series of interviews with the representatives of the boards of the umbrella association and its daughter associations. However, I also had access to the project archives, which facilitated the construction of the rich description of the Ifè literacy program necessary to case studies. I examined the history of the program and each association, in the process also looking at how each organization functions. My expectation was that knowing these things would help my organization, an international development NGO, better tailor its training programs and technical support for national literacy personnel and their programs. During the process of data analysis, I realized that the question of motivation was also extremely important, which is true for all organizations that rely on volunteers. Representations of illiteracy, literacy, and language seem to be the primary source of motivation for the people interviewed. I came to appreciate the importance these representations also have in the decision-making of program leadership vis-à-vis program activities and emphases.

However, due to a massive influx of external funding a few years prior to my visit, the original strategy of developing one local association at a time had been abandoned by the time of my arrival in Togo to carry out the research. This was not recognized, even by the ACATBLI literacy officers, until my first interview with them. The goal is still to have local associations carry out the bulk of the work. Now, however, regardless of their stage of development, all the associations have been put on the same footing. While this makes my original evaluation plan impossible to carry out, the situation did reveal other aspects of the management and leadership of large literacy (and development) programs dependent on external funding that may help guide other programs.

In this final chapter, the answers to the research questions will be summarized. Next, contributions to theory will be summarized, and several implications for policy and practice will be highlighted. Limitations of the study will then be described. After that, directions for future research will be indicated before my closing comments.

## 9.1 Summary of findings

The main thrust of the research questions was to determine, first, what representations of leadership and literacy circulate among the Ifè; second, to determine what types of capacity building have occurred in and through the literacy program and, according to participants, what types still need to happen; and finally, to determine the impact those representations have had on capacity building in the Ifè literacy program. These findings will have implications for theoretical development and lead to suggestions for policy and practice.

### 9.1.1 Representations of leadership

A significant degree of convergence was found in the representations of general leadership that emerged in the interviews. For the Ifè, it is essential that leaders be patient and faithful to their group and their work. They must listen well, receive all that is said and then be capable of synthesizing what is said in order for the group to make a decision together, but they must never dictate what should be done. This, along with other aspects of group management, is part of the competence leaders are expected to display. This competence should also be seen in how they manage their household. Leaders must also be model citizens, exemplifying the values of Ifè society. Most Ifè interviewed also want their leaders to care about everyone and to be humble and available. Some Ifè also expect their leaders to be forgiving and serious about their work. Finally, in view of current societal needs, many believe leaders should be literate.

Literacy program leaders should manifest all of the above characteristics while also possessing other qualities necessary for the effective achievement of the program goals. The most important one is creativity, which is needed for all those with program responsibilities *(responsables d'alphabétisation)* as well as for literacy association board members, in order to overcome the challenges encountered.

Representations for literacy program heads—coordinators and supervisors—do not seem to be socially shared, implying that a *responsable d'alphabétisation* is not (yet) a social object. A few characteristics were nonetheless shared between groups. For instance, literacy program heads are expected to be respectful both of time and of work in order to build trust between themselves, subordinates, and students. They also should be teachable and be able to teach, as they are both participants in and providers of continuing education, as well as developers of future leaders. Two other qualities listed pertain to relationships: a cooperative spirit and awareness of the personalities of one's followers. A final one is a willingness to sacrifice even one's personal funds for the good of the program.

Board members also are expected to have the characteristics listed above for all leaders. In addition to these and creativity, three other qualities were specifically listed by more than one group for a board. Foremost is solidarity, a common value in sub-Saharan Africa. Possession of this quality helps a board to be well regarded in the community and be able to function smoothly. Discretion, likewise, is important for the reputation and effective operation of the board. A final quality valued in boards is deliberation in making decisions, as this prevents hasty reactions that would damage relationships unnecessarily.

The representations of subordinates also offer insights into leadership, as a leader cannot exist without followers. In these interviews, a subordinate was generally understood to be a person immediately under the authority of a leader, thereby putting him or her in the role of a mediator between the leader and the larger group. This requires that the relationship between the two be close: the subordinate must be attached to the leader, obedient, respectful, and listening closely to him or her. The resulting understanding generally promotes harmony and a collaborative relationship. It also facilitates the subordinate's role as a mediator, reporting to the leader on the activities and on the thinking of the group, and reporting to the group on the activities and plans of the leader. As a subordinate exemplifies these qualities, projects will advance. However, some participants stressed that the leader must be willing to share with and teach his or her subordinates in order for these qualities to develop or to be maintained.

### 9.1.2 Representations of literacy, illiterates, and language

The representations of literacy, illiterates, and the language of literacy held by literacy workers also are significant to the leadership of the literacy associations, providing these workers at all levels with the motivation needed to commit to the program regardless of whether or not remuneration occurs. Many of these representations are formed through personal experience, although some are also circulated through the media.

Links between literacy and development were seen in many of the representations that emerged during the interviews. Literacy is seen as creating an attitude of openness that permits development, whether economic, social, cultural, or spiritual; as a correlation, illiterates are perceived as blocks to development. They are presumed to be living in darkness and ignorance. Literacy is assumed to free them from this bondage and the distrust it generates, and permit full participation in society. One aspect of this participation is that certain roles in the community are now open primarily, if not exclusively, to the literate. This includes some roles, including leadership positions, that in the past did not require competence in text literacy.

Acquisition of mother tongue literacy is perceived to be important for all Ifè. First, mother tongue literacy is seen to promote the maintenance and development of the Ifè language. Second, it is viewed as encouraging the preservation and transmission of the Ifè cultural heritage. It also allows communication between Ifè living away from their hometown and their families still in the area. Those Ifè who know French well are urged by the interview participants to learn to read and write their own language in order to be able to translate works that will help their rural brethren develop, thereby fulfilling their responsibility to their people and demonstrating their solidarity with them. Biliteracy is also deemed helpful for improving the work of interpreters, so that they can maintain a good standing in the community and communicate the original message more accurately.

French in both its oral and written forms is considered to be a much more difficult language to learn than Ifè. Ifè is seen by research participants to be far more comprehensible, even among those Ifè who speak French fairly well. The use of French in the villages reinforces feelings of mistrust and insecurity among the non-schooled population. However, since it is a prestigious language and practical for use outside the language area, many people are motivated to learn it. Literacy is thus also seen as access to another language, whether one's own mother tongue for those literate in French, or a language spoken in the region, whether French or Éwé.

One association also regards literacy in Ifè as a prerequisite to participation in some aspects of the program. They have used it to reserve paid positions in the development activities for Ifè program graduates, such as those of beekeeper and shepherd. Also, it only allows those who can produce their diplomas for Cycle 2 classes to enroll in the French course. These conditions to program participation provide motivation to villagers who otherwise see no reason to invest time and money in learning to read Ifè, as well as creating a visible link between literacy and development.

### 9.1.3 Capacity building and representations

Capacity building in the Ifè program occurs at three levels: personnel, organizational, and community. Representations of leadership and of literacy influence many of the choices made at each level. Competence is a common theme to all areas, as training in the program has sought to develop competence in the literacy, management, and development domains.

Qualities important to the development and maintenance of relationships, such as patience, faithfulness, caring, and an exemplary life, also influence capacity building at all levels. Training of personnel occurs both in workshops and through mentoring. This last, to be effective, requires that leaders have good relationships with those whom they are mentoring.

These relational qualities are also of primary importance in the building of organizational and community solidarity. Organizational solidarity is important for the healthy functioning of the board. The building of community solidarity helps to validate the leaders and program in the eyes of the Ifè community. As this solidarity is built, trust develops. It is this trust that has allowed the program to enter individual villages formerly reluctant to permit it access, and, as attitudes are changed and skills developed, to have the desired impact. Other representations of leadership that facilitate the building of trust between Ifè literacy program leaders and local communities are respect, and a willingness to listen and to work with others to find workable solutions to problems faced by the group.

## 9.1 Summary of findings

The representation that leaders should be literate leads trainers to include time during training sessions for participants to build reading fluency. Supervisors and teachers, although not the primary decision-makers in the program, are seen as community leaders and future program leaders. The representation that literacy leaders must be teachable and be able to teach supports all the training that occurs in and through the program, whether in literacy classes, at teacher-training workshops, at writers' workshops, or during the practical lessons given at teachers' meetings, which are open to the community.

Finally, the theme of creativity is seen as a key component of leadership in organizational capacity building. This is needed for all literacy program leaders as they seek to develop strategies to carry out their association's vision. It also helps them adjust to changing realities in their environment. Most importantly, this quality assists them in finding ways to motivate illiterates to learn to read and write their own language, as well as to keep new literates motivated to build on their skills.

Although representations of leadership affect the effectiveness of the associations, capacity-building choices seem to have been impacted more obviously by representations of literacy. In the area of organizational capacity building, the representation of literacy as openness and development affected the development of each association's vision and mission statements: each chose a focus that was broader than literacy per se, encompassing economic, social, cultural, and/or spiritual development.

This representation of literacy as openness and development has also influenced the strategies and activities chosen at personnel and community levels. For instance, explicit training in agricultural and health topics is offered both to teacher trainees and to community groups during teacher meetings. The program's reforestation efforts are also undertaken largely because of this representation, although the scarcity of water during the long dry season has also played a role in this particular decision. The representation of literacy as openness and development has also affected the topic choice of several writers' workshops where the focus was on translating or adapting religious and/or development literature.

Writers' workshops are one of the ways in which the representation of mother tongue literacy as a means to maintain and develop the language is manifested. This representation is also shown in the use of Ifè in all training and meetings hosted by ACATBLI and its daughter associations. In using Ifè at such events, the associations also demonstrate another representation of mother tongue literacy, that of its preserving and transmitting Ifè culture and identity. This representation has led to the use of cultural material such as proverbs in reading books, and to the teaching of traditional herbal remedies during teacher-training sessions, which is then passed on to literacy students.

Literacy is also viewed as providing access to other languages. Those who become literate first in their mother tongue often desire to learn to read and write a more socially and economically advantageous language. In fact, a number of testimonies have emerged over the course of the program of new literates figuring out how to read Éwé and/or French on their own. This representation of literacy as access to other languages has caused the program to offer a course to their graduates that, building on the literacy skills in Ifè already acquired, teaches French, oral and written.

Meanwhile, Ifè already literate in French are periodically offered a class that would help them transition to reading and writing Ifè. Besides being linked to the representation of literacy as providing access to additional languages, this class offering reveals the representation of mother tongue literacy as preservation and transmission of culture and of identity. It also builds on the representation of biliterates having a responsibility to help develop those who do not have access to materials written in global languages such as French or English.

The final representation of literacy that has had an impact on capacity building and other decisions in the program is that of literacy as full participation in society. Participants noted a number of community leadership roles that new literates have taken. These include leadership roles in the literacy program itself, which are open to all literate Ifè, including women. Other roles include elected community positions and church positions.

## 9.2 Contributions to theory

This study used the theory of *représentations sociales* in order to study representations of leadership and of literacy among the Ifè. This theory, not yet well known outside of francophone academic circles, has the potential to provide useful insights to researchers seeking to develop or refine theories of leadership and literacy. Social representations are specific to a social group and object, being constructed in and studied through discourse (Moore and Py 2008). Although this theory has been used in the field of formal education, to my knowledge, this is the first time this theory has been applied to a study of leadership or of literacy as conceived by leaders of a nonformal education program. It certainly has never been applied before to this particular social group. This study is also one of the few available in English that are based on this theory.

Leadership theories were also discussed in this project. Current theories of leadership are based primarily on Western institutions, with some input from Asian and African business leadership studies (Blunt and Jones 1997; Dym and Hutson 2005). This study provides valuable data for those theoreticians desiring to develop a theory of leadership useful across cultures and outside the business environment, giving as it does information on representations of leadership and followership in nonprofit organizations in a little-studied West African group. It should also enrich theories that examine traits and skills, as these figure prominently in Ifè representations of leadership, particularly as some qualities prized by the Ifè, such as patience and faithfulness, do not figure in lists developed through the study of Western leaders. This project also reveals many situational constraints common to literacy organizations serving minority groups, and thus may help theoreticians working on contingency theories to account for such constraints in their models more adequately. Since contingency theories also consider the needs and characteristics of subordinates (Dym and Hutson 2005; Northouse 2007), the information on representations of subordinates in this group may also prove valuable.

However, most, if not all, theories of leadership fail to take into account one of the most important dynamics of nonprofit leadership: the relationship to stakeholders. Stakeholders include employees, volunteers, the governing body, clients or beneficiaries, funders, technical advisors, and even governments. This case study, with its descriptions of problems faced and solved by local associations (see section 6.1.1), of the impact of massive outside funding on a program that had been running for well over a decade, of the effect of inadequate rural infrastructure, and of the influence of government policy on primer content, provides data that may assist in the development of such a theory component.

As noted in section 5.1.3, the theory of social representations has much in common with the view of literacy as social practice prevalent in situated literacy theory. This case study supports Cheffy's (2006) contention in his study of literacy in rural Cameroon that situated literacy studies should go beyond social practices to examine conceptions of literacy because of their power to motivate and influence. It is this power to explicate that interpretive framework, which motivates and influences actions and attitudes, that makes SRs so valuable to the study of literacy in its social context, as has been seen in this study linking representations of literacy to aspects of capacity building in the Ifè literacy program.

This study may also be helpful as researchers theorize the relationship between literacy and development. The Ifè literacy work has incorporated development activities since the early years of the program, which has facilitated its access to communities traditionally closed to outsiders, including Ifè from different areas. In addition, the literacy program has been a catalyst for opening the Ifè community to accept, or at least to consider, new ideas and ways of doing things. This project and its impacts as perceived by program leaders support the view that the relationship between the two is recursive, with activities in literacy supporting development efforts and development activities providing uses for literacy.

Finally, the theory of investment (Norton 1997, 2000) seems to have been primarily applied to language learners, including those acquiring a specific type of literacy (Angélil-Carter 1997), in order to explain their relationship to the target language. Although to apply it fully to the context of literacy workers would have required additional, personal interviews, it seems to have relevance in this context as well. Substituting 'literacy worker' for '(language) learner' and 'literacy acquisition and literacy work' for 'target language' in Norton's explanation of this notion yields, "The construct of investment conceives of the [literacy worker] as having a complex history and multiple desires. An investment in [literacy acquisition and literacy work] is also an investment in a [worker's] own social identity, which changes across time and space" (Norton 1997:411). This extension of the theory may prove useful to other researchers seeking to understand motivational forces for those working in volunteer and other organizations.

## 9.3 Implications and recommendations

Various implications and recommendations may be drawn from this study. This section will discuss in turn implications and recommendations for the Ifè

## 9.3 Implications and recommendations

program and its associations; for other literacy programs attempting to serve a large, dispersed population; for partners; and for government policy makers.

### 9.3.1 Recommendations for associations of the Ifè program

This literacy program has been blessed by having many dynamic, passionate leaders committed to the development of their people and willing to work as a group, in solidarity, to achieve their goals. It has helped that the program has had the means to provide benefits to their teachers, supervisors, and coordinators through development training and small remuneration amounts at various times, which contribute to the motivation of these volunteers. Additionally, the Ifè literacy program's training strategy is a strength, meeting the needs of relationship development and of personnel development.

The diversity of ACATBLI's income-generating activities has been another strong point. With the creation of ACA, this diversity has been greatly reduced. It would be wise, however, for the local associations to add activities to reduce dependence on outside funding and to hedge against changes in the markets and government controls that periodically affect agriculture-based IGAs. However, external funding will be needed for some time to come in order to maintain the current level of service. Thus, if possible, several leaders across the local associations should receive training in grant-writing and be mentored through the process.

All the associations, the umbrella association included, would benefit from stronger relationships with the Ifè who have left the rural areas and joined the educated cadre of their respective countries, whether they are professionals or civil servants. This group has the potential to be a resource of both financial and technical aid. All the associations also ought to strengthen their ties with the ministries attending to adult literacy in their areas as well as with NGOs with complementary interests, even becoming active partners with them in service provision as the occasion arises.

A final recommendation for the Ifè program is in the area of leadership succession. This issue should be addressed by those associations that are currently dependent on only one or two strong personalities. It is one that is made easier when a large pool of leadership candidates is available, so these associations should also examine how they might expand their membership bases.

## 9.3.2 Implications of lessons learned for other literacy programs

In order to determine the usefulness of the zone strategy for other large language communities desiring to provide literacy access to all adults, several factors must be considered. It seems that the foremost factor is not the strategy per se, but the involvement of creative, motivated personnel, willing to invest substantial time and effort for uncertain financial rewards, who also fit their own culture's definition of good leaders. These people will need to be found and trained for each area where a local association is needed to carry out the literacy work. Attention should also be given to the factors that will encourage them to invest themselves in the association, in order to ensure the continuation of their involvement. Also, decision-making procedures must be put into place that are congruent with the local culture's norms of governance.

Financial considerations must be taken into account. While small funding projects are beneficial for limited purposes, a donor organization which will commit to paying, at a minimum, salaries and transportation costs for the umbrella organization's leaders over several years until a stable source of internally generated funds has been established, appears to be crucial to the establishment of literacy work throughout the language area. However, a careful assessment of potential donors' priorities and reporting and other requirements should be made to ensure that these mesh with the current needs and priorities of the program and with the capabilities and energy levels of the program leaders.

The search for viable income-generating activities ought to begin early and be on-going, regularly providing opportunities for participation in these projects by local community members. Two significant reasons for having multiple IGAs exist. The first is to spread the risk; in case of financial loss due to environmental catastrophes or other causes for one activity, income may still be generated by the others. The second is to increase the income-earning potential for local people who learn from the example of and through participation in these activities. However, these IGAs generally will require a certain amount of seed money, or initial capital; thus someone associated with the program will need to learn early on how to approach potential partners, whether members of their ethnic group's elite, national organizations, or international organisms.

Both leadership development and funds development require significant amounts of time to make the progress necessary to sustainability. Therefore, programs seeking to develop multiple local associations should plan to spend several years, not just three or four, in establishing these associations. This is particularly important for financial stability, as rarely can several locally viable income-generating activities be started at once, and successful procurement of external funds is never certain.

One factor that is generally outside the control of the local people but that needs to be considered when determining program strategies is the infrastructure available, from roads to telecommunications. Poor roads and communication services may make a multiple association strategy very attractive, but also require stronger, well-trained local association leadership from the outset, as local leaders may need to act independently more quickly. An umbrella association located in a town with e-mail and Internet access may need to be the primary seeker of external funding if the communities where the local associations are headquartered do not have this access, at least until such services become available in or near those communities.

Finally, capacity for literacy includes the generation of a literate environment. It has frequently been said during education and literacy conferences and courses that in order to want to learn to read, there must be materials for a person to read. The Ifè program has an uneven track record in this area, but with the publication and distribution of the New Testament in 2009, in addition to the booklets and leaflets on various topics that have been produced through the years, interest in learning to read Ifè has increased dramatically. Any literacy program desiring to inspire its target population with the desire for mother tongue literacy therefore should consider literature production to be an integral part of the overall program and strategy, and encourage the use of this literature in multiple community institutions, such as health centers, churches, and where government policy permits it, schools.

### 9.3.3 Recommendations for external partner organizations

As noted in chapter 5, partnerships carry risks. In order to reduce the risks for the local associations, their partners should endeavor to give priority to local concerns where possible, letting the local partners lead. During decision-making, the weight of the local associations' primary concerns should influence the priorities of the external partners, even when the former are not on the radar of the international community. International partners in particular ought to be prepared to adjust their expectations of what ought to happen and how long it should take. They should communicate regularly, not just in order to receive progress reports, but so that they may listen and learn from their field partners. Among things the local partners may reveal are changes in the environment of the program, unexpected obstacles, and negative as well as positive side effects of the programs. Open, regular communication facilitates adjustments to the partnership parameters, which should improve relationships and offer additional security to the local associations, assuming the external partner has made a long term commitment. These parameters should include appropriate follow-up to initial activities. As the ADCIBA coordinators noted, without proper support to sustain learning, outside NGOs are essentially throwing their money away (see section 7.1.4 for the complete discourse reguarding this point).

In addition, financial partners should be aware of the workload their expectations are putting on the local actors and particularly the program leaders, remembering that communities also have time- and energy-consuming expectations of these same people. In the Ifè program, for example, the ACATBLI leaders frequently are requested for help in acquiring official documents such as birth certificates, or for help in setting up bank accounts. They spend time and energy meeting these requests because elements of the Ifè representation of leadership, specifically caring and solidarity, require that they do so. So, if yearly goals are frequently not met, this might be an indicator that cultural leadership requirements are overriding donor requirements. In this situation, it may be prudent to consider either providing for the salary of another part- or full-time worker, or eliminating certain goal(s) from the plan.

Another area of capacity building that is often inadequate is in the area of funding development. Most nonprofit organizations, even in financially wealthy countries, require some level of external funding. Organizations that partner with local associations in developing countries should provide training for these leaders to assist them to discover and to develop ties to additional organizations that have the resources necessary to make progress towards the vision of their associations. Additional strengthening in the area of financial training to international standards is also helpful. This is particularly useful in sub-Saharan Africa where cultural norms are often contrary to those standards (Maranz 2001), creating conflict for leaders and a need for strategies and tools that can help them resolve this conflict.

Finally, partner organizations involved in providing leadership training should be sensitive to local conceptions of what constitutes good leadership. This may mean doing a preliminary survey of representations before beginning a course, to decide how the underlying theory can be adapted to the situation. Alternatively, trainers may design a course that leads participants to identify those representations, to decide how to maximize their strengths in and develop other competencies of leadership and then to discern how to apply them in their particular context.

### 9.3.4 Recommendations for government policy makers

Economic and social development has been a goal of most, if not all, governments in sub-Saharan Africa. However, as one of the ADCIBA literacy coordinators interviewed said, if a government truly wants an equitable and rational development for the benefit of all its citizens, it needs to think about literacy. Policies that support mother tongue literacy and education facilitate the involvement of all citizens in education and development initiatives, which may make them better citizens. Additionally, policies and funds that promote the creation and maintenance of rural infrastructure would aid the work of both government and private or community literacy and development workers. In particular, attention to road building and maintenance, and extension of access to national electric grids and of telecommunications would be of great help to those working to improve the standard of living, access to markets. and access to information of rural populations. Policy makers who are able to promote these objectives would be rendering a great service to their country.

## 9.4 Limitations of the research

While my relationships with several of the program leaders and my background knowledge of the linguistic and environmental situation in Togo and Benin proved to be major strengths, a number of constraints affected what I was able to accomplish during this research project. Foremost was my lack of Ifè language skills. These added a filter that affected communication. On-the-spot interpretation, for instance, often missed nuances and occasionally even content that transcriptions and written translations revealed. However, due to the limited amount of time that I had in the language area and that my translator had available to work on transcription, a significant portion of discourses in Ifè were neither transcribed nor translated. Some were, however, verbally reinterpreted and noted after he and I listened to the recordings together. The lack of complete fluency in French on my part and on the part of most participants also at times hindered communication and may have affected analysis.

Another limitation of the research was the small size of its comparison group and the lack of female participants. Finances and time were the primary constraints here. It would have been better if I could have had access to additional villagers or other Ifè speakers, preferably including several who were not involved in the literacy program. The research proposal had however only called for one such comparison group, and the time necessary to gain approval from my university's ethics committee for a modification made such an addition unfeasible. Additionally, I was paying a gratuity to the research participants and had neither budgeted for such an increase, nor for the amount needed to pay for transportation to another site outside of Atakpamé. I would have had access to a larger group of teacher participants had I learned that my proposal had obtained the ethics committee's approval just after my arrival in Atakpamé. That would not, however, have provided me with any participants with no program responsibilities, such as I had in Itséré.

Finally, although the Ifè live in both Togo and Benin, all research took place in Togo, again for time and financial reasons. In order to travel to Benin, I would first have needed a visa for that country, which would have required travel to Lomé, a minimum two-day stay there, and the payment of a fee. Then the practical difficulties of travel to Doumé or Tchetti would have arisen; there are no direct taxis between Atakpamé and the Savalou Region, and renting a taxi would have been prohibitively costly. So instead, the ACATBLI leaders suggested (and I agreed) to ask the ADCIBA board members to meet me at a point more or less halfway between us in Togo, which they did. I had visited Doumé in 2003, though, so felt I had some knowledge of the area and situation of the Ifè there. However, it would have been potentially enlightening to have had a separate control group of Beninese as part of the research project.

## 9.5 Directions for further research

In this final section, I will address areas in which further research would be helpful to theoreticians of leadership and of literacy, and to literacy practitioners. These include research among the Ifè on aspects of leadership and literacy, and research among other groups of West Africa on social representations of leadership.

As was discussed in the chapters concerning representations of leadership and literacy, certain facets of these were not explored, as they required a larger sample than was available to me given the circumstances of my time in Togo. The first aspect to explore are the apparent differences between men and women in the representations of leadership. Were these differences anomalous or would they hold up with a larger sample, particularly if women in leadership positions as well as those who are not were interviewed?

Another area noted was that certain leadership themes seem to have much in common with those promoted in Christianity. A second research project that ensures representative participation of all three major religious persuasions found in the area could shed light on whether Christianity has influenced these representations or whether they have deep roots in Ifè culture in general.

Research on representations of leadership in other ethnolinguistic groups of Africa would also contribute to knowledge and practice. Research projects of this type would provide additional information to those seeking to develop models of leadership applicable to Africa, which would potentially be more useful for leadership training on the continent than what tends to occur now. They would also be valuable to those attempting to develop theories of leadership that take cultural elements into account.

The representations of literacy and of illiterates were solely derived from interviews with literacy leaders. It would be valuable to discover whether current students or those with no interest in learning to read and write would construct the same representations, or whether, as in Cheffy's (2006) research in Cameroon, significant differences in the conception of literacy and its usefulness exist between the groups. If there are significant differences, this could affect awareness-raising activities as well as other program content and activities.

I also did not have the time or resources to explore the actual uses of literacy beyond the examples that emerged during the interviews. A research project that focused on the actual personal and communal uses of literacy in all languages used in the community would contribute to theories of situated literacy and has the potential to suggest future directions for literature development in the community. Such a project could also explore the culture's change in position along the continuum of oral-literate practices in this culture where many people are the first in their family to learn to read and write in any language.

## 9.6 Closing comments

This research project satisfied my yearning to understand better the Ifè literacy program and how it has developed over the years. Certainly my relationships with the various association leaders have benefited from my time with them, as did my understanding of the particular constraints of the Ifè context. In addition, this project has contributed to a better understanding of how leadership, literacy, and capacity building are viewed and practiced in this West African group, while opening up further avenues of research into the issues of leadership, literacy, and development.

Practically, I have been able to use this knowledge in the development and revision of training courses with my African colleagues since my return to West Africa. Knowledge of the strengths and weaknesses of the Ifè strategy has also been of benefit in my role as a consultant, as I work with other mother tongue literacy programs who are struggling to serve dispersed and/or large populations. The awareness of the importance of representations in mentoring relationships also serves as an excellent reminder to me of the qualities to focus on, as I enter into or continue these types of relationships with African colleagues.

Finally, this case study has shown how mother tongue literacy programs can be a catalyst for community development. Through the Ifè program, rural communities have been empowered to affirm their identity and to choose their own path towards the future. May communities throughout Africa do the same.

# Appendix A: Interview protocols

This appendix gives the questions used in each of the four types of interviews conducted in this research.

>   Interview A:  the co-coordinators of the umbrella organization
>   Interview B:  the members of the board of each local association, first meeting
>   Interview C:  the members of the board of each local association
>   Interview D:  the literacy workers and/or members of the language community

**Interview A: the co-coordinators of the umbrella organization**
*Entretien A : les co-coordinateurs de l'organisation chapeau*

When did you begin to work with the SIL team?
> *Quand avez-vous commencé à travailler avec l'équipe de la SIL ?*

Why did you choose to do this work?
> *Pourquoi avez-vous choisi de faire ce travail ?*

What did you bring to this work in the way of personal, educational, and work experience qualifications?

*Qu'est-ce que vous avez apporté à ce travail en qualifications personnelles, éducationnelles et expérientielles ?*

When did you take on a role involving responsibility for the program?
*A quel moment étiez-vous chargé des responsabilités ?*

How were you prepared for these program responsibilities?
*Comment étiez-vous préparé pour vos responsabilités au programme ?*

When and why was the strategy of developing affiliated organizations conceived?
*Quand et pourquoi la stratégie des associations affiliées a-t-elle été conçue ?*

Whose idea was this strategy?
*Qui était l'auteur principal(e) de cette stratégie ?*

What are the steps you take for each association? (in preparation, to start it up, to develop it)
*Quels sont les étapes que vous faites pour chaque association ? (en préparation, pour l'entreprendre, pour la développer)*

Did the money from *Folk et Språk*\* change your strategy? If so, how?
*L'argent de Folk et Språk\* a-t-il modifié votre stratégie ? Si oui, comment ?*

Since the beginning of the literacy program, what has changed in the Ifè environment?
*Depuis le commencement du programme d'alphabétisation, qu'est-ce qui a changé dans l'environnement ifè ?*

How have you managed in the face of these changes?
*Comment avez-vous fait face à ces changements ?*

What unexpected events, challenges, and opportunities have there been?
*Quels imprévus, défis et opportunités y avaient-ils ?*

How do you define success for the local associations?
*Comment définissez-vous la réussite pour les associations locales ?*

---

\**Folk et Språk* is a Swedish development organization.

## Interview B: the members of the board of each local association, first meeting
*Entretien B : les membres du conseil administratif de chaque association locale, première rencontre*

[The questions with * may be omitted if the response was included in the answer to another question, such as the first question.]

*[Les questions avec un * sera supprimées si la réponse est sortie lors de la réponse à une autre question, telle que la première.]*

*Tell me a little about the history of your association.

*Racontez-moi un peu de l'histoire de votre association.*

What are the goals of your organization?

*Quels sont les buts de votre organisation ?*

How do you work towards the goals of your organization?

*Comment réalisez-vous les buts de votre organisation ?*

*When did (each of you) become involved in this association?

*À quel moment étiez-vous impliqué dans cette association ?*

*How was the board chosen? How were positions decided upon?

*Comment le C.A. a-t-il été choisi ? Et les rôles pour chaque personne ?*

How were you prepared for your responsibilities in the association?

*Comment étiez-vous préparé par vos responsabilités au programme ?*

*What were the challenges
- in the beginning?
- at the time of transition to less support from SIL/ACATBLI?

*Quels étaient les défis*
*- au commencement ?*
*- au moment de la transition à moins de soutien de la SIL/ACATBLI ?*

What challenges does your association currently face? Tell me about a time when you overcame a challenge in your association.

*Racontez-moi un moment où vous avez dû surmonter un défi dans votre association.*

What support do you expect to get from ACATBLI?

*Quel soutien attendez-vous de l'ACATBLI ?*

What is your relationship with the Office of Literacy and Adult Education?

*Quel est votre relation avec la Direction de l'alphabétisation et l'éducation des adultes ?*

Do you have any relationships with other associations or NGOs in your zone? If so, please describe their nature.
> *Avez-vous des relations avec d'autres associations ou ONGs dans votre zone ? Si oui, veuillez les décrire.*

What are the resources of your association?
> *Quelles sont les ressources de votre association ?*

How do you manage these resources?
> *Comment gérez-vous ces ressources ?*

In order to move forward, what capacities do you need to acquire?
> *Afin de progresser, de quelles capacités avez-vous besoin ?*

How do you define success for your association?
> *Comment définissez-vous la réussite pour votre association ?*

To whom does responsibility for the success of your association belong—to your president, to ACATBLI [the umbrella organization], to all the members of the association, or to the entire community?
> *À qui appartient la responsabilité pour la réussite de votre association ?—à votre président, à ACATBLI, à tous les membres de l'association ou à toute la communauté ?*

What rituals (ceremonies) does your association have—for example: recognition of success or of transition?
> *Quels rites (cérémonies) votre association a-t-elle—par exemple : reconnaissance des succès ou de transition ?*

Appendix A: Interview protocols

## Interview C: the members of the board of each local association
*Entretien C : les membres du conseil administratif de chaque association locale*

### Theme 1: Leadership
*Thème 1 : Le leadership*

A. How do you define a leader, what are the most important characteristics he should show?
*Comment définissez-vous un chef, quelles sont les qualités les plus importantes qu'il doit montrer ?*
What are the most important characteristics of a literacy program leader? Why?
*Quelles sont des qualités les plus importantes d'un responsable d'un programme d'alpha ? Pourquoi ?*
What are the most important characteristics of an association board? Why?
*Quelles sont des qualités les plus importantes d'un conseil administratif d'une association ? Pourquoi ?*
What are the most important responsibilities of a subordinate or of a colleague in an organization? Why?
*Quels sont les responsabilités les plus importantes d'un subordonné ou d'un collaborateur dans une organisation ? Pourquoi ?*

B. Tell me about a time when you had to resolve a conflict in your association (involving board members, the community, teachers, supervisors and/or students).
*Racontez-moi un temps quand vous avez dû résoudre un conflit lié à l'association (impliquant des membres du conseil, de la communauté, des moniteurs, des superviseurs et/ou des apprenants).*

### Theme 2: Organizational theory and capacity building
*Thème 2 : La théorie organisationnelle et le renforcement des capacités*

C. Would you please choose one of these statements, either because you find yourself in agreement with it or because you disagree? Explain:
*Veuillez choisir une de ces affirmations, soit parce que vous vous sentez en accord ou en désaccord. Expliquer :*

1. An organization that has a well-structured hierarchy is the best for directing a literacy program.
   *Une organisation qui a une hiérarchie bien structurée est la meilleure à diriger un programme d'alphabétisation.*

2. A literacy program will best succeed when all its members have a say when decisions must be made.
   *Un programme d'alphabétisation réussira le mieux lorsque tous les membres ont leur mot à dire lorsqu'il faut prendre les décisions.*

3. The president of a literacy and development association should watch out for the well-being of all the members of the association as well as that of class participants.
   *Le président d'une association de développement et d'alphabétisation doit surveiller le bien-être de tous les membres de l'association ainsi que celui des participants des classes.*

4. A literacy and development association should build the capacities of all the individuals who participate in the activities of the program.
   *Une association de développement et d'alphabétisation doit renforcer les capacités de tous les individus qui participent dans les activités du programme.*

5. "The continuity of the life of organizations depends on the creative action of human beings." (Morgan 1999:66)
   *« La continuité de la vie des organisations dépend de l'action créatrice d'êtres humains. »* (Morgan 1999:66)

D. How do you improve life for the Ifè people?
   *Comment améliorez-vous la vie pour le peuple ifè ?*

E. What is the point of developing literacy in local languages? Why is this important for you? How does this go along with the learning of other languages, such as Éwé, Yoruba, or French?
   *A quoi sert de développer la littératie (ou l'alphabétisation) dans les langues locales ? Pourquoi est-ce important pour vous ? Comment s'articule avec l'apprentissage des autres langues, telles que l'éwé, le yorouba ou le français ?*

## Interview D: literacy workers and/or members of the language community
*Entretien D : les alphabétiseurs et/ou membres de la communauté linguistique*

### Theme 1: Leadership [large group discussion]
*Thème 1 : Le leadership [discussion en plénière]*

How do you define a leader, what are the most important characteristics that he should have? Why?
*Comment définissez-vous un chef, quelles sont les qualités les plus importantes qu'il doit montrer ? Pourquoi ?*

What are the most important characteristics a literacy program leader should have? Why?
*Quelles sont les qualités les plus importantes d'un responsable d'un programme d'alpha ? Pourquoi ?*

What are the most important characteristics of an association's board?
*Quelles sont les qualités les plus importantes d'un conseil administratif d'une association ? Pourquoi ?*

### Theme 2: Capacity building [only for literacy workers]
*Thème 2 : Le renforcement des capacités [seulement pour les alphabétiseurs]*

Describe the most important literacy or development training that you have taken.
*Décrivez la formation en alphabétisation ou en développement la plus importante que vous avez suivie.*

Describe the most useless literacy or development training you have taken.
*Décrivez la formation en alphabétisation ou en développement le plus inutile que vous avez suivie.*

# Appendix B: Interview excerpts

This appendix offers the original French texts. The French was the basis for all analysis and, as the actual voice of most participants (the exceptions are those given in Ifè and interpreted on the spot), is, thus, the authoritative text.

Conventions used in the French and Ifè transcriptions, below, are the same as those used in the English translations in the body of the book (see p. xiii). Direct quotes from interviews, both those in the English translation in the body of the book, and those in French and Ifè in this appendix, are coded as follows:
- The first letter indicates which of the four interview protocols was used (see Appendix A).
- For interviews beginning with A, the number following the A indicates in which of the three audio files (covering two interviews) the citation is found. For interviews beginning with B or C, the following number identifies the local association. For interviews beginning with D, the literacy teachers in the village group were each assigned a number according to the order in which they first responded to the questions. However, for the village discussion groups on leadership qualities, the representative for the men is indicated as *Rep. men.*

- For some interviews beginning with B, supplementary interviews are indicated by *si*. I had two supplementary interviews with ADCIBA, distinguished by *si1* and *si2*.
- A numeral followed by *m* indicates how many minutes into the interview the citation begins; a numeral followed by *s* indicates the second within the first minute of the interview; *ff*. signifies that the quote follows immediately after the one shown immediately above it.
- There are two audio files for the first interviews with ACATBLI and AVID, which are indicated by *af1* and *af2* followed by the time stamp.
- For the first interview with *Jésus le Chemin,* the data are summaries of what the participants said (based on notes, their recapitulation of important points, and the translator's memory of the interview). Consequently there are no time stamps.

### Interviews with ACATBLI: A

| | |
|---|---|
| First part | A.1.[individual's code] af# time stamp |
| Second part | A.2.[individual's code] time stamp |
| Supplementary interview | A.3.[individual's code] time stamp |

### Interviews with the local associations, focus on organizational history: B

| | |
|---|---|
| AVID | B.1.[individual's code] af# time stamp |
| AVADI | B.2.[individual's code] (si) time stamp |
| AMIADA | B.3.[individual's code] (si) time stamp |
| ADCIBA | B.4.[individual's code] (si#) time stamp |
| *Jésus le Chemin* | B.5.[individual's code] (si) time stamp |

### Interviews with the local associations, focus on representations: C

| | |
|---|---|
| AVID | C.1.[individual's code] time stamp |
| AVADI | C.2.[individual's code] time stamp |
| AMIADA | C.3.[individual's code] time stamp |
| ADCIBA | C.4.[individual's code] time stamp |
| *Jésus le Chemin* | C.5.[individual's code] time stamp |

Appendix B: Interview excerpts

## Village group interview: D

D. [representative/literacy teacher's number] time stamp

### Table B.1. Individual codes

| SURNAME and Given Name(s) | Code | Position |
|---|---|---|
| AFFONFERE Novignon Abdel | ANA | literacy coordinator and head treasurer, ADCIBA |
| AGAYI Ama | AgA | coordinator, AVID |
| AGBÉMADON Akoété | AgbA | head of literacy, ACATBLI |
| AMOUSSOU Akoété | AmA | president and literacy coordinator, AMIADA |
| BASSAN Komla | BK | moderator, *Jésus le Chemin* |
| ÐEÐZI Omanɔlá | ÐO | advisor, *Jésus le Chemin* |
| EDOH Koffi | EK | literacy coordinator, *Jésus le Chemin* |
| FONTCHÉ Akoété | FA | advisor, AVID |
| GÚDÙ Ðzègbó | GÐ | 2nd treasurer, ADCIBA |
| JeDene REEDER | JR | researcher |
| KOUMONDJO Labité | KL | literacy coordinator and president, ADCIBA |
| KPONDZA Jean | KÐ | advisor and supervisor, ADCIBA |
| MAFON Kokou | MK | treasurer, AMIADA |
| MONKITI Léon | ML | vice president, ADCIBA |
| N'TCHOU Kowouvi | NK | president, AVID |
| ODAH Kodjo | OK | project and missions director, *Jésus le Chemin* |
| ODIN Kossi David | OKD | secretary, AMIADA |
| SÁÀNYÀ Yàwùfí | SY | vice president and supervisor, AMIADA |
| SÉTODJI Kodjo | SK | literacy coordinator, ACATBLI |
| YAOU Messan Afadja | YMA | secretary, AVID |

NB: The members of AVADI opted for anonymity. Therefore, they each have a number, based on the order of their first responses, as follows:

VA1 – literacy coordinator
VA2 – secretary
VA3 – president (who is also a village chief)
VA4 – advisor

# Representations of leadership (Chapter 6)

## Social representations of a leader (section 6.1)

### Patience (section 6.1.1)

**p. 86**

A.3.SK 30m   Là où je dirai encore, là où le Seigneur nous a beaucoup bénis, pour nos forces, c'est vraiment il nous a donné la patience .. Sinon, si on n'avait pas cette force, {il rit} on ne pouvait pas continuer= on ne pouvait pas faire le travail. Parce que les moniteurs ils ne sont pas faciles hein ? Ça c'était très dur mais, Dieu nous a beaucoup aidés à acquérir, cette compétence de patience, et de temps en temps, eux-mêmes le disent, que: vraiment, quand ils viennent avec des décisions, ils s'engagent, ils font des réunions, de se préparent, quand ils amènent, mais quand les parlent seulement {claquement de langue}

**p. 87**

A.3.AgbA ff.   Ils sont désarmés ! [{il rit}]
A.3.SK ff.                              [Ils sont désarmés !] {les deux rient}
C.3.AmA 9m   Bon, dans le cas de l'alphabétisation, pour pouvoir élire un chef {d'un programme d'alpha}, les qualités les plus nécessaires ou importantes, je vois d'abord la première qualité, c'est la patience. Il faut qu'il soit beaucoup patient avant d'être un responsable. Donc, dans le cas où un responsable n'a pas n'a pas assez de patience, il faut que la= sa patience domine sa colère . qu'il soit un peu lent en colère. Ça c'est une première qualité ça. Première qualité ça la patience.
C.3.MK 13m   puisque c'est l'alphabétisation, ce sont les GRANDS, ils vont même faire quelque chose même il y a des gens qui vont te demander, des parents qui vont te .. te lancer des paroles tu n'est pas PATIENT, tu ne peux PAS recevoir mais il faut être patient.
C.3.AmA 20m   *Bí ò dzé ɔ̀gá ŋu έ, àtèsi ŋu nákó kpɔ ni quoi.*
             Si tu es chef la patience doit être grande quoi.

Appendix B: Interview excerpts 261

C.3.All ff.   *Nn!*
              Effectivement !
C.3.AmA 29m   Si . il s'agit d'un chef . du village, avant d'élire un chef . dans un village, je vois que ces qualités aussi sont importantes . à un chef d'un village. D'abord le chef doit aussi {être} patient. Si un chef n'est pas patient on ne peut pas l'élire, parce que . on va dire que bon, notre chef-là . il n'est pas patient est-ce qu'il peut encore régner sur nous, il peut diriger ce village, voire que il a de l'argent, il a tel tel mais, c'est l'impatience qu'il au= qu'il a. Donc, si le chef n'est pas patient selon moi, ça ne peut pas bien calé.

**p. 88**

C.5.OK 6m    Je disais que, la qualité la plus importante pour un chef de programme d'alphabétisation, c'est la patience. Il doit avoir beaucoup de patience envers les adultes . parce qu'il faut du temps pour les comprendre . étant dit que peut-être vous êtes lettré, certains comportements vous allez trouver ça bizarre ... vraiment, il faut les accepter tels qu'ils sont, pour pouvoir aller xx je propose la patience pour gérer un tel groupe.

C.4.ANA 34m  Quelques fois même on peut aller jusqu'à vous dire que, ah toi tu ne vois pas tel que ton patron est en train d'évoluer pourtant lui il est en train d'évoluer à ton détriment c'est ce qu'il doit te donner là et il ne te donne pas et il est en train de construire quelque chose et bien il est en train d'acheter tout ceci, donc, vas-y il faut gréver contre lui, il faut revendiquer ce droit-là, il faut faire ceci, il faut faire ceci, oui, ça arrive souvent et si toi subordonné tu n'es pas .. patient, tu n'arrives pas à analyser bien, ces provocateurs-là tu risques de ton bien ou de bloquer le travail, c'est-à-dire ce qu'il vous attend.

**p. 89**

C.1.NK 17m   Et .. par des investigations, on a su que le superviseur a de tel problème. Maintenant, lorsqu'on l'a interpellé au au au sein de [YMA : du bureau] du bureau, il a reconnu les faits.

C.2.VA1 32m  Donc, c'est après tout on s'est réuni avec les autres moniteurs qui se sont présentés, et dans l'association, et nous sommes dit bon voilà le problème est posé, que pensez-vous ? Ils ont dit bon d'accord, et les autres qui étaient moniteurs, on a écouté leurs idées,

C.2.VA1 34m  Donc, là, on va sur le terrain de temps en temps pour régler de tels problèmes réunir les apprenants ET les moniteurs, discuter avec eux et relancer la classe.

C.3.AmA 49m  Et à la fin de la campagne 2002 maintenant, nous nous sommes réunis ici et nous avons, nous nous sommes décidés que bon tel que nous travaillons ensemble avec les frères, les superviseurs, le superviseur qui est de l'autre côté, des moniteurs, et il a fallu que c'est suspendu, donc nous allons revoir cet aspect. Et on a convoqué une réunion et nous sommes allés vers eux. Et on a .. on s'est réuni, et chacun a dit ce qui ne va pas.

**p. 90**

C.4.JR 47m  Donc, cette entente c'était arrivée pendant une réunion comme l'as [semblée générale, pendant]

C.4.ANA ff.  [oui, plusieurs réunions nous-mêmes] on a fait plusieurs réunions pour discuter de cela.

C.4.GÐ 54m  (interprété par ANA) on a débattu de ces problèmes-là, on a traîné ça pendant {sourire dans la voix} pratiquement un mois avant de pouvoir élire le bureau. On a discuté d'ici et de loin là est que vraiment, si on ne fait pas attention, on risque . de de de faire une association mort-née.

C.4.GÐ 59m  (interprété par ANA) Bon, c'est résolu, c'est résolu, on nous coordinateurs, superviseurs, d'abord coordinateurs on a tant expliqué ça aux superviseurs et ensemble avec superviseurs on a fait des réunions sur des rumeurs avec les anciens moniteurs-là pour pouvoir vraiment les amener à raison, pour leur dire .. ce qui il faut pour qu'ils puissent continuer à travailler.

C.5.OK 21m  Donc, c'est par la la voie de négociation et à plusieurs reprises par ce moyen nous sommes arrivés . à faire revenir . beaucoup, certaines qui sont en voie de dérailler.

## p. 91
*Faithfulness (section 6.1.2)*

AgbA 10 Oct 07 (pour un leader) Il est fidèle. Il gère correctement les fonds, il est impartial, ouvert aux innovations de développement.
(explanation of the importance of this quality for a leader) Savoir gérer le personnel, le matériel didactique, roulant, du bureau et les fonds du programme. Avoir une comptabilité saine pour pouvoir gagner la confiance des bailleurs.

SK 10 Oct 07 (explication de l'importance de cette qualité pour un leader) Il est impartial à tel point que les villageois lui font confiance. Il aime assumer sa responsabilité.
(et pour un responsable d'alphabétisation) Savoir gérer le personnel et les fonds du programme. Avoir une comptabilité saine.

## p. 92

C.1.NK 4m    Fidélité dans ses actions d'abord, fidélité dans la gestion … de de l'entreprise, fidélité aussi en parole tu ne peux pas dire autre chose et le lendemain dis autre chose . ou bien ce que tu vas dire, peut-être vous avez posé un acte que vous avez tous .. eh . discuté, décidé donc, être fidèle aussi dans sa conduite dans son accomplissement. Voilà.

C.2.VA2 11m  ou bien justesse rentre dans la fidélité, je ne sais pas,

C.1.YMA 3m   *Bí ò wà tsòtítɔ́, bí ò wà tsòtítɔ́ nàa dzáfɔ̀-ɔ̀nyà kpó.*
             Si tu es fidèle, si tu es fidèle, tu aimeras tout le monde.

C.1.AgA ff.  *Nàa nyáa wà tsòtítɔ́, tsí ò kòó dzáfɔ̀-ɔ̀nyá kpó.*
             Tu peux être fidèle sans aimer tout le monde.

C.1.YMA ff.  *Ni ò kò wà tsòtítɔ́ ńnèɛ́.*
             Alors là tu n'es pas fidèle.

C.2.VA3 6m   *Ètítɔ́ ó wà kpataki, bí ò dzɛ́ ɔ̀gá tsí ò kò wà tsòtítɔ́, kò sã̀.*
             La fidélité est très importante, si tu es chef, et tu ne pratiques pas la fidélité, c'est mauvais.

C.2.VA1 ff.  C'est ça. *Náa fɔ́ égbé.*
             C'est ça. Ça détruit l'association.

C.3.AmA 25m  Ò rí fee, ó wà ní fee, bí ɔnyà-kã̀ dzɛ́ ɔ̀gá fee, tsí esprit de fidélité kò wà ńnɛ̀ fee, itsɛ́ ɛ́ kò bòkó rɛ̀̃.
Tu vois, il faut que, si quelqu'un est chef, ne possédant pas l'esprit de fidélité, le travail ne pourra pas marcher.

C.5.EK 13m  S'il n'y a pas la fidélité, bon, nous allons chuter dans le travail.

**p. 93**

C.3.SY 8m  (interprété) Le chef c'est lui la tête. Et quand la tête est ma-lade, tout le corps ne se sent pas bien. Par exemple, un père de famille qui est mou, qui n'est pas éveillé, qui ne réveille pas qui ne fait pas travailler bien ses enfants, les enfants sont derrière lui, quand papa parle, on fait, il ne parle pas, ils restent là. Alors, un chef de groupe, un groupe quoi ce soit, il doit être quelqu'un qui soit vraiment dynamique et aider le groupe à se mouvoir.

C.1.NK 10m  Donc, ces membres du comité, le comité-là, doit être aussi un comité .. ho .. fidèle.

C.1.YMA ff.  actif

C.1.NK ff.  actif .. et ... fidèle actif,

*Exemplary (section 6.1.3)*

**p. 94**

C.1.AgA 3m  Ó kó dzɛ́ ɛnɛ yèé dzɛ́ àrítse ɔ̀nyàŋa gbo.
Être un modèle pour les autres aussi.

C.2.VA2 3m  Si je peux ajouter, je veux dire, ce qu'il vient de le dire, il doit être exemplaire, comme il {VA3} l'a dit

C.4.ANA 3m  Et il faudrait aussi qu'il ait un bon comportement, une bonne moralité, .. puisque c'est lui qui doit donner exemple aux au-tres, un bon leadership doit montrer comment faire et non dicter ce qu'on doit faire.

C.4.GĐ 20m  Tsí ó kpã̌dzú ní kó léèbè fú ara-ɛ̀, tsí ká máa wà gbɔ́ afɔ-gbèsè nára-ɛ̀, ńnɔ́-owó dzídzɛ ti ńnɔ ilú gìdì wá ńnɔ́-egbé. Tsí ó wà ní òŋu gbo, sèkèrètéɛ́ gbo, tèrèsɔríyè gbo aŋa kó né ìlò kàntso, àrũ-ŋa kó ɖé, arũ-ŋa kó dzɛ́ arũ kàntso.
Il doit savoir bien se comporter, éviter des rumeurs de dette à son égard, que ce soit ailleurs ou dans l'association. Il faut que le président,

|             | le secrétaire et le trésorier aient le même comportement positif, être unis, que leurs paroles ne diffèrent pas les unes des autres. |
|---|---|
| C.2.VA2 14m | Donc uhn bon, notre travail-là, si tu: . bon: tes comportements . ne ho n'est pas .. doux, pour attirer les autres, tu auras beaucoup de problèmes. Donc, il faudrait que tu sois exemplaire, et: partant de là, bon, tu peux quand même attirer les gens et faire passer aisément . ho: tes= c'est-à-dire .. le message quoi. |
| C.2.VA1 ff. | Il doit il doit avoir aussi une portion d'une vie morale saine. |
| C.2.VA2 ff. | Mmm. Oui, xx |
| C.2.VA1 ff. | Ça c'est, je vois ça important .. sa vie . dans le milieu . joue beaucoup. Donc uhn il doit quand même . adopter certains comportements, comme on vient de le dire, qu'ils vont: qu'ils ne seront pas, ne feront pas obstacle . à ce programme d'alphabétisation. |

**p. 95**

| | |
|---|---|
| C.2.VA2 ff. | C'est ça. |
| C.4.ANA 4m | Chez nous ici, en Afrique surtout, il ne faudrait pas que ça soit quelqu'un qui commet l'adultère, il ne faudrait pas ça soit quelqu'un qui vole. Le vol=.. ce n'est pas quelqu'un qui est trop arrogant, qui .. est agressif et qui vraiment qui se bagarre avec beaucoup de personnes, il ne faudrait pas que ce soit quelqu'un= un soûlard. Quelqu'un qui soûle et dit des choses sans s'en rendre compte que, ce que je dis n'est pas bon. Surtout cette première part-là, c'est, disons, bon .. ce catégorie-là, l'Africain surtout au niveau de l'adultère, l'Africain est trop rigoureux sur ça. Et c'est que ça met TROP de temps à ce qu'on puisse diriger pour oublier. Tu commets adultère . cette année maintenant dans vingt ans, les familles ne vont pas laisser tomber. C'est pourquoi on aussi se méfie beaucoup de ça là. |
| C.4.GĐ 22m | {interprété} Il faut que en .. au sein du BE ou bien du bureau exécutif qu'il y ait l'amour entre les membres, pour éviter aussi l'adultère comme l'autre l'avait dit et éviter de prendre la femme d'autrui. Quand ça là ça intègre le groupe-là ça ne peut jamais marcher. C'est comme nos anciens le dit, c'est comme un bouteille dans le sol, qui ne pourrit jamais. {petites rires |

de plusieurs} Voilà, donc, il faut tout faire pour éviter cette situation.

**p. 96**

C.2.VA2 17m  Bon, comme on dit le pourquoi, bon moi, je, normalement, pour un homme comme ça, il ne c'est pas un alphabète, qui va chercher à courir les femmes des autres ou bien quelqu'un bon qui sait bon .. qui qui vole, par exemple. Si tu as ce caractère, donc, tu n'es pas bien placé pour ce travail.

C.3.AmA 1m  Il ne faut pas qu'il soit un chef aussi violent.

C.2.VA2 5m  *Eeh! Ó wà ní kó tse nam gbo, ilò-re, bon, ńkɔ-re, avec bon, ŋyèŋè ŋu έ, ńkɔ-re ní nɔ̀?*
Oui ! Il faut qu'il fasse chose aussi, bon comportement, bon, un beau nom, avec bon, ça là, un beau nom n'est-ce pas ?

C.2.VA1 ff.  *Ńkɔ-re. Ɛ̃ɛ̃! Ɛnɛ yèé wà balɛ-ara-è έ. Iŋé nyèŋè ŋa ná nyáa wɔ ń nɔ́ è gé ni ..* parce que *bí ɔ̀gá-kã̀ wà tsí tsí iŋé yèé, ó fɔ̀ έ, ńǹtá-è gé ní à kó tse έ, nyèŋè ŋu.*
Un beau nom. Oui, qu'il soit celui qui s'humilie. Tout cela doit rentrer dedans obligatoirement .. parce que s'il y a quelqu'un et s'il dit quelque chose, il veut que cela soit sans doute fait, alors ça.

**p. 97**

C.2.VA1 21m  Ils doivent être humbles, ils doivent écouter des autres, ils ne doivent se prononcer comme des ... des parfaits qui connaissent tout, qui veulent faire tout à leur gré.

C.5.ĐO 9m  {interprété} Un tel chef de programme doit éviter l'orgueil et .. plutôt faire preuve d'humilité. Dans cette humilité, ça fera que tout ce qu'il dirige ils vont vraiment vouloir à tout moment s'approcher de lui et acquérir la connaissance qu'il a. Sinon, en voulant faire savoir que c'est lui seul qui connaît, c'est que lui qui est la tête, ça fait que les gens vont se retirer.

C.5.OK 11m  Parce qu'ici .. au sein d'un groupe qu'ils dirigent, s'ils ne sont pas patients, ne sont pas humbles, s'ils ne sont pas sobres, eh, s'ils ne sont pas ouverts, ils ne peuvent pas diriger un groupe .. sur lequel ils sont établis.

*Appendix B: Interview excerpts* 267

## *Competent in work (section 6.1.4)*

C.3.AmA 1m  Quand on dit que quelqu'un est un chef dans une association, ou soit il est responsable d'une association, d'abord, on doit avoir en lui . eh la compétence . de son travail. Est-ce que celui-là, la responsabilité à qui on le confie là, est-ce qu'il est compétent dedans. Est-ce qu'il a la compétence. Ça c'est une première qualité chez moi.

C.5.BK 2m  Donc, le chef c'est celui-là qui est censé .. avoir la compétence, la maturité et l'esprit de coordination, pour avoir .. une manière de gérer par concert, donc, lui il prend les idées et les= il les travaille afin d'avoir un produit pour pouvoir amener à bien le groupe sur lequel il est établi chef.

**p. 98**

C.1.NK 9m  Bon, les qualités, moi je vois le bureau exécutif .. est l'organe qui est capable, c'est-à-dire qui qui a toutes les: .. les qualités possibles pour diriger.

AgbA 10 Oct 07  Un chef est sage. Il sait prendre des décisions, il a l'aptitude professionnelle (savoir diriger, coordonner les activités, avoir le sens de l'organisation).

C.1.NK 13s  Je disais que le chef-là bon il doit savoir écouter ses collaborateurs, il doit pouvoir distribuer au cours de la réunion les paroles à ses collaborateurs, il doit être aussi, comme la dame l'a dit, pardonner, savoir pardonner . et .. savoir aussi diriger les réunions dans le sens est-ce que chacun puisse . envoyer ses idées et maintenant il doit savoir aussi AGIR, agir en quelque sorte que, si quelqu'un donne peut-être ses idées, il ne doit pas le rejeter inxxment comme ce n'est pas fondé. Donc il doit accepter TOUT et ensemble analyser l'idée-là d'abord.

p.99

C.3.SY 6m  {interprété} Alors, il reçoit beaucoup de choses, c'est-à-dire de gauche à droite, lui il reçoit il sait comment maintenant administrer pour que ça puisse marcher.

C.5.ĐO 4m   {interprété} tout le monde vient déposer ce qu'il a, bien comme le mal, et lui reçoit. Et, c'est au chef maintenant de mettre une différence entre tout ce qu'il reçoit et choisir ce qui est bien.

C.4.GĐ 2m   *Kó dzέ ɔ̀nyà-kā̀ yèé bí ó bòkó wũ̂nyὲ ńwádzú-ɔ̀nyà ni odzo kà tse é, tsí bí ó bòkó wũ̂nyὲ fú ɔ̀nyà ni náa máa fɔ̂ɔ, tsí bí afɔ̀ έ le gìḑì tsí ó bàkó dzέ oŋù fú ɔlέὲ ni nákó nyáa nyíi fɔ̀ έ.*
Un bon chef doit avoir le courage de parler devant les gens sans peur. Il doit savoir s'adresser aussi aux gens, savoir parler, ne parler pas avec arrogance en répondant aux questions mais avec sagesse et douceur quand bien même la question est d'un ton dur ou fort.

C.4.ANA 6m   il faut vraiment un responsable . qui arrive à bien gérer tout ce qui arrive, et dans une condition difficile, ça dit quand il y a difficultés, c'est-à-dire au cours de l'exécution de . de d'un programme, quand une difficulté rentre dedans. Ça dit qu'une situation difficile vient, il faudrait que celui-là soit en mesure quand même de diriger, de diriger ça, d'une manière à ce que l'association ne soit pas bloquée. C'est très important pour le leadership.

## p.100
### *Does not dictate (section 6.1.5)*

C.1.NK 1m   Donc il doit accepter TOUT et ensemble analyser l'idée-là d'abord. Donc, il ne doit pas être un dictateur. Il doit pas être dictateur.

C.2.VA2 36m   Ils {adultes} ne veulent pas qu'une seule personne décide que bon, aujourd'hui on doit faire ceci et ainsi de suite comme ça. Un adulte n'aime pas une situation comme ça.

C.5.EK 5m   Il ne doit pas aussi décider de quelque chose en lui-même, en lui seul, disons que je suis chef, donc je vais agir comme je veux. Il doit appeler ses membres et et poser la question, poser la situation et ensemble ils vont discuter et trouver la meilleure solution.

C.3.AmA 43m   c'est-à-dire le chef doit considérer les subordonnés, il ne faut pas que le chef prenne les décisions seul. Il ne faut pas que le chef soit un chef dictatorial. Lui seul va prendre des décisions comme tel, c'est ça que je veuille qu'on fasse .. sans avoir l'avis des subordonnés, sans recueillir leurs informations, leurs idées .

*Appendix B: Interview excerpts* 269

alors, si c'est comme ça, si les subordonnés sont mal traités, le travail ne peut pas avancer.

**p. 101**

C.5.ĐO 32m  {interprété} Bon, dans un groupe ou bien dans une association, c'est le chef est là, et qu'il amène un problème, il doit désirer recevoir l'opinion de chacun. Et recueillir les idées, débattre ensemble afin de prendre une décision. Et sans ça, l'association ne peut pas évoluer. Et quand les subordonnes ou bien ses collaborateurs finiront par découvrir que non, notre chef, notre patron est en train de faire le .. il se faire de s'autoproclamer, ou bien il décide seul ce qu'il veut, finalement, ils vont désister ou bien se décourager, se retirer et le travail ne peut plus avancer. Là, il faut la collaboration.

C.5.EK 30m  c'est bien à ce que si un groupe veut faire un travail, bon le chef de ce groupe, il ne faudra pas qu'il ait, bon, qu'il se regarde déjà .. trop haut, il dise c'est moi qui suis le chef, donc, je vais prendre seulement, seul ma décision pour conduire le travail, donc ça ne va pas marcher. Il faut appeler les membres et vous asseyez et chacun donne son opinion, et à base de cela, on retranche ce qui n'est pas bon, et ceux qui sont ceux qui sont bon, on les ajoute, et c'est enSEMble qu'on peut faire évoluer un groupe.

**p. 102**

C.2.VA2 4m  Il doit se soumettre, pour que la chose passe bien et au moment important, c'est à lui d'agir quand même.

C.2.VA1 ff.  Il doit avoir aussi la qualité d'écouter les autres. Il doit, comme notre frère vient= le président vient de le dire, il doit être toujours disponible à écouter les autres et à analyser les idées des autres et avoir comment on peut quand même .. pratiquer certaines idées que les autres ont amené.

C.2.VA1 5m  *Nákó balɛ-ara-ɛ̀, nákó ɖi ɔmatsɛ́ fú ɛnɛ atí bɔ̀ ŋa.*
Il doit soumettre, devenir serviteur aux autres.

C.2.VA2 ff.  *Ó ɖi ɔmatsɛ́, nn.*

|           | Il devient serviteur, oui. |
|---|---|
| C.2.VA1 ff. | *Béɛ̀ ní ɔ̀dáyé gìdì fɔ̀ fú wa á ńnèɛ́. Enɛ yèé dzɛ́ ɔ̀gá á, ó wà ní kó dzɛ́ ɔmatsɛ́ fú enìkéèdzì-è ni, nn!* |
|           | C'est ce que Dieu lui-même nous dit. Celui qui est chef, il faut qu'il soit serviteur aux autres, oui ! |
| C.2.VA2 ff. | *Ó wà ní kó dzɛ́ ɔmatsɛ́ gìdì ni, nn!* C'est ça, se soumettre. *Eeh! Ó wà ní kó tse nam gbo, ìlò-re, bon, ńkɔ-re, avec bon, ŋyèŋè ŋu ɛ́, ńkɔ-re ní nɔ̀?* |
|           | Il faut qu'il soit vraiment serviteur, oui! C'est ça, se soumettre. Eeh ! Il faut qu'il fasse chose aussi, bon comportement, bon, un beau nom, avec bon, ça là, un beau nom n'est-ce pas ? |
| C.2.VA1 ff. | *Ńkɔ-re. Ɛ̃ɛ̃! Enɛ yèé wà balɛ-ara-è ɛ́. Iŋɛ́ nyèŋè ŋa ná nyáa wɔ̀ ń nɔ́ è gé ni ..* parce que *bí ɔ̀gá-kã̀ wà tsí tsí iŋɛ́ yèé, ó fɔ̀ ɛ́, ńǹtá-è gé ní à kó tse ɛ́, nyèŋè ŋu.* |
|           | Un beau nom. Oui, qu'il soit celui qui s'humilie. Tout cela doit rentrer dedans obligatoirement .. parce que s'il y a quelqu'un et s'il dit quelque chose, il veut que cela soit sans doute fait, alors ça. |
| C.4.ANA 4m | un bon leadership doit montrer comment faire et non dicter ce qu'on doit faire. |

## p. 103
### Some of the secondary features (section 6.1.6)

*Caring (section 6.1.6.1)*

| C.3.MK 3m | il faut que la personne {chef}, premièrement, *compassionne de tout le monde. |
|---|---|
| C.3.AmA 10m | La deuxième qualité, il faut qu'il soit aussi amour il faut aimer le= il faut qu'il il faut que la personne {responsable} aime d'abord le travail qui est devant lui il faut qu'il aime aussi celui= cela cela qu'il veut gouverner, ceux qu'il veut diriger, il faut qu'il les aime. Donc, il ne peut pas travailler sans l'amour. Ça c'est la deuxième qualité. |
| C.1.AgA 3m | *Ɛ̀kɛ́ɛta á, ó kó dzɛ́ enɛ yèé naá dzáfɔ̀-ɔ̀nyà kpó.* |
|           | La troisième, être celui qui aime tout le monde. |

## p. 104

| | |
|---|---|
| C.1.YMA ff. | Bí ò wà tsòtítɔ́, bí ò wà tsòtítɔ́ nàa dzáfɔ̀-ɔ̀nyà kpó. |
| | Si tu es fidèle, si tu es fidèle, tu aimeras tout le monde. |
| C.1.AgA ff. | Nàa nyáa wà tsòtítɔ́, tsí ò kòó dzáfɔ̀-ɔ̀nyá kpó. |
| | Tu peux être fidèle sans aimer tout le monde. |
| C.1.YMA ff. | Ni ò kò wà tsòtítɔ́ ńnèɛ́. |
| | Alors là tu n'es pas fidèle. |
| C.3.AmA 20m | Ǹhṹ, àmúɖɔ̀̃. |
| | Et ensuite, l'amour. |
| C.3.MK ff. | Àtèsi è fee, òŋu àmúɖɔ̀̃ ɛ́ ... |
| | Je veux savoir, entre la patience et l'amour ... |
| C.3.AmA ff. | Gbèɖé, ó wà nũ̀kã̀ ni. |
| | Jamais, c'est différent. |
| C.3.SY ff. | Àtèsi fee, nàa nyáa né àmúɖɔ̀̃ fú ɔnyà tśi ò kàa né àtèsi. |
| | Pour la patience, tu peux aimer quelqu'un et ne pas avoir la patience. |
| C.3.AmA ff. | Oui ! |
| C.3.SY ff. | Ó wà yé ɛ báàyũ̀? Náa nyáa, náa nyáa, ìwɔ ɔ̀nyà méèdzí nákó wà kpàɖé bé, tsí nákó wà tsàmúɖɔ̀̃ fú ŋé, àmá bí ó wá a tó ńŵèrè-itsɛ, náa ké-ara-è. Òŋu ní dzé bé ɛ́, bi ó ké afɔ-kã̀ wá, à kà gbàá si ńnè fúu. |
| | Comprends-tu maintenant ? Tu peux, tu peux, toi tu te familiarises avec quelqu'un qui vous aime, mais s'il s'agit de travailler, ce dernier devient hautain. C'est lui qui se voit au-dessus, alors si tu avances une idée, on ne l'accepte pas. |
| D.Rep.men 16s | Et s'il aime tout le monde aussi, même si ses ennemis viennent, il va bien juger. |
| C.4.GƉ 21m | Ɛnɛ yèé dzé éwo-ɛgbé ɛ́, ó wà ní náàŋírĩ ŋa, ó wà ní àmúɖɔ̀̃ kó wà náŋírĩ ŋa, bí ó dzé ní àmúɖɔ̀̃ kò wà, ɛgbé ɛ́ kà lɔ. |
| | L'amour est très indispensable entre les membres du BE, sans cela, l'association ne réussira pas. |

## p. 105

| | |
|---|---|
| C.4.GƉ 22m | Yàtɔ fú nyɛ̀ŋɛ̀ gbo ró ɛ́, bí ó dzé ní, náaŋírĩ àŋa méèta nyɛ̀ŋɛ̀, bí ó dzé òkpi-afɔ̀ gbígbɔ́ kò wà, fú ɔ̀nyà-kã̀ náàŋírĩ ìlú ɛ́, tsí bódzé à wũ̀nyè gé, ɛnɛ nyɛ̀ŋɛ̀ gé ní kà gbɔ́ òkpì-afɔ̀ fú ìlú ɛ́, náa tse tsí ìlú ɛ́ náa kpɛ̃́ méèdzì. À náa kpɛ̃́ tori ɔ̀nyà nyɛ̀ŋɛ̀ tsí à kà nyáa tse ɛgbé ɛ́ gbo ró. |

Autre chose à remarquer, si l'un des membres du BE n'aime pas ou n'a pas l'habitude de comprendre écouter les membres de l'association, ceci neutralise les efforts des autres et il y a division. Ils deviennent divisés à cause de cette personne puis ils n'arrivent plus à continuer la vie en association.

C.3.MK 27m  Bon, ça serait différent. {discussion d'autres qualités} Donc . là-bas il faut .. premièrement, il y a des chefs dans bon dans le milieu qui n'ont pas l'amour.

C.3.AmA 29m  Moi je vais aller un peu . dans un sens contraire à ce que le frère vient de dire. Si . il s'agit d'un chef . du village, avant d'élire un chef . dans un village, je vois que ces qualités aussi sont importantes . à un chef d'un village. {discussion concernant la patience et la disponibilité} {claquement de langue} Moi je veut dire automatiquement que selon moi, dans mon humble avis d'œil que, cet étape= ces trois= ces quatre qualités-là . sont aussi importantes à un chef du village . selon moi. Mais contrairement, on voit le côté opposé . de chef . dans nos villages. Donc, normalement, il faut que ces qualités soient . dans le chef.

C.3.JR ff.  Donc, si j'avais demandé les qualités d'un BON chef, est-ce que ça aurait changé votre ..

C.3.MK ff.  Oui, si on dit un bon chef, donc, automatiquement, ces sont ces qualités-là. Mais si on dit le CHEF, ça c'est vague. I= donc c'est un bon chef, automatiquement, c'est ça.

**p. 106**

C.3.OKD 30m  Je veux ajouter, un chef doit avoir ces qualités-là. Les quatre xx un bon chef doit avoir ça. Même si c'est un chef de village, il fait ces quatre qualités-là xx, et c'est fini.

C.3.SY 32m  {interprété} Il dit que, ce que les frères ont dit, que c'est vrai et souvent ces qualités on les retrouve dans des responsables des services administratifs. Et souvent ils essaient de les mettre en pratique pour que tous le personnel puisse bien travailler. Mais de l'autre côté, quand on voit nos chefs aujourd'hui, ils ne font que le contraire.

A.3.AgbA 34m  Eh . notre force, comme je l'ai dit que . il n'y a pas d'orgueil, ça ce ça s'est fait voir au moment où ILS nous abordent ..

|  | et ils viennent à nous présenter leurs problèmes de la maison même. Donc, il y a une . confiance qui est là, qu'il peut amener son problème de la maison avec sa femme, ses enfants, bon, souvent on essaye de . les diriger un peu. [C'est ça.] |
|---|---|
| A.3.SK ff. | [C'est ça que] je dis même que actuellement avec nos moniteurs, nous ne sommes plus .. pour dire leurs chefs de travail, mais nous sommes devenus des frères. Nous sommes devenus des frères, n'importe qui vient maintenant à Atakpamé, veux voir eh va aller chez Akoété, va aller chez Kudjo, ou bien chez Akpovi. On est devenu des frères mêmes. On est trop lié. |

**p. 107**

| A.3.AgbA ff. | Il y a un ancien moniteur qui est chez moi depuis trois jours maintenant [SK : Voilà] aujourd'hui il va partir. |
|---|---|
| A.3.SK ff. | Oui donc, vraiment. |
| A.3.AgbA ff. | Cela est venu je lui a aidé à épargner son argent dans une . dans une des petites banques-là. Donc, ce matin il va partir. |

*Forgiving (section 6.1.6.2)*

| C.1.NK 25s | il doit être aussi, comme la dame l'a dit, pardonner, savoir pardonner. |
|---|---|

*Literate (section 6.1.6.3)*

**p. 108**

| C.4.ANA 9m | Bon, aussi, une aptitude très important, c'est que celui-là pour ce nouveau monde, il doit être lettré {il rit}. Mais dans le cas contraire, il ne peut pas avancer. Il doit être lettré, c'est obligatoire. |
|---|---|
| C.4.KÐ 1h12m | {interprété} C'est vrai, aujourd'hui un dirigeant, quelqu'un peut avoir ces qualités et premièrement diriger un groupe, mais il a la lacune de ne pas avoir l'alphabétisation ou bien, il n'est pas lettré. Alors, les gens pensent que celui-ci, il peut le faire, mais voilà il est bloqué à ce niveau il n'est pas lettré, il ne connaît pas papier. |

Celui-là qu'on voit qui ne peut même, qui n'a pas ces qualités mais qui connaît papier, c'est lui qu'on peut laisser à ce poste-là.

D.Rep.men 22s S'il est lettré, tout ce qu'il juge, il va faire ses rapports.

## p.109

SK 10 Oct. 07 Il doit être lettré pour mieux s'informer, habileté à assister à réunion, avoir accès à la lecture sur le développement, pouvoir transcrire des innovations, lire les documents sur la législation.

C.4.ANA 25m Donc, comme ça c'est pourquoi c'est maintenant nécessaire, d'après l'évolution du monde, c'est vraiment nécessaire que le trio-là, président, trésorier, secrétaire, tous ce trois-là, sachent lire et écrire, tout au moins. On ne va pas exiger un diplo ou un haut niveau, puisque on n'a pas souvent la chance surtout dans les villages ou bien les localités rurales de trouver des gens qui qui sont vraiment lettrés, c'est-à-dire qui ont un niveau élevé, et qui vont se donner à faire évoluer les autres c'est-à-dire aider les autres. Souvent c'est des gens qui pensent déjà comment construire des grandes maisons comment acheter la belle voiture, et ceux-là n'ont plus le temps d'aider les autres. Ehen, donc ceux-là aussi pensent surtout déjà au grand salaire, donc, ceux-là n'ont plus le temps de faire face à l'évolution de leur localité, vous voyez. Donc c'est souvent des gens qui ont à peine le niveau . euh . primaire ou bien à peine, bon, à peine le niveau secondaire par exemple jusqu'au troisième ou plus en a, c'est c'est souvent des gens-là, parmi les gens-là qu'on trouve les gens qui se donnent au développement pour leur communauté.

## p.110

B.3.AmA 1h11m Que je vois que maintenant, grâce à l'alphabétisation et grâce à .. à ce travail que nous faisons d'alphabet= dans ce domaine d'alphabétisation, j'ai vu que .. euh beaucoup de gens occupent de petits, des petits postes des petits postes petits postes. C'est-à-dire que, par exemple, lui {en indiquant SY}, il est diacre maintenant dans une église. Il était inconverti quand on a commencé le travail. Mais, il a vu que le travail-là c'est bon. Et il s'est converti.

*Appendix B: Interview excerpts*

Maintenant, il est devenu un diacre dans no= dans son église. Et il est aussi .. aussi programmé prédicateur. Il prêche correctement et les autres interprètent dans d'autres langues. Ça c'est un fruit. Et il n'est pas le seul. Il y a aussi d'autres exemplaires. Il y a aussi d'autres gens plutôt que, on ne peut pas tous les citer. L'autre que vous voyez là-bas. {en indiquant quelqu'un qui s'assied vers le fond de la salle}. Lui, c'est un superviseur. Il est à Affolé, il est à la frontière {au Bénin}. Quand il y a un projet .. qui concerne le développement, quand le projet arrive, on doit l'atteindre d'abord. Et c'est lui qui accueille les étrangers. C'est lui, quand on dit on veut évoluer, on veut on veut .. euh .. on veut travailler sur le développement au niveau de l'école, on veut avoir telle vision, telle vision sur le plan.

B.3.SY 43m {interprété} Il veut, c'est toujours le même point sur le bien fait de ce que l'alphabétisation a *produise en sa vie, quoi. Bon, en tant que, les gens lui connaissaient comme illettré, analphabète, mais au travers de l'alphabétisation ifè, il arrive maintenant à lire et écrire, et déchiffrer certains mots français. Il peut lire certains mots, mais peut-être ne pas avoir bien le sens. Ça c'est déjà un point. Et c'est par la grâce aujourd'hui, de Dieu aujourd'hui, il arrive à commencer par lire français couramment devant les gens. Tous ceux qui sont retournés, se sont reculés, par cette lecture, cette expression en français, ça peut les faire revenir. Donc, c'est déjà un grand pas, donc aujourd'hui étant superviseur, partant de zéro atteint superviseur c'est un grand pas.

**p. 111**

C.5.ÐO 48m {interprété} Il dit que là l'alphabétisation est très important du moment où, lui-même il est d'abord un témoignage parce qu'il était complètement, il était illettré, à l'arrivée de l'alphabétisation il s'est impliqué et voilà qu'aujourd'hui il peut faire beaucoup de choses et qu'il est en train de faire d'ailleurs. Donc, ça l'a beaucoup aidé, ça l'a sorti de de beaucoup de choses d'ignorance, mais il peut aujourd'hui calculer, si c'est de l'argent, dix millions, trente millions, il peut le faire. Il peut se tenir à la banque aujourd'hui, quand le caissier fait mal, fait un calcul, il peut lui dire que non, qu'il n'a que reprendre, parce qu'il est sûr de ce qu'il est en train de faire devant lui.

*Serious (section 6.1.6.4)*

D.Rep. men 11s  s'il est sérieux, il ne va pas prendre de l'argent auprès de quelqu'un pour mal juger les affaires.

## p. 112

C.2.VA4 39m  Bon, exactement, le président de l'association doit être bien surveiller les classes. {pause de 3 secondes} Bon, il doit naître qui= .. qu'il travaille beaucoup, à celui qui amenait . faire tout le monde a compris que tout le travail. Donc, il doit être bon, premièrement, sérieux et surveiller les classes des adultes.

*Available (section 6.1.6.5)*

C.2.VA3 3m  Un chef doit être disponible puisque si on appelle une réunion c'est un chef, et si le chef dit qu'il est occupé, donc qui va aller ? Donc, le chef doit être disponible aussi.

C.3.AmA 21m  *Kíbí àa wá nɔ́bɛ́ báàyí ɛ́, káfárà, tsí idza á kò wá ŃŃdzɛ́ɛló gbo kò wá. Bí à kpè kpàdɛ́-kã̀ gbo kò wà lɔ, báàyí bí à kó tse fáà tsí kɛ́ɛ fú tsɛ́ ɛ́.* Supposons, comme nous sommes ici aujourd'hui, excusez-moi, qu'on dise que lui type n'est pas venu, l'autre fois aussi, il n'était pas là. Quand on convoque une réunion, il n'y va pas, alors, comment peut-on te confier une tâche à faire.

## p. 113

C.3.MK ff.  *Òŋu ní kpɑ́́dzú gìḍì ɛ́.*
C'est ça qui est très important.

C.3.SY ff.  *Òŋu ní dzɛ́ kó dzáfɔ-tsɛ́.*
C'est ça aimer le travail.

C.3.AmA ff.  *Ńǹń, ká dzáfɔ-tsɛ́ wà lɔ fú ayè ni, ó ḍi* disponibilité *fe, Ká né ayé-tsɛ́, ayè-tsɛ́ kó wà. Ònyà nákó nyáa né àmúḍɔ̃́ fú tsɛ́ tsí kókó wà rí ayè tsí wà wá nɛ́?*

| | |
|---|---|
| | Non, aimer le travail, ça marche avec avoir du temps, pour ce qui concerne la disponibilité. C'est avoir le temps, disposer un temps pour le travail. L'on peut avoir l'amour pour le travail et ne pas avoir du temps pour y venir ? |
| C.3.SY ff. | Ńnè ní èmi ǹ wà wí ní ká dzáfɔ-tsɛ́ ɛ́. Bí ó dzɛ́, ò dzáfɔ-tsɛ́ fee, náàsòkò-kã̀ kpó, yèé ní tse tsí ǹ kò làkó ńnè ɛ́ kò wà. Ká dzáfɔ̀-tsɛ́ yàtɔ̀ fú ká nɛ́ àmúɖɔ̃̀ fú tsɛ́. Ká nɛ́ àmudɔ̃̀ fú tsɛ́ fee, ó dzɛ́, itsɛ́-àwa adzɔ́ bɛ́ kpó, ó ɖi bí ó dzɛ́ ò dzáfɔ-itsɛ́ fee, bí ó dzɛ́ ìwɔ nũ̀ìkã̀ gìɖì nàa wà lɔ ńnè, ǹ kó rí enìkéèdzì-mi kò wà ńnè. |
| | C'est pourquoi moi je dis qu'il faut aimer le travail. Si, réellement, tu aimes le travail, à tout moment, ceci empêche, ça ne pourra jamais te bloquer le chemin du travail. Aimer le travail, c'est différent de avoir l'amour pour le travail. Avoir l'amour pour le travail, c'est collectif d'une part, mais, si individuellement tu aimes le travail, même étant seul, tu vas y aller, « je n'ai pas vu mon second » ne sera pas dedans. |
| C.3.AmA ff. | Ǹhṹ, fɔ tɛ̀ɛ. |
| | Oui, parle. |
| C.3.MK ff. | Iŋɛ́ yèé ǹ wà gbɔ́ ńnɔ-ti |
| | Ce que je comprends dans |
| C.3.AmA ff. | Wũ̀nyɛ kũkũ wũ̀nyɛ kũkũ! |
| | Parle à haute voix, parle à haute voix ! |
| C.3.MK ff. | Iŋɛ́ yèé ǹ wà gbɔ́, iŋɛ́ yèé ǹ wà gbɔ́ ńti yèé ò wà fɔ báàyí ɛ́. Nàa nyáa dzáfɔ-itsɛ́, tsí itsɛ́ yèébɛ́, à kɛ́ɛ sí ńnè ɛ́, dzɛ́ ayè kò wà fɛ́ɛ, iŋɛ́ yèé tse ɛ́ ńbí ò làkóò ɛ́, itsɛ́ kɛ́ ní ò là kó káà tse ɛ́. |
| | Ce que tu as, ce que je comprends en ce qu'il dit maintenant. Tu peux aimer le travail, et le travail devant lequel tu es laissé il faut que tu ais du temps, car là où tu vas, c'est le travail que tu vas faire. |
| C.3.AmA ff. | Ò dzáfɔ-ɔnyà gbo. |
| | Tu dois aimer aussi les gens. |
| C.3.MK ff. | Ɛ̃hɛ́ɛ̃̀, óɖi, ǹhũ̀, òŋu ní àa tì fɔ dzɔ́ɔ́ ɛ́ nɔ̀? Ò rũ̀, ayè rírí fú tsɛ́. Bí ó dzɛ́ ò dzáfɔ-itsɛ́, báàyí, tsí ò gbɔ́ ní itsɛ́-kã̀ wà ńbòmírɛ̀̃ tsí ò ǹde tsí lɔ. Bí ɛnɛ yèé ŋa wáa wá ńǹdí-yèébɛ́, ǹdzɛ́ ní ò dzáfɔ-tsɛ́ ró ńnɛ̀ɛ́ è? Ò kò dzáfɔ-tsɛ́. Donc, ɛ́ iŋɛ́ yèè wà bɛ ɛ́, ayè rírí fú tsɛ́ ńnɛ̀. Oŋu gé ní inàbí-iwa fɔ ɛ́, wo ayè fú tsɛ́, òŋu ní dzɛ́ ǹdì èkɛ̃́ɛ̃́rɛ̃ ɛ́. Ayè rírí wà ńɛɛ̀, iŋɛ́ ŋa a kpó wà ńnɔ́-afɔ ɛ́ bè. |

Exactement, c'est ça que nous avons dit, n'est-ce pas ? Tu vois, avoir du temps pour le travail. Si tu aimes le travail, puis tu apprends qu'il y a un autre travail ailleurs et tu es parti, et si les gens viennent à ton absence, est-ce qu'on peut dire là que tu aimes le travail ? Tu n'aimes pas le travail. Donc, ce qui est là, c'est avoir le temps disposé pour le travail. C'est ça que les frères ont dit, trouver du temps pour le travail, c'est ça le quatrième {point}. La disponibilité est inclue, toutes les autres sont dedans.

**p. 114**

C.4.KĐ 11m   {interprété} ce responsable de programme doit être disponible à tout moment. S'il y a une nouvelle, un travail à faire, il doit se donner corps et âme pour que cette occasion qui se présente ne soit pas .. comment là ? emportée. Il doit tout faire pour ramener les choses de bien à l'association. Et plus encore, il demande un service, ou bien un sacrifice, il doit se donner pour le faire, il ne doit pas attendre, qu'il va dire celui-ci n'est pas là, l'autre aussi n'est pas là, alors je les attends, au moment où ils seront là, nous allons commencer ensemble le travail, non. Un chef de programme doit se donner et doit se sacrifier pour faire le travail afin que, pour que l'association ou bien le programme puisse bien marcher.

C.4.KĐ 12m   {interprété} Un chef de programme doit se donner et doit se sacrifier pour faire le travail afin que, pour que l'association ou bien le programme puisse bien marcher.

C.4.GĐ 51m   (interprété par ANA) on a débattu de ces . problèmes-là, on a traîné ça pendant {sourire dans la voix} pratiquement un mois avant de pouvoir élire le bureau. On a discuté d'ici et de loin là est que vraiment, si on ne fait pas attention, on risque . de de de faire une association mort-née. Puisque quand on va élire les premiers responsables-là, qui ne seront pas disponibles d'abord, et qui ne vont pas vouloir s'investir cœur et âme comme ceux il y aura d'autres qui seront en train de s'investir cœur et âme, et c'est d'autres qui seront en train de profi= de profiter, ou bien de .. de faire ce qu'ils pensent de l'association, ça ne va pas marcher. Donc, on a juré donc vraiment on sera

Appendix B: Interview excerpts

obligé d'élire ceux-là qui s'investissent déjà ceux-là sur qui on a senti le ZÈLE .. de faire marcher vraiment l'alphabétisation dans le cas contraire, on va créer une association mort-née.

**p. 115**
**Features specific to literacy program leaders (section 6.2)**

C.2.VA1 23m   L'exécutif doit être des gens qui ont des visions et qui apportent surtout les nouvelles choses pour que l'association puisse vivre et tout ceci quand ils ont des visions ils ont des nouvelles choses, ils doivent revenir à la source, discuter avec l'association, avant de savoir comment on peut mener ce plan d'action comme le frère vient de le dire.

**p. 116**

C.2.VA1 36m   Il dit, la continuité de la VIE .. des organisations dépend de l'action créatrice .. d'êtres humaines. C'est vrai, on peut commencer quelque chose aujourd'hui. Et .. on peut ne pas avoir des bonnes résultats .. s'il n'y a pas des idées .. nouveaux qui rentrent dans le programme .. des idées nouvelles. Donc, je je tiens à cela parce que aujourd'hui, .. dans un programme d'alphabétisation, on a .. xx chez nous on a commencé. Donc, des années s'écoulent. Pour que ce programme puisse durer, puisse continuer, il faut qu'il y ait des personnes qui amènent d'autres idées, qui créent encore d'autres choses pour toujours renforcer ce programme que nous avons commencé depuis. Et que la continuité y existe . parce que c'est important. S'il y a pas d'autres choses .. que . de savoir lire et écrire, on va se demander à quoi nous sert bon de savoir lire et écrire, s'il n'y a pas d'autres choses que on va encore faire .. à base de savoir lire et écrire. Quand on a appris à lire et à écrire, on va faire quoi avec ? Donc, il faut qu'il y a des idées, il faut qu'il y a de créativité, il faut qu'il y a des choses qui puissent démontrer que réellement, ce n'est pas partie de la base de lire et écrire, on n'allait pas arriver ici.

C.2.JR ff.   Okay. Merci. {je regarde la prochaine personne}

C.2.VA3 ff.   Bon, ici c'est le cinq que j'ai choisi comme le pasteur a dit. Par exemple, dans notre association, nous avons des rencontres des moniteurs .. qui nous aident beaucoup. Bon je vais dire comme on ne l'a pas encore fait . dans cette année, ça nous empêche beaucoup . puisque . certains lieux de rencontres pour tous les moniteurs, et ce que tu as comme problème dans ta classe, tu vas exposer dans = ça devant tous les moniteurs, et tout le monde .. va t'aider par leur pensée, comment il a fait dans son village et ça marche bien. Donc ça ici, on nous a = .. on a demandé que tout le monde puisse donner sa contribution pour le développement, donc, je vois que le cinq m'intéresse beaucoup. Il faut avoir toutes les pensées de tout le monde afin que toi aussi ailles de l'avant.

**p. 117**

C.4.ANA 1h1m   Bon, cette idée, j'ai pour ça . je suis d'accord avec ça, parce que vraiment j'ai senti que ... dans une association . surtout pour mener c'est-à-dire pour traîner . des adultes à un changement de comportement, ou bien, aller de l'avant ou bien à sortir de .. aller sortir de l'ornière. Quand toi, leadership, c'est-à-dire le conducteur ... tu n'es = tu n'as pas vraiment = tu n'es pas animé d'un esprit créatif, on n'arrive pas à mener à bien .. le programme. Puisque l'homme, étant ce qu'il est .. il change toujours ... euh de je ne sais pas vraiment, l'homme change vite. L'homme change à chaque moment, devant chaque situation-là, l'homme change. Donc, toi le conducteur, si vraiment il y a . euh . devant une difficulté peut-être qui veut bloquer .. euh .. l'évolution ou bien, que vraiment dévier . ton objectif ou bien le but principal de l'association, vraiment quand on n'a pas .. on n'a pas .. l'esprit créatif, quand on n'est pas animé des idées créatives, vraiment, on ne peut pas surmonter. On ne peut pas vraiment mener .. à bien .. l'objectif, sinon le but, qu'on est = qu'on s'est fixé. Donc, c'est cette idée-là vraiment je l'approuve. Ça ça ça m'intéresse beaucoup {sourire dans la voix} puisque j'ai j'ai vraiment des des cas comme ça, {rires} j'ai vu que seul la créativité de de de certaines, de de certaines idées qui m'ont sauvé. {rires}

**p. 118**

C.4.KĐ 1h07m  {interprété} Donc, de telle manière que tout ce que l'homme fait si nous voyons le monde au début, dès la création, il n'est= le monde n'est plus à ce stade. Le monde évolue. Et nous devons chercher aussi à évoluer. Il faut cultiver, il faut chercher de nouvelles idées, pour élargir le champ, et comment amener l'homme à agrandir, c'est-à-dire élargir notre intelligence, notre connaissance. S'il faut rester toujours dans le xx c'est que nous faisons depuis un certain temps, c'est comme ÇA que nous faisons. Quand les gens vont savoir que bon, quand c'est ça, aujourd'hui, nous faisons la même chose↓ demain c'est la même chose↓ . qu'est-ce que je vais aller encore chercher. Mais quand il y a des nouvelles idées, d'autres vont chercher à venir voir à découvrir ce qu'il ait de nouveau. Donc, c'est pourquoi lui aussi a choisi le cinquième formule.

C.4.JR ff.  Okay. À ajouter ?

C.4.KL ff.  Moi, je ne ferai que, répéter ce que les autres ont dit. Sinon, pour faire que, dans notre association nous sommes en train de . de créer .. bon . euh l'élevage de de volailles maintenant, selon, là donc, pour faire revivre surtout ceux qui sont . un peu ennuyés, ceux qui sont . dedans, ceux qui étaient dedans il y a longtemps et il n'y a pas de changement donc, on a fait emmener ça là pour les faire réveiller encore de leur sommeil. Aussi pour . faire plaire les autres . qui ne sont pas encore là, que s'ils sont allés là, ils peuvent découvrir autres choses.

**p. 119**

A.3.AgbA 28m  Bon, je pense que . {il tape la table} voilà, c'est nos forces, et ... fait que si= nous avons aussi .. bon ça rentre dedans quand nous avons des innovations .. des nouvelles idées, on partage toujours avec les autres.

A.3.SK 29m  Je dirai que la vraie force encore, c'est que . on a vraiment soif pour le peuple ifè de leur faire réussir. Ça fait que, nuit et jour, on a en train de réfléchir . qu'est-ce qu'on peut faire, comment nous pouvons passer . pour pouvoir faire sortir le peuple donc, de temps en temps, c'est pourquoi il vient de parler des innovations, on a des innovations d'encouragement, des idées de . d'encourager nos moniteurs, nos s= les villages à pouvoir continuer le travail.

## Qualities of literacy program heads (section 6.2.1)

**p. 120**

*Respectful of work and of time (section 6.2.1.1)*

C.3.SY 15m  {interprété} Quand un chef est là, il a établi un programme, il doit le respecter, il doit le compléter comme ça, ça fera de la joie à toute l'association, à tout le groupe . parce que ils diront que non, notre chef, s'il dit quelque chose, il le fait.

**p. 121**

C.3.OKD 24m  *Respect nákó nyáa gbàḍì – disponibilite.́*
Le respect peut occuper la place de la disponibilité.

C.3.SY ff.  *Ká né àrísá fú tsé ńnèé nɔ?*
C'est avoir du respect pour le travail, n'est-ce pas ?

C.3.All ff.  *Nn!*
Oui !

C.3.OKD ff.  *Ò mà ní nákó nyáa gbà ìḍì-yèébé tsí yèébé ó kó nɔ, tsí respect é gbo á, ó wà gbewo fú iŋé ɔkằlɔ́ɔ̀kằ kpó.*
Sache que ça peut prendre la place de ceci, puis ceci s'efface et le respect aussi devient plus important que tout.

C.3.AmA ff.  *Kòkó nyáa nɔ ìḍì-disponibilité, disponibilité ŋu wà nĩkằ,* c'est un temps, temps de travail *ni, àsòkò-itsé ńnèé. Asòkò-tsé nákó nyáa wà nĩkằ.*
Ça ne peut pas faire perdre la place de disponibilité, la disponibilité, elle autre est à part, c'est un temps, c'est le

| | |
|---|---|
| | temps de travail, c'est ça le temps de travail. Le temps de travail peut être à part. |
| C.3.OKD ff. | xx {il parle aussi} |
| C.3.AmA ff. | Ò gbɔ́ ò kpì-è báàyfî? |
| | Me comprends-tu maintenant ? |
| C.3.OKD ff. | O gbɔ́ afɔ̀ yèé èmìgbo ǹ wà fɔ̀ ɛ́, bí ò respecter temps á, ó kó yáa tse tsí nàa yáa lɔ ńtsɛ́ ɛ́. Bí ǹ kò respecter nɔ́mbɔ́ báàyí, ǹ kòkó wá; ó dzɛ́ ǹ kò rí ayè fú tsɛ́, mais ǹ nɛ́ respect fú ŋɛ́ yèé à fɔ̀ ɛ́, fú ǹwèrè yèé à ɖá á tsí ǹ wá, ò wà rfî? |
| | Écoute ce que moi aussi je dis, si tu respectes le temps, cela vas faire que tu vas aller au travail à temps. Si je ne respecte pas aujourd'hui par exemple, je viendrais pas, et c'est que je n'ai pas de temps pour le travail, mais j'ai du respect pour ce qui a été dit, pour le temps fixé, et je suis là, vois-tu ? |
| C.3.AmA ff. | Nn! Ǹ kò wà kɔ iŋɛ́ yèé ò wà fɔ̀ ɛ́ náa. Ò rí fee, ó wà ní fee, bí ɔ̀nyà-kã̀ dzɛ́ ɔ̀gá fee, tsí esprit de fidélité kò wà ńnè fee, itsɛ́ ɛ́ kò bòkó rɛ̃̀. |
| | Oui ! Je ne refuse pas du fait ce que tu dis. Tu vois, il faut que, si quelqu'un est chef, ne possédant pas l'esprit du fidélité, le travail ne pourra pas marcher. |
| C.3.OKD ff. | Tì fidélité ǹ kò kɔ̀. |
| | Pour ce qui concerne la fidélité, je ne refuse pas. |
| C.3.MK ff. | Nn! Ń si bè. Iŋɛ́ yèé ò wà fɔ̀ kpó ŋa á ò gbɔ́ɔ̀. |
| | Oui, mets ça là. Tout ce que tu dis, tu comprends ? |
| C.3.AmA ff. | Yèé ò fɔ̀ ɛ́ ó kó dzɛ́ cinquième rubrique. |
| | Celui que tu as touché sera pour la cinquième rubrique. |
| C.3.MK ff. | Iŋɛ́ yèé è wà fɔ̀ ŋa kpó kéŋúkéŋú ŋa á. Yèé è wà fɔ̀ ŋa kpó ɛ́, ó wà ńnè. |
| | Tout ce que vous êtes en train de dire. Tout ce que vous dîtes est dedans. |

**p. 121**

| | |
|---|---|
| C.3.AmA ff. | À nákó rfî, ó wɔ̀ má kpó ńnè. Ó wɔ̀ má kpó kékéŋú lɔ ni. Ó wɔ̀ nára ara-ŋa lɔ. |
| | On peut le trouver, c'est un ensemble. Tout est combiné. C'est une interdépendance. |

| | |
|---|---|
| C.1.AgA 5m | Ó kó dzɛ́ ɛnɛ yèé bí ó bòkó tsitsɛ́, kà kó dzɛ́ ɛnɛ yèé náa tsiyɔ̃̀ nɔmí ɔ̀gẽ́ nára itsɛ́ ɛ́. Nɔmí nákó nyáa mú tsɛ́ ɛ́ tsí [YMA : voilà] ń kpe tsɛ́ ńǹwèrè ɔ̀kã̀lɔ́ɔ̀kã̀ kpó. |
| | Il doit être quelqu'un, s'il veut travailler, ne devra pas paresser. En d'autre termes, il doit donner de la valeur à son travail à tout moment. |
| C.1.NK ff. | Ɛ̃́ɛ̃́! |
| | Oui ! |
| C.1.YMA ff. | Iŋé yèé tse, kò tsi ɔ̀nyà kpó ní dzɛ́ akɔ́nɛ tsí wà mú itsɛ́ ɛ́ tsí wà ń kpe tsɛ́ ɛ́. |
| | Car ce n'est pas tout le monde qui est moniteur et qui accorde de l'importance au travail. |
| C.1.AgA ff. | Kó mú tsɛ́ ɛ́ tsí ń kpe tsɛ́. |
| | Il doit accorder de l'importance au travail. |
| C.2.VA3 18m | puisque nos apprenants ce sont des adultes. Respecter les heures aussi qu'on a fixées pour les enseignements. Donc, si quelqu'un qui est déjà plus âgé que toi s'il arrive dans la classe toi à l'heure fixée et toi tu n'es pas arrivé, il te voit, il est ton apprenant mais il te voit que tu es déjà en retard. Donc, il doit être juste ça par rapport au jour |
| C.2.VA1 ff. | des heures |
| C.2.VA3 ff. | et aux heures aux jours des apprenants et aux heures aussi fixées. |
| C.4.KL 17m | Mais, un responsable d'abord il doit être à l'heure quand on parle de réunion. Il doit être à l'heure pour montrer le bon exemple aux autres membres. |

**p. 123**
*Teachable and able to teach (section 6.2.1.2)*

| | |
|---|---|
| C.1.NK 5m | Ó kó ma ɛkpa-akɔ́nɛ rere. Tsí ó kó máa kɔ́ nɛ, |
| | Il doit connaître les conditions/règles d'un bon moniteur. Et il doit savoir enseigner à quiconque, |
| C.1.YMA ff. | nókó máa tse ɛ̀kɔ́. |
| | doit savoir présenter une leçon. |
| C.1.NK ff. | nákó máa tse ɛ̀kɔ́. Ó kó ma ɛkpa-akɔ́nɛ tsí ó kó máa tse ɛ̀kɔ́. |

*Appendix B: Interview excerpts* 285

|  |  |
|---|---|
|  | doit savoir présenter une leçon. Connaître les règles d'un bon moniteur, il doit savoir présenter une leçon. |
| C.3.AmA 1h15m | La fois= hier il y a un frère qui est venu {il baisse la voix} il fait l'internat c'est celui qui a fait tout ceci-là au tableau-là {le tableau est couvert des formules mathématiques} et ce matin j'ai j'ai enseigné nos élèves, c'est-à-dire ceux-là qui forment le troisième cycle ici à Adogbenou ici, c'est moi qui les enseigne. |

**p. 124**

|  |  |
|---|---|
| C.3.AmA 41m | Donc, quand je suis revenu de Kara le jour-là, je me dis Ah, d'accord je dois transférer ma compétence je dois avoir l'esprit de transfert de compétences aux autres, il faut leur partager le travail. Souvent quand on va aux réunions de moniteurs, bon, le coordinateur fait des enseignements pratiques. Donc, à partir de ce jour-là, quand on dit il y a une réunion de dans ce mois, il y a une réunion des moniteurs dans le mois prochain, je dis Ah, toi, prépare-toi, prépare un enseignement pratique que tu vas dispenser. Toi, le mois sur prochain, prépares un enseignement pratique tu vas dispenser et ce n'est plus moi qui vais tout faire. {petite rire} |
| C.2.VA1 18m | C'est quelqu'un quand même .. bon, je ne sais pas si on veut en venir là. Il y aura toujours besoin de formation parce que il faut certaines choses aussi pour que ce programme puisse évoluer. Bon, par exemple, en matière de gestion, des .. des personnes ou bien de gestion de finances .. ce responsable de programme d'alpha doit être formé la-dessus. Il doit avoir ces qualités professionnelles, en matière de gestion des personnes et de gestion des matériels, de gestion de finances. |

**p. 125**

|  |  |
|---|---|
| B.4.GĐ 14m | {interprété} Son expérience propre, c'est qu'il a commencé au niveau {de l'église} il a été élu le prés{ident lacune} |
| B.4.ANA ff. | président d'une église .. locale |
| B.4.GĐ ff. | (interp.) Une église . locale, donc ça lui a permis aussi de faire des expériences et de s'en sortir de certaines {épreuves} et de plus, depuis que là on l'a choisi pour être membre de ce comité de d'association d'alpha {lacune ad}ministration, ça |

là a aussi beaucoup aidé, et vraiment, comme les anciens le disent, beaucoup de viande ne gâte pas la sauce. {rires de tous} Alors, s'il peut avoir aussi l'opportunité d'en a[voir]
B.4.ANA ff. [compléter]
B.4.GÐ ff. (interp.) de compléter, ça le ferait du bien.

*Other qualities (section 6.2.1.3)*

**p. 126**

C.3.SY 15m {interprété} un chef doit avoir l'esprit de . un esprit coopératif il doit avoir des relations avec d'autres associations et ça fera que son travail peut connaître d'épanouissement.

C.4.ANA 1h44m quelques rares fois que d'autres viennent de d'autres ethnies ou bien de d'autres localités ou bien de d'autres pays . pour venir nous parler des choses, après leur départ, on oublie tout .. Puisque il n'y a pas une organisation-là qui met ça, qui traduit ça .. en textes. Comme ça là, ce qu'on a écouté oralement, COMbien de jours combien de mois cela peut faire . la mémoire peut la garder pendant combien de temps ? {petit rire} Vous savez que la capacité de la mémoire est limitée . {petit rire} et quand on parle beaucoup, on oublie beaucoup de choses on garde peu. Donc, si vraiment ceux qui viennent, comme ça là les ONG des organisations gouvernementales même aussi, qui veulent vraiment former .. les gens sur certaines pratiques . culturales ou bien que ça soit . euh changement des comportements tout ça là, qu'ils nous impliquent nous .. acteurs à l'alphabétisation pour que si possible s'ils peuvent nous expliquer cela plus profondément pour que ça nous soit facile à traduire de rendre ça textuel, et ce serait maintenant maintenue cette formation sera maintenue éternellement .. puisque une formation dont on a les . les fascicules, ou bien les brochures qui parlent de ça qui expliquent cette formation, c'est devenue immortelle cette formation est devenue à jamais durable.

**p. 127**

B.1.NK af1 10m Donc, nous savons que, SI nous arrivons à organiser une classe, par exemple, en groupement, donc pour nous comme on n'a pas la capacité, nous allons maintenant demander des appuis techniques auprès des ONG qui va intervenir maintenant dans notre programme pour pouvoir les aider, aider maintenant ce groupement.

C.4.KÐ 12m (interprété par ANA) quelque fois il arrive des moments où le responsable, sinon le leader dans le xx de programme d'alphabétisation met ses propres FONDS dedans. En attendant peut-être si la communauté ou bien les membres vont l'aider, vont à cotiser pour qu'il puisse remplacer. Si celui-là ne veut pas mettre ses propres intérêts au profit du groupe, ça ne marche pas. Il y a d'autres qui ne veulent pas vraiment prendre son propre argent pour aider le groupe, non. Quelqu'un comme ça ne peut pas conduire un programme d'alphabétisation puisque il arrive des moments vraiment, si tu n'aimes pas sortir l'argent de ta poche, ça ça risque bloquer du programme, ça bloque, donc il faut que ça soit quelqu'un vraiment qui a l'idée de faire progresser coût coût coût ce programme.

C.5.EK 8m Donc, moi je dirais que il doit s'efforcer aussi à connaître la situation de ses .. de ses membres. Bon, par exemple, dans un groupe donné, il faut savoir, qui est celui-ci, bon, qu'est-ce qu'il aime, qu'est-ce qu'il n'aime pas, comment faut-il aller envers lui pour pouvoir le faire venir à toi ou pouvoir le faire comprendre bien ce qui va se passer, donc, .. voilà les qualités qu'il doit assumer, un chef de groupe d'alphabétisation.

p. 128
*Qualities of board members (section 6.2.2)*

*Solidarity and discretion (section 6.2.2.1)*

p. 129
C.4.GÐ 20m *Tsí ó wà ní òŋu gbo, sèkèrètɛ́ɛ̀ gbo, tèrèsɔ̀ríyè gbo aŋa kó nɛ́ ìlò kàntso, àrū-ŋa kó ɖɛ́, arū-ŋa kó dzɛ́ arū kàntso. Kó máa dzɛ́ ní bí à gbɔ́ ɔtɔ̀ ńdi présidɑ̄̂ɑ̂ ká káà gbɔ́ ɔ̀tɔ̀ ńdi sèkèrètɛ́ɛ̀ tsí gbɔ́ ɔ̀tɔ̀ ńdi tèrèsɔ̀ríyè. Nyèŋè náa tse tsí bí ɔma-ɛgbé ŋa kpé nyèŋè gbígbɔ́, náa tse ní à wà dzowú ni; ńǹsérè-ɔ̀nyà ɖúɖú bí.*

|   |   |
|---|---|
|   | Il faut que le président, le secrétaire et le trésorier aient le même comportement positif, être unis, que leurs paroles ne diffèrent pas les unes des autres. Ils ne doivent pas permettre que les paroles du président diffèrent de celles du secrétaire, de celle du trésorier ce sera très mauvais. Quand les simples membres apprennent de ces choses, ils disent qu'il y a jalousie ou mésentente entre les leaders selon leur analyse. |
| C.5.OK 22m | Parce que nous voulons comme nous l'avons dit la fois passée, sauvegarder l'union par la culture et tout ce qui nous unit. Et surtout de cette manière nous sommes plus forts que d'être divisés . parce que notre association comme on l'avait indiqué la fois passée, ce qui fait vraiment notre force, c'est ce qui nous unit ensemble, que nous partageons ensemble et il est bien de préserver cela. |

**p. 130**

| | |
|---|---|
| C.2.VA2 22m | et .. comment, comment dire, {il faudrait qu'ils soient} unis et ho avoir l'idée aussi d'écouter ho l'association, les membres quoi de l'association et bon pour mettre en application ces choses ho leur décisions et bon . bon il faudrait mettre en application ce qu'ils ont pris comme décisions dans bon dans l'association que je vais dire. Et en bref, je vais dire que il faudrait quelqu'un aussi comme on l'a dit, qui se comprenne, qui n'a pas de tiraillement et ainsi de suite quoi. |
| C.3.AmA 36m | le bureau exécutif doit aussi avoir la qualité de la solidarité. Il faut que le bureau ait la solidarité du travail parce que quand nous travaillons ici, ce qui .. ce qui nous manque, ou soit ce= beaucoup de choses qui rentrent là où les fuites passent pour influence= pour là où vient les fuites pour empêcher l'évolution du travail les aspects de scandale, pour pouvoir les les les surmonter il faut qu'on soit solidaire. Qu'il ait l'esprit de solidarité en nous, là, s'il y a la solidarité, le travail ça va tranquillement il n'y a pas assez de problèmes. |

**p. 131**

| | |
|---|---|
| C.5.BK 12m | De l'autre côté, ils doivent traiter avec confidence, d'où la sobriété, confidence, les dossiers de du groupe, il doit être |

*Appendix B: Interview excerpts*  289

confidentiel. À tel point que si on a traité un sujet concernant .. une église une tierce personne que cela ne sert pas de d'occasion pour déjà divulguer l'idée qu'on a construite ensemble. Donc, il faudrait qu'ils soient, ils géraient confidentiellement les dossiers qu'ils leur sont soumis. Afin de ne pas créer des préjugés.

*Study a situation before reacting (section 6.2.2.2)*

C.2.VA1 20m l'exécutif maintenant doit avoir du temps pour étudier certaines idées avant de les mettre en exécution.

Plus tard au même discours:

**p. 132**

Ils doivent toujours se fier . à la volonté du peuple. Ce que . les autres veulent, et c'est ça qu'ils doivent étudier . pour euh savoir comment faire pour aboutir . à ce que EUX ils ont énoncé

C.4.GĐ 18m  Ó wà ní ɛnɛ yèé dzɛ́ ɔgá nɔmí pèrèsìdáā̀-á, tắná kó wûnyɛ̀, ó wà ní kó rí òkpì-afɔ ɛ́ gbɔ́ rere. Tori, ńbí ɛgbé wàá, iŋɛ́ kpó náa wà bɛ̀, otítɔ́ gbo òdòbò gbo náa wà bɛ̀.

Avant qu'un président ne convoque une réunion sur une affaire, il doit être sûr et bien étudier d'avance le problème. Car dans une association, il y a un peu de tout, le mensonge de même que la vérité.

**p. 133**

C.2.VA1 32m Et voilà, bon, c'est ce qu'on a fait, et des fois on était sur place pour voir la situation écouter les autres et que par eux-mêmes on a essayé de trouver des solutions à ce problème qui est né.

**p. 134**
**Representations of subordinates (section 6.3)**

C.4.GĐ 30m  Ègbè náàynì-nɛ ɛ́ fee, ó dzɛ́ òŋu gbo wà ń buróò nàmíí?
Le subordonné dont on parle, est-il membre du BE ou comment ?

C.4.ANA ff.   *Ká fɔ̀ní kíbí ìwɔ Làbíté wà báàyí ɛ́, ȇhɛ̑ɛ̄ɛ̄, kí wo dzú-tɛ̀ɛ? Ki ò dólá tse. Fú èdè-àbínɛ bí ɛ́, ìwɔ gbo ní wà sɔ́má ɔ̀gá á, kí ŋa ó wà ní ò ḍólá tse, tsí kí ŋa ò kò ḍólá-tse?*

Supposons, tel que tu es avec Labité par exemple, il est coordinateur et superviseur, quelles sont tes devoirs en tant que subordonné à Labité ? Dans le domaine d'alphabétisation, c'est toi par exemple qui es après le chef, alors là que dois-tu faire et que ne dois-tu pas faire ?

C.1.YMA 13m   *Afúfɛ̀ɛnɔ́.*

Le conseiller.

C.1.NK ff.   *Ńǹń!* Subordonné, c'est-à-dire .. *ká fɔ̀ ní, ǹ dzɛ́* responsable, *èŋɛ è dzɛ́* subordonnés-*mi ŋa, itsɛ́ yèésí wodzú-*subordonné *ɛ́?*

Non ! Subordonné, c'est-à-dire .. disons je suis responsable, vous, vous êtes mes subordonnés, quels devoirs incombent au subordonné ?

**p. 135**

C.1.JR ff.   Les autres membres de l'association
C.1.NK ff.   de l'asso [ciation]
C.1.JR ff.   [quelles s]ont, quelles sont leurs responsabilités.
C.1.YMA ff.   Là, {en Ifè, pas transcrite}
C.1.JR ff.   Ou bien, vous comme membres d'un village, et vous êtes sous un chef je suppose, quelles sont les responsabilités [de quelqu'un qui]
C.1.NK ff.   *[Ò rí nyèŋè ɛ́,] àa ti gba ɛkɔ́ nyèŋè wáa lɔ.*

[Tu vois,] à ce sujet, nous avons été initiés déjà.

C.4.KĐ 37m   {interprété} le premier responsable doit écouter, doit considérer son subordonné. En d'autres sens, le subordonné est comme son oreille, parce que, ici en le .. dans la race noire ou bien en Afrique souvent l'homme n'aime pas s'approcher du premier responsable. C'est son subordonné qu'on pousse, s'il y a quelque chose, c'est au subordonné qu'on le dit.

C.4.ANA 39m   si le chef .. n'aime pas que ses subordonnés connaissent ses activités, connaissent dans ce que lui il fait, sinon, une seule personne, on dit en en en chez nous, qu'une seule personne est: souvent .. c'est quelqu'un qui peut mourir:

ou bien c'est-à-dire c'est quelqu'un qui est proche de la mort. Mais si on dit le groupe, le groupe ne meurt jamais d'un coup.

**p. 136**
*Willingness and obedience (section 6.3.1)*

C.5.BK 16m  Oui, le: le subordonné ou: celui sur qui on est établi doit afficher sa volonté en toute choses. Il doit être disposé . à .. à être MEMbre . avec euh . tous ce que: tout ce que exige de lui= tout ce qu'on attend de lui à accomplir dans . dans l'œuvre qui nous tous ont signé. Donc, il faudrait qu'il soit disposé. C'est sa bonne volonté qui va lui prédisposer à faire à accomplir sa responsabilité. Donc, il n'est pas facile d'être subordonné mais, si on affiche la volonté, l'enTIÈre volonté, on on s'y met.

C.5.EK 17m  le subordonné il doit aussi connaître que . il a un un supérieur. Il doit connaître qu'il a un supérieur, et toute la tâche qu'il va confier le supérieur, il doit les assumer.

**p. 137**

C.3.SY 45m  {interprété} un subordonné doit être disponible de recevoir d'auprès de chef, et après avoir reçu, il faut qu'il exécute, il met en valeur ce qu'il a reçu.

C.2.VA4 26m  Ó wà ní kó wà rēti gbè-ɛnɛ yèé wà ńwádzú fúu, nɔ̀mí ɛnɛ yèé dzé ɔ̀gá-ɛ̀ ɛ́. Ó wà ní kó wà mú tsɛ́ ɛ́ kpe tsɛ́ kóya kóya.
Il faut qu'il obéisse à celui qui lui est établi chef. Il doit à tout moment accorder une grande importance à son travail.

C.2.VA2 ff.  Ó wà ní kó wà mú tsɛ́ ɛ́ kpe tsɛ́ négbé ɛ́.
Il doit considérer son travail dans l'association.

C.1.AgA 14m  que c'était notre chef, si il dit quelque chose, il faut= il faut que nous soumettre,

*Collaboration (section 6.3.2)*

C.2.VA1 26m  Comme il dit que le chef ou bien le responsable doit être quelqu'un qui collabore, il faut le sujet aussi accepte cette collaboration et qu'il se collabore avec aussi le responsable et que leurs idées soient les mêmes pour mener un même combat faire le réussit le projet qu'ils ont mis en place.

**p. 138**

C.5.ÐO 32m  {interprété} Et quand les subordonnés ou bien ses collaborateurs finiront par découvrir que non, notre chef, notre patron est en train de faire le .. il se faire de s'autoproclamer, ou bien il décide seul ce qu'il veut, finalement, ils vont désister ou bien se décourager, se retirer et le travail ne peut plus avancer. Là, il faut la collaboration.

C.4.ANA 38m  eh: il faudrait que vraiment il y a la bonne compréhension entre les subordonnés . et: le chef. Surtout d'une manière que le chef . sache que . ce qui celui qui est sous lui là aussi {le registre monte} doit comprendre, si possible même, connaître même ce que lui il est en train de faire. Comment il fait ? Puisque quand lui n'est pas là là, c'est: son subordonné qui doit continuer l'œuvre . qu'il ait quand même la volonté de libérer . euh la tâche au: = à son subordonné.

**p. 139**
*Attention and respect (section 6.3.3)*

C.2.VA3 25m  Ó wà ní kó wà rē̄tígbè-ɔ̀gá-ɛ̀.
Il doit écouter son chef.

C.2.VA1 ff.  Kó rɛ̃̀ si ńǹtá-ìŋé yèé àfɔ fú ɛ́.
Il doit respecter ce qu'on lui a dit de faire.

C.2.VA2 ff.  Ò kpì-afɔ gbígbɔ́ kó gbe ńnɔ́-ɛgbé ɛ́ fú ŋa.
Il leur faut la compréhension dans l'association.

C.1.NK 14m  Le subordonné . aussi écoute .. son chef, le subordonné aussi .. eh . respecte .. son = le responsable, et .. lui soumet . ses idées, il soumet, il respecte, il écoute, et il lui rend service.

*Harmony and loyalty (section 6.3.4)*

C.2.VA1 27m  Donc, la responsabilité c'est .. c'est de d'être en communion avec l'exécutif ou bien avec le responsable qu'ils sont devant. Donc, le membre doit être en communion avec lui, il doit partager les mêmes idées que les autres pour que le projet puisse réussir.

**p. 140**

| | |
|---|---|
| C.2.JR ff. | Autres choses à compléter, ajouter ? |
| C.2.VA2 ff. | Sinon, ho, l'entente, s'il y a l'entente, donc le travail va bien évoluer. Donc, les décisions prises, qu'ils soient en entente et dans des ho avoir une même idée alors ça peut faire avancer le groupe et ainsi de suite. |
| C.4.KÐ 37m | {interprété} Donc, s'il n'y a pas une entente entre le premier responsable et son subordonné, le travail va marcher difficilement. |
| C.3.SY 45m | {interprété} Là, c'est là où il donne l'exemple de l'évangile selon Jean, chapitre 15, et on a donné un exemple là-bas que, toute branche qui n'est pas attachée au tronc ne peut pas porter du fruit. Alors, s'il veut rester indépendant, il va noyer. Alors, il faut que les subordonnés aussi soient attachés au patron pour profiter du bien qui= que le patron détient, ou bien le chef détient comme ça eux aussi ils peuvent évoluer. |
| C.4.GÐ 33m | {interprété} Il doit aimer son respon=. son premier responsable, il doit aimer aussi le travail qui lui est confié et être ami du responsable. En aimant le premi= quand le premier responsable et le subordonné aime le premier responsable, vraiment le travail peut avancer. |

**p. 141**

| | |
|---|---|
| C.4.Interpr. ff. | Et je pense que c'est ce que j'ai retenu, si j'ai oublié un côté, il faut me dire. |
| C.4.ANA ff. | Moi, je vois que c'est un relais très important parce que quand on est sous quelqu'un les gens essaient de vouloir casser le lien qui est entre vous subordonné et le responsable. Quelque fois même on peut aller jusqu'à vous dire que, ah toi tu ne vois pas tel que ton patron est en train d'évoluer pourtant lui il est en train d'évoluer à ton détriment c'est ce qu'il doit te donner là et il ne te donne pas et il est en train de construire quelque chose et bien il est en train d'acheter tout ceci, donc, vas-y il faut gréver contre lui, il faut revendiquer ce droit-là, il faut faire ceci, il faut |

faire ceci, oui, ça arrive souvent et si toi subordonné tu n'es pas .. patient, tu n'arrives pas à analyser bien, ces provocateurs-là tu risques de ton bien ou de bloquer le travail, c'est-à-dire ce qu'il vous attend. Vraiment que, c'est pourquoi il est nécessaire qu'il exige un un amour et vraiment, une bonne compréhension entre le chef et le subordonné ou bien celui qui est sous.

## *Report giver (section 6.3.5)*

C.5.EK 17m  Il donne un bon rapport à son supérieur.

**p. 142**

C.5.OK ff.  Voilà. Ça c'est ce que j'allais ajouter. Il a la responsabilité de rendre compte.

C.5.EK ff.  C'est ça.

C.5.OK ff.  de rendre compte

C.4.ANA 40m  Donc, comme ça là il faut vraiment apPRENDre à son subordonné comMENT il faut faire. Et même, leur lancer à le faire, et toi responsable maintenant, tu corriges . au cas où c'est mal fait. Comme ça, eux aussi, ils sont plus= ils sont plu= ils ont plus le cœur gai de se rapprocher de vous responsable. puisque tu les as confié . une une session d'activité à faire, {registre plus haut} après avoir finir il doit tenir compte, et comme ça tu lui apportes . les ajoutes ou bien: des *correctives que lui-même il aussi il sait Ah, moi aussi je connais un peu ce que le chef fait. Donc lui aussi, ça ça ça le fait grandir, et comme ça, la franche collaboration peut exister.

C.4.KƉ 37m  {interprété} C'est son subordonné qu'on pousse, s'il y a quelque chose, c'est au subordonné qu'on le dit. Avec l'intention que c'est lui qui peut le rendre, qui [xx]

C.4.ANA ff.                                        [xx]

C.4.KƉ ff.  (interp.) qui peut rendre compte de ce que c'est qui est fait.

**p. 143**

C.4.GƉ 32m  {interprété} En ce sens que, quand il y a un problème, ou bien on l'a parlé du responsable par exemple la masse

Appendix B: Interview excerpts

                n'aime pas aller directement vers le responsable, le premier responsable pour l'accuser. Ces sont des rumeurs. Et le subordonné celui qui est sous le responsable, lui il est plus proche de la masse. Donc, étant éveillé, il peut écouter aussi la masse, et là, il peut recueillir les informations. Ces informations maintenant, à lui de les juger, les analyser et savoir comment les présenter au responsable et comment au travers de son subordonné le responsable aussi sera préparé.

C.4.KL 35m  Donc, il doit être éveillé et suivre tout ce qui se passe. Et sera en mesure aussi de répondre quand il y aura des questions et .. par les membres qui ne sont pas dans le bureau.

p. 147

## Motivations of literacy workers: Representations related to literacy (Chapter 7)

p. 148

C.1.NK 31m  L'importance de faire l'alphabétisation dans les langues locales . c'est que aujourd'hui, nous: = tout le monde, quelque soit le rang social de chaque communauté, que, la vie de nos vieux, de nos ancêtres, ce qu'ils ont mené est différent que celle que nous retenons aujourd'hui. Comme d'habitude on dit qu'il y a la mondialisation et tout ça là, donc tout est changé.

p. 149

C.1.NK 32m  Donc, on ne peut pas vivre .. sans connaître à lire et écrire maintenant, même nos parents ou bien les = . la communauté ifè avec qui nous travaillons aujourd'hui, reconnaît, ils voient l'importance maintenant de s'alphabétiser,

B.2.VA2 13m  puisque tout le monde veut, peut xx connaître euh savoir écrire sa langue et parle couramment . et lire, c'est ça.

## Representations of nonliterates (section 7.1)

### p. 150
*Handicapped (section 7.1.1)*

C.2.VA2 40m  En premier lieu, moi je vais dire que: c'est important parce que: eh le: quelqu'un . l'adulte . qui: bon .. il est *handicap . parce qu'il ne connaît pas . à écrire et à lire.

A.2.AgbA 9m  Donc, le prédominant, c'est l'alphabétisation .. Quand la personne n'est pas alphabétisée, tu peux lui donner un million de francs, il va dilapider ça.

C.2.VA1 43m  Quelqu'un qui ne sait pas lire et écrire, NE PEUT PAS s'autosuffire. Il ne peut pas s'autosuffire.

### p. 151

C.3.MK 13m  mais il faut être patient et ait compassion de ces gens-là . puisqu'ils sont comme des aveugles, ils sont sourds aussi ils ne connaissaient rien. C'est là, pourquoi moi j'aime toujours la compassion de ces gens-là et qui= la personne vont voir que les gens qu'ils ne *connaient rien et c'est lui, c'est à lui de le faire sortir dans les tunnels où ils sont.

C.4.ANA 1h20m  Comment celui qui n'est pas lettré .. peut se retrouver .. dans: euh: . peut= peut reconnaître SA PART {accentuée mais doucement} . dans le fruit de la démocratie ? Voilà qu'il ne sait pas lire les textes .. Même les textes électoraux . ils ne comprennent rien de cela.

*In darkness and ignorance (section 7.1.2)*

### p. 152

C.1.NK 33m  Donc, les gens ont pris conscience maintenant de connaître à lire et écrire, même savoir calculer maintenant pour gérer leur propre exploitation, leurs propres affaires, et maintenant, de ne pas être encore dans l'obscurité . de ce monde lettré.

C.1.NK 34m  même au niveau du média, tout ce qu'on dit maintenant sensibilisation, tout ce qui se dit que tout le monde doit sortir de

Appendix B: Interview excerpts

l'obscurité et être maintenant ouvert maintenant, à ce monde lettré qui interpelle tout le monde. Voilà.

C.4.KL 1h15m   Donc, aujourd'hui lui il vient m'encourager de continuer, qu'on faire ev= que moi je vais les sortir maintenant . eh . de l'obscurité.

**p. 153**

C.5.EK 41m   Bon, aujourd'hui par exemple, si nous allons voir nos raisons par exemple, ceux qui connaissent papier .. ne sont pas égaux à ceux qui ne connaissent pas papier.

C.5.BK 43m   Je peux dire que l'alphabétisation a pour intérêt le la civilisation. Un homme alphabétisé est égal à un homme civilisé. Ça veut dire que, il a quitté, il a franchi les barrières locales et maintenant il peut être en contact avec l'extérieur. Pour le le le fait que le frère a expliqué. Donc, quand qu'il reçoit quelque chose de l'extérieur et qu'il arrive à gérer ça de lui-même, il est civilisé.

C.4.GĐ 1h10m   {interprété} Alors, ils étaient aussi comme des esclaves . ou bien je dirais même des bêtes, exécution avant réclamation. Est-ce qu'il avait même réclamation, d'ailleurs

C.4.ANA ff.   non, tu ne comprends rien

C.4.GĐ ff.   (interp.) pour toi devant quelqu'un qui est lettré, quand il te parle, c'est pour dire oui. Et tu exécutes, que ce soit bon ou mauvais, c'est lui qui a dit que c'est vrai ou pas, ce qu'il a dit, tu ne vois rien.

**p. 154**

C.4.GĐ 1h11m   {interprété} Et c'est pourquoi, nuit et jour, il se force pour que ce programme puisse continuer.

C.5.BK 44m   Donc, l'alphabétisation va amener les apprenants à être éclairés. Ils peuvent lire, écrire, transmettre tout ce qu'ils veulent de manière ordonnée, logique et ordonnée. Avant, sans le le l'alphabétisation, le raisonnement était .. flou, mais par= euh avec l'arrivée de l'alphabétisation, eux ils qui se sont appliqués, ils ont su exploiter cette formation.

C.3.SY 1h21m   {interprété} Du moment où avant, dans le temps, on était .. tout le peuple était dans l'ignorance. Tout ce qu'on pouvait faire, de un laps de temps, un petit temps pour gagner quelque chose on utilisait assez d'énergie et on ne gagnait rien. Mais à base de l'alphabétisation, les yeux sont ouverts, les gens ont compris,

**p. 155**

C.5.ĐO 48m {interprété} parce qu'il était complètement, il était illettré, à l'arrivée de l'alphabétisation il s'est impliqué et voilà qu'aujourd'hui il peut faire beaucoup de choses et qu'il est en train de faire d'ailleurs. Donc, ça l'a beaucoup aidé, ça l'a sorti de de beaucoup de choses d'ignorance.

*Distrustful (section 7.1.3)*

C.1.YMA 30m Moi je vois l'importance si: il y a l'alphabétisation . et: nos: parents vont sortir de l'obscurité .. s'ils sont analphabètes . cela instruit, et de là, ils n'ont pas de méfiance. Si je parle de méfiance, si moi, lettré, si je lis mon livret choisir une de ces= bon, et si un analphabète, un illettré est avec moi ici, lui .. il va se demander qu'est-ce que je dis. Est-ce que je parle de lui. Mais si je dis « Ɛgbé-kã̀ = Ɛgbé-kã̀ yèé » donc, elle, lui aussi doit comprendre aussi ce que je voulais dire. Donc, c'est pourquoi je parle de méfiance. Il n'y aura pas de=de méfiance.

**p. 156**

C.4.GĐ 1h10m {interprété} vraiment l'alphabétisation est très importante . du moment où, on les avait tellement trichés quand ils étaient analphabètes, dans le temps, quand ils ne connaissaient pas papier, ils étaient trichés . et leurs intérêts étaient vraiment bafoués.

*Blocks to development (section 7.1.4)*

A.2.AgbA 8m l'idée primaire c'est: tout développement n'est possible que .. la personne est lettrée.

A.2.SK ff. C'est ça. Tout le monde devraient être lettrés.

C.2.VA2 42m et partant de là aussi, il sait que, bon si on n'apprend pas, on ne peut pas évoluer.

## p. 157

B.1.NK af1 29m   c'est au départ .. comme ça a fait que le nombre des Ifè illettrés est très très très important dans notre milieu. Même aujourd'hui. Donc, ça a freiné beaucoup de choses. Vous savez, des .. les gens ne comprennent p= quand tu n'es pas lettré, ça fait que tu ne connais pas l'importance de de ton enfant, qu'il faut introduire à l'école formelle.

C.2.VA1 45m   Et je peux dire .. dans le cadre de … de ce= nos nos parents, comme nous le disons, puisque nous sommes dans notre .. cadre. d'alphabétisation, ils ont= ils avaient beaucoup travaillé, mais ne sachant pas comment améliorer .. les techniques à: .. exploiter, ils ont été toujours .. eh restés au bas d'échelle.

C.4.ANA 1h18m   Mais si … un gouvernement veut vraiment . que le développement soit réel .. harmonieux . et que le bien, c'est-à-dire le fruit de l'effort d'un gouvernement soit reparti .. correctement, .. rationnellement, . à tous les citoyens, il faut que ce gouvernement-là PENSE . d'abord à l'alphabétisation. {pause de 5 secondes} TOUS les responsables . qui tiennent réunions devant la population, ils leur SOIT ils les leur parlent leur langue, OU bien, ils cherchent un interlocuteur, ou bien interprète, .. pour pouvoir aller traduire. Même . {petit rire} voilà que, les choses publiées, dans les radios↓ . dans les journaux↓ .. les populations ne sont pas impliquées c'est-à-dire les populations ne trouvent pas leur part dedans↑. Ils ne peuvent pas lire . dans les journaux, ils n'écoutent pas le français ils ne comprennent pas le français qui est parlé . dans les radios .. Est-ce que l'information de ce gouvernement-là PASSE pour la grande majorité ? Non pour la petite minorité. {pause de 3 secondes}

## p. 158

C.4.JR ff.   Donc

C.4.ANA ff.   DONC, SANS QUE vraiment .. un gouvernement . n'attache pas d'importance . à l'alphabétisation, le développement dont on parle là, on va toujours parler de cela, mais ce ne sera pas réa= réaliste. C'est ce que moi j'ai compris.

B.4.ANA si2 5m Il y a des ONGs qui avaient tenté vraiment de d'aider, de venir en aide aux populations rurales. Et à cause de l'analphabétisme, puisque les gens ne savent pas écrire, ils ont presque: jeté de l'argent parce que .. la formation qu'ils: l'auront donné ne les=. n'est pas à leur . euh motivation c'est-à-dire ils ne peuvent pas vraiment . euh maintenir cette formation-là et le mettre en pratique [KL : oui] strictement comme cela se doit pour qu'ils puissent bénéficier . [JR : Mmhm] de cela.
B.4.JR si2 ff. Okay. Okay ..
B.4.KL si2 ff. Ils ont investi on a [fait la formation mais,]
B.4.ANA si2 ff.                            [Ils ont investi on a fait la formation]
B.4.KL si2 ff. la formation n'était pas reçue et mise en pratique.
C.4.ANA 1h21m TEL QUE l'espace culturel se réduit de jour en jour, on doit changer de comportement. Et le changement de cet= de ces comportements-là, SANS QUE l'homme ne puisse lire . sur papier, ou bien les noter sur papier, on ne peut pas suivre strictement. Pour pouvoir gagner, on a un petit portion . pour pouvoir cultiver. Tu n'as pas l'argent pour acheter un grand espace. Comment maintenir cet espace-là toujours riche pour pouvoir te donner euh un bon résultat, un bon rendement .. Je vois que, quand on va te dire ça oralement, dans la pratique, tu vas oublier d'autres choses et au lieu d'augmenter ton rendement tu vas encore .. diminuer ton rendement que tu avais là.

p. 159
**Representations of literacy and language (section 7.2)**

p. 160
*Literacy as openness and development (section 7.2.1)*

p. 161
B.1.NK af2 16m Or, nous sommes= on se dit que nous sommes des agents de développement. Le développement . social et le développement économique. C'est ça qui importe. Ça, ça me tient toujours à cœur.
B.1.AgA 15m Mais moi . je CHERCHE le bien-être de mes frères.

Appendix B: Interview excerpts

B.4.KL si1 10m   Maintenant ce dernier bureau qu'on a pris maintenant, on a dit, c'est CEUX . QUI . VEULENT . faire le travail, donc ceux qui sont .. aptes pour le travail qu'on a pris.

C.4.ANA 27m   Donc, il faut que ça soit vraiment des gens .. qui vont se donner, qui vont se donner vraiment . qui vont laisser leur propre évolution en quelque sorte, et vouloir l'évolution du groupe, sinon de la commu = de toute la communauté.

C.4.GÐ 55m   {interprété by ANA} Donc, on a juré donc vraiment . on sera obligé d'élire ceux-là qui s'investissent déjà . ceux-là sur qui on a senti le ZÈLE .. de faire marcher vraiment l'alphabétisation.

**p. 162**

B.1.NK af1 6m   et nous, l'objectif visé que normalement, c'est d'abord, nous savons que tout développement dépend de .. de certaines connaissances. Donc, quelqu'un qui est dans l'ignorance, ... dans l'ignorance d'une manière .. globale, mais↑ spécifique, nous savons que dans notre milieu ifè, surtout dans les villages, les villages reculés, on n'a PAS été à l'école. Donc, ce .. l'alphabétisation, d'abord, est la base d'abord du développement, c'est ce qu'on avait compris.

C.2.VA1 43m   moi je dis souvent que ... la lecture et l'écriture .. font la base d'un développement . d'un individu, d'une association, ou bien d'une communauté parce que c'est très important de savoir lire et écrire. Ça c'est la base. Quelqu'un qui ne sait pas lire et écrire, ne peut pas s'autosuffire. Il ne peut pas s'autosuffire. Nous avons les moyens, mais parce que nous les, nous les connaissons pas, nous ne les utilisons pas, et la pauvreté gagne toujours le terrain.

C.3.SY 1h21m   {interprété} Tout ce qu'on pouvait faire, de un laps de temps, un petit temps pour gagner quelque chose on utilisait assez d'énergie et on ne gagnait rien. Mais à base de l'alphabétisation, les yeux sont ouverts, les gens ont compris, les consciences sont réveillées, les gens ont commencé par comprendre quelque chose et la discipline est arrivée.

**p. 163**

D.H4 6m   Èmi ŋu ǹ rí ní gbà tì ńǹtá-ìwé-ifɛ̀ yèé à ké wá fú wa á, ó tsódzú fú wa kpíkpɔ kpíkpɔ, ó tsí odzú fú wa kpíkpɔ. Iŋé yèé tse tsí ó tsí *odzú fú wa kpkpɔ ɛ́ ní wà dzɛ́ ní; kíbí èmi gbo ǹwa'a wɔ̀ ńnɔ́ɔ nɔ́dɔ̃́ àtsɛ̀tsɛ̃̀ yèé à kɛ́ ɛ̀kɔ́ ɛ́ tsí ń wá ń d̬i-tiwa ŋa bí ɛ́, èmi ǹ kɛ́ɛ sí ńǹtá-ara-mí ní ɔ̀, bon, ǹlú-wa ni, èd̬è-ti àwa káa wa ni, ti ara wa ni « kòa », ńbí ǹbòkó tse sùkúrù ɛ̀ títí kó wáa gbɛ̃́ mi tsí ń lɔ? Vɔ̀à nɔ́mbé báàyí ɛ́ ń rí ní ǹ wà gba nfɛ̀ɛnɔ́ kpíkpɔ ńnɔ́-è.*

Moi, j'ai vu qu'au travers de l'alphabétisation ifè qu'on nous a apportée, ça nous a tellement ouvert les yeux, cela nous a beaucoup ouvert les yeux. La raison pour laquelle cela nous a beaucoup ouvert les yeux est que comme moi aussi j'ai intégré, la première année quand on a apporté l'alphabétisation aux nôtres ici, moi je me disais en moi-même, quoi, bon, c'est notre langue, c'est notre propre langue, c'est pour nous même quoi, je vais faire cette école pour qu'elle m'amène où ? Mais, de nos jours maintenant, je vois que j'apprends assez de connaissances au travers de cela.

C.5.EK 43m    Et encore par chose, le commerce, par exemple, il y a certaines femmes qui m'ont donné témoignages la fois passée, qui .. à base de l'alphabétisation maintenant, elles sont dans la classes de cycle 2. Mais aujourd'hui elles arrivent à calculer. Elles arrivent à calculer. Quand elles vont à chose, au marché maintenant, si elles vendent quelque chose, c'est elles-mêmes qui calculent, elles n'ont plus besoin aller chercher quelqu'un, vient m'aider calculer ce que j'ai vendu ou autre là. Donc, maintenant, elles ont trouvé que c'est bon d'être alphabétisée. Donc, à base de cela, l'alphabétisation peut nous développer.

**p. 164**

C.5.BK 39m    Par nos actions, par les les classes d'alphabétisation qui va leur permettre d'être en contact avec le= euh la vie actuelle, par la lecture, et: la capacité d'écrire. Donc, tous cela va permettre au peuple ifè d'émerger, comme d'autre peuple qui dans le temps . euh: se sont vus des restes. On peut noter le peuple chinois, dans les années au seizième siècle qui était un peuple, un des derniers peuples de la terre et qui par l'effort de. de s'appliquer, à étudier sa propre langue, a émergé et influence le monde entier aujourd'hui. Donc, nous espérons voir que, le peuple ifè va émerger et selon ce que Dieu voudra, d'ici là.

A.1.SK af1 44m  Je vois vraiment que .. l'alphabétisation parmi les Ifè est fonctionnelle. C'est-à-dire il y a des compétences dans la lecture, dans l'écriture, dans le calcul . et puis aussi avoir vraiment assez de réflexion, c'est-à-dire que l'alphabétisation amène les Ifè maintenant à mieux réfléchir sur leur situation de vie pour pouvoir les gérer . et il a y beaucoup de connaissances, c'est-à-dire, on veut voir l'application. intégrale de l'alphabétisation dans la vie des Ifè . parmi le peuple ifè.

**p. 165**

C.1.NK 32m  donc il vaut mieux maintenant de profiter pour que . ils aussi soient ouverts maintenant et à la société . lettrée . donc, tout le monde peut être ouvert maintenant à cette société lettrée pour que tout ce qu'ils pensent, ils peuvent l'écrire. Tout ce qu'ils entendent, ils peuvent l'écrire. Tout ce qu'ils voient, ils peuvent lire, et cela va changer beaucoup de choses dans la conduite .. ho de chaque jour, dans leur programme dans leurs activités, dans leurs quoi je ne sais pas donc il y a maintenant beaucoup de choses qui entourent ce ce cette phénomène. Donc, les gens ont pris conscience maintenant de connaître à lire et écrire, même savoir calculer pour gérer leur propre exploitation, leurs propres affaires, et maintenant, de ne pas être encore dans l'obscurité . de ce monde lettré. Donc, c'est un peu près, selon les témoignages, ce qu'on voyait sur le terrain qui témoigne la volonté manifeste maintenant de .. des personnes analphabètes qui veulent être maintenant des néoalphabètes pour être maintenant ouvert à ce monde lettré . pour bénéficier beaucoup de choses, à travers les affiches maintenant, il y a beaucoup de choses qui se fait. même au niveau du média, tout ce qu'on dit maintenant sensibilisation, tout ce qui se dit que tout le monde doit sortir de l'obscurité et être maintenant ouvert maintenant, à ce monde lettré qui interpelle tout le monde. Voilà.

A.3.SK 9m  Ça veut dire que, la base du développement c'est l'éducation. Donc, on devrait dire le développement, c'est l'éducation.

## p. 166
*Mother tongue literacy as preservation and transmission of cultural knowledge and identity (section 7.2.2)*

C.2.VA1 49m   Donc, moi je vois que c'est important. parce que surtout qu'il y a aussi des choses .. des richesses ... culturelles .. dans CHAQUE langue locale, qui sont exprimées . dans certains livres.

C.4.ANA 1h31m   D'autre part, c'est que↑ . les richesses culturelles sont cachées sous la langue PARLÉE de cette communauté-là .. SANS avoir appris cette langue, vous ne pouvez pas maintenir . ces richesses culturelles-là ... Vous ne pouvez même pas les exploiter ... S'il n'y a pas l'écriture . dans une langue pour une ethnie .. les richesses culturelles de cette ethnie-là diminuent de jour en jour ... Voilà.

## p. 167

C.4.ANA 1h22m   Il y a toujours brassage maintenant des ethnies . des peuples. Et ceux-là, notre comportement, ils viennent rester chez vous, tout ça là, QUEL est: leur comportement original ? Toi, vous, toi-même tu as un comportement original, en tant que homme ifè par exemple ou bien en tant que homme fon, en tant que homme kabiyè, QU'est-ce que vous avez l'habitude de faire, qu'est-ce que vous ne de = vous ne faites pas dans votre ethnie ? .. On n'a écrit nul part ces choses-là. Ça diminue et ça fait que . chacun fait ce qu'il veut maintenant.

C.1.NK 37m   les gens s'intéressent parce qu'ils veulent garder leurs coutumes.

C.2.VA3 47m   Donc, moi je peux dire aussi que . d'autres . aujourd'hui qui peuvent écrire des choses .. au temps de leur vieillesse pour les enfants .. pour comme le partage des héritages comme ça .. Et ils peuvent leur écrire en ifè. C'est déjà une: grâce pour eux.

## p. 168

A.2.AgbA 0m   Quand nous étions dans les villages, on a vu le chef, et nous sommes approchés pour le dire nous sommes là pour .. euh .. faire la sensibilisation, ouverture des CLASSES d'alphabétisation dans leur village. Il dit, vous êtes la bienvenue. Mais je voudrais

Appendix B: Interview excerpts

vous mettre en garde. Que chez moi ici, dans ce village, on n'a même pas . question d'église. Nous, nous sommes les païens, nous sommes les ido= . idolâtres, on ne peut pas entendre parler de l'église. Et si jamais j'entends cela, je vous mets à la porte. O: soit, il y avait quelqu'un qui était venu pour évangéliser le village, mais par la suite, il était mort. Et je l'ai dit, Chef, merci pour cet avertissement. Mais je suis venu pour vous parler de la langue ifè et non de christianisme. Et ici, je suis venu pour vous parler comment nous pouvons nous de= . développer, comment nous pouvons développer notre village. Étant dit que moi aussi, je suis un enfant de=. d'un parent .. idolâtre, je vais vous dit que, avant d'être un charlatan, il faut suivre la formation. Et la formation de charlatan fait que vous restez là au moins trois mois, et vous recevrez des enseignements. Et, je l'ai expliqué TOUT ce qui se passe là, et je l'ai dit c'est la même manière d'être alphabétisé parce que, chez les charlatans, ils ont leur écriture ce ne sont que les traits, et chez le . l= mm . disons .. les .. l'alphabétisation, nous avons les traits, mais ce sont les traits bien préparés .. et .. plus jolies. Et je l'ai expliqué, il dit Ah, donc, si c'est n'est ainsi, allez-y.

B.3.AmA 26m  Bon, ça a vraiment un peu agi sur le travail au départ, mais avec le temps, eux-mêmes ont compris que Ah être lettré ce n'est pas affaire de la religion. Nous retravaillons la sensibilisation, encore nous les demandons est-ce qu= quand vous envoyez vos enfants à l'école, est-ce que l'État ou soit les enseignants demandent à vos enfants inscrits s'ils sont les chrétiens ou pas ? S'il n'est pas religieux, est-ce que c'est ça qui est l'objectif des enseignants. Leur objectif, c'est que, si tu es religieux ou pas, il faut être lettré. C'est ce qui nous réunit.

## p. 169

C.1.AgA 34m  Et l'avant hier-là, un féticheur m'a dit . comme: .. ils ils savent écrire et lire maintenant, il va faire . un testament pour garder pour le fétiche. Si quelqu'un vient . il va regarder le fétiche-là si on veut tuer, eh . une poulet . un coq-là, tu vois= on fait comme ça, comme ça ça ça ça avant de tuer ça. Il faut prier il

|  |  |
|---|---|
|  | faut prier comme ça comme ça comme ça avant de faire c'est qu'il va écrire tout et garder sous {rires} le fétiche avant de partir. C'est pourquoi il est en train de . de fréquenter. |
| C.1.NK ff. | un un témoignage |
| C.1.AgA ff. | un témoignage [c'est un témoignage.] |
| C.1.NK ff. | [parce que] .. ça me mène aussi à dire un, un jour j'étais dans un village, et c'est: un: féticheur qui m'a posé la question que nous voulons leur apporter . la parole de Dieu . {AgA rit} et je lui dit, même si nous= nous allons vous apporter la parole de Dieu, ce n'est pas une mauvaise chose. Toi, tu es maintenant: l'adepte de ce fétiche. Est-ce que, là où est l'origine de ce fétiche, tu le connais ? Il dit non Pourquoi tu ne le connais pas ? Que ces aïeux n'ont pas . écrit quelque chose déposée que: l'origine de ce fétiche c'est à tel à tel. Il dit Ahan. Comment on prie ? Les= tes aïeux priaient pour le fétiche, et tu le sais maintenant Il dit non, Tu connais même celui qui a= qui est parti chercher le fétiche non voilà c'est le pourquoi nous avons amené l'alphabétisation. Pour que, dès maintenant eh, ce que toi tu connais, tu le matérialises . comme ça, le jour où tu n'es plus celui qui viendra de succéder saura que Ah c'est comme ça que mon successeur priait, c'est comme ça qu'il faisait, les cérémonies, jusqu'à de tel . moment, tel moment, il faut faire ceci de tel moment il faut faire ceci. Donc, c'est comme ça. Il a dit Ahan. Vraiment, si c'est ça, ça les intéresse maintenant. Ahan. Donc, il y a beaucoup de choses unh que la communauté ifè maintenant comprend sur l'importance de l'alphabétisation [JR : uhun] .. dans leur langue locale. |

**p. 170**

|  |  |
|---|---|
| B.2.VA1 10m | Donc, pour le moment, nous avons essayé, nous avons des idées sur eh la santé, sur eh . le développement même culturel, parce que .. avant, au temps de nos aïeux, on réunissait les enfants pour les faire les contes:, pour les faire des choses:, et avaient les aupara= aujourd'hui, il n'y a plus ça. Donc, nous nous sommes dit, si on pouvait aider chaque village, ou bien chaque .. agglomération avoir un centre culturel, et que les gens puissent venir et puissent s'exprimer. |

*Appendix B: Interview excerpts* 307

C.4.ANA 1h35m   C'est pourquoi on écrit des livres des livrets, des trucs des idées des quoi quoi quoi, des histoires des contes, tout ça là. Il y a des contes aujourd'hui .. qui traduisent d'une manière comme on peut faire pour développer une communauté. Et que les les aïeux conter oralement. Si on pouvez simplement le.s écrire . dans, dans la langue, on peut = puisque il y a tant de . d'alphabétisés maintenant, ils peuvent lire aussi et comprendre que Ah c'est comme ça qu'on peut faire vraiment pour développer notre milieu, notre localité. C'est ça.

**p. 171**

C.2.VA3 53m   moi j'ai pris le papier c'est l'ifè que j'ai lu en même temps . et je n'ai pas lu le français puisque je sais que je suis moniteur en ifè,

C.2.VA1 54m   Et bon, aujourd'hui même, certains mêmes, certains Fon qu'ils disent Ah, nous serons converti en ifè plus tard parce que bon ils parlent l'ifè aujourd'hui: ils xx en ifè, et puis ils écrivent en ifè

B.3.AmA 37m   Et on prend les notes = on prend le papier maintenant, on écrit les phrases en ifè, on les demande de lire et c'est difficile pour eux, et nous les disons euhunh, c'est comme ça, les blanches ils sont nées ils se sont exprimés en français mais ils vont à l'école, il y a les gens aussi qui sont âgées chez eux mais qui n'ont pas jamais mis pied à l'école, quand on les amène les notes, ils appellent les toutes petites, et les lisent. Anhan.

**p. 172**

C.1.NK 36m   C'est que les gens veulent .. lire et écrire dans leur propre langue. Même quand tu connais une langue étrangère, et tu ne connais pas ta propre langue, ça te manque beaucoup de choses. C'est pourquoi dans nos centres dans nos classes, vous allez voir que les gens qui ont fait les classes françaises et ils sont inscrits maintenant POUR s'alphabétiser

B.4.KL si1 1m   Mais, il y a un sixième qui ne veut pas se comporter ifè.
B.4.JR si1 ff.   Ahan.
B.4.KL si1 ff.   dans Savalo.
B.4.JR si1 ff.   Ahan {ton étonné}.

B.4.KL si1 ff. Oui, dans la commune de Savalo il y a un autre arrondissement. C'est: . Pataba.
B.4.JR si1 ff. Mmhm. Okay.
B.4.KL si1 ff. Oui. Ils parlent ifè rapproché de .. comment appelle, itcha.
B.4.JR si1 ff. Mmhm
B.4.KL si1 ff. Oui, leur ifè est rapproché d'itcha, donc, ils ne veulent se comporter ou bien accepter, ifè proprement dit.

### p. 173
*Literacy as full participation in society (section 7.2.3)*

C.2.VA2 41m Bon: ensemble, bon, de de= au cours de d'une réunion, il peut prendre la parole même si c'est sa langue locale, puisqu'il sait . ce qu'il veut dire. Il sait l'imp= IL Y A {accentuée mais doucement}, il a appris, une idée donc l'importance des choses, il a appris ça, dans: dans dans l'éducation. Et comme ça, il n'est plus= il n'a plus peur de la population. Il se= le fait de aussi rester ensemble apprendre toutes ces idées va au tableau: et ainsi de suite tout ça là, c'est bon .. [on va dire que]
C.2.VA1 ff.                                      [Il n'a plus peur] des autres.
C.2.VA2 ff. Il n'a plus peur des autres, quoi. Donc, ÇA c'est un avantage,
C.3.SY 1h22m {interprété} Alors, aujourd'hui, ceux qui sont alphabétisés, ils peuvent prendre notes, ils peuvent être en contact avec les documents, et lire eux-mêmes savoir et avoir le message qui est le contenu du message. À une réunion par exemple, les gens, quand ils= on va les convoquer, ils n'ont plus besoin de rester bras croisées pour attendre qu'un autre viendra leur faire le rapport eux-mêmes ils peuvent prendre le bic prendre notes de ce qui a été dit, écouter à la réunion.

### p. 174
C.5.BK 45m Donc moi, pour témoigner, ma femme n'a pas eu cette chance de d'être instruit à l'école séculaire. Mais avec l'alphabétisation en tant que madame du pasteur, elle arrive à faire le ministère de visites avec la lecture des portions de Jacques traduites qu'elle a, avec ça, elle encourage les femmes, les malades, et bien d'autres

                personnes encore. En mon absence, ou que je sois, si je= si je suis empêché de faire le ministère, il suffit de l'indiquer faire ceci faire ceci, elle arrive à le faire de manière .. euh efficace. Donc, c'est vraiment du bien que cela va faire à la société.

C.5.ĐO 48m {interprété} Il peut se tenir à la banque aujourd'hui, quand le caissier fait mal, fait un calcul, il peut lui dire que non, qu'il n'a que reprendre, parce qu'il est sûr de ce qu'il est en train de faire devant lui.

C.5.ĐO 50m {interprété} Et la fiche de de questionnaire que vous venez de sortir là, la partie d'en haut c'était, c'est en français. Il dit que si ce qui était dit là-bas n'était pas traduit de l'autre côté, il serait complètement dans le noir. Donc, à base de ÇA, il arrive aussi à répondre à la question.

**p. 175**

B.4.ANA si2 12m O, oui, oui, je disais que .. eh ça .. l'alphab= grâce à l'alphabétisation, on a maintenant des gens . qui ont fait politique, et qui sont: eh élus, qui sont devenus maintenant élus soit ils sont conseillers dans leur village, soit ils sont conseillers dans la commune, soit ils sont conseillers dans l'arrondissement c'est-à-dire chefs de villages dans leur village ils sont chefs de leur village et cetera. Il y a quelqu'un qui est chef de l'arrondissement maintenant, dans mon arrondissement de Doumé-là.

C.4.ANA 1h43m on a déjà traduit beaucoup de livres de médecine, historique .. qui peuvent vraiment aider les gens . dans le changement de comportement pour que vraiment les gens, on puisse renforcer les capacités des néoanalphabetes, afin de pouvoir augmenter le rang des actifs au développement communautaire . puisque nous avons besoin à l'instant-là . des actifs au développement de notre communauté.

B.3.SY 43m {interprété} Donc, c'est déjà un grand pas, donc aujourd'hui étant superviseur, partant de zéro atteint superviseur c'est un grand pas.

## Ifè literacy as language maintenance and development (section 7.2.4)

**p. 176**

A.1.AgbA af1 2m  Et plus tard, j'aurais bien vu que, c'est plutôt un appel pour moi . de faire ce travail, parce que j'ai à cœur .. mon ethnie .. Il faut que quelqu'un développe . la langue. Il faut que quelqu'un soit un pionnier pour que la langue soit reconnue national ou bien, a son poids.

A.3.AgbA 24s  C'est .. de faire évoluer la langue ifè. Donc, et ils ont vu que, pour é= faire évoluer, la langue ifè, ils ne peuvent pas aller en rangs dispersés, il faut qu'ils se réunissent . en association . pour faire développer ça. Et c'est ce qui a fait que .. les= cette motivation, ou bien le prestige de la langue, a fait que . on sait . maintenant .. on a oublié nos différences .. que tu sois musulman, que tu sois païen, que tu sois chrétien, que tu sois: bouddhiste je ne sais pas, {rire court} que tu sois polit= politicien ou pas, que tu sois de RPT ou du RPFC . non, c'est l'ifè qui nous réunit .. Et c'est ça, c'est un grand atout . pour la réussite de ces associations. Et, et partant de là, tous: les autres Ifè qui ne sont pas de... de l'équipe ici, tous attendent de nous . que nous faisions= fassions quelque chose pour développer la langue. Et ils sont prêts au moins pour nous soutenir même s'ils n'ont pas l'argent. Et ils nous encouragent . à évoluer. À tel point que, quand un Ifè parle l'ifè, et quelqu'un d'autre entend un mot étranger-là il dit, non↑, ça ce n'est pas ifè, il faut parler l'ifè .. Voilà. Si bien qu'ils nous incitent à [fouiller {la porte sonne}]

A.3.SK ff.  [faire des recherches]

A.3.AgbA ff.  même sur des mots, des mots même, fouiller des mots-là même s'il faut créer, il faut créer, qu'il= ce soit ifè. Là c'est c'est . c'est un atout.

**p. 177**

C.4.KƉ 1h29m  {interprété} vraiment l'alphabétisation, c'est un, je disais, un signe de réveil. Ça a réveillé vraiment le peuple ou bien c'est ça qui continue pour nous réveiller. Pourquoi il le dit, il dit comme ça, parce que, il y a certaines . certaines expressions, certains mots . en ifè qui sont là que nos vieux parents, nos aïeux utilisaient.

Appendix B: Interview excerpts

>  Aujourd'hui, où se trouve soit illettré ou celui qui va à l'école formelle, on n'arrive plus ces ces ces ces expressions ou bien ces noms ne sont plus conservés. Tout est oublié. Mais au travers de l'alphabétisation, les gens ont fait des recherches pour retrouver ces mots-là, retrouver ces expressions, et ils nous les a emmené aujourd'hui donc lui qui s'intèg= s'adhère à l'alphabétisation, il est automatiquement, il va redécouvrir ces expressions et ces termes-là et ça fait que la vie ce qu'il est, la source même, on retourne à la source, et la langue serait gardée sur la plan .

C.4.ANA ff. original

Interpreter ff. original ou originel, s'il faut le dire.

B.3.MK 14m où je peux un peu ajouter, c'est que auparavant là, les moniteurs sont éloignés de nous ici. Et avoir leurs vélos pour les atteindre, on a laissé le sein de l'association de se rencontrer pour les attein= pour les atteindre vite, jusqu'au beau milieu, là s'appelle Patala. Puis, en ce moment-là, comme ils n'ont ils n'ont pas eh . obéit, ils ne sont pas eh .. ou bien, savoir ce que nous voulons faire là, ils= quand vous allez dire de venir d'ici là, ça sera difficile de déplacer du même temps .. puis qu'on les approchait, et nous, on se déplace ici, pour aller là-bas les rencontrer, et puis c'est là-bas centre, et ils viennent vite. Leur, comme on les approche, ils viennent, ils nous donnent des idées et des outils ils sont intéressés, que donc notre propre langue que là ça ne va pas échouer donc on va évoluer.

**p. 178**
*French as a more difficult language than Ifè (section 7.2.5)*

C.1.AgA 29m Si nous exprimons dans dans nos langues, on comprend . bien, mieux que, d'autres langues. Si je parle ifè maintenant . euh . une personne ifè, en tant ce que je suis en train de dire en ifè, elle va comprendre mieux . de lire .. ou de de par= parler autre langue .. Eux-aussi, si on écrit en ifè, bon .. ça nous arrange, on lit bien. Mais en français pour expliquer aussi, le français-là, m?m. Ça tourne comme ça, donc tourne comme ça mais ça nous dit la même chose .. et dans autre langues aussi c'est comme ça si c'est en ifè, c'est en ifè si on dit maintenant en ifè *tsaka tsaka*, c'est *tsaka tsaka* ça n'a pas changé. Si on dit *okpa*, c'est *okpa*.

**p. 179**

C.3.SY 1h21m {interprété} De nos jours, lui par exemple, le document qu'on vient de nous remettre, la fiche de renseignements, avant de ça, c'est une partie en français, l'autre est en ifè, mais il a laissé la partie française il a lu ce qu'il est en ifè il a compris et il arrivait aussi à donner son opinion à propos de ce qui a été demandé.

C.2.VA1 48m parce que↑ .. tout de suite quand vous avez présenté ce papier . le français est écrit en haut, j'ai lu ces cinq . déclarations en français, et que je n'ai PAS PU en même temps saisir . le sens . de tout ce que vous voulez= on veut dire dans chaque phrase. Et en même temps je suis descendu en bas. J'ai lu en ifè, et, automatiquement, j'ai tout compris. Et c'est un= voilà donc c'est de ça qu'on va parler ici. Et puis vous allez voir en français on a fait presque: . une seule ligne, mais en ifè c'est jusqu'à trois lignes↓ ce qui veut dire . qu'on veut expliquer beaucoup de choses. Et j'ai en même temps compris.

**p. 180**

C.2.VA2 51m Franchement: bon comme moi aussi j'ai pris le papier, moi j'ai lu seulement en français. Comme: il a failli cinq, et je l'ai lu le cinq, je regrette à avoir choisir le deux {rires de tous} parce que si j'ai lu ça en ifè, vraiment c'était= . c'est très clair et je vois que c'est vraiment . important. Et des deux . si tu sais quelqu'un . qui se croit lettré hein↑.. il dit bon je connais déjà le français pourquoi apprendre encore ma langue locale même si on écrit moi je peux lire. Il se trompe. Sinon: franchement moi: . bon: je disais ça, que bon, si je prends: bon le fra= l'ifè je peux lire. Et je lis, j'ai des difficultés, de fait même↑ . si je ne comprends pas la langue je ne peux pas lire. Donc, si je lis ça il ne sonne pas bien donc c'est comme ça il faut tourner, et j'ai= je= avant le tourné, j'efforce, et ça sonne. Donc je ne savais pas que, donc les flèches là ça va dire ceci, {quelqu'un rit avec un petit grognement} dire comme ça et ainsi de suite {il rit avec un petit grognement}. Or je n'ai pas rédigé. OR, réellement comme il vient de le dire, il y a certains, qui peuvent lire sont forts dans les mathématiques et c'est comme ça↓ mais ils n'ont pas les verbes faciles. Parce qu'ils n'ont pas de milliers ils n'ont pas . beaucoup de verbes. Mais dans notre langue locale, on a les verbes faciles, donc l'exprimer c'est facile, donc on peut même rédiger la remarque . ça nous permette bon, on dit maintenant bon, si les Ifè bon . on va avoir beaucoup de choses. Puisque quand de temps disaient xx aisément faire sortir dans ta: langue locale. Sinon c'est très important si même, le mieux même, les lettrés sont mieux placés que même: . bon je veux dire que . que les: ceux qui ne comprenaient . n'ont pas l'importance du papier.

C.2.VA3 53m   il n'y a rien qui peut me= je vais lire s'il demandait l'interprétation encore, j'ai lu, j'ai tout compris . et: . c'est une joie pour moi puisqu'il y a des choses que je vais lire en français ici et je n'arrive pas .. {petit rire} à: bien comprendre les mots.

**p. 181**

C.2.VA1 48m   Il y a certains: eh . quand même .. portions de la Bible traduites déjà en ifè↑. et que quand je veux préparer mon sermon↓ moi je suis pasteur↑ . je lis en français, et, ça m'aide beaucoup s'il y a cette portion en ifè.

C.2.VA2 ff.   en ifè oui

C.2.VA1 ff.   Quand je prends en ifè et je LIS .. eh= eh= vraiment, c'est c'est .. ça m'a dirigé à beaucoup de choses.

C.2.VA1 49m   et que: tu= moi je sais lire seulement le français, et que je ne sais pas lire= tu ne peux pas lire ma langue . maternelle, je PERDS {doucement mais accentuéé}. Je perds parce que en lisant la langue maternelle, on comprend . en même temps . ce qu'on lit, et en français il faut encore des dictionnaires↑, il faut les chercher↑, il faut= cer= certains mots sont: pour la première fois venus et puis, on est embarrassé et certaines phrases sont formées de plusieurs manières . dans la langue française .. une seule= une seule phrase est formulée de plusieurs manières ↑et que tu vas lire la même phrase et on va écrire dans l'autre manière que tu ne peux pas comprendre . que c'est la même chose qu'on veut dire. Alors qu'en ifè, il n'y a pas de quoi te dire on peut changer n'importe comment, comme tu lis, tu comprends.

**p. 182**

C.2.VA1 50m et surtout .. et= et quand je veux rédiger par exemple . un TEXTE .. je le rédige . en français, mais:↑ je mets mes idées en ifè. Et des fois↑ . ce que je PENSE je n'arrive même pas à l'exp = met sur le papier, parce que je manque des mots↓ . je manque d'expressions↓ . pour l'exprimer entre alors que si c'était en ifè, j'allais les transmettre en même temps directement et que, ceux qui veulent lire peut me comprendre en même temps.

### 7.2.6 Biliteracy as responsibility

C.4.ANA 1h31m Moi je dis même que c'est obligatoire qu'il sache lire et écrire sa propre langue . parce que d'une part, on dit chez nous que, si tu ne sais pas . mettre au propre ton ménage c'est-à-dire ta maison, faut pas te hasarder aller balayer la rue. {l'interpreté rit} Mm↑. Toi qui ne sais pas . lire . écrire . en ta propre langue et tu fais: le pédant en une autre langue, .. c'est que tu t'injuriais d'abord.

**p. 183**

C.3.AmA 1h26m Donc, il est important à celui-là qui connaît déjà le français de connaître aussi à lire dans sa propre langue. On entend ce problème surtout= ce problème-là, c'est on les rencontre beaucoup dans les églises. Dans les églises c'est difficile. Il y a le pasteur qui parle le français. Si euh: . l'interprète est Ifè, il ne sait pas lire l'ifè, c'est difficile ça ne passe pas bien l'information. L'information, ça ne sent= ça ça ne pénètre pas les membres. Quand le l'interprète interprète mal, il y a des rumeurs, il y a des jurons, les gens xx o non non non, lui il n'interprète bien ce que le pasteur lui dit. Donc, quand celui-là qui sait déjà lire le français doit se ressourcer un peu en ifè . pour pouvoir faire bien .. passer son message ou soit faire bien passer ce qu'il a reçu, quoi. C'est nécessaire, c'est très nécessaire.

Appendix B: Interview excerpts

## p. 184

C.3.SY 1h28m {interprété} Quel que soit le niveau de ton français, tu as eu ton bac, ta maîtrise ou quoi que ce soit, les gens aujourd'hui sont là ils ont bien maîtrisé le français, ils viennent, ils donnent, ils font un exposé, ils peut faire l'exposé en français, on leur demande de transmettre le message dans leur langue maternelle, ils sont bloqués. Ils ne peuvent pas le faire. Là, c'est une lacune. Alors, à ce moment, il est important que toute personne, quelque soit son niveau de connaissance en langue française, il faut qu'elle revienne pour étudier sa propre langue, le maîtriser et donner les messages là-dedans et c'est plus pénétrant quoi.

C.4.GƉ 1h27m {interprété} Pourquoi, par exemple il y a certains noms en ifè . que, si quelqu'un = si vous indiquez quelque chose à quelqu'un par exemple en ifè et qui veut aller rapporter .. ce nom , si la personne connaît le nom en ifè il peut faire un bon rapport. Par exemple quelqu'un qui a appris seulement et qui connaît français, il se parlait un peu la langue, mais quand vous lui parlez, vous lui donnez ce nom .. en ifè arriver maintenant, quand il veut faire le rapport en français ou bien il prend la rapport en français arriver il veut rapporter ça en ifè, là au niveau-là il est bloqué. Il ne connaît pas le nom. C'est pourquoi il est important que, quel que soit son = ton niveau, en français ou en telle langue, il faut retourner à l'origine . pour étudier sa langue maternelle, à lire et à écrire, comme ça ça va aider même à avoir les termes originaux. C'est ça l'importance.

## p. 185

C.5.ƉO 49m {interprété} Donc, il demande, il souhaiterait, que les frères qui sont devant fournissent encore d'effort d'amener les livres d'autres livres dans d'autres langues, à les traduire en ifè, et comme il y a des bonnes choses dedans, ils peuvent aussi profiter.

C.4.ANA 1h32m Maintenant on dit que il y a .. de de nouvelles techniques culturales .. Il y a des livres qui sont déjà édités soit en anglais soit en français. Il y a des livres qui traitent = qui parlent de beaucoup de maladies en anglais, en français .. Toi maintenant .. qui comprends bien . l'anglais, même, tu as évolué tu comprends deux langues comme ça anglais français. Tu veux . aider . ta population. Tu veux aider ton peuple .. Comment tu pourras le faire .. Ton peuple est bien = bel et bien alphabétisé voilà que toi-même tu ne sais pas écrire . cette langue. Tu ne sais pas la lire. Est-ce que tu peux faire la traduction ? Je dis non.

C.4.ANA 1h33m Donc moi je vois que c'est même plus important . pour ceux-là qui . connaissent déjà . le français ou bien l'anglais ou bien d'autres langues étrangères . de VITE rattraper. Ceux-là doivent vite rattraper pour que vraiment on puisse s'unir pour aider . notre population sinon notre communauté. C'est ceux-là qui trouvent . comment ça se passe ailleurs, souvent. C'est eux qui ont eu la chance d'évoluer peut-être dans les pays des autres mais, soit en France aux États-Unis, ou bien qui ont beaucoup la chance de voyager beaucoup qu'on trouvait des nouvelles idées, de nouvelles pratiques, de nouveaux comportements, qui vont maintenant vouloir l'écrire dans leur langue pour vulgariser cela dans leur communauté, et quand vous ne savez pas . écrire votre langue, ce serait fiasco vous ne pouvez pas. Vous pouvez avoir bel et bien la volonté d'aider votre peuple mais, vous ne pouvez pas .. Que TOI . naTIF . d'une ethnie ou bien d'un peuple .. d'une langue et que tu trouves encore d'interprète, moi je trouve que c'est {claquement de langue} .. c'est vraiment mauvais de sa part {rires} que tu trouves que tu cherches d'interprète afin de pouvoir aller . parler à tes parents, vraiment ce n'est pas bon.

**p. 186**

C.4.ANA 1h35m  Et c'est souvent des gens qui ont eu la chance de comprendre autres langues, c'est ceux-là que, s'ils trouvent une idée ils peuvent le développer vite. Ils peuvent développer . l'idée-là, la petite idée que les vieux vont dire là, eux-autres peuvent le développer ça et rendent ça plus .. euh: usuelle .. un↑ . puisque c'est plus facile à utiliser = à être utilisé pour les autres selon le monde d'aujourd'hui, selon l'évolution du monde. Donc, sans que . nos frères qui savent lire et écrire dans une autre langue ne reviennent pas .. apprendre leur propre langue, vraiment l'alphabétisation encore serait bloqué ↑d'une manière que, si ton parent veut t'écrire . voilà que lui il ne comprend pas français, il sera obligé d'aller voir quelqu'un d'autre que, dont il ne voudrais pas qu'il .. il sache ce qu'il voudrais te dire. Même s'il t'écrit en sa langue= en ta langue tu pourras pas lire . là où tu es en France peut-être ou bien aux États-Unis. Alors que c'est lui qui t'a mis au monde, tu ne comprends pas sa langue . quand il s'agit de l'écrit, mais ça c'est gauche ! {petite rire} Si toi tu veux écrire à ton papa ou bien à ta maman .. qui comprennent ta propre langue, tu seras obligé de l'écrire en français .. Et c'est un autre, {il claque des doigts deux fois} le fils d'un autre ou bien d'une autre mais qui va lire, qui va comprendre ce que toi tu es en train d'apprendre à ta maman ou bien à tes parents, et qui peut-être . dit autre chose, traduit autre chose et allais mettre ça en pratique dans sa propre famille d'abord. Et ta famille sera obligé de tricher auprès de lui. Est-ce que, ce n'est pas s'injurier ? Je vois que vraiment et je suis en train d'exhorter nos frères nos grands frères qui savent lire dans d'autres langues de venir nous aider. Ceux eux qui devraient nous aider, et s'ils n'apprennent pas la langue ils ne peuvent pas nous aider.

**p. 187**

C.4.KL 1h37m  Chez moi, ceux qui savent lire .. déjà le français, ceux qui .. euh ceux qui connaissent le papier déjà, et: . il est très important à eux aussi de revenir . apprendre à écrire et lire leur propre langue. Sinon, nous qui faisons maintenant aujourd'hui l'alphabétisation↓ nous faisons l'alphabétisation de BASE. Mais, SI CEUX-là qui sont évolués en études ne reviennent pas apprendre encore la langue avec nous, nous ne pouvons plus évoluer nos pas, ne pouvons plus évoluer plus que nous sommes aujourd'hui nous serons toujours comme ça. Mais eux autres ils ont déjà étudié ils sont déjà allés à haut niveau. Donc, comme ça, s'ils apprennent aussi à lire et écrire, ils peuvent FAIRE développer aussi notre langue, pour que nous aussi nous

|            |                                                                                                                              |
|------------|------------------------------------------------------------------------------------------------------------------------------|
| C.4.JR ff. | puissions évoluer et même . travailler .. faire tous ce que eux autres font en langue étrangère aussi dans notre langue. |
| C.4.JR ff. | Mmhm |
| C.4.KL ff. | Oui, donc c'est pourquoi il est aus= il est très important que eux autres reviennent apprendre .. eh à lire et écrire la langue. Oui. Sinon bon, nous maintenant qui sommes acteurs aujourd'hui, nous= nous pensons, nous rêvons |
| C.4.ANA ff. | Mmhm |

**p. 187**

| C.4.KL ff. | que notre langue ce soit une langue .. administrative .. |
|---|---|
| C.4.ANA ff. | dans notre [communauté toute au moins] |
| C.4.KL ff. | [dans notre communau]té au toute au moins. Donc, SI eh: ceux qui sont évolués ne= bon, voilà, nous nous n'avons pas un niveau élevé, donc, c'est ceux qui ont beau= bien étudié qui peuvent revenir, traduire eh: |
| C.4.ANA ff. | les textes |
| C.4.KL ff. | les textes, et nous aussi nous pouvons évoluer. |

*Literacy as access to another language (section 7.2.7)*

| C.5.EK 52m | Bon, si nous prenons maintenant, chose-là en langue locale ifè, si nous prenons . la lettre a. Donc, en langue, on dit aa. Déjà ce a en français. Donc nous voyons que c'est la même . lettre. Quelqu'un qui a fait euh l'alphabétisation, en voyant déjà en français la lettre a, reconnaît en même temps que c'est la lettre a et il peut lire. Donc, si nous voyons dans les lettres-là, bon, il y a plusieurs lettres . qui se sont . bon, qui sont les mêmes. Par exemple, la lettre b aussi, bon . plusieurs dans le= dans l'alphabétisation. Oui. Donc, je sais vraiment qu'il y a une relation . dans des . autres langues aussi. |
|---|---|

**p. 189**

| B.3.SY 43m | {interprété} Bon, en tant que, les gens lui connaissaient comme illettré, analphabète, mais au travers de l'alphabétisation ifè, il arrive maintenant à lire et écrire, et déchiffrer certains mots français. Il peut lire certains mots, mais peut-être ne pas |
|---|---|

              avoir bien le sens. Ça c'est déjà un point. Et c'est par la grâce aujourd'hui, de Dieu aujourd'hui, il arrive à commencer par lire français couramment devant les gens. Tous ce qui sont retournés, se sont reculés, par cette lecture, cette expression en français, ça peut les faire revenir.

B.3.AmA 6m  Et aujourd'hui maintenant, c'était la semaine passée qu'on a entamé une troisième cycle parce que ceux-là qui ont appris l'ifè à écrire et à lire, et aussi à faire le calcul et la rédaction, eux qui sont un peu parfait dans le cours, on a souhaité qu'on ait un troisième cycle pour pouvoir nous aider à xx un peu en français. Et c'est ça qui a été le désir de nos apprenants.

**p. 190**

C.3.AmA 1h14m Les rapports que j'ai recueillis . sur le troisième cycle {claquement de langue}, que .. le cours = le cours français qu'on vient de commencer là {claquement de langue}, ça donne assez de lumière .. d'abord .. aux moniteurs .. qui: ont fait la classe formelle ils disent que, c'est maintenant même qu'eux autres comprennent . le sens des grammaire, le vocabulaire, l'orthographe .. le son, les sens des mots son orthographe vocabulaire bon qu'ils ont ils ont beaucoup de lumière sur ce cours . par rapport à ce qu'on leur avait appris sur le banc. La fois = hier il y a un frère qui est venu {il baisse la voix} il fait l'internat c'est celui qui a fait tous ceci-là au tableau-là {le tableau est couvert des formules mathématiques}

{explication de son enseignement de la classe du troisième cycle là-bas}

Il les a beaucoup .. il a beaucoup apprécié les documents que, c'est maintenant que, {claquement de langue} il semble que, c'est nous qui sommes .. sur la vraie étude quoi. Que, le document, ça va, ça va, ça ça va plus clair, plus abordable que par par rapport à ce que on a enseigné . à l'école .. formelle . et nous nous principalement, nous qui représentons↓ nous qui sommes moniteurs pour enseigner .. les les gens pour troisième cycle, vraiment ça nous a beaucoup apporté PLUS de lumière. Ça on ne peut pas tout dire. {petit rire} Ça nous aide.

B.3.AmA 31m  Il y a des anciens moniteurs même, qui ont beaucoup travaillé au départ, et ils se sont repliés, retirés, et quand ce troisième cycle arrivait maintenant, ils disent que Ah comme ils ont souhaité troisième cycle depuis ça on n'a pas réussi, c'est pourquoi quand ils vont, ils vont voyager, ils voyagent, ils arrivent au niveau des frontières, les soldats les posent des questions en français là, ils n'arrivent pas à s'exprimer là, c'est ça qui fait que eux ne pouvaient plus continuer le travail avec nous en tant que tel. Donc, heureusement que le cycle trois est là, ça va les aider un peu.

**p. 191**

B.3.AmA 52m  Quand je suis arrivé= mon enfant a quatre ans j'ai dit qu'il aura cinq ans, il va aller à l'école formelle de fois, quand je trouve un peu de temps, je je l'ai je je l'initie un peu sur {l'alphabétisation dans} la langue maternelle. Pour les deux, quand il va arriver à l'école formelle, ça va vite passer quoi.

B.3.SY 49m  {interprété} Il nécessitera l'engagement des alphabétiseurs au niveau des écoles formelles afin d'entretenir les élèves, pour que les enfants dès leur bas âge commencent par étudier la langue qu'ils arrivent déjà à parler. Comme ça à l'écrire. Et arrivée, en évoluant, ils n'auront plus de blocage. Parce qu'ils ont constaté aujourd'hui que, quand les enfants commencent avec le français, à un certain moment, on fait revenir des idées qu'ils leurs demandent d'aller faire des recherches encore de leur naissance, ils sont bloqués en ce moment, alors, s'ils avaient fait ça dans le bas âge, ils ne seraient pas bloqué à ce niveau. Il faut qu'on fasse de ces enfants, des enfants faits des hommes faits dès le bas âge parce que, à six ans déjà, l'enfant commence l'école formelle, et d'abord l'ifè n'est pas encore il n'est pas ancré dedans, et avec l'école française, ou bien l'école formelle, ils évoluent, ils ne comprennent pas bien l'ifè, ni bien français et ils sont entre l'étau et, comment là, l'enclume et le marteau, et ne savent plus quoi faire. Quand on leur demande de revenir au plan ifè, on leur dit certains mots, ils n'arrivent pas à comprendre, voilà qu'ils ont aussi les difficultés un jour alors il faut une bonne fondation que le bâtiment soit bien posé.

## p. 192
### Ifè literacy as a qualification (section 7.2.8)

B.3.AmA 38m   Maintenant, les gens ont appris dans les villages, ils sont spécialistes dans l'élévation pour l'élevage de des abeilles mais ils ne se sont pas alphabétisés. Et ils nous viennent solliciter auprès de nous qu'on va les impliquer dans le comité on les dit NON, unhun, c'est un exemple, quoi. Bon, d'autres aussi, quand par exemple, le projet demande est-ce qu'on engage un berger. Voilà les gens viennent de gauche et à droit, que c'est eux qui vont suivre le berger, pardon, la bergerie pour que s'il y a une petite pension qu'ils prennent ça mensuellement. On les dit non, on vous a apporté l'alphabétisation ici vous avez refusé, vous voyons déjà, non ?

## p. 193

C.3.AmA 1h23m   Deuxième aspect, il faut que son moniteur ait un niveau de deuxième cycle. Niveau d'alphabétisation deuxième cycle. Parce que↑ .. tout ce que vous allez rencontrer en français, il faut transmettre en ifè. ↑Il faut .. oui, il faut il faut transmettre ça aux autres en ifè.

B.3.AmA 41m   Bon, déjà *ma aspect le troisième cycle maintenant qu'on vient de la dire qu'on vient de dire maintenant, il y a les gens quand ils ont compris que c'est le français, ah↑ ils ne font que me gêner. Ils ne font que gêner les superviseurs et les superviseurs viennent me dire tout. Et la critère, la barré que moi j'ai *mis, et que si quelqu'un n'a pas eu son diplôme, du deuxième cycle, il ne doit pas s'inscrire au troisième cycle. Pas de question. Ils peuvent venir avec des présents, pas de question.

## p. 197
# Enhancing capacity (Chapter 8)

## p. 199
### At the personnel level (section 8.1)

## p. 202

B.2.VA1 25m    Donc, c'est pourquoi ils ont xx demandé à même temps il faut = nous avons besoin de formation, nous avons besoin de des d'autres choses pour pouvoir bien situer les choses.

B.2.JR ff.    Quelqu'un veut ajouter ? {pause de 3 secondes}

B.2.VA3 ff.    Pour ajouter, on veut suivre la formation. Sinon on a besoin de la formation, pour gérer une association il faut la formation. Donc, on a besoin quand même de la formation.

B.3.AmA 21m    Bon, s'il vous plaît, en 2006, l'ACATBLI est venue nous former. Le rôle du président . le rôle du secrétaire, le rôle du trésorier. Mais la formation-là, c'est bien, mais elle nous est insuffisante. Et nous réclamons que, il faut que l'ACATBLI revienne encore nous former.

## p. 204
### At the organizational level (section 8.2)

## p. 205

B.3.AmA 1h04m    Moi, par exemple, dans notre association, nous devons = nous voulons avoir encore de formation sur le rôle de leadership. Comment gérer l'association. Comment était, pardon, le comité, le comité, former le comité, où le comité de l'association doit recevoir une formation ENSEMBLE. Et chacun saura ce qu'il ATTEND, ce qu'il le FAUT, quelles compTENCES il doit AVOIR, donc c'est le = un premier objectif pour moi.

## p. 206

B.2.VA1 26m    Euh . oui, bon, pour .. comment la formation surtout .. très nécessaire. Et, après cette formation, il faut qu'on nous .. a {petit rire} il faut qu'on nous mette sur le terrain à plein pied ..

Appendix B: Interview excerpts

|  | et: .. nous fait travailler .. et nous suivre. Donc, ça nous les = nous le désirons beaucoup, et, essayer de nous définir .. qu'est-ce que le président fait, et le coordonnateur qu'est-ce qu'il fait, le secrétaire qu'est-ce qu'il va faire, former former les gens là-dessus et nous .. encore nous stimuler nous donner encore certaines idées plus, qui peuvent conquérir, qui peuvent venir au développement des Ifè. |

B.2.VA2 12m   Surtout côté gestion: . bon c'est ça, on ne sait pas gérer, c'est ça nous pouvons faire que de fois: on a touj= bon des pertes partout .. unhan .. d'accord.

B.3.AmA 58m   Donc, c'est la formation sur la gestion et le rôle de de leadership-là qui nous a ouvert les yeux à avoir l'ouverture de la caisse. Nous ne savions pas il faut ouvrir une caisse par un compte bancaire, et avant on a laissé l'argent dans la chambre on dort avec l'argent, que ce n'est pas prudent. Donc quand on a l'argent là-bas on est libre.

**p. 207**

B.1.NK af146m   Bon .. avec uh: . cette suspension, et c'est ça qui nous a emmené à s'organiser avec ACATBLI pour que ACATBLI cherche les fonds, {il tape la table} et qu'ils gèrent les fonds, {il tape la table} avec les associations. Donc, aujourd'hui nous ne sommes pas autonome. Parce que nous ne décidons rien .. Ce que .. ils décident, {doucement} avec nos membres, c'est ça que nous exécutons .. C'est ça. Donc, nous ne sommes PAS autonome. Bien sûr que l'ACATBLI est notre chapeau, il nous sommes = c'est tout comme c'est un réseau de tous les associations qui sont encore relevé {?}. Mais aucune association, que vous allez trouver aujourd'hui, là qui dit il est autonome, non. Quand on parle de l'autonomie, il faut avoir d'abord l'autonomie financière. Quand tu n'as pas l'autonomie financière, tu n'es pas autonome .. Donc, on n'a pas d'autonomie financière, on n'est pas autonome. Bien sûr qu'on peut= nous faisons nos nos réunions au sein de l'association:, nous avons des suggestions nous faisons

comment . faire ceci cela. Mais en matière de: de gestion ..
nous ne sommes pas là-bas.

**p. 212**

B.3.MK 1h09m  Si je peux ajouter aussi, c'est ce que .. euh .. personnellement, nous, l'association, quand nous allons aussi, par avant, c'est que les supérieurs vont venir pour nous dire faire ceci .. pour aller .. suivre les moniteurs maintenant aller faire les services ont techniques au niveau xx qui vont venir nous guider. Faire ceci. Faire ceci. Donc, à notre niveau . maintenant, nous avons, nous aussi, nous-mêmes nous avons des idées qui .. qui .. et ces idées-là ne viennent pas .. c'est .. de de nos .. superv={claquement de langue} de nos supérieurs et nous-mêmes qui avons des idées que nous lançons déjà avant et puis faisant des choses et les mon= les apprenants et les moniteurs nous voient PLUS et on sait que donc notre association AMIADA c'est ça qui déroule maintenant, ça qui travaille, et puis nous .. nous amenons des rapports, des choses savoir qui donc, aussi, là où nous sommes aussi, nous allons faire quelque CHOSE. Puis nous voyons bon que là où nous sommes maintenant, ça va. Ce qui nous MANQUE, c'est ça qu'on avait déjà demandé ça nous encore former plus plus de là nous allons évoluer.

**p. 213**

B.2.VA2 41m  Bon, la solidarité, bon, comme on le dit, et de fait c'est nous on ne le fait comme on nous sait, bon, on dit, il faut chaque fois arroser le fruit et bon ou bien, nettoyez .. hoo toute autour de fruit qui= de l'arbre qui produit.

**p. 214**
**At the community level (section 8.3)**

**p. 115**

A.1.AgbAaf2 40m  Et ce que nous faisons, souvent c'est que, on voit le problème ensemble avec eux, et on les donne des approches de

|  |  |
|---|---|
|  | solutions. Et comme on n'a pas d'argent, quand ils mettent ça en pratique, ils peuvent régler le problème. |
| A.2.AgbA 7m | Tout cela c'est le développement. Et: .. |
| A.2.SK ff. | communautaire |
| A.2.AgbA ff. | communautaire, nous travaillons dans la communauté {il rit}. Et, c'est c'est un travail qui se fait en masse, pas individu. Donc, euh . ça fait que, il y a certains villages, ils ont initié . des = des entraides, cinq ou six personnes se réunissent, et ils travaillent en groupe. Et il y a même les classes qui ailleurs qui deviennent de petits groupements. |
| A.2.SK ff. | C'est ça. .. Les petits groupes d'entraide, quoi. |
| A.2.AgbA ff. | Mmm. Donc, c'est communautaire, parce que, LÀ quand il y a le problème d'eau, ils s'asseyent et ensemble ils discutent tout le monde discutent. Oui. |

**p. 217**

|  |  |
|---|---|
| B.2.VA1 18m | Nous reconnaissons aujourd'hui, tout a changé avec l'ACATBLI qui essaie de donner des informations, essaie de leur donner des communications comment faire les sensibiliser, on va payer tout a changé. Et surtout les enfants aujourd'hui↑ . vouent à l'école plus qu'avant. Le taux d'instruction dans les écoles formelles a augmenté. Et il y a maintenant des écoles qui sont nées récemment un peu partout . dans des villages, il y a des écoles pour les enfants aujourd'hui, et les enfants essaient d'y aller. Et les enfants aussi acceptent aider les enfants = et les parents acceptent aujourd'hui aider leurs enfants à l'école sinon, avant, il dit non {il bat les mains}, ça nous donnera rien, l'enfant n'a qu'à rester pour aller au champ. Mais maintenant, ils acceptent envoyer leurs enfants à l'école, ils acceptent acheter du pétrole que les enfants puissent apprendre à la maison. Parce qu'il a abordé, certains parents m'ont dit, Aah pasteur, je ne savais pas que c'est ça ! Avant comme mon enfant échoue à l'école, ooo {ton tres élevé}, je prends le bâton. Je dis qu'il est paresseux alors quand il revient de l'école, je lui dit faire ceci faire cela je ne lui donne le temps d'apprendre. Mais quand même, moi-même, j'ai été |

alphabétisé, j'ai su que, AH, si on n'apprend pas à la maison, on ne peut pas réussir à l'école. Donc à partir d'aujourd'hui, je vais aider mon enfant à apprendre ses leçons à la maison afin de réussir. Donc, on a vu que, nous sommes en train nous sommes sur la bonne voie . ee, dans le milieu ifè.

**p. 218**

B.1.NK af1 31m Donc, ceci nous a fait dire que, nous nous fait voir que, AH, les gens maintenant ont compris le BIEN de l'alphabétisation parce que ça leur fait beaucoup de choses. D'abord, POUR leur propre vie, pour la vie de leurs enfants, et les gens ACCEPTENT maintenant envoyer leurs enfants à l'école. Imaginez. Une femme, une femme disons paysanne qui va accepter emmener ses enfants ici en la ville, et c'est elle-même qui va transporter de charbon, la nourriture pour mener à son enfant, avant, la femme ne va pas le faire ! Qu'est-ce que l'enfant viendra le faire. Et elle autre a souffert surtout. Aujourd'hui c'est les femmes mêmes qui vraiment qui se mobilisent pour chercher de places à leurs enfants à l'école ici.

B.1.AgA af1 37m Maintenant, nous sommes fières, parce que nos femmes aussi veulent être comme moi aussi, aller au bureau {il rit} partout, partout, elles intéressent .. et eux aussi, sont en train de .. faire d'effort pour arriver là. {rires}

**p. 219**

B.1.NK af1 1h4m Bon, parce que . il y a un changement, au niveau d'abord . du groupe de population de base . qui nous alphabétisons. Il y a un changement . {FA répond à son portable} au niveau même des des individus .. On avait parlé comment: les gens maintenant vraiment: . luttent pour la la la vie de leurs enfants dans les dans les les les .. dans l'école classique. Que ce soit filles ou bien garçons .. D'abord, là on a vu vraiment .. les avancés que nous avons fait. Au sein même de nos moniteurs . il y a maintenant du *bousculage. Les gens luttent maintenant pour être moniteur. Les gens luttent pour être monitrice. Parce que ils savait que AH↑

Appendix B: Interview excerpts

les femmes aussi peuvent être monitrices ? Parce que nous avons vu .. notre formatrice, la supervi=. notre superviseure. Elle est femme comme moi mais pourtant elle est pilote . de vélo, elle est sur la moTO↑, elle est venu de chez moi aussi je peux l'être. Donc, déjà on a vu que, au moins en partie, on a ces changements .. bon.

B.1.AgA af1 15m {petit rire} Parce que, dans notre association, il n'y a pas de femmes, qui ont .. leur qui ont leur vision sur l'alphabétisation ou bien travailler volontairement comme ça. On cherche ce qu'on va manger aujourd'hui, nous dire, chez nous, nos femmes, mais moi, je cherche le bien-être de mes frères.

**p. 220**

C.3.SY 1h11m {interprété} Il y a un autre document aussi qui s'appelle Ɔ̀nyaɖɔ̰̀ tsoko náàrìmáa dzɛnɛ̀ . c'est-à-dire Comment gérer un foyer. Lai= ne pas laisser abandonner son mari à d'autres femmes et cetera comment il y aurait entente entre la femme et son mari entre le mari et sa femme, comment éviter des désordres, et il dit que, à base de ces documents, vraiment les foyers, ou bien la vie aux foyers sont améliorées et là où il y avait des difficultés, aujourd'hui il y a l'entente, il y a l'amour, il y a le développement qui a commencé. Donc, c'est ainsi que on a ajouté un plus à la vie du peuple ifè.
{pause de 3 secondes avec des murmures}

C.3.OKD ff. Pour ajouter encore, xx ceci-là, à base de des ces documents, maintenant, ça a changé beaucoup dans ma vie .. Avant, moi je veux que hein on circule avec la femme seulement. [les autres : hah] Mais comme je suis devenu encore moni= devenu moniteur maintenant j'ai appris qu'il faut beaucoup de patience, si la femme circulait maintenant moi je la regarde comme elle ne *save pas ce qu'elle dit. {les autres rient doucement} Et voilà qu'actuellement . dans ma vie ça ça faisait beaucoup de choses.

**p. 221**

B.4.ANA si2 13m {petite rire} Donc, grâce à ça {alphabétisation} aussi, on a compris que la politique, la démocratie, s'enracine vraiment.

[JR : ahan] C'est-à-dire les gens ont commencé par comprendre on arrive, c'est une opportunité de leur expliquer plus posément ce qu'ils ont besoin, leurs droits et devoirs de citoyen quoi. Donc, eux-mêmes aussi comprennent, même au niveau du jour d'élection, qu'est-ce qu'on ne doit pas faire, qu'est-ce qu'on doit faire, on arrive à leur expliquer toutes ces choses-là.

**p. 222**

B.4.GĐ 39m {interprété} C'est la remarque paraît que {auparavant} les gens qui n'ont pas mis pied à l'école n'étaient pas considérés . dans la politique {lacune d'enregistrement} on voudrait leur faire le choix {lacune d'enregistrement} d'eux mais telle vue .. quand les gens de l'autorité ont envoyé certaines personnes pour pouvoir faire certaines choses . ils se disaient en eux mais, les gens-là ils ne connaissent rien, on peut les tourner n'importe comment, mais comme les alphabétiseurs, les coordinateurs et autres ils étaient vraiment veillants ils ont préparé les gens malgré qu'ils n'ont pas fait l'école formelle, ils étaient préparés de telle manière que tu ne peux pas les contourner. Alors, ils ont voulu se dévier vers ces gens qui n'ont appris que leur langue maternelle . peut-être pour les truquer, mais finalement, ils ont vu qu'ils n'ont pas pu, ils n'ont pas réussi leur *mentade {?}.

# References

Abdi, Ali A. 2006. Historical and current analyses of Africa. In Ali A. Abdi, Korba P. Puplampu, and George J. Sefa Dei (eds.), *African education and globalization: Critical perspectives,* 13–30. Lanham, Maryland: Lexington Books.

Abric, Jean-Claude. 2001. Méthodologie de recueil des représentations sociales [Methods of data collection in social representations]. In Jean-Claude Abric, (ed.), *Pratiques sociales et représentations* [Social practices and representations], 59–82. Third edition. Paris: Presses Universitaires de France.

Abric, Jean-Claude. 2003. La recherche du noyau central et de la zone muette des représentations sociales [Research of the core and of the silent zone of social representations]. In J. Abric (ed.), *Méthodes d'étude des représentations sociales* [Methods of study of social representations], 59–80. Ramonville Saint-Agne, France: Érès.

Affala, Foundoumi. n.d. *Pour découvrir les Ifè d'Atakpamé : Origines, Odon-itser, vie religieuse et politique* [To discover the Ifè of Atakpamé: Origins, Odon-itser, religious and political life]. Second edition. Atakpamé, Togo: privately published.

Aire, J. U. 1990. The private sector: Thoughts on African leadership. In Obasanjo and d'Orville, 209–215.

Ajayi, J. F. Ade, and Michael Crowder, eds. 1974. *History of West Africa*. London: Longman.

Ajulu, Deborah. 2001. *Holism in development: An African perspective on empowering communities.* Monrovia, Calif.: MARC.

Allen, John. 2006. *Rabble-rouser for peace: The authorized biography of Desmond Tutu.* New York: Free Press.
Anantharaman, A. 1990. The private sector: Interest in leadership. In Obasanjo and d'Orville, 206–209.
Angélil-Carter, Shelley. 1997. Second language acquisition of spoken and written English: Acquiring the skeptron. *TESOL Quarterly* 31:263–287.
Ansu-Kyeremeh, Kwasi. 2005. Communication in an Akan political system. In K. Ansu-Kyeremeh (ed.), *Indigenous communication in Africa: Concept, applications and prospects,* 178–193. Accra: Ghana Universities Press.
April, Kurt, and Marylou Shockley, eds. 2007. *Diversity in Africa: The coming of age of a continent.* Houndsmills, Hampshire: Palgrave Macmillan.
Archer, David, and Sara Cottingham. 2007. *Manuel de conception de REFLECT : Alphabétisation freirienne régénerée à travers les techniques de renforcement des capacités et pouvoirs communautaires* [REFLECT training manual: Regenerated Freirian literacy through empowering community techniques]. London: ActionAid.
Awokou, Kokou. 1997. L'enseignement dans l'Ogou : Analyse et perspectives [Teaching in the Ogou: Analysis and perspectives]. In T. Gbéasor (ed.), *Espace, culture et développement dans la région d'Atakpamé,* 83–90. Lomé: Les Presses de l'UB.
Baker, Victoria J. 1998. Literacy in developing societies: Native language versus national language literacy. In Aydin Yücesan Durgunoğlu and Ludo Verhoeven (eds.), *Literacy development in a multilingual context: Cross-cultural perspectives,* 21–35. Mahwah, NJ: Lawrence Erlbaum.
Bane, Martin J. 1956. *Catholic pioneers in West Africa.* Dublin: Clonmore and Reynolds.
Barton, David, and Mary Hamilton. 1999. Literacy practices. In David Barton, Mary Hamilton, and Roz Ivanic (eds.), *Situated literacies: Reading and writing in context,* 7–15. London and New York: Routledge.
Bellier, Irène. 2008. Le développement et les peuples autochtones : Conflits de savoirs et enjeux de nouvelles pratiques politiques [Development and indigenous peoples: Conflicts of knowledge and issues of new political practices]. In Géronimi, Bellier, Gabas, Vernières, and Viltard, 119–139.
Bennis, Warren. 2007. The challenges of leadership in the modern world: Introduction to the special issue. *American Psychologist* 62:2–5.
Bess, James L., and Paul Goldman. 2001. Leadership ambiguity in universities and K–12 schools and the limits of contemporary leadership theory. *The Leadership Quarterly* 12:419–450.
Blunt, Peter, and Merrick L. Jones. 1997. Exploring the limits of Western leadership theory in East Asia and Africa. *Personnel Review* 26:6–23.
Bolman, Lee G., and Terence E. Deal. 1996. Repenser les organisations : Pour que diriger soit un art. Adapted by the authors and translated by Marie-Agnès

Schmitt. Paris: Maxima. Originally published as Reframing organizations: Artistry, choice and leadership (San Francisco: Jossey-Bass, 1991).
Bonardi, Christine, and Nicolas Roussiau. 1999. *Les représentations sociales*. Paris: Éditions Dunod.
Bourdieu, Pierre. 1991. Language and symbolic power. Cambridge: Polity Press.
Bourdieu, Pierre, and A. Spire. 2002. « *Si le monde social m'est supportable, c'est parce que je peux m'indigner* » ["If I can bear the world, it's because I can be indignant"]. Paris: Éditions de l'Aube.
Bourdieu, Pierre, and Jean-Claude Passeron. 1970. *La reproduction : Eléménts pour une théorie du système d'enseignement* [Reproduction: Elements for a theory of a system of teaching]. Paris: Les Éditions de Minuit.
Bourges, Hervé. 2006. *Léopold Sédar Senghor : Lumière noire* [Leopold Sedar Senghor: Black light]. Paris: Menges.
Boutros-Ghali, Boutros, George Bush, Jimmy Carter, Milail. Gorbachev, and Desmond Tutu. 1998. *Essays on leadership*. Washington DC: Carnegie Corporation of New York.
Boyer, Henti. 2003. Introduction : Le paradigme représentationnel [Introduction: The representational paradigm]. In H. Boyer (ed.), *De l'autre côté du discours : Recherches sur le fonctionnement des représentations communautaires* [On the other side of speech: Research on the function of community representations], 9–15. Paris: L'Harmattan.
Brudney, Jeffrey L. 2005. Designing and managing volunteer programs. In Robert D. Herman and Associates (eds.), *The Jossey-Bass handbook of nonprofit leadership and management*, 310–344. Second edition. San Francisco: Jossey-Bass.
Burke, Seán J. 2007. Introducing leadership in development. UNDP-SNV. Accessed October 14, 2008. www.capacity.org.
Busia, Kofi A. 1968. *Purposeful education for Africa*. The Hague: Mouton.
Carrington, Vicki, and Allan Luke. 1997. Literacy and Bourdieu's sociological theory: A reframing. *Language and Education* 11:96–112.
Cavalli, Marisa, and Daniela Coletta. 2003. Représentations sociales : Traits fondamentaux, traits contextuels et contextes. In Cavalli, Coletta, Gajo, Matthey, and Serra, 61–73.
Cavalli, Marisa, Daniela Coletta, Laurent Gajo, Marinette Matthey, and Cecilia Serra, eds. 2003. Langues, bilinguisme et représentations sociales au Val d'Aoste. Aoste, Italy: IRRE-VDA.
Cheffy, Ian. 2006. Conceptions of literacy in context: Situated understandings in a rural area of northern Cameroon. Ph.D. dissertation. Lancaster University, UK.
Chhokar, Jagdeep Singh, Felix C. Brodbeck, and Robert J. House, eds. 2007. *Culture and leadership across the world: The GLOBE book of in-depth studies of 25 societies*. Mahwah, NJ: Lawrence Erlbaum.
Coquery-Vidrovitch, Catherine, Daniel Hemery, and Jean Piel, eds. (1988) 2007. *Pour une histoire du développement : Etats, sociétés, développement*. Paris: L'Harmattan.

Cosway, Nancy, and Steven A. Anankum. 1996. Traditional leadership and community management in northern Ghana. In Peter Blunt and D. Michael Warren (eds). *Indigenous organizations and development,* 88–96. London: Intermediate Technology.

Dagenais, Diane, and Marianne Jacquet. 2008. Theories of representation in French and English scholarship on multilingualism. *International Journal of Multilingualism* 5:41–52. doi:10.2167.

Davis, Patricia M. 2004. *Reading is for knowing: Literacy acquisition, retention, and usage among the Machiguenga.* Publications in Language Use and Education 1. Dallas: SIL International.

Davison, Cathy. 2008. Literacy in cultures of oral tradition. In Mutaka, 82–87.

Diagne, Mamousse. 2005. *Critique de la raison orale : Les pratiques discursives en Afrique noire* [Critique of oral reasoning: Discursive practices in black Africa]. Paris: Éditions Karthala.

Doise, Willem. 1986. Les représentations sociales : Définition d'un concept. In W. Doise and A. Palmonari (eds.), *L'étude des représentations sociales,* 81–94. Neuchâtel and Paris: Delachaux and Niestlé.

Doronila, Maria Luisa C. 1996. *Landscapes of literacy: An ethnographic study of functional literacy in marginal Philippine communities.* Hamburg, Germany, and London: UNESCO Institute for Education and Luzac Oriental.

Droar, Dave. 2006. Expectancy theory of motivation. Accessed March 16, 2006. www.arrod.co.uk/archive/concept_vroom.php.

Droz, Yvan, and Jean-Claude Lavigne. 2006. *Ethique et développement durable* [Ethics and sustainable development]. Paris and Geneva: Éditions Karthala and IUED.

Drucker, Peter F. 1990. *Managing the non-profit organization: Principles and practices.* New York: HarperBusiness.

Duluc, Alain. 2008. *Leadership et confiance.* Second edition. Paris: Dunod.

Durkheim, Émile. 1898. Représentations individuelles et représentations collectives. *Revue de Metaphysique et de Morale* VI (mai). Accessed 2002. http://classiques.uqac.ca/classiques/Durkheim_emile/durkheim.html database.

Duveen, Gerard. 2000. Introduction: The power of ideas. In Serge. Moscovici and Gerard. Duveen (eds.), *Social representations: Explorations in social psychology,* 1–17. Cambridge: Polity Press.

Dym, Barry, and Harry Hutson. 2005. *Leadership in nonprofit organizations.* Thousand Oaks, Calif.: Sage.

Eade, Deborah. 1997. *Capacity-building: An approach to people-centred development.* Oxford: Oxfam Publishing.

Eade, Deborah. 2007. Capacity building: Who builds whose capacity? *Development in Practice* 17:632–639. doi:10.1080/09614520701469807.

Edmunds, Stahrl. W. 1978. *Basics of private and public management: A humanistic approach to change management.* Lexington, Mass.: Lexington Books.

Edoho, Felix. 1998. Management capacity building: A strategic imperative for African development in the twenty-first century. In Valentine Udoh James, (ed). Capacity building in developing countries: *Human and environmental dimensions,* 228–251. Westport, Conn.: Praeger.

Fairclough, Norman. 1992. *Discourse and social change.* Cambridge: Polity Press.

Ferdman, Bernardo M. 1999. Ethnic and minority issues in literacy. In Wagner, Venezky, and Street, 95–101.

Finnegan, Ruth. 1999. Sociological and anthropological issues in literacy. In Wagner, Venezky, and Street, 89–94.

Fisher, James. C., and Kathleen M. Cole. 1993. *Leadership and management of volunteer programs: A guide for volunteer administrators.* San Francisco: Jossey-Bass.

Fraenkel, Béatrice, and Aïssatou Mbodj. 2010. Introduction: Les New Literacy Studies, jalons historiques et perspectives actuelles [Introduction: the New Literacy Studies, historical milestones and current perspectives]. *Langages et Société* 133:7–24. doi:10.3917/ls.133.0007.

Freire, Paulo. 1970. *Pedagogy of the oppressed.* Translated by M. B. Ramos. New York: Seabury Press. Originally published as *Pedagogia do Oprimido* (Rio de Janeiro: Edições Paz e Terra, 1970).

Fullan, Michael. 2003. *Change forces with a vengeance.* New York: Routledge.

Furniss, Graham. 2004. *Orality: The power of the spoken word.* New York: Palgrave Macmillan.

Gajo, Laurent. 2000. Disponibilité sociale des représentations : Approche linguistique [Social availability of representations: A linguistic approach]. *Travaux neuchâtelois de linguistique* [Linguistic works from Neuchâtel] 32:39–53.

Gayibor, Nicoué L. 1997. *Histoire des Togolais, Volume 1 : Des origines à 1884* [History of the Togolese, Volume 1: From the origins to 1884]. Lomé: Les Presses de l'Université du Bénin.

Gee, James Paul. 1990. *Social linguistics and literacies: Ideology in discourses.* Hampshire, UK: Falmer Press.

Gee, James Paul. 1996. *Social linguistics and literacies: Ideology in discourses.* Second edition. London: Taylor and Francis.

Géronimi, Vincent, Irène Bellier, Jean Gabas, Michel Vernières, and Yves Viltard, eds. 2008. *Savoirs et politiques de développement : Questions en débat à l'aube du XXIe siècle* [Development knowledge and policies: Issues being debated at the dawn of the 21st century]. Paris: Karthala and GEMDEV.

Graeff, Claude L. 1983. The situational leadership theory: A critical view. *Academy of Management Review* 8:285–291.

Groupe Technique du Travail de Ministère de la Culture, de l'Alphabétisation et de la Promotion des Langues Nationales (MCAPLN). 2009. *Document* cadre du mise en oeuvre de la stratégie du faire-faire au Bénin (Options, mécanismes, procédures et outils d'operationnalisation) [Framework document of the implementation of the outsourcing strategy in Benin (Options, mechanisms, procedures and tools of operationalization)]. Ms.

Gubbels, Peter, and Cathryn Koss. 2000. *From the roots up: Strengthening organizational capacity through guided self-assessment.* Oklahoma City: World Neighbors.

Hargreaves, John D. 1974. The European partition of West Africa. In J. F. Ade Ajayi and Michael Crowder, (eds). *History of West Africa,* 402–423. London: Longman.

Harris, Theodore L., and Richard E. Hodges. 1995. *The literacy dictionary: The vocabulary of reading and writing.* Newark, Del.: International Reading Association.

Helame, Esoh. 2009. Contribution pour une approche interculturelle du développement. In Fabien Grumiaux and Patrick Matagne (eds.), *Le développement durable sous le regard des sciences et de l'histoire, volume 2, Politiques publiques, utopies ou nouveau paradigme, un concept aux références multiples, gestion des ressources et des risques* [Sustainable development in the light of science and history, volume 2, Public policy, utopias or a new paradigm, a concept with multiple references, management of resources and of risks], 61–84. Paris: l'Harmattan.

Hope, Anne, and Sally Timmel. 1995. *Training for transformation: A handbook for community workers, book I.* Revised edition. London: ITDG.

House, Robert J. 1996. Path-goal theory of leadership: Lessons, legacy, and a reformulated theory. *The Leadership Quarterly* 7:323–352.

Ilsley, Paul J. 1990. *Enhancing the volunteer experience: New insights on strengthening volunteer participation, learning, and commitment.* San Francisco: Jossey-Bass.

Imdieke, Ben. 2003. The rest of the world: Capacity building in the international context. *New Directions for Philanthropic Fundraising* 40:89–101.

Jodelet, Dénise. 1989. Représentations sociales : Un domaine en expansion. In Dénise Jodelet (ed.), *Les représentations sociales,* 47–70. Paris: PressesUniversitaires de France.

Johnson, Hazel, and Alan Thomas. 2004. Professional capacity and organizational change as measures of educational effectiveness: Assessing the impact of postgraduate education in development policy and management. *Compare: A Journal of Comparative Education* 34:301–314.

Johnson, Hazel, and Alan Thomas. 2007. Sustainable development and African local government: Can electronic training help build capacities? *Compare: A Journal of Comparative Education* 37:447–462.

Jones, Robert B. 2003. Capacity building in human service organizations. *New Directions for Philanthropic Fundraising* 40:15–27.

Kambhampati, Uma S. 2004. *Development and the developing world*. Cambridge: Polity Press.
Katz, R. L. 1955. Skills of an effective administrator. *Harvard Business Review* 33(1):33–42.
Kingsbury, Damien. 2004. Community development. In D. Kingsbury, J. Remenyi, J. McKay, and J. Hunt (eds.), *Key issues in development*, 221–242. Basingstroke, Hampshire: Palgrave Macmillan.
Kinsey, David J., and J. Russell Raker, III. 2003. Capacity building: A primer. *New Directions for Philanthropic Fundraising* 40:5–14.
Koba, Anani 1996. L'approche fonctionnelle des proverbes ifè. M.A. thesis. University of Benin, Lomé, Togo.
Kossi-Titrikou, Komi. 1997. Culture et société à Atakpamé. In T. Gbéasor (ed.), *Espace, culture et développement dans la région d'Atakpamé*, 69–82. Lomé: Presses de l'UB.
Kouzes, James, and Barry Posner. 1987. *The leadership challenge: How to get extraordinary things done in organizations*. San Francisco: Jossey-Bass.
Kramsch, Claire. 2008. Contrepoint de chapitre 6. In Geneviève Zarate, Danielle Lévy, and Claire Kramsch (eds.), *Précis du plurilinguisme et du pluriculturalisme*, 319–323. Paris: Éditions des archives contemporaines.
Kress, Gunther 1985. *Linguistic processes in sociocultural practice*. Victoria, Australia: Deakin University Press.
Lacey, Anita, and Suzan Ilcan. 2006. Voluntary labor, responsible citizenships, and international NGOs. *International Journal of Comparative Sociology* 47(1):34–53.
Lamboni, Arzouma Thomas 2008, Sept.–Oct.. Libre opinion : Quel développement faisons-nous ? [Free opinion: Which development do we do?] *Info-Reseau* 2:2.
Landy, Frédéric. 2008. Du « développement rural » à la « gestion concertée des ressources » [From "sustainable development" to "joint resource management"]. In Géronimi, Bellier, Gabas, Vernières, and Viltard, 187–208.
Latouche, Serge. (1988) 2007. Contribution à l'histoire du concept de développement. In Coquery-Vidrovitch, Hemery, and Piel, 41–60.
Lewis, David. 2001. *The management of non-governmental development organizations: An introduction*. New York and London: Routledge.
Lewis, M. Paul, ed. 2009. Ethnologue: Languages of the World, sixteenth edition. Dallas: SIL International. Online version: http://www.ethnologue.com/16.
Lewis, M. Paul, Gary Simons, and Charles D. Fennig, eds. 2013. *Ethnologue: Languages of the world*. Seventeenth edition. Dallas: SIL International.
Lewis, M. Paul, Gary Simons, and Charles D. Fennig, eds. 2016. *Ethnologue: Languages of the world*. Nineteenth edition. Dallas: SIL International.
Littrell, Ronnie F., and Peter Baguma. 2005. Education, management, and the world's work: Leadership traits of educators in undeveloped and

developing countries, focusing on Uganda in sub-Saharan Africa. In J. R. McIntyre and I. Alon (eds.), *Business and management education in transitioning and developing countries: A handbook,* 301–322. Armonk, New York: M. E. Sharpe.

Maathai, Wangari. 2009. The challenge for Africa. New York: Pantheon Books.

Mabogunje, Akin L. 1990. African agricultural production. In Obasanjo and d'Orville, 92–110.

Maddox, Bryan. 2001. Literacy and the market: The economic uses of literacy among the peasantry in north-west Bangladesh. In Street, 137–149.

Malunga, Chiku. 2006. Learning leadership development from African cultures: A personal perspective. *INTRAC Praxis Note* 25:1–13.

Mandela, Nelson Rolihlahla. 1994. *Long walk to freedom: The autobiography of Nelson Mandela.* Boston: Little, Brown.

Manning, Susan Schissler. 2003. *Ethical leadership in human services: A multi-dimensional approach.* Boston: Allyn and Bacon.

Maranz, David E. 2001. *African friends and money matters: Observations from Africa.* Publications in Ethnography 37. Dallas: SIL and the International Museum of Cultures.

Martin-Jones, Marilyn. 2000. Enterprising women: Multilingual literacies in the construction of new identities. In Marilyn Martin-Jones and Kathryn Jones (eds.), *Multilingual literacies: Reading and writing different worlds,* 149–169. Amsterdam and Philadelphia: John Benjamins.

Matemba, Lawrence. 2007. Diversity challenges in community research and action. In April and Shockley, 238–262.

Matthey, Mariette. 2003. Aspects théoriques et méthodologiques de la recherche [Theoretical and methodological aspects of the research]. In Cavalli, Colette, Gajo, Matthey, and Serra, 47–55.

Mbigi, Lovemore. 2007. Rethinking leadership and wealth creation in Africa. In April and Shockley, 3–9.

McClelland, David C. 1976. *The achieving society: With a new introduction.* Second edition. New York: Irvington.

Mintzberg, Henry. 1973. *The nature of managerial work.* New York: Harper Collins.

Moliner, Pascal, Patrick Rateau, and Valérie Cohen-Scali. 2002. Introduction et éléments théoriques. In Pascal Moliner, Patrick Rateau, and Valérie Cohen-Scali (eds.), *Les représentations sociales : Pratique et études de terrain* [Social representations: Practices and studies on the ground], 11–28. Rennes: Presses Universitaires de Rennes.

Moore, Danièle. 2001. Les représentations des langues et de leur apprentissage : Itinéraires théoriques et trajets méthodologiques [Representations of languages and of their learning: Theoretical directions and methodological routes]. In D. Moore (ed.), *Les représentations des langues et de leur apprentissage : Références, modèles, données et méthodes* [The representations of languages and of their learning: References, models, data and methods], 7–22. Le Mesnil-sur-l'Estrée, France: Didier.

Moore, Danièle, and Bernard Py. 2008. Introduction : Discours sur les langues et représentations sociales. In Geneviève Zarate, Danielle Lévy, and Claire Kramsch (eds.), *Précis du plurilinguisme et du pluriculturalisme,* 271–279. Paris: Éditions des archives contemporaines.

Morgan, Gareth. 1999. *Images de l'organisation.* Translated by Salonge Chevrier-Vouve and Michel Auden. Quebec: Les Presses de l'Université Laval and De Boeck. Originally published as *Images of Organization.* Second edition (Beverly Hills: Sage, 1997).

Moscovici, Serge. 1989. Des représentations collectives aux représentations sociales : Éléments pour une histoire [From collective representations to social representations: Elements of a history]. In Dénise Jodelet (ed), *Les représentations sociales,* 70–103. Paris: Presses Universitaires de France.

Moulton, Jeanne, and Karen Mundy. 2002. Conclusion: Paradigm lost? Synthesis and discussion. In Jeanne Moulton, Karen Mundy, Michel Walmond, and James Williams (eds.), *Education reforms in sub-Saharan Africa: Paradigm lost?,* 179–212. Westport, Conn.: Greenwood Press.

Mumford, Michael D., Stephen J. Zaccaro, Frances D. Harding, T. Owen Jacobs, and Edwin A. Fleishman. 2000. Leadership skills for a changing world: Solving complex social problems. *The Leadership Quarterly* 11:11–35.

Mumford, Michael D., Stephen J. Zaccaro, Mary S. Connelly, and Michel A. Marks. 2000. Leadership skills: Conclusions and future directions. *The Leadership Quarterly* 11:155–170.

Mutaka, Ngessimo M., ed. 2008. *Building capacity: Using TEFL and African languages as development-oriented literacy tools.* Mankon, Bamenda, Cameroon: Langaa Research and Publishing CIG.

Mutaka, Ngessimo M., and Lilian M. Attia. 2008. Introduction: Issues in the teaching of languages as a prop to a development-oriented literacy. In Mutaka, 1–12.

Negura, Lilian 2006. L'analyse de contenu dans l'analyse des représentations sociales [Content analysis in the analysis of social representations]. *Sociologies, Théories et Recherches* (October 2006). Accessed March 2, 2010. http://sociologies, revues.org/index993.html.

Nkasa, Grace Akukwe, and David W. Chapman. 2006. Sustaining community participation: What remains after the money ends? *Review of Education* 52:509–532. doi:10.1007/s11159-006-9009-9.

Northouse, Peter G. 2007. *Leadership: Theory and practice.* Fourth edition. Thousand Oaks, Calif.: Sage.

Norton, Bonnie. 1997. Language, identity, and the ownership of English. *TESOL Quarterly* 31:409–429.

Norton, Bonnie. 2000. *Identity and language learning: Gender, ethnicity and educational change.* Harlow, UK: Pearson Education.

Nyerere, Julius K. 1967. *Freedom and unity / Uhuru na umoja : A selection from writings and speeches 1952–65*. London: Oxford University Press.

Nyerere, Julius K. 1973. *Freedom and development / Uhuru na maendeleo: A selection from writings and speeches 1968–1973*. Dar es Salaam: Oxford University Press.

Obasanjo, Olusegun, and Hans d'Orville, eds. 1990. *Challenges of leadership in African development*. New York: Crane Russak.

Pell, Arthur R. 1972. *Recruiting, training, and motivating volunteer workers*. New York: Pilot Books.

Planche, Jeanne 2004. Accompagner l'émergence et le renforcement des sociétés civiles [To accompany the emergence and the strengthening of civil societies]. *Coopérer Aujourd'Hui* 38:1–51.

Py, Bernard. 2003. Introduction. In Cavalli, Colette, Gajo, Matthey, and Serra, 15–33.

Py, Bernard. 2004. Pour une approche linguistique des représentations sociales. *Langages* 154:6–19.

Rassool, Naz. 2009. Literacy: In search of a paradigm. In J. Soler, F. Fletcher-Campbell, and G. Reid (eds.), *Understanding difficulties in literacy development: Issues and concepts*, 7–31. London: Sage.

Reader, John. 1998. *Africa: A biography of the continent*. New York: Alfred A. Knopf.

Robichaud, Suzie. 1998. *Le bénévolat : Entre le coeur et la raison* [Voluntary work: Between the heart and the mind]. Chicoutimi, Quebec: Les Éditions JCL.

Rogers, Alan. 2001. Afterword: Problematising literacy and development. In Street, 205–221.

Russell, Craig J., and Karl W. Kuhnert. 1992. Integrating skill acquisition and perspective taking capacity in the development of leaders. *The Leadership Quarterly* 3:335–353.

Schanely, Leon. 1983. *Developing community potential*. Edited by Larry Yost and Willa Yost. Dallas: Summer Institute of Linguistics.

Schatzberg, Michael G. 1993. Power, legitimacy and "democratisation" in Africa. *Africa* 63:445–461.

Serra, Cecelia. 2000. Traitement discursive et conversationnelle des représentations sociales [A discourse and conversational processing of social representations]. *Travaux neuchâtelois de linguistique* 32:77–90.

Silverthorne, Colin P. 2005. *Organizational psychology in cross-cultural perspective*. New York and London: New York University Press.

Smith, David M. 1986. The anthropology of literacy acquisition. In B. B. Schieffelin and P. Gilmore (eds.), *The acquisition of literacy: Ethnographic perspectives*, 261–275. Norwood, NJ: Ablex.

Smith, Linda Tuhiwai 1999. *Decolonizing methodologies: Research and indigenous peoples*. London and Dunedin, NZ: Zed Books and University of Otago Press.

St-Germain, Michel. 2002. Le leadership constructiviste : Une solution au paradoxe de l'individualité et de la normalisation [Constructivist leadership: A solution to the paradox of individuality and of standardization]. In L. Langlois and C. Lapointe (eds.), *Le leadership en éducation : Plusieurs regards, une même passion*, 113–151. Montreal: Chenelière/McGraw-Hill.

Street, Brian V. 1990. *Cultural meanings of literacy: Literacy lessons.* Geneva: International Bureau of Education. Accessed June 12, 2007. http://proxy.lib.sfu.ca/login?url=http://search.ebscohost.com.proxy.lib.sfu.ca/login.aspx?direct=true&db=eric&AN=ED321040&site=ehost-live.

Street, Brian V. 1995. *Social literacies: Critical approaches to literacy in development, ethnography and education.* London: Longman.

Street, Brian V., ed. 2001. *Literacy and development: Ethnographic perspectives.* London: Routledge.

Tadadjeu, Maurice. 2008. Enhancing the role of African languages in local development projects. In Mutaka, 66–81.

Tandon, Rajesh. 1988. Management of voluntary agencies: Some issues. *Asian-South Pacific Bureau of Adult Education Courier* 44:17–27.

Theimann, Nadine M. 2007. The lions mark their territory: The African thought system. In April and Shockley, 93–105.

Theimann, Nadine M., and Kurt April. 2007. Cave canem! The art (or science?) of Western management in an African context. In April and Shockley, 10–34.

Tutu, Desmond. 1998. Leadership. In Boutros-Ghali, Bush, Carter, Gorbachev, and Tutu, 67–70.

Ugwuegbu, Denis C. E. 2001. *The psychology of management in African organizations.* Westport, Conn.: Quorum Books.

UNDP (United Nations Development Program). 2013. Sustaining human progress: Reducing vulnerablities and building resilience. 2014 Human Development Report. Accessed 2014. http://hdr.undp.org/en/content/table-1-human-development-index-and-its-components.

UNESCO. 2006. *L'alphabétisation, un enjeu vital (Education pour Tous - Rapport Mondial de Suivi)* [Literacy for Life]. Paris: UNESCO.

UNESCO. 2010. Reaching the marginalized (EFA Global Monitoring Report). Paris and Oxford: UNESCO Publishing / Oxford University Press.

UNESCO. 2014. *Enseigner et apprendre : Atteindre la qualité pour tous (Education pour Tous - Rapport Mondial de Suivi)* [Teaching and Learning; Achieving Quality for All]. Paris: Éditions UNESCO.

Vernières, Michel. 2003. *Développement humain : Economie et politique* [Human development: Economy and politics]. Paris: Economica.

Vernières, Michel. 2008. L'éducation dans les processus de développement. In Géronimi, Bellier, Gabas, Vernières, and Viltard, 209–229.

Viltard, Yves. 2008. Etats, savoirs et politiques de développement [States, knowledge, and development policies]. In Géronimi, Bellier, Gabas, Vernières, and Viltard, 22–43.

Vroom, Victor. 1964. *Work and motivation.* New York: John Wiley and Sons.

Wagner, Daniel A., Richard L. Venezky, and Bryan V. Street, eds. 1999. *Literacy: An international handbook.* Boulder, Colo.: Westview Press.

Wagner, Lilya D. 2003. Why capacity building matters and why nonprofits ignore it. *New Directions for Philanthropic Fundraising* 40:103–111.

Warren, D. Michael, Remi Adedokun, and Akintola Omolaoye. 1996. Indigenous organizations and development: The case of Ara, Nigeria. In Peter Blunt and D. Michael Warren (eds). *Indigenous organizations and development,* 43–49. London: Intermediate Technology.

Webster, J. B. 1974. Political activity in British West Africa, 1900–1940. In J. F. Ade Ajayi and Michael Crowder (eds). *History of West Africa,* 568–595. London: Longman.

Willis, Katie. 2005. *Theories and practices of development.* London and New York: Routledge.

Windham, Douglas M. 1999. Literacy and economic development. In Wagner, Venezky, and Street, 342–347.

Woronoff, Jon. 1972. *West African wager: Houphouet versus Nkrumah.* Metuchen, NJ: Scarecrow Press.

# Index

## A

ACA 32, 210, 214, 216, 241
ACATBLI 31, 108, 118, 146
  activities of 21, 26, 29, 30, 32, 164, 168, 200, 202, 205, 207, 209, 210, 212, 217, 221, 226, 227, 238, 241
  funding of 32, 205, 210
  goals of 170, 175, 225
  leadership 11, 18, 23, 26, 31, 32, 86, 91, 98, 106, 109, 123, 147, 156, 165, 191, 201, 206, 208, 210, 215, 222, 225, 226, 244, 246
  relationship with local associations 23-25, 27, 30, 32, 90, 125, 191, 202, 205, 207-209, 212, 213, 224, 232
ADCIBA 27-29, 31, 95, 104, 108, 112, 114, 117-119, 122, 125-127, 130, 132, 133, 135, 138, 142, 153, 155-158, 161, 166, 170, 177, 185, 187, 200, 207, 211, 214, 220, 221, 226, 244-246

advisor
  association board 111, 120, 134, 138
  technical xiv, 199, 239
Akan 57
Akposso 16
AMADPENI 24, 25, 31
AMI 22, 24, 31
AMIADA 25,-27, 31, 103, 105, 112, 120, 121, 133, 168, 177, 189, 191, 192, 202, 205-207, 211, 212, 213, 221, 226
Atakpamé 18, 20, 27, 30, 32, 106, 246
AVADI 23, 29-31, 94, 101, 111, 112, 117, 122, 124, 130, 132, 137, 139, 144, 146, 170, 171, 179, 181, 202, 206, 218, 219, 221
AVID 23, 31, 32, 91, 92, 103, 107, 111, 121, 123, 126, 132, 134, 137, 139, 144, 145, 155, 161, 165, 167, 169, 207, 218, 226, 227
awareness-raising 80, 151, 165, 168, 214, 225, 248

## B

Bago 16
Benin xiv, 16–18, 28, 29, 72, 214, 216, 226, 246
  history 6, 71, 79, 151
  infrastructure 18, 195, 228
  linguistic situation 5, 6, 15, 20
  literacy in 2, 9, 19, 27, 28, 152
  literacy work in 5, 79, 208
  policies of 9, 16, 19, 20, 27, 28, 65, 67, 79, 164
biliterate(s) 183, 184, 203, 238
board members 128, 204, 212
  representations of 93, 96, 104, 105, 108, 114, 115, 128, 129, 131, 212, 234
  responsibilities of 129, 131–133, 161, 207, 210, 221, 227
  roles of 202, 205
  training of 201, 202, 205, 227
book(s)
  importance of 166, 170, 184, 185
  literacy program 175
  production of 21, 200
  topics available 20, 26, 175, 220–222, 238

## C

Cabe 27
capacity building xiii, xiv, 3, 49, 69, 98, 195, 223, 224, 233, 236, 238, 240
  African 248
  community 199, 214, 222
  definitions xiii, 4, 5
  organizational 11, 22, 44, 148, 198, 199, 204, 211, 212, 214, 227–229, 237, 244
  personnel 125, 199, 200, 202, 229
CENALA 19
chief(s) 18, 57, 84, 85, 87–89, 104–106, 112, 132, 135, 144, 168, 174, 175, 211
church(es) 21, 33, 70, 90, 131, 168, 216, 222, 226, 228, 243
  and literacy 1, 20, 25, 152, 167, 170, 183, 188
  denominations 18, 24, 152, 226
  leadership of 109, 110, 125, 201, 222, 238
CNL 9, 10, 31
Congo 6, 57
coordinator(s) 2, 11, 23, 25, 31, 90, 95, 109, 115, 119, 123, 124, 126, 133, 134, 137, 138, 141, 142, 145, 146, 151, 157, 158, 161, 163, 165, 168, 170, 171, 181, 185, 187–189, 191, 193, 199–201, 205–209, 211, 212, 218, 219, 221, 222, 225, 226, 234, 241, 244, 245
cultural capital 78–80, 194

## D

development xiv, 3, 4, 53–55, 58, 63, 64, 71, 74, 75, 77–81, 84, 91, 109, 118, 119, 126, 128, 145, 148, 150, 154, 156, 157, 159–161, 164–166, 175, 183, 188, 194, 195, 199–201, 206, 211, 213, 215, 220–224, 226, 232, 235, 236, 240, 241, 248
  cultural 68, 76, 162, 170, 194, 203, 235
  definitions of 68–70, 76, 156
  economic 22, 23, 26, 30, 32, 67, 70–73, 76, 78, 79, 117, 161, 162, 163, 164, 194, 210, 214, 216, 229, 235, 236, 245
  holistic 24, 25, 29, 32, 33, 162, 214, 237
  language 18, 19, 33, 126, 175, 194, 203, 225, 229, 235
  leadership 3, 46, 47, 49, 51, 53, 60, 226, 243
  literacy program 55, 81, 117
  organizational 10, 31, 43, 60, 198, 199, 214, 225–228, 232, 237
  social 26, 65, 67, 72, 73, 76, 78, 79, 110, 117, 161, 164, 194, 203, 214, 218, 229, 235, 245

spiritual 24, 162, 194, 203, 235
sustainable xiii, 72, 76
DNAEA 9, 20, 28

# E

education 8, 17, 38, 53, 165, 173, 191, 198–201, 234, 239, 243
 and development 23, 29, 69–72, 76, 79
 colonial era 6, 7
 formal 4, 30, 168, 218
 impact of Ifè literacy program on 216, 217, 225, 228
 language of 6, 7, 8, 30, 245
 nonformal 2, 11, 123
Education for All 2, 63, 150
English
 as language of wider communication 185, 188, 195, 201, 238
 in education 6
Espoir pour l'Avenir 30, 31
evaluation(s) 209
 of literacy students 201
 of programs and personnel 47, 48, 54, 71, 77, 214, 226, 232
Éwé
 as language of wider communication 16, 236
 in Togolese literacy policy 8
 language in education 7
 leadership 57
 national status 7
 transfer to reading 19, 238

# F

Fon
 customs 167
 people 171
 relationship with the Ifè 16, 171
France 6–8
Freire 9, 65, 66, 79
French 20
 as language of formal education 7, 8, 30, 171, 172, 182, 191, 192
 as language of research 11, 12, 39, 84, 85, 91, 103, 116, 174, 179, 180, 246
 as language of wider communication 80, 151, 155–157, 181, 183–185, 190, 194, 195, 235, 238
 bilingualism with 160, 179, 180, 184–186, 190, 192–194, 235
 in the Ifè literacy program 123, 189, 190, 192–195, 203, 208, 236
 in Togolese literacy policy 8
 literacy in 144, 181, 183, 186, 187, 194, 225, 236, 238
 people 171
 representations of 159, 178, 179, 181–183, 188, 189, 194, 235
 scholarly research in and theories 36, 40, 44
 status of 6, 171, 194
 transfer to reading in 110, 189, 238
French West Africa 8, 9
funders xiv, 23, 72, 201, 203, 204, 208, 213, 239
funding 25
 external 4, 22, 23, 27, 55, 73, 198, 204, 205, 207–209, 211, 212, 227, 231, 232, 239, 241–244
 internal 194, 205, 209, 227, 241, 242, 244
fundraising 55, 201

# G

Gambia 56, 57
gender 16, 75, 145, 225
German
 language in education 7
 missions 7
Germany
 colonial language policy 6, 7
Ghana 7, 57, 58, 73, 76, 201
globalization 68, 72, 75, 76, 144, 148, 149

# H

Houphouët-Boigny 58, 59
Human Development Index 2, 70

## I

Ica 27, 172
Idaasha 27
identity 7, 40, 53, 66, 68, 148, 159, 160, 166, 171, 172, 194, 225, 228, 238, 240, 248
ideology/ies 40, 58, 65, 68, 71, 76, 77, 79
Ifè 193, 216
  associations, local 231
  culture 16, 18, 33, 39, 40, 47, 57, 84, 89-91, 93, 95, 97, 100, 102, 104, 128, 132, 133, 135, 137, 138, 141, 144, 159, 167-170, 172, 192, 202, 203, 220, 223, 227, 228, 233, 235, 238-240, 244, 247
  environment of 1, 5, 17-19, 21, 28, 30, 152, 162, 172, 212, 214, 220, 228, 246, 248
  impact of 240
  language 12, 16, 18, 19, 21, 28, 30, 84, 85, 103, 110, 120, 134, 144, 148, 159, 160, 166-168, 170-172, 175-185, 188-195, 202, 203, 225, 235-238, 243, 246, 257
  leaders 133, 224
  literacy program xiii, xiv, 1, 2, 5, 10, 18-20, 22-25, 27-33, 49, 66, 79, 81, 125, 126, 148, 153, 159, 163-165, 173-175, 189, 192, 194, 199-203, 209, 211, 212, 214, 215, 217, 218, 223-226, 228, 229, 231-233, 236, 238, 240, 241, 243, 244, 248
  people xiv, 11, 15, 16, 23, 24, 26, 27, 29, 30, 32, 33, 119, 128, 132, 145, 149, 157, 160, 164, 170, 171, 176, 177, 183, 185, 194, 206, 211, 214, 217, 218, 222-225, 229, 233, 235, 236, 238, 240, 241, 246, 247
illiteracy 2, 4, 10, 157
  rates 8, 9, 16, 60, 159
  representations of 152, 232

income-generating activities (IGA) 23, 208
  agricultural projects: 26, 29, 30, 210, 227
  other projects 23, 26, 210, 227
  problems and challenges 210, 227, 241, 242
investment(s)
  theory of 66, 67, 148, 240

## J

Jésus le Chemin 24, 25, 31, 129, 133, 146

## K

Kabiyè
  customs 75, 167
  in Togolese literacy policy 8
  language in education 7
  national status 7, 8
  people 171
  relationship with the Ifè 171

## L

leadership xiii, 4, 10, 11, 41, 73, 83, 164, 198, 222, 232, 235, 238, 239, 241, 243, 245
  African 3, 4, 35, 43-45, 53, 55-59, 73, 85, 93, 100, 128, 146, 219, 239, 247, 248
  collaboration in 143
  definitions of 3, 57, 58
  development of 3, 44, 46, 48, 52, 53, 56, 60, 205, 206, 226, 228, 243, 245
  Ifè representations of xiv, 39, 45, 84, 86, 88, 90, 92-94, 96-104, 106,-112, 114-118, 120, 122-126, 128, 130, 132, 134, 136, 138, 140-142, 144-146, 197-199, 202, 212, 213, 215, 223-225, 227, 228, 232, 233, 235-239, 244, 247

Index 345

of volunteer organizations 41, 44, 47, 50, 52–55, 59, 60, 203, 206, 214, 225, 226, 228, 229, 232, 239
theories xiv, 44–46, 55, 59, 84, 134, 201, 232, 239, 247
  path-goal 47, 49–51, 54, 72
  situational 48-50, 59
  skills 46–48, 59, 65, 239
  traits 45, 46, 59, 239
  transformational 51–54
  Western 43, 44, 55, 115, 239
literacy xiii, 5, 18–20, 22, 114, 162, 166, 200, 211, 224, 243, 247, 248
  as power 64, 65, 68, 80
  as skills 47, 64, 65, 67, 68, 108, 149, 159
  as skills (traditional) 4, 224, 225, 238
  as social practice 64, 66–68, 239, 240
  associations 2, 3, 10, 23–33, 35, 41, 64, 112, 116, 119, 120, 125, 126, 145, 147, 198, 199, 207, 208, 209, 212, 214, 223, 224, 226–229, 232, 234, 235, 239, 241, 242
  church-based 20, 152
  community-based 20, 24
  functional 32, 67, 78, 79, 164
  government requirements, Benin 28
  government requirements, Togo 20
  ideological 65, 66
  impact of 1, 30, 65, 78–81, 109–111, 154, 156, 159, 160, 162–164, 167, 170, 172–175, 177, 178, 184, 194, 214–223, 225, 235, 238
  in development topics 210
  language of 8, 16, 18, 25, 27, 28, 30, 35, 66, 80, 108, 110, 148, 149, 159, 163, 166, 168, 170, 172, 174, 175, 177–179, 182, 186–195, 203, 222, 225, 231, 235–238, 243, 245, 248
  leaders xiv, 2, 10, 11, 18, 23, 31, 32, 39, 47, 84, 86–88, 90, 91, 94, 96, 98, 101, 103, 104, 109, 111, 112, 115–125, 127–129, 131, 134, 145, 148, 149, 154, 156, 161, 174, 193, 195, 200–202, 209, 210, 212, 215, 218, 219, 221, 223, 225, 228, 232–234, 236, 237, 245
  method(s) 199, 201
    Freire 9, 66, 79
    Gudschinsky 79
    pedagogy of the text 9
    REFLECT 65
  practices 65–68, 228
  program(s) (general) xiii, xiv, 2, 4, 8–10, 27, 43, 49, 55, 65, 75, 80, 81, 96, 101, 127, 133, 147, 148, 199, 200, 231, 232, 241–243, 248
  rates (levels) 2–4, 6, 8, 10, 16, 22, 33, 77, 109, 216
  relationship to development xiii, 24, 26, 29, 63, 64, 68, 77–81, 119, 157–166, 183, 187, 194, 195, 201, 203, 210, 216, 223, 227, 235–237, 240, 245, 248
  representations of xiv, 3, 10, 39, 64, 65, 67, 78, 81, 108, 148–184, 186–195, 197–199, 202, 203, 214, 222, 223, 225, 232, 233, 235–240, 247
  research 10, 11, 44
literacy class(es) 2, 16, 24, 25, 30–33, 89, 156, 164, 167, 168, 188, 189, 200, 203, 216, 218, 220, 237
literate environment 32, 228, 243
literates 238, 243, 247

M

Maathai 58
management 4, 21, 53, 74, 92, 107, 124, 125, 198–200, 204, 206, 208, 216, 223, 226, 232, 236
  activities of 205
  conflict 47
  financial 124, 205–207

group  86, 90, 91, 98, 99, 124, 233
leadership  201
models  43, 53
program  2, 35, 48, 56, 200, 201, 209
styles  43, 55
Mandela  57
Ministry of Primary, Secondary, and Technical Instruction and Professional Training  8
Ministry of Social Action  8
mission(s)
  organizational statement  3, 5, 55, 75, 204, 214, 223, 237
  religious  6, 7, 24
Moba
  beliefs  146
  in Togolese literacy policy  8
motivational  45, 49
  factors  45–47, 53, 54, 60, 147
  theory  47, 50
motivation(s)  58, 231, 235
  importance in volunteer organizations  53, 54, 232, 240
  in leadership theories  46, 49, 50, 53, 59, 60
  of leaders  148, 149
  of literacy leaders  176, 219
  of literacy learners  78, 167, 236
  of literacy workers  35, 148, 149, 167, 232, 241

## N

New Literacy Studies  66, 67
Nigeria  16, 18, 56, 79
Nigerian  211
Nkrumah  58, 59
Nyerere  57, 69–71

## O

orthography  19, 20, 126, 201

## P

Pagabete  57

parameters  244
partnership(s)  2, 72, 74, 75, 77, 243
Portugal  6
post-literacy  20, 195, 200, 201
printer(s)  21, 199
proverb(s)  37
  Ifè  95, 125, 135, 182, 213
  use in literacy program  20, 222, 238

## R

*représentations sociales* (see also social representations [SR])  35, 36, 67, 238

## S

schools  1, 6, 7, 9, 16, 24, 30, 70, 191, 200, 217, 243
Senghor  58, 70, 74
SIL  xiii, 2, 5, 10, 18–20, 22–25, 27–31, 33, 48, 55, 79, 154, 160, 200, 201, 203, 207, 210, 214, 226
social representation(s)  38–40, 67, 81, 83, 85, 87, 89, 91, 93, 95, 97, 99, 101, 103, 105, 107, 109, 111, 113, 120, 144, 197, 223, 232, 238, 239, 247
  theory of  xiv, xv, 36, 37, 41, 60, 195
solidarity  18, 25, 57, 127–131, 134, 183, 185, 188, 194, 195, 213, 223, 224, 228, 234–236, 241, 244
SOTOCO  8, 23
Spain  6
stereotype(s)  37, 39, 151
subordinate(s)  11, 41, 47, 54, 55, 84, 97–101, 103, 106, 107, 124, 138, 202, 224, 225, 234
  in leadership theories and models  4, 46, 48–51, 53, 59, 134, 239
  representations of  88, 134–144, 234
  responsibilities of  137, 139–144, 234
supervision  50, 92, 99, 200, 201, 208, 209
supervisor(s)  20, 23, 89, 90, 107, 110, 111, 115, 120, 123, 124, 132, 134,

175, 193, 199–201, 203, 209, 211, 219, 221, 225, 234, 237, 241
sustainability 5, 23, 73–75, 198, 208–210, 226, 243

## T

teacher(s) xiii, 7, 8, 11, 22, 24–27, 30, 47, 66, 71, 81, 89, 90, 106, 107, 119, 120, 122, 123, 132, 133, 144, 145, 161, 163, 169, 189, 190, 192–194, 199–203, 209, 210, 216–218, 221, 223–225, 237, 238, 241, 246
teachers' meeting(s) 11, 26, 116, 124, 201, 209, 223, 224, 237
Tem 8
Togo xiv, 8, 17, 18, 72, 75, 151, 226, 246
  history 6, 7
  infrastructure 18, 21, 33, 73, 195, 228
  linguistic situation of 5–7, 15, 16, 19, 20, 57, 146
  literacy work in 2, 5, 8, 22, 24, 27, 31, 65, 79, 151, 201, 208
  policies of 7, 20, 67, 164
  training 5, 6, 23, 27, 29, 35, 44, 54, 147, 154, 199, 211, 212, 216, 224, 232, 236, 241, 244, 248
  development of 205
  formal 50
  in development topics 23, 30, 32, 125, 126, 154, 158, 201, 210, 211, 216, 224, 237, 238, 241

leadership xiv, 41, 47, 48, 50, 125, 205, 206, 245, 247
literacy-related 25–28, 47, 120, 124, 133, 165, 200–203, 209, 210, 213, 221, 225, 237
of literacy learners 158
program management 2, 48, 56, 124, 125, 147, 200–202, 204, 206, 207, 245
religious 6, 24, 144, 168
Tutu 45, 57

## U

UNESCO 2, 28, 64, 164

## V

volunteer(s) 53–55
  organizations that use 23, 29, 44, 47, 49, 50, 52, 53, 55, 59, 60, 204, 232, 240
  program personnel 24, 81, 199, 204, 226, 239, 241

## W

writers' workshops 200, 202, 203, 237

## Y

Yoruba 19
  as language of wider communication 16
  in Beninese literacy policy 16, 27
  linguistic relationship with Ifè 27, 28
  people, relationship with the Ifè 16

## SIL International Publications
Additional Releases in the **Publications in Language Use and Education Series**

6. **Developing Orthographies for Unwritten Languages,** edited by Michael Cahill and Keren Rice. 2015, 265 pp., ISBN 978-1-55671-347-7
5. **The Early Days of Sociolinguistics: Memories and Reflections,** reprint, edited by Christina Bratt Paulson and G. Richard Tucker, 2010, 259 pp., ISBN 978-1-55671-253-1
4. **Language Contact and Composite Structures in New Ireland,** by Rebecca Sue Jenkins, 2005, 275 pp., ISBN 1-55671-156-5
3. *Namel Manmeri:* **The In-Between People—Language and Culture Maintenance and Mother-Tongue Education in the Highlands of Papua New Guinea,** by Dennis L. Malone, 2004, 263 pp., ISBN 1-55671-147-3
2. **And I, in My Turn, Will Pass it On: Knowledge Transmission among the Kayopó,** by Isabel I. Murphy, 2004, 235 pp., ISBN 1-55671-155-7
1. **Reading is for Knowing: Literacy Acquisition, Retention, and Usage among the Machiguenga,** by Patricia M. Davis, 2004, 343 pp., ISBN 1-55671-094-0

SIL International Publications
7500 W. Camp Wisdom Road
Dallas, TX 75236-5629 USA

General inquiry: publications_intl@sil.org
Pending order inquiry: sales_intl@sil.org
www.sil.org/resources/publications